TABLE OF CONTENTS

World Records for National Libraries

World Records for Public and Subscription Libraries

World Records for University and Academic Libraries

World Records for Specialty Libraries and Archives

Miscellaneous World Records for Libraries

World Records for Books, Periodicals and Bookstores

World Records for Library Buildings

World Records for Library Catalogs, Databases and Technology

World Records for Library and Information Science Organizations

ACKNOWLEDGMENTS

The British Library and the academic libraries of the University of London and City University in London (my alma maters) and several public libraries in London have always been the first places for me to go for my initial research work for *Library World Records*. That was the case for the first edition of this book. With the opportunity to travel overseas during the course of finishing the later stages of the book, repeat visits to several libraries in western Europe helped build up comparative statistical data. For those libraries I could not visit, their websites were the best places for gathering further information.

Particular thanks go to the reference libraries and press offices of the embassies of the United States, Germany, France, Turkey, China, South Korea, and Japan, as well as the Australian, South African, and Nigerian High Commissions. They all provided general reference sources.

I want to say a big thank you to all the librarians who responded to my request for votes on the most fascinating library buildings in the world.

Many photographs used in this book are from libraries, bookstores and universities around the world and I am very grateful for permission to reproduce them.

A personal thank you goes in particular to my neighbor Vivian Williams for finding the precious time to help me do some typing work.

Finally I want to extend my appreciation to everyone else who has corresponded with me by e-mail, has provided me with answers to specific questions I raised, or has sent in numerous tips that have helped to fill in the gaps.

Godfrey Oswald
(infolibrary@yahoo.co.uk)

PREFACE TO THE SECOND EDITION

Since the first edition, *Library World Records* has established itself as an indispensable reference work on libraries and books not just for librarians or library users but also researchers and students. This second edition provides updates on the first edition as well as numerous new and useful facts. The format is similar to that of the first edition, with the use of entry numbers (also used in the index). Since this edition contains a great deal of new information, there are many more entries. Also used again are notes (in italicized type) containing further interesting facts and some essay-style entries rather than listings. Data and other information are current through the end of 2007.

The books that help you the most are those which make you think the most.

—*Theodore Parker, U.S. theologist*
and transcendentalist

A book is a version of the world. If you do not like it, ignore it; or offer your own version in return.

— *Salman Rushdie, British author*

The reading of all good books is like conversation with the finest men of past centuries.

— *René Descartes, French philosopher*

INTRODUCTION

Have you ever wondered which university in the world has the largest library? Do you know the name of the oldest public libraries in the Americas? In Europe? What year was the first CD-ROM book released? In what year was the first book in the United States printed? When was the first major computer database released? To find the answers to these questions, you could spend days skimming hundreds of reference sources in libraries for this kind of information. Or you might think about the *Guinness Book of World Records*, but it does not cover a lot of information specifically about libraries. However, all the answers can be found in the present work.

Library World Records is not just a book about library and book comparisons, it is a remarkable story of libraries and books from the earliest times to the present. The hundreds of facts about libraries, periodicals, books and reference databases around the world illustrate just how significantly things have evolved from crude and simple to complex and sophisticated. Necessity, it is said, is the mother of invention. From the time humans learned to write, they have not stopped improving the way they communicate their ideas, thoughts, knowledge and inspirations.

The arrangement of specific lists and entries (with regard to geographic area or continent) are in no particular order of preference, but the following should be noted. A general rule I adopted when organizing specific lists and entries on libraries was to start first with the geographic area with the most numerous libraries (including the largest number of library books) and end with the geographic area with the fewest libraries.

For this arrangement, entries and lists for most libraries in the United States and Europe will appear first, followed by those for libraries in Latin America and Asia, and those for libraries from the Middle East and Africa will appear last.

University and public libraries combined in the West have a greater number of books for each specific country than do libraries in countries from other continents or geographic regions. So there are more lists pertaining to individual countries in the West than the other continents or geographic areas covered in the book.

This arrangement is also used in the lists on "World Records for Books, Periodicals and Bookstores." Because Western languages are widely spoken (officially or unofficially) and understood on an international level around the world, there are more entries, for instance, on the oldest books written in Western languages.

I have tried to ensure that, at least on a continental level, facts and figures on major libraries for each continent (Africa, Europe, the Asia-Pacific region, North and South America) were covered.

If, after reading the book, you know of any official or factual information on libraries and books in any country that is missing from this book, please e-mail me (infolibrary@

yahoo.co.uk) the details, including the source of the information. Such information will be useful for a future edition.

Every effort has been made to ensure accuracy. In particular all dates and total numbers of books are either official, or estimated and verified from several independent and reliable sources. *Library World Records* is for anyone who appreciates the important role libraries have played and continue to play in the development of our modern society.

How to Use This Book

Each separate entry or list within each chapter is given a number to facilitate use of the table of contents and the index. Items within each numbered list are themselves numbered according to their numerical rank. Entry numbers are used for the index.

As the book covers mostly world records on libraries, books, etc., the word "world" has been omitted for each record entry where applicable, thus the entry "Largest National Libraries" covers the largest national libraries in the world.

But records for national or continental entries, "largest university libraries in France"

or "oldest public libraries in Europe," for example, will have the appropriate name of the country or continent.

Where possible, if English is not the official language or one of the official languages of a country, then the name of the national, university or public library in the official language (with transliteration where necessary) is given alongside the English version.

For some entries, additional information has been provided. These notes, written in italics, will provide either useful background information or additional interesting facts.

WORLD RECORDS FOR NATIONAL LIBRARIES

1
Fifteen Oldest National Libraries

For most countries of the world, the number one library is always the national library, which is also a very important cultural institution. For each country the national library normally has a legal right to be given a copy of every book published in that country. For this reason national libraries tend to have large collections. And in some countries the national library is the largest library or the only major library available to the public. Many national libraries around the world began as public libraries such as the national libraries in Russia, South Africa, India, Argentina, and Bulgaria. In other countries such as Finland, Denmark, Macedonia, Croatia, Slovenia, Mexico, and Israel, a major university library also functions as the national library. The National Library of Singapore began as a subscription library. In Burma (Myanmar) and the Philippines, the national library also serves as a public library. In Japan and the U.S. the national library bears the same name as the parliamentary library (i.e., Diet Library and Library of Congress). Some national libraries are the result of an amalgamation of libraries founded much earlier in history, some of which were libraries of the monarchy, religious libraries, or private libraries of public figures. In many large countries that are divided into several provinces (e.g., Canada, South Africa and China) and states (e.g., the U.S., Australia and Germany), apart from the main national library in the country's capital,

there may also be several state or provincial libraries. These libraries in essence function as the main library for the state or provincial government, so like national libraries, they tend to be large libraries as well.

The Alexandria Library founded around 305 B.C. by Greek Macedonian king of Egypt, Ptolemy I Soter, is probably the earliest significant national library in the world, and undoubtedly the greatest library in existence from the time of Alexander the Great's Empire to the fall of the Western Roman Empire. Expanded by other kings after Ptolemy I Soter, its first two librarians (great scholars of the day) were Zenodotus of Ephesus (famous for writing a critical review of the works of the mysterious Greek author Homer), and Callimachus, who created a subject catalog of the library's holdings called the *Pinakes*. This catalog was a masterpiece and was composed of over 100 scrolls. One of the goals pursued by the owners of the Alexandria Library was to have a copy of every single book in the world — an ambitious but impossible task given to one of the librarians, a former governor of Athens named Demetrius. King Ptolemy I himself wrote letters to sovereign leaders and statesmen, requesting books by prominent writers, poets, doctors, soothsayers, and people in other important professions. At the same time the library sent out literary experts to search the cities of Europe, North Africa and the Asia Minor region for important manuscripts, maps and other items to loot. And being a major harbor at the time, foreign ships passing through Alexandria or moored at the port were thoroughly searched (sometimes with force) for anything significant to add to the library's growing collection. The library did not reach its ultimate goal. Nevertheless, at its peak, the library did house over 750,000 parchment and papyrus scrolls, a huge collection for a library of its era. Many of these documents were in several languages, such as ancient Egyptian, Greek, Hebrew and Latin, written by some of the greatest experts of the day in astronomy, medicine, law and science. Famous users of the library included Euclid and Archimedes. The library was destroyed around A.D. 638 (after existing for almost 1000 years) as Arab armies overran North Africa, and the circumstances of this destruction have been controversial ever since.

In 1989 the United Nations Educational, Scientific and Cultural Organization (UNESCO) initiated work to recreate the ancient Alexandria Library as the Bibliotheca Alexandrina. The new Alexandria Library is located near the Alexandria University Faculty of Arts campus, in Shatby, close to the Mediterranean Sea. The completed building, costing over $230 million, now has space for over 4 million books. Many of the books and manuscripts were contributions and donations received from individuals and governments from around the world, and so far the total items in the library are just under 300,000. Bibliotheca Alexandrina opened to the public October 19, 2002. In 2004 a Polish-Egyptian archeological team led by Zahi Hawass, the prominent Egyptian Egyptologist, announced they had discovered remnants of the original site of the Alexandria Library.

The following are the oldest national libraries founded before 1700, which exist today.

Ptolemy I Soter, as the first King of Egypt from the Ptolemaic dynasty, set up the first national library in the world, which also became the greatest library in the ancient world. A new Alexandria Library was opened in 2002.

1. National Library of the Czech Republic, Prague (*Národní Knihovna České Republiky*). Founded 1366. The most fascinating sight is the baroque architecture of the Klementium Complex in which the library is situated.

The national library began with a donation of books by King Charles IV. The history of the library is closely related with the foundation of the Charles University in 1348.

2. National Library of Austria, Vienna (*Österreichische Nationalbibliothek*). 1368. The national library of Austria (Department of Papyri) has over 180,000 papyri and parchments, making it the library with the biggest papyrus collection in Europe and the second largest collection in the world after the one at the Egyptian Museum in Cairo. A huge digitization program aided by the UNESCO Memory of the World Register is already underway in Vienna to make them available via a database to scholars.

It was founded from the royal collections of Austrian Dukes (starting with Archduke Albrecht III) as part of the later Imperial Court Library (Kaiserliche Hofbibliothek), during the early period of the Habsburg dynasty. This royal family ruled Austria from 1278 up to 1918, after the end of the First World War. The library contains the most beautiful atlas in the world, the 17th century Dutch manuscript Blaeu-Van der Hem. The interior of the library has more space for decorations and artifacts than books itself, including a big baroque state hall (Prunksaal) with statues of King Charles IV and several princes of the Habsburg dynasty.

3. Marciana National Library, Venice, Venetian Republic (*Biblioteca Nazionale de Marciana*). 1468.

The National Library of Austria in Vienna is the second oldest national library in the West — and the second oldest in the world.

Cardinal Bessarione started the library with his own collection of important religious manuscripts. The Venetian Republic is now part of Italy, and the library still exists under the same name, a legacy of the time Italy was not a united country, but made of city-states like Genoa and Venice. Today while most countries have one main national library, ten institutions in Italy are given the title of National Library, at Bari, Rome, Florence, Milan, Naples, Palermo, Turin, Venice, Potenza and Cosenza. However, those at Rome and Florence are the most prominent.

4. National Library of France, Paris (*Bibliothèque Nationale de France*). 1480.

The legal status of the National Library of France was acquired in 1617, and the library opened for the public in 1735. But actual foundation of the library goes back to 1480 when the library was known as the Bibliothèque du Roi and was part of King Louis XI's royal library. A collection of books belonging to King Charles V "the Wise" (a patron of the arts and of learning), and now part of the national library, dates back further to 1368.

5. National Library of Malta, Valetta (*Biblioteka Nazzjonali ta' Malta*). 1555.

Books belonging to the Knights of the Order of St. John of Jerusalem started the library. Descendants of the Knights of the Order of St. John were originally in Jerusalem in the 12th century to defend Jerusalem, with help from the Knights Templar, against Arab forces during the 2nd Crusade. After the crusades ended, the Knights of the Order of St. John were forced to leave Palestine, so moved onto Cyprus in 1291, before being granted sanctuary in Malta in 1530 by Emperor Charles V.

6. Bavarian State Library, Munich. Germany (*Bayerische Staatsbibliothek*). 1558.

Duke Albrecht V founded the library as the Wittelsbach court library during the time Bavaria was a kingdom and Germany was made up of several city-states and then part of the Holy Roman Empire. Today the library is not part of the German national library, but it is one of the three largest and most important libraries in Germany.

This old building housed the National Library of France for a long time, until a new national library building was opened in 1996.

The Bavarian State Library in Munich was the most important library of the Wittelsbach dynasty, which dominated the German kingdom of Bavaria until the last king of Bavaria, Ludwig III, abdicated in 1918.

7. National Library of Belgium, Brussels. Royal Library Albert I (*Koninklijke Bibliotheek van België/Bibliothèque Royale de Belgique*). 1559.

The Dukes of Burgundy laid the foundation for the national library starting with a collection of important manuscripts. Belgium is one of the few countries in Europe that are bilingual, so her libraries tend have two titles; in French and Flemish (Dutch). Books in the libraries are in both of these languages as well.

8. National and University Library of Slovenia, founded 1595. The university joined with the national library is called Edward Kardelja University Library, Ljubljana (*Edvarda Kardelja* Knjižnica *Univerza v Ljubljani*).

9. National Library of Croatia, Zagreb (*Nacionalna i Sveučilišna* Knjižnica). 1606.

Jesuits first established the library collections; it is also part of the Zagreb University Library.

10. National Library of Finland, Helsinki (*Helsingin Yliopiston Kirjasto*). 1640.

It also forms part of the Helsinki University Library, and was first founded in Turku, the old capital of Finland (formerly called Åbo, when Finland was then part of Sweden). The library moved to Helsinki in 1828 after the Great Fire of Turku.

11. National Library of Denmark, Copenhagen (*Det Kongelige Bibliotek*). 1653.

King Frederick III originally founded the library. It is also part of the Copenhagen University Library founded in 1482. There are two other locations of the library at Amager and Fiolstræde, but these are part of the Copenhagen University library. The old national library building of the Slotsholmen site was built in 1906 and is a copy of Charlemagne's Palace

The National Library of Denmark is now housed in a an enthralling new building, known locally as the "Black Diamond." It was opened in 1999.

Chapel in the Aachen Cathedral. In 1999, a new building was opened at Slotsholmen, known as the "Black Diamond," or Den sorte diamante, in Danish. It is so named for its outside cover of black marble and glass (shown in the photograph). It houses a concert hall in addition to the library.

12. National Library of Sweden, Stockholm (*Kungliga Biblioteket*). 1661.

This national library began as a collection of books originally belonging to the first Swedish king, Gustavus Vasa (Gustavus I). Between 1397 and 1523, Sweden had been part of a political union with Denmark and Norway, but with a Danish monarch (Union of Kalmar). When Sweden left the union in 1523, Norway remained united with Denmark until the 1814 Congress of Vienna ceded it to Sweden.

13. Prussian State Library, Berlin, Germany (*Staatsbibliothek zu Berlin. Preussischer Kulturbesitz*). 1661. The renovated library building, which opened in 1978, is part of the Kultur-forum, a complex of buildings including the Philharmonie, the Kammermusiksaal and the Neue Nationalgalerie. The library was fea-

tured in Wender's classic film *Wings of Desire*. Generously financed by successive German governments, the building housed the largest library in post-war Germany, until the former East and West German national libraries merged in 1990. Today it is the second largest library in Germany and called the Berlin State Library. Architects were Scharoun and Wisniewski.

Prussia is now part of Germany and Poland, and the library is now known as the Berlin State Library. Frederick William, ruler of Brandenburg, founded the library. Like the Bavarian State Library, it is not part of the German national library in Frankfurt, but it is one of the three main important libraries in Germany.

14. National Library of Scotland, Edinburgh. U.K. 1682.

It was formerly part of the Library of the Faculty of Advocates, which is still in existence, but now as a law library. The separation of the library to become a national library occurred in 1925.

15. National Library of Colombia, Bogotá (*Biblioteca Nacionale de Colombia*), 1777.

The National Library of Scotland (with 7 million books) is the oldest national library in the United Kingdom and third largest library in the United Kingdom, after the British Library in London and the Bodleian Library at Oxford University (© Trustees of the National Library of Scotland).

2
Oldest National Libraries in Africa

The two oldest national libraries in Africa are the National Library of South Africa, Cape Town branch, founded 1818, and the National Library of Tunisia, Tunis, founded 1845.

3
Oldest National Libraries in the Americas

The five oldest national libraries in the Americas are:

1. National Library of Colombia, Bogotá (*Biblioteca Nacional de Colombia*). Founded 1777.

2. Library of Congress, Washington D.C., U.S. Founded in 1800.

Joint 3rd. National Library of Argentina, Buenos Aires (*Biblioteca Nacional de la República Argentina*) and National Library of

Brazil, Rio de Janeiro (*Biblioteca Nacional de Brasil*). Both founded 1810.

4. National Library of Chile, Santiago (*Biblioteca Nacional de Chile*). Founded 1813.

Joint 5. National Library of Mexico, Mexico City (*Biblioteca Nacional de México*) and National Library of Venezuela, Caracas (*Biblioteca Nacional de Venezuela*). Both founded 1833.

4
Oldest National Libraries in Asia

The two oldest national libraries in Asia are the National Library of Georgia, Tbilisi, founded 1846 and the National Library of India, Calcutta (Kolkata), founded 1902.

5
Oldest National Libraries in the Middle East

1. National Library of Egypt, Cairo (*Dâr el-Kutub Al-Misrîyya*). Founded 1870.

2. National Library of Israel, Jerusalem. Founded 1925.

6
Largest National Libraries with Over 10 Million Books

When considering the size of a library's collections, only the number of books is taken into account throughout this book; other library materials such as manuscripts, serials (newspapers, journals and so on), microfilms, and maps are disregarded. In 1964 during an UNESCO conference, it was agreed internationally that a book was defined as *a non-periodical printed publication of at least 49 pages.* Many libraries say of their collections that they have so many "items" but this includes all kinds of library materials as well as books.

1. Library of Congress, Washington, D.C. 30 million books. Founded 1800. The national library with the biggest annual budget, currently about $462 million. The Library of Congress grows at a rate of about 10,000 items a day.

Among the treasured maps at the Library of Congress is the only remaining copy of German geographer Martin Waldsemüller's original map of 1507, which was the first to show the American continent and the first to use the word "America" in honor of Italian explorer Amerigo Vespucci. In the summer of 2001 the German government gave permission for the former owners of the map (Prince Johannes

*Waldberg-Wolfegg-Waldsee library in Wolfegg, Baden-Württemberg) to sell it to the Library of Congress for $10 million. The map had been re-discovered in 1901 by Joseph Fisher, a Jesuit historian, after nearly 400 years during which it was listed as "missing." There were other maps made before 1507 that included the Americas (see list **63**). The Library of Congress was the most expensive library building before the 20th century, when the Jefferson Building, the oldest part of the three buildings that make up the library, opened in 1897 at a cost of $10 million. Storage of its huge collections of books has meant going to extraordinary lengths such as constructing 500 miles of underground rooms beneath the library building. The rate at which the book collection in the Library of Congress has grown in size is staggering. In 1900 it had just over 2 million books. The first full time librarian of the Library of Congress was George Watterson in 1815. During the Second World War the original copies of the 18th century Constitution and the Declaration of Independence (engrossed upon parchment), were taken from the Library of Congress to Fort Knox (ordinarily used for storing U.S. gold bullion) in Kentucky for safekeeping. Both documents are today housed in helium-filled glass cases (this time to protect them against decay) in the National Archives building in Washington, D.C. In times of war, revolution or political*

Jefferson Building of the U.S. Library of Congress. Even though the U.S. national library bears the name of the U.S. legislative body, the Congress, the U.S. Senate has its own library (called the Senate Library), with about 253,000 books; it was founded in 1871 (photograph by Stephan Erfurt, courtesy Library of Congress).

unrest, other important documents around the world have had similar instances of contingency plans for protection. For instance it is believed that the famous Dead Sea Scrolls found in secret caves were actually hidden there to protect them during the first Jewish revolt that occurred between A.D. 66 and 70. During the clashes between the Roman army and rebel Jews, it was feared the scrolls would be destroyed if the Romans got hold of them. After Roman Emperor Titus put down the rebellion, the scrolls remained hidden and forgotten until a chance discovery in 1947. Each of the 50 states in the U.S. has a state library. The three largest are the New York State Library (founded 1818 in Albany) with more than 3 million books and the oldest in the U.S.; the California State Library (founded in 1850 in Sacramento); and the Library of Michigan (founded in 1828 in Lansing). Texas State Library in Austin

(fourth largest) used to be called the National Library of the Republic of Texas between 1839 and 1848.

2. National Library of China, Beijing (Zhongguo Guojia Tushugan). Founded 1911. 27 million.

It was previously called the Metropolitan Library of Beijing. A new building for the library was added in 1987. The are 21 provinces in China, each with one large main provincial library. The three largest such libraries are the Zhejiang Provincial Library, Sichuan Provincial Library and the Hubei Provincial Library.

3. Russian State Library, Moscow (Rossiskaya Gosudarstvennaya Biblioteka). 24.2 million.

The National Library of China is now the largest in Asia and second largest in the world (courtesy Ben Gu, National Library of China).

Known affectionately as the "Leninska," its 42 million bibliographic items of all kinds would make it the second *largest library in the world (after the Library of Congress). It is also Europe's largest library. It is the third largest library in the world in number of actual books (24.2 million). Formerly called the Lenin State Library of the USSR (until 1991), it was founded in 1924, a few years after Vladimir Ilyich Lenin's October revolution. But the origin of the library goes back to 1862, when it was part of the private collection of Count Nickolai Rumyantsev. It was then the first public library in Moscow.*

4. National Library of Germany, Frankfurt, Leipzig and Berlin (*Die Deutsche Bibliothek*). 17 million. Founded in 1990 following the merging of the former East German National Library in Leipzig (*Deutsche Bücherei,* founded 1912) with the *Deutsche Bibliothek* in former West Germany (founded 1946). The third location of the national library is in Berlin, where music materials are kept in the *Deutsches Musikarchiv.*

Two other large state libraries also exist in Germany and are comparable with the national library

in Frankfurt. The first one, the Bavarian State Library in Munich, currently holds 8 million books. The other, the Berlin State Library (Staatsbibliothek zu Berlin), holds about 11 million books. Smaller state libraries also exist in Stuttgart (Baden Württemberg State Library) and Dresden (Saxony State Library). The latter is home to the famous Dresden Codex *(see list* **126***).*

5. National Library of France, Paris (*Bibliothèque Nationale de France*). 15.3 million. Third largest in Europe. A new library building opened to the public in 1996, but the library's actual foundation goes back to 1480.

Among the millions of photographs at the French national library is the world's oldest photograph, taken by Nicéphore Niepce in 1825 (which took 8 hours to develop!). In 1997 the French national library was the first library to provide full-text access to a great deal of its collections via the Internet. The special catalog called Gallica also provides photographs and illustrations from the publication (cover page digital image and/or digital images from inside the publication). In total over 80,000 digitalized books were available to access, including access to important publications that had once had restricted access such as the French Academy of Sciences publications (*Procès Verbaux de l'Académie des Sciences*). Normally a library's catalog only provides brief bibliographic details of its book collections, so Gallica was a unique deviation from library tradition. Other national libraries around the world have already begun initiatives to provide full-text access to some of their collections, such as the one between Google and several large academic libraries in the U.S. and the one at the British Library providing access to its rarest incunabula. The Google project will be released as Google Book Library. The project involves several large U.S. university libraries collaborating to provide up to 10 million books from their collections available for digitization and access through Google's search engine. The bulk of the universities are in the U.S. Outside the U.S. libraries of Keio University in Japan and Ghent University in Belgium are recent additions.

6. The British Library, London. 14.5 million. It is also Europe's fourth largest national library, containing 920,000 journals and newspapers (the largest such collection in Europe), as well as 3 million sound recordings.

Although the British Library was part of the British Museum founded in 1753, it became separate in 1973, and officially different entities in 1998. The British Museum Library itself developed from the Royal Library of King Henry VII. The new British Library building was opened to the public in 1997. Prior to this, the collections of the library were housed in several buildings in central London. There are also two other British national libraries: in Scotland (Edinburgh), founded in 1682, with 7 million books, and in Wales (Cardiff), founded in 1911 and with 5 million books.

7. Vernadsky National Library of Ukraine, Kiev (*Natsional'na Biblioteka Ukraïny*). 13 million. Founded 1918.

8. National Library of Russia, St. Petersburg (*Rossiiskaya Natsionalnaya Biblioteka*). Formerly M.E. Saltykov-Shchedrin State Public Library. 12.1 million.

Empress Catherine the Great founded the library in 1795.

9. National Library of Canada, Ottawa (*Bibliothèque Nationale du Canada*). Founded 1953.

The National Library of Russia in St. Petersburg is the third largest in Russia after the Russian State Library in Moscow and the Russian Academy of Sciences Library in St. Petersburg (© Joyce N. Church).

11 million. All national libraries and national archives around the world are normally two separate cultural institutions. But in 2004, following new legislation, the National Library of Canada was the first to merge with its National Archives (founded in 1872) into one organization as the Library and Archives Canada. As librarians and library users in Canada debated the merits of such a merger, one of the reasons given for the merger was that the differences between national libraries and national archives could no longer be explained, such as the simple question: does a map belong in a library, or an archive? Since the merger, national libraries worldwide have been watching with interest, but to date none have followed suit.

A second national library of Canada also exists in Montreal, as the Bibliothèque Nationale du Québec. The above figure is the total for both libraries.

10. National Library of Japan, Tokyo (*Kokuritsu Kokkai Toshokan*). Founded 1948. 10 million books. Three buildings comprise the National Library of Japan, or National Diet Library. The *Nagata-cho* main building, adjacent to the National Diet (Japan's parliament), opened in 1968, and an Annex was added in 1986 to keep up with the expanding book collection. The *Nagata-cho* main building is based on a stack system, with the stack space unit measuring 45m by 45m with 17 vertical levels. The Annex has four floors above the ground, and 8 floors below ground level. Both buildings are in Tokyo, while a third building, *Kansai-kan,* in the Kansai Science City, outside Kyoto opened in 2002. The winners of an open international architecture competition held in 1996 designed the new building. A notable feature of the new library will be its "light and chameleon effects" in which abundant greenery and the transparency of the glass exterior blend well with the surroundings. The illumination of the building is governed by the time of the day and the season.

It was originally founded in 1872 during the Meiji period as the Imperial Library or Teikoku Toshokan, but after the end of the Second World War and following adoption of a new constitution, it was renamed Kokuritsu Kokkai Toshokan or Diet Library.

7

Five Largest National Libraries in Africa and the Middle East

1. National Library of Israel, Jerusalem. 4.8 million books. Founded 1925.

Also part of the Hebrew University Library in Jerusalem.

2. National Library of Egypt, Cairo (*Dâr el-Kutub Al-Misrîyya*). 2 million. Founded 1870.

It began as the royal Khedival Palace Library belonging to Khedive Ismael, one of the rulers of Egypt. His son Khedive Tawaf later expanded the library. During the time Egypt was ruled by the Turkish Ottoman Empire from 1517, the rulers of Egypt between 1867 and 1914 were called Khedive and were under the orders of the Sultan of Ottoman Turkey.

3. National Library of South Africa, Pretoria and Cape Town. 1.4 million. The Cape Town branch was founded 1818, while Pretoria branch was founded in 1887.

4. National Library of Turkey, Ankara. (*Türkiye Milli Kutuphane*). 1.3 million. Founded 1948.

5. National Library of Tunisia, Tunis. 1.2 million. Founded 1845.

The largest national library in Africa can be found at the National Library of South Africa in Cape Town (© courtesy National Library of South Africa, Cape Town).

8
Ten Largest National Libraries in Asia

1. National Library of China, Beijing (*Zhongguo Guojia Tushugan*). 27 million. See also list **6**.

2. National Library of Japan, Tokyo (*Kokuritsu Kokkai Toshokan*). 10 million. See also list **6**.

3. National Library of Australia, Canberra. Founded 1901. 7.3 million.

   It was the first national library to set up its own website back in 1994. The library played a leading role in the establishment of the National Library of Papua New Guinea, when in 1975 the then Prime Minister of Australia announced its Independence gift to people of Papua New Guinea would be a national library building and its contents. This was possible after consultations with Papua New Guinea leaders. In addition to advising on the design of the building, the National Library of Australia developed the initial collection. By the end of 1977, huge quantities of ordered materials were arriving, signaling the beginning of the huge job of processing books, government publications, films and equipment. A special gift from the National Library of Australia was Papua New Guinean books, films and maps, some of which were valuable historic items not otherwise available. In 1978, the Australian government formally handed over the keys to the building in Port Moresby. There are six states in Australia, each with one main state library. The largest is the New South Wales State Library in Sydney.

The National Library of Australia in Canberra is the third largest in the Asia-Pacific region (© Joyce N. Church).

4. National Library of Armenia, Yerevan. 7 million. Founded 1919.

5. National Library of Kazakhstan, Almaty. 6.5 million. Founded in 1931.

6. National Library of Georgia, Tbilisi. 6 million. Founded 1846.

7. National Library of India, Calcutta (Kolkata). Founded 1902. 4.5 million.

The national library is the result of the amalgamation of the Calcutta Public Library founded in 1835, with the Imperial Library in 1903.

8. Akhundov M.F. State Library of Azerbaijan, Baku. 4.5 million. Founded 1923.

9. National Library of New Zealand, Wellington (*Te Puna Manatauranga O Aotearoa*). Founded 1856. 4.4 million.

10. National Library of Korea, Seoul. 4 million. Founded 1923.

Several of the former Asian members of the Soviet Union, such as Armenia and Kazakhstan, had very large national libraries, which they inherited when the USSR was dissolved in 1991.

9
Ten Largest National Libraries in Europe

More details of most of the libraries noted below are given at list **6**.

1. Russian State Library, Moscow (*Rossiskaya Gosudarstvennaya Biblioteka*). 24.2 million.

2. National Library of Germany, Frankfurt, Leipzig and Berlin (*Die Deutsche Bibliothek*). 17 million. It is the largest national library in Western Europe.

3. National Library of France, Paris (*Bibliothèque Nationale de France*). 15.3 million.

Top: As the largest library in France, the National Library of France is based in one of the most intriguing buildings: four tall glass towers each resembling an opened book. *Bottom:* The Marciana National Library, based in the San Marco Museum building in Venice, is the third largest and oldest of Italy's ten national libraries spread throughout the country.

4. The British Library, London. 14.5 million.

5. Vernadsky National Library of Ukraine, Kiev (*Natsional'na Biblioteka Ukraïny*). 13 million. Founded 1918.

6. National Library of Russia, St. Petersburg (*Rossiskaya Natsionalnaya Biblioteka*). 12.1 million.

7. National Library of Italy, Rome and Florence (*Biblioteca Nazionale Centrale*). 11 million. The Rome branch was founded in 1876, and is called *Biblioteca Nazionale Centrale Vittorio Emanuele II*. While the Florence branch

Biblioteca Nazionale Centrale was founded in 1747.

8. National Library of Romania, Bucharest (*Biblioteca Naţională a României*) 8.3 million. Founded 1836. See also list **34** for details on the Romanian Academy Library.

9. National Library of the Czech Republic, Prague (*Národní Knihovna České Republiky*). 6.3 million. Founded 1366.

10. National Library of Austria, Vienna (*Österreichische Nationalbibliothek*). 6 million. Founded 1368.

10
Five Largest National Libraries in Latin America

1. National Library of Chile, Santiago (*Biblioteca Nacional de Chile*). 4 million. Founded 1813.

2. National Library of Mexico, Mexico City (*Biblioteca Nacional de México*). 3.3 million. Founded 1833. The building of Mexico's number one library is based on tiled mosaic facades, with Aztec culture themes. The mosaic-decorated stackroom tower by Diego Rivera is fantastic. Juan O'Gorman, the architect of the library, who was inspired by the works of U.S. architect Frank Lloyd Wright, is one of Mexico's famous architects. The 10 story and almost windowless library building opened in December 1979, is located along the famous Insurgentes Avenue (*Avenida Insurgentes*), and rubs shoulders with the also famous Olympic Stadium.

It is also part of the National Autonomous University Library.

3. National Library of Argentina, Buenos Aires (*Biblioteca Nacional de la República Argentina*). 3 million books. Founded 1810.

4. National Library of Venezuela, Caracas (*Biblioteca Nacional de Venezuela*). 2.7 million books. Founded 1833. The National Library of Cuba (*Biblioteca Nacional José Marti*) in Havana has about the same number of books. It was founded in 1901.

5. National Library of Brazil, Rio de Janeiro (*Biblioteca Nacional de Brasil*). 1.8 million books. Founded 1810.

The first collection of books of the National Library of Brazil belonged to the Portuguese royal family, who took the books with them when they fled to Brazil, after Napoleon Bonaparte and his forces invaded Portugal in the late 18th century.

World Records for Public and Subscription Libraries

A public library is usually a library open to the public that is funded by the government. In many cities and towns several branches of a main library may exist in different locations. For instance New York Public Library has over 80 branches in the city. Precursors of public libraries in many countries were called circulating or subscription libraries. Some were part private and part public. Today some subscription libraries have become full public libraries.

11
Fifteen Largest Public Libraries

Los Angeles and New York are the two cities in the world with the largest combined collection of public library books (all library branches in the city), and the largest annual budgets in the world. Below are the largest public libraries with more than 5 million books.

1. Boston (Massachusetts) Public Library, U.S. 14 million. Founded 1848.

2. Los Angeles County (California) Public Library, U.S. 10.4 million. Founded 1912.

3. Cincinnati & Hamilton County (Ohio) Public Library, U.S. 9.6 million. Founded 1856.

4. Shanghai Library, China (*Shanghai Tushugan*). 9.5 million. Founded 1952. See list **14** for more information.

5. Detroit Public Library (Michigan), U.S. 7.5 million. Founded 1865.

6. Toronto (Ontario) Public Library, Canada. 7.65 million. Founded 1884.

It has 9 million items and an annual circulation of 28 million (probably giving it the highest public library circulation numbers in the Americas).

7. Nanjing Library, China (*Nanjing Tushugan*) 7.4 million. Founded 1908.

8. Russian State Public Library for Science and Technology, Moscow. 7.3 million books. Founded in 1958. It is the largest specialized public library in the world.

9. Queens Borough Public Library, New York City, U.S. 7 million. Founded 1896.

10. Philadelphia (Pennsylvania) Free Public Library, U.S. 6.5 million. Founded 1891.

11. Los Angeles City (California) Public Library, U.S. 6.4 million. Founded 1872.

12. Carnegie Library of Pittsburgh (Pennsylvania), U.S. 6.3 million. Founded 1897.

13. Chicago (Illinois) Public Library, U.S. 6 million. Founded 1873.

*Because the existing library building did not have enough space for the expanding book collections, a new central library called the Harold Washington Library Center opened to the public in 1991, and it is now the second largest public library building in the world. See list **241**.*

Top: As the second largest public library in the United States, Los Angeles County Public Library has 84 branches. This is the East Los Angeles County branch (courtesy of Los Angeles County Public Library). *Bottom:* Shanghai Library in China, with more than 9 million books, is the largest public library in the world, outside the United States (courtesy Ben Gu, National Library of China).

14. New York Public Library, U.S. Has about 5.9 million books and 84 separate branches. Founded in 1895.

15. Brooklyn Public Library, New York City, U.S. 5 million. Founded 1897.

12
Largest Public Libraries in the U.S. and Canada

Eleven U.S. public libraries are given in list **11**. The next 5 largest public libraries with 4 million or more books are: San Diego (California) Public Library, 4.5 million; Dallas (Texas) Public Library, 4.3 million; Miami-Dade (Florida) Public Library, 4.2. million; Cleveland (Ohio) Public Library, 4.1 million; and Houston (Texas) Public Library, 4 million.

Apart from Toronto Public Library above, the next three largest public libraries in Canada are: Ottawa Public Library (Ontario) with 2.5 million books, founded 1906; Vancouver Public Library (British Columbia) 2.3 million books, 1887, and Montréal City Library (*Bibliothèque de Montréal*) in Québec province with 2 million books. Vancouver Public Library has a unique sight. The exterior of the library building designed by Moshe Safdie resembles the remnants of the ancient Roman Coliseum in Italy.

Vancouver Public Library in Canada probably has the most recognizable face in the world: It is shaped like the famous Roman Coliseum in Italy (courtesy Diana Thompson and Oi-Lun Kwan).

Miami-Dade Public Library in Florida is one of several very large public libraries in the United States that are able to provide nearby outdoor café, so users can take a break after using the library (© Miami-Dade Public Library System).

13
Largest Public Libraries in Africa and the Middle East

In the Middle East, the two largest libraries are the Tel Aviv Central Public Library (*Shaar Zion*) founded 1958 with 950,000 books and the Jerusalem City Public Library founded 1961 with 810,000 books. Both are located in Israel. King Abdul-Aziz Public Library in Riyadh, Saudi Arabia, has over 310,000 books. It was founded in 1985.

In Africa, Johannesburg Public Library, founded in 1959 has 1.7 million books. Cape Town City Library, founded in 1947, has 1.2 million books. Both are in South Africa.

The Cape Provincial Library Service of South Africa, based in Cape Town, has over 200 affiliated public libraries and over 70 depot libraries, giving a total collection of over 5 million books. The Transvaal Provincial Library in Pretoria, founded in 1943, contains over 4.5 million books.

14
Largest Public Libraries in Asia

In China, Shanghai Library (*Shanghai Tushugan*), founded in 1952, has 9.5 million books, while Nanjing Library (*Nanjing Tushugan*), founded in 1908, has 7.4 million books.

Beijing Society of Library Science Capital Library, founded 1913, owns over 4.1 million books. In addition to the above three Chinese libraries, several large public provincial libraries with over 2 million books also exist in China.

The largest Asian public library outside China is the Delhi Public library in New Delhi, India. It was founded in 1951 in association with UNESCO and has about 1.7 million books. Bangladesh Central Public Library in Dhaka, founded in 1958, has just over a million books and is the main public library in the capital.

The five largest public libraries in Japan are the Tokyo Metropolitan Central Library, with 1.4 million books, founded 1939; the Aichi Prefectural Library in Nagoya, holding just over 990,000 books; Kanazawa City Library, 980,000 books; Kanagawa Prefectural Library, 930,000 books, founded 1954; and the Osaka Prefectural Library with over 900,000 books. The largest public library in South Korea is the Pusan Civil Library with about 850,000 books. It was founded in 1968.

In Malaysia, the three largest public libraries are Selangor Public Library, 1.6 million books, founded 1971; Kedah Public Library, Alor Setar, 710,000 books, founded 1974; and Penang Public Library, 550,000 books, founded 1817. The largest public library in Taiwan is the Taipei City Library, founded in 1952, with 164,000 books. In Singapore, the largest public library is the Woodlands Regional Library with just over 400,000 books. The new building for the library opened in 2001.

In Australia the largest public library is the Sydney Public Library with 1.7 million books. The largest public libraries in New Zealand are Auckland City Library (1.1 million, founded 1880) and Wellington Public Library (710,000 books, founded 1893).

15
Ten Largest Public Libraries in Europe

The current 10 largest libraries in Europe are:

1. Russian State Public Library for Science and Technology, Moscow. 7.3 million books. Founded in 1958. It is the largest specialized public library in the world.

2. Mitchell Library, Glasgow, Scotland, U.K. 4.5 million. Founded in 1874.

3. Birmingham Central Public Library, U.K. 3.3 million. Founded 1852.

4. Munich City Library, Germany (*Münchner Stadbibliothek*). 3.2 million. Founded 1843.

5. Berlin Central Library, Germany (*Zentral und Landesbibliothek Berlin*). 3.1 million. Founded 1901.

6. Zurich Central Library, Switzerland (*Zentralbibliothek Zürich*). 3 million. Founded 1914.

7. Malmö City Library, Sweden (*Malmö Stadsbibliotek*). 3 million. Founded 1905.

8. Liverpool Public Library. 3 million. Founded 1852.

9. Prague City Library, Czech Republic (*Městká Knihovna v Praze*). 3 million. Founded 1891.

10. Helsinki City Public Library, Finland (*Helsingin Kaupunginkirjasto*), founded in 1860, and Lyons Municipal Library (*Bibliothèque Municipale de Lyon*) in France, founded 1527, both presently have over 2.8 million books.

The total collection of all the individual libraries in the 32 boroughs that make up Greater London is now 12 million. The largest ones are the Westminster and Barnet borough public libraries. The London Library, set up in 1841 by Thomas Caryle, today has about 650,000 books. There are 39 counties in the U.K, the 4 largest county libraries are: Hampshire (Winchester) public libraries, 3.8 million books; Kent (Maidstone) public libraries, 3.5 million; Lancashire (Preston) public libraries, 3 million and Essex (Chelmsford) public libraries, 2.8 million.

Malmö City Library in Sweden is the largest in Scandinavia and also has the largest single public library building in Europe (photograph by Johan Kalén, courtesy of Malmö City Library, Sweden).

In France, Bordeaux Municipal Library (*Bibliothèque Municipale de Bordeaux*) has about 1.2 million books. It was founded in 1740. The combined book collection of public libraries in Paris (including the Georges Pompidou Center Library) is just over 5 million volumes. The largest is the Paris City Library (*Bibliothèque de la Ville de Paris*).

In Germany, apart from Munich Public Library listed above, the other large public library is the Hamburg Public Library (*Hamburger Öffentliche Bucherhallen*) owns about 2.6 million books. It was founded in 1899. There are several public libraries in the German capital Berlin, most beginning with the title Stadtbibliothek. The Berlin Central Library (*Zentral und Landesbibliothek Berlin*) is the largest.

Other major large public libraries in Europe (excluding those in the U.K., Germany and France) and the foundation year are Stockholm City Public Library, Sweden (Stockholms Stadsbibliotek), 2.2 million books, founded 1927; Dublin City Library, Ireland, 2.1 million, 1884; Rotterdam Municipal Library, Netherlands (Gemeentebibliotheek Rotterdam), 2 million, 1604; Moscow City Public Library, Russia (Moskva Publichnaya Biblioteca), 2 million, 1919; Bucharest City Library, Romania (Biblioteca Municipale Bucuresti), 1.6 million, 1935; Espoon City Public Library, Finland (Espoon Kaupunginkirjasto), 1.5 million, 1869; Barcelona Public Library, Spain, 1.5 million, 1918; Oslo Deichman Public Library, Norway (Deichmanske Bibliotek), 1.5 million, 1785; Vienna Public Library, Austria (Büchereien Wien), 1.3 million, 1945; Oporto Public Library, Portugal (Biblioteca Pùblica Municipal Porto), 1.4 million, 1833; Metropolitan Ervin Szabo

There is so much space in Sweden's Malmö City Library that the free, spacious seats are everywhere, even in the library's verandah (photograph by Johan Kalén, courtesy Malmö City Library, Sweden).

Lyons Municipal Library is the oldest and largest public library in France. The tall building behind the library is also part of the library building. See list **246** on the most fascinating public library buildings.

Library, Budapest, Hungary (Ervin Szabo Könyvtár), 1.2 million, 1904; Warsaw Public Library, Poland (Biblioteka Publiczna Warszawy), 1.2 million, 1907; Antwerp Central Public Library, Belgium (Antwerpen Openbare Bibliotheek), 1 million, 1866; Tampere City Public Library, Finland (Tampereen Kaupunginkirjasto), 1 million, 1861; Central Library of Sofia, Bulgaria, 938,000, 1886; Eindhoven Public Library, The Netherlands (Openbare Bibliotheek Eindhoven), 851,000, 1916; Panizzi Municipal Library, Via Emilia, Italy (Biblioteca Municipale Panizzi), 710,000, 1796.

16
Largest Public Libraries in Latin America

The five largest public libraries in Latin America are: São Paulo Municipal Library (*Biblioteca Municipal Mario de Andrade*), Brazil, 630,000 books, founded in 1925; Mexico Public Library, Mexico City (*Biblioteca de México*), 510,000, founded in 1946; Rio Grande Public Library, Brazil (*Biblioteca Pública Rio Grandense*), 450,000, founded in 1846; Bernardino People's Library, Buenos Aires, Argentina (*Biblioteca Popular Bernardino Rivadavia*), 159,000, founded in 1949; and Bahia State Public Library, Salvador, Brazil (*Biblioteca Pública do Estado da Bahia*), 114,698.

Public libraries in many Latin American countries such as Argentina are known as popular libraries (biblioteca popular*), but the English equivalent is "people's libraries."*

17
Busiest Public Libraries

New York Public library in the United States is the busiest in the world, receiving over 10 million visitors a year and having over 3 million registered members. Toronto Public Library in Canada receives an average 7 million visitors and processes 28 million books and other items such as CDs annually, probably giving it the highest public library circulation numbers in the world.

18
Busiest Public Library in Latin America

The São Paulo Municipal Library in Brazil has been the busiest for decades. The largest library in South America receives roughly half a million visitors each year.

Since January 2004, every Friday, Mexico City's subway lends books to commuters to read for their journey.

19
Busiest Public Library in Asia

At the 2006 Northumbria International Conference on Performance Measurement in Libraries and Information Services (sponsored by the International Federation of Library Associations), statistics data from library research papers indicated that Japanese public libraries were the busiest in Asia, including Australia.

20
Busiest Public Library in Europe

Opened in 1977, the Georges Pompidou Center's state-of-the-art multimedia Public Information Library or BPI (*Bibliothèque Publique d'Information*) always seems to draw record number of crowds, with at least 14,000 people a day (or 5 million a year) visiting the library. This figure is about half the total number of people who visited the New York Public Library. If it isn't the free access without membership cards that attracts the crowds or the 1,800 reading desks, 450,000 books, 2,600 periodicals, and 2,400 DVDs and videos, then it's the yearly Festival of Reality, dedicated to documentary and ethnological film.

Using the standard set by the U.K. Chartered Institute of Public Finance & Accounting or CIPFA, which is the national body responsible for the collection of data on public and local authority services, Birmingham Central Public Library currently receives 2.3 million visits per year (just under 7,000 a day). This makes it the most visited public library in the U.K.

21
Public Libraries with the Largest Budgets

U.S. public libraries share the largest budget in the world, with just over $10 billion made available for the libraries to spend in the fiscal year 2005. The money came from local, state and federal sources. The five biggest single recipients of public funding in rank order for the fiscal year 2004 were: New York Public Library (largest single public library budget in the world); Los Angeles County Public Library; Chicago Public Library; Cincinnati & Hamilton County Public Library; and Miami-Dade Public Library.

22
U.S. States with the Largest and Smallest Library Budgets

According to the U.S. Department of Education, for the fiscal year 2005, the five U.S. states with the largest library budgets were: California ($995 million); New York ($903 million); Ohio ($608 million); Illinois ($528 million); and Florida ($437 million). The five states with the smallest budgets were: North Dakota ($9 million); Vermont ($15.7 million); South Dakota ($16 million); Montana ($16.2 million); and Wyoming ($19 million).

23
Countries with the Largest Number of Public Libraries

Abbreviations: PL=public libraries, NL=national libraries, HEL=higher education libraries.

In 2006, Russia had more than 14,100 public and government funded libraries. The U.S. had over 10,300 public libraries. According to a UNESCO survey in 2005 and other sources the countries with the largest number of libraries in the major regions of the world are:

Africa: South Africa, 2 NL, 520 PL; Egypt 357 PL and Algeria 102 PL.

Asia: China, 2,689 PL; Japan, 2,742 PL; Australia, 548 PL; South Korea, 320 PL.

Europe: Russia, 14,100 PL, 42 NL, 339 HEL; Germany, 9,800 PL, 6 NL, 256 HEL; Ukraine, 6200 PL; U.K. 3, NL, 5000 PL; France 3,884 PL, 396 HEL; Spain, 3,832 PL; Poland, 3107 PL; Finland, 2700 PL.

Latin America: Brazil, 2,740 PL; Argentina, 2,300 PL; Colombia, 721 PL.

Middle East: Israel, 1,186 PL; Turkey 873 PL; Egypt 357 PL; Kuwait, 27 PL.

North America: U.S., 10,300 PL; Canada, 3700 PL.

By the start of the 21st century, Russia had a total of almost 64,500 libraries, making it the country with the largest number of libraries in the world. The American Library Association estimated that there are more public libraries in the U.S. than McDonald's restaurants. The large number of sophisticated public libraries in the U.S. can sometimes mean public libraries are subject to surveillance by the government agencies. For instance in the 1980s, during the Ronald Reagan administration and at the height of the Cold War, the FBI under its Library Awareness Program tried to recruit public librarians in the U.S. as freelance agents to help in identifying "suspicious" use of library materials in U.S. public libraries. But after a few months of fierce opposition from the American Library Association, the FBI finally abandoned the idea. But in a further case of Big Brother, in October 2001, the U.S. Congress passed the Patriot Act. This law, among other things, allows the FBI to serve search warrants to public libraries and to enable them to access the confidential records of targeted library users under suspicion of being involved in terrorism. Once again the American Library Association is fighting the law because, while the law can be beneficial in investigating terrorism, it can be abused and infringes privacy. The U.K. has a similar law to the Patriot Act called the Regulation of Investigatory Powers Act, which allows surveillance operations to be conducted on libraries, while another law allows law enforcement agencies to access confidential library records. Reports seem to suggest the U.K.'s library association (CILIP) is supportive of some aspects of the laws.

24
Ten U.S. States with the Largest Number of Public Libraries

According to the Institute of Education Sciences National Center for Education Statistics annual report published in 2006, *Public Libraries in the United States*, and supportive data from the American Library Association and other sources, there are now 10,300 public libraries in the U.S., making it the second largest in the world, behind those in Russia. Total circulation of library materials was 2 billion, the largest in the world. The five states with the largest number of public libranches (not largest book volumes of the branches) were: New York (largest number); Illinois; Texas; Pennsylvania; and Massachusetts. Wyoming, Hawaii, Nevada and Rhode Island had the fewest.

25
Countries with the Largest and Smallest Number of Public Libraries per Capita

The U.K. has more than 5,000 libraries for a population of 60 million. Norway has over 1000 public libraries for a population of 4.5 million, while Finland has over 2700 public libraries for a population of 5 million. Finland clearly has the largest number of public libraries per capita. List **15** above also shows that Finland has some of the biggest individual public libraries in Europe, for its population size. Japan only has just over 2700 libraries for a population of over 120 million, making it the OECD country (or industrialized country) with the smallest number of public libraries per capita. The explanation for this is that traditionally, the Japanese do not borrow books from publicly funded libraries. One reason for the small number of public libraries was that the cultural idea of public libraries only became significant after the Second World War, when legislation was passed to begin the establishment of public libraries in Japan. And only then were funds made more readily to build public libraries. And every April 30 (the date when the library bill became law) is celebrated as "Public Library Day."

In Europe having a large number of public libraries can be translated to mean that the country has a large number of avid book readers. A survey in 2002 showed that the largest numbers of book readers in Europe are in the U.K., Finland, Iceland and Sweden. All four have the largest number of public libraries in Europe per capita. Not surprisingly the most enthusiastic book readers in the world are in the U.S., while it is Iceland that has the world's highest literacy rate. UNESCO calculates that Iceland also publishes the largest number of books per capita.

26
Oldest Public Libraries in Africa and the Middle East

Koprulu Library established in Istanbul, Turkey, in 1678 with public funds (see list **73**, on the oldest university libraries), while the Beyazit State Library, also in Istanbul, was opened in 1884. In Israel, the Tel Aviv Central Library (*Shaar Zion*) was founded in 1958. In Africa, Luanda Municipal Library in Angola (*Biblioteca Municipal*) was founded in 1873 by the Portuguese colonial government. In South Africa, Cape Town City Library was founded in 1947, while Johannesburg Public Library was founded in 1959.

The first African public library act to legalize the role of public libraries in Sub-Saharan Africa was the 1948 Ghana Library Board Act. The first major Sub-Saharan general library board, handling the daily running of public and state university libraries as well as the national library, was the one set up in 1959 in Sierra Leone. Subscription libraries in South Africa were first set up in 1838; many later became public libraries.

27
Oldest Public Libraries in Asia

Penang Library, Malaysia, was founded in 1817 by the British colonial government. It is now part of the Penang Public Library Corporation (*Perbadanan Perpustakaan Awam Pinang*). On the Indian subcontinent Hardayal Municipal Public Library, New Delhi, India, was established in 1862. While in Japan, the Kyoto Public Library (*Kyoto Koukai Toshokan*) was founded in 1873. In China, the first public library opened in 1905 in Hunan Province. The Chinese Tianyi Ge Library building in Ningbo, China, although not a public library, is the oldest existing non-academic library in Asia, outside the Middle East. See list **236** for more details.

Sir Stamford Raffles, the founder of Singapore, was also instrumental to the founding of the Raffles Subscription Library in 1823, which later became the National Library of Singapore.

In Australia, Melbourne Public Library was founded 1853 and Brisbane Public Library in 1896. The oldest Australian subscription library was the Sydney Subscription Library, founded in 1826. It is now known as the State Library of New South Wales. In New Zealand the three oldest public libraries are Christchurch City Library (1859); Auckland City Library (1880) and Wellington Public Library (1893).

28
Oldest Public Libraries in Europe

The Pisistratus Public Library in ancient Athens, Greece, was set up by Greek scholars circa 540 B.C. The library was later destroyed when soldiers of the Roman Empire overran Greece. The first Roman public library was set up circa 40 B.C. in Rome by Gaius Asinius Pollio, the Roman general, historian and poet.

The following are the 11 oldest existing major public libraries in Europe. Due to the early foundation date of these libraries, many also stock vast collections of old and rare manuscripts produced on paper (incunabula), parchment, vellum, and papyrus. More details on libraries with large incunabula can be found at list **165**.

1. Vatican Library, Rome, Vatican City (*Biblioteca Apostolica Vaticana*). It was founded in A.D. 1451 by Pope Nicholas V (as a public library), but the original founding date actually goes back to the 14th century. At this time the construction of the library in Rome was interrupted by the removal of the popes from Italy to France, when Pope Clement V (French Archbishop of Bordeaux) moved the papal court from Rome to Avignon in 1305, the event called the "Babylonian Captivity." The Vatican Library was completed when the popes returned to Rome in 1377 with the initiative of Pope Gregory XI. However, the problems of having the papacy in the two cities continued with the

Although the Vatican Library was started as a public library, it has since become a research library, and scholars need to make an appointment to use it (© Biblioteca Apostolica Vaticana).

election of rival popes or the "The Great Schism," until 1417, when Rome was once again the official seat of the Vatican. The Avignon papal library (*Bibliothèque Palais des Papes*), the largest library in Europe in the 14th century, still exists today in France. The Vatican Library's collection includes over 75,000 rare manuscripts, 8000 incunabula and over 1.5 million books. The Vatican librarians are among the best translators working in a library today. One former librarian, Cardinal Giuseppe Caspar Mezzofanti, who worked in the nineteenth century, was fluent in 49 languages.

The Vatican Archives, containing the "state papers" of the Vatican as a civil and ecclesiastical government, are distinct from the Vatican Library. By the 15th century the Vatican Library was the largest library in world, until university libraries in Europe began to expand their libraries, with the influence of both the Renaissance and the invention of printing. Troops of Napoleon Bonaparte once raided the Vatican Library and the Vatican Archives and transferred several priceless manuscripts (many related to the Inquisition, which were subsequently lost) back to Paris, only to be returned after the 1815 Congress of Vienna. As the Vatican Library is a manuscript library, many important historical non-paper manuscripts, such the Codex Vaticanus, *a 4th century* A.D. *Greek Bible, are still preserved in the library, alongside books printed before 1501 (i.e., incunabula). One interesting collection of items in the Vatican Library are the several personal letters written by statesmen over the centuries. One such collection is the love letters written in 1536 by English King Henry VIII to his new lover Anne Boleyn before he married her, one of the six wives he had in all.*

2. Magdeburg Public Library, Germany (*Stadsbibliotek Magdeburg*). 1525.

3. Lyons Municipal Library, France (*Bibliothèque Municipale de Lyon*). 1527.

4. Bern Public Library, Switzerland. 1528.

5. Deventer Athenaeum Library, The Netherlands. 1560. It has over 700 incunabula.

6. Laurentian Library, Florence, Italy (*Biblioteca Mediceao Laurenziana*). 1571. It owns

over 3000 papyrus documents and 6000 incunabula.

The Library has the oldest accurate map of Africa (Portolano Laurenziano Gaddiano) *made circa 1351 which has left historians baffled about who were the first explorers of the African coast. See also list* **137**.

A number of Italian public, religious and private libraries with large collections of incunabula (paper and parchment versions) and papyri such as the Ambrosian Library in Milan and the Biblioteca Comunale dell'Archiginnasio *in Bologna (see list* **165***) exist today. The oldest is the San Domenico Library (Biblioteca "Studium" San Domenico) in Bologna, founded in 1218 in honor of St. Dominic, who established the Roman Catholic Dominican order (the Dominicans). He had arrived in Bologna to establish a friar in 1218. It has over 2000 incunabula, and 20,000 manuscripts.*

7. Rotterdam Municipal Library, The Netherlands (*Gemeentebibliotheek Rotterdam*). 1604.

8. Ambrosian Library, Milan, Italy (*Biblioteca Ambrosiana*). 1609.

The library contains the largest collection of Leonardo da Vinci's notebooks, collectively called the Codex Atlanticus *(the second largest such collection are at the Windsor Castle Library in the U.K.). The library was founded by Cardinal Federigo Borromeo as Italy's first official public library and owns 2100 incunabula. A large proportion of the very rare ancient Greek manuscripts at the Ambrosian Library were acquired by Cardinal Borromeo from the famous library of the prominent bibliophile and intellectual Gian Vincenzo Pinelli, just a few months after Borromeo founded the library. A photograph of the library can seen at list* **120**.

9. Mazarin Library, Paris, France (*Bibliothèque Mazarine*). 1643. It owns just over 1000 incunabula

Several European libraries in France and Italy with some sort of public library function were founded in the 16th and 17th century, influenced by the invention of printing and/or the Reformation, such as the Luciano Benincasa Library in Ancona, Italy, founded in 1669. One public library in France that attracts rare book researchers is the Nancy City Library in France which has the oldest existing hand-copied edition (1427) of Claudius Ptolemy's Geographia (Cosmographia).

The Laurentian Library in Florence dates to the fourteenth century, but it was destroyed in 1494. Since being refounded, it has Italy's most important and valuable manuscripts, especially classical and biblical manuscripts.

France's oldest public library is the proud owner of the oldest original Gutenberg Bible (1455), which today bears its name: **Mazarin Bible.** It was acquired for the library by the famous French doctor and librarian, Gabriel Naudé.

10. Chetham Library, Manchester, Britain. 1653.

Even though it started out originally as a subscription library, it later became a public library and is often referred to as the oldest public library in the English-speaking world

11. Marsh Public Library, Dublin, Ireland. Founded in 1701 by Irish Archbishop Narcissus Marsh. It is the oldest public library in Ireland.

Several other prominent British libraries (not circulating or subscription libraries) do not qualify to be listed as public libraries. Some were not necessarily open to everyone (e.g., some were barred to women and children or the working class), while others had books mostly on religion. The oldest of these founded before the 1700s were:

1. Francis Trigge Grantham Library, 1598. Essentially a parish library, and famous for its fabulous chained books (see list **144**).

2. Norwich City Library, England. It opened in 1608 as a public library, but it only stocked theological books and publications.

3. Innerpeffray Library in Crieff, Perthshire, Scotland. 1680. Founded by David Drummond, 3rd Lord Maddertie. Oldest non academic library in Scotland.

4. Kirkwell Library, Orkney, Scotland. 1683.

5. Leignton Library, Dunblane, Scotland. 1688. In 1734 it was reconstituted as a public library.

The standard legal status for public libraries in Europe (public libraries as they are today) was only finally implemented from the 19th century, with the U.K. leading the way. Officially public libraries in the U.K. came into being with the passing of the 1850 U.K. Public Library Act. Both Canterbury and Warrington public library (listed below) users had to pay a small admission fee of around 1*d* to the library before they could use the library, so technically Salford Public library below is the oldest public library in the U.K. The British Museum Library, founded in 1753, was actually a public library, but it is today one of the U.K.'s national libraries, the British Library. The 10 oldest public libraries in the U.K. are:

1. Canterbury Public Library. 1847.

2. Warrington Public Library. 1848.
   Records show that it was founded in November 1848 under the 1845 U.K. Museums Act, 2 years before the 1850 U.K. Public Library Act. It is nevertheless officially the first public library in the England.

3. Salford Public Library. 1849.

4. Norwich Public Library. 1850.
   It was formerly a subscription library, then renamed Norwich Public Library in 1850, when it became the first public library to adopt the 1850 U.K. Public Library Act.

5. Winchester Public Library. 1851.

6. Liverpool Public Library. 1852.

7. Manchester Public Library. 1853.

8. Bolton Public Library. 1854.

9. Oxford Public Library. 1855.

Joint 10. Kidderminster Public Library and Cambridge Public Library. 1856.

Prior to the creation of free public libraries in the U.K., it was common for members of the public to subscribe to commercial circulating libraries. The largest of these libraries were based in London. There were more than fifty such circulating libraries in the U.K. by 1750. By the end of the century such circulating libraries were widespread. In 1801 it was estimated that there were no fewer than a thousand such libraries. Three candidates for the title of U.K.'s oldest subscription libraries are:

1. Chetham Library, Manchester, England. 1653.

2. Edinburgh Circulating Library, Scotland. 1725.

3. Linen Hall Library in Belfast, Northern Ireland. 1788.
   The oldest and only residential library in the U.K. was founded in 1889. Its book collections grew from a donation of books by the 19th century prime minister William Gladstone. The library is named St. Deiniol's and includes a hostel. Today it has over 200,000 books. Based in Hawarden in Flintshire, readers pay an annual subscription fee.
   The London Library, a private subscription library formed in 1841, is the most important surviving subscription library remaining in the capital. Its collection includes several 19th century books on literature.

In Russia, the M.E. Saltykov-Shchedrin State Public Library (later National Library of Russia) was founded in 1795 by Empress Catherine the Great. The Russian State Library in Moscow was originally the first public library in Moscow in 1828. In Germany, the first official German public libraries (*Volksbibliotheken*) were established in 1840 in Berlin. In Bosnia and Herzegovina, the Grazi Husrebegov Library in Sarajevo (*Biblioteca Grazi Husrebegova*) was founded in 1537, but mostly has religious (Islam) books and manuscripts.

29
Oldest Public Libraries in Latin America

The oldest public libraries in Latin America are:

1. Palafox Library (*Biblioteca Palafoxiana*), Puebla, Mexico. Founded 1645. Its library

building is the oldest existing one in the Americas.

2. Santa Fe Public Library, Bogotá, Colombia (*Biblioteca Pública Santa Fe*). 1777.

3. Buenos Aires Public Library, Argentina (*Biblioteca Buenos Aires*). 1812. Later became the National Library of Argentina in 1884.

4. Oaxaca Public Library, Mexico (*Biblioteca Pública Oaxaca*). 1826.

5. Chihuahua Public Library Mexico (*Biblioteca Pública Chihuahua*). 1829.

6. La Paz Municipal Library, Bolivia (*Biblioteca Municipal Mariscal Andres de Santa Cruz*). 1838.

The oldest public library in Brazil is the Pelotas Public Library (Biblioteca Pública Pelotense) founded in 1875, the city also contains Brazil's oldest university library. San Jose Seminary Library (Biblioteca Seminario Concilar de San José) in Bogotá, Columbia was founded in 1581. St. Benedict Monastery Library (Biblioteca do Mosteiro de S. Bento) in Rio Janeiro, Brazil, was founded in 1600, but both are religious public libraries.

30
Oldest Public Libraries in the U.S. and Canada

Generally speaking, the simplest definition of a public library from U.S. state and federal statute books is: "a public library is an administrative entity, the agency that is legally established under local or state law to provide public library service to the population of local jurisdiction." Peterboro Public Library in New Hampshire, established under these rules, is thus the oldest in the U.S., but it was not initially free to use as explained below.

The 10 oldest public libraries in the U.S. are:

1. Peterboro Public Library, New Hampshire. Founded 1833.

2. Buffalo & Erie County Public Library, New York. 1836.

3. New Orleans Public Library, Louisiana. 1843.

4. Boston Public Library, Massachusetts. 1848.

Boston Public was the first true tax-supported public library in the U.S. because Peterboro, New Orleans, and Buffalo & Erie public libraries initially all charged an admission fee. Boston Public Library was also the first public library to allow people to borrow books.

5. Cincinnati & Hamilton County Public Library, Ohio. 1856.

6. Cleveland Public Library, Ohio. 1869.

7. Los Angeles Public Library, California. 1872.

8. Chicago Public Library, Illinois. 1873.

9. Houston Public Library, Texas. 1875.

10. Pasadena Central Public Library, California. 1882.

In Canada, Quebec City Library (*Bibliothèque de Québec*) set up in 1779 by Governor Frederick Haldimand, began as a subscription library. It stocked books in both French and English. Toronto Public Library (*Bibliothèque Publique de Toronto*) was founded in 1884. Since Quebec City Library is now a public library, Toronto Public Library is regarded as the second oldest public library today.

The very first subscription library in the U.S. was the Library Company of Philadelphia, set up by Benjamin Franklin in 1732. The Franklin Public Library, in Wrentham, Massachusetts, named in honor of Benjamin Franklin, is America's first lending library, having been established in 1778. The oldest subscription library in the U.S. in continuous service is Darby Library Company, since 1743.

31
Oldest Public Libraries in the Caribbean Islands

The 5 oldest public libraries in the Caribbean Islands are:

1. Dominican Public Library, Santo Domingo, Dominican Republic (*Biblioteca Dominicana*). Founded 1729.

2. Nassau Public Library, The Bahamas. 1837.

3. Bridgetown Public Library, Barbados. 1847.

It is also the largest public library in the Caribbean islands, with over 165,000 books.

4. Port of Spain Public Library, Trinidad and Tobago. 1851.

5. Carnegie Public Library, San Juan, Puerto Rico. 1916.

32
First Public Library Commemorative Coins of the Millennium

In 2000, the Royal Mint in Llantrisant, which makes all the coins used in the U.K., celebrated the 150th anniversary of the U.K. Public Library Act by issuing a special 50 pence coin.

In 2000 the U.S. Mint in Washington, D.C., issued two special commemorative coins. Both of the coins are honoring the Library of Congress. One of them was a beautiful ten dollar bimetallic (platinum and gold) coin, the first ever issued by the U.S. One side of the coin shows the hand of Minerva raising the torch of learning over the dome of the Jefferson Building. The other commemorative coin was a silver one dollar coin, the first such commemorative U.S. coin of the millennium.

33
First Public Library Commemorative Postage Stamp

The New York Public Library in the U.S. was the first public library to be featured on a postage stamp, issued in 1920.

The Library of Congress first appeared on a U.S. stamp in April 1981, designed by Bradbury Thompson and based on a 1898 photograph of the Thomas Jefferson Building. The National Postal Museum Library and Research Center has over 40,000 books and manuscripts, making it the world's largest philatelic and postal history library facilities. The Smithsonian Institution Libraries operates the library. The postage stamp itself was invented in 1840, with the introduction of the "Penny Black" in 1840 in London, U.K.

WORLD RECORDS FOR UNIVERSITY AND ACADEMIC LIBRARIES

Yet the reverence for size continues. The library that has the most books is likely to be regarded as ipso facto, the best.

Herman Fussler, U.S. academic librarian. 1949.

Universities can be made up of several campuses, either in the same city or in different cities. For instance, the University of California has branches in 9 cities in the state, but each one is a university in its own right. It follows that a university may have several libraries in different buildings and locations. It is common for even a single-campus university library to have a central collection and other collections divided among different faculties and departments. Hence all numbers of books given below are the total in aggregate of books in all libraries of each specific university listed, including departmental and faculty libraries.

When considering lists for the oldest university libraries, where the actual opening date of the library is not known, the foundation date of the university is used. But bear in mind that some university libraries may actually open on the same day a university is officially opened (in many cases after the foundation date), or after the university is opened, in this case from a few months to a few years. Some of the earliest universities had no building dedicated to a library; for instance the U.K.'s Oxford University in the 13th century kept its book collection in St. Mary's Church nearby until the 14th century.

34
Twenty Largest University Libraries

N.B. This chapter covering largest university libraries also includes the largest libraries of academies, which were particularly numerous in the former communist countries of Eastern Europe. It excludes U.S. university libraries with less than 8 million books. See list **35** for the 20 largest U.S. university libraries.

1. Harvard University Library, Cambridge, Massachusetts, U.S. 15 million books. Founded in 1636 with 300 books bequeathed to the university by John Harvard. Also the oldest university library in the U.S. Apart from Cambridge, Harvard University also has libraries in Boston, Washington, D.C., and Florence, Italy. Altogether there are just over 90 Harvard University libraries.

The Harvard University student population currently numbers about 19,600 students. In comparison, the State University of New York, the largest university in the U.S., has over 250,000 students. Its largest library, at Buffalo campus, contains about 3.2 million books. The first full-time librarian at Harvard was Solomon Stoddard in 1643.

2. Russian Academy of Sciences Library, St. Petersburg, Russia (*Biblioteka Rossiskaya Akademii Nauk*). 14.2 million. Founded in 1714 by Tsar Peter I.

It was the first state-owned public library of Russia. Another large Russian academy library is the Russian Academy of Sciences Library for Natural Sciences with 11 million books, founded in 1934 in Moscow and the INION library (listed below).

3. Yale University Library, New Haven, Connecticut, U.S. 12 million. Founded 1701.

4. Institute for Scientific Information on Social Sciences Library, Moscow, INION (*Insitut Nauchnoi Informatsii po Obshchestvennym Naukam*) 12.8 million books. Founded 1918.

5. Lomonosov Moscow State University Library, Russia *(Nauchnaia Biblioteka Universiteta Lomonosova)*. 11 million. Founded 1756.

It was for several years the only major library in the 18th century available to the public in Russia, till the M.E. Saltykov-Shchedrin State Public Library (later National Library of Russia) was founded 1795 by Empress Catherine the Great in St. Petersburg.

6. University of Illinois Library, Urbana-Champaign, U.S. 10.5 million. Founded 1867. Third largest U.S. university library, after the libraries at Harvard and Yale universities.

7. University of California Library, Berkeley, U.S. 10 million. Founded 1868.

It has the largest university student population in the U.S. after the State University of New York (SUNY) and City University of New York (CUNY). The MELVYL catalog (the combined University of California libraries union catalog), is larger than the Harvard University library catalog.

8. Romanian Academy Library (*Biblioteca Academiei Române*), Bucharest, Romania. Founded 1866. 9.8 million.

Technically this is one of Romania's three national libraries.

9. University of Toronto Robarts Library, Canada. 9.5 million, Founded 1891.

10. University of Tokyo Library, Japan (*Tokyo Daigaku Toshokan*). 9.2 million. Founded 1893. Nihon University in Tokyo, has the largest student population in Japan.

11. Columbia University Library, New York City. 9.2 million. Founded 1784.

12. Oxford University Bodleian Library, U.K. 9 million. See list **36**.

13. University of Texas Library, Austin, U.S. 8.9 million. Founded 1839.

It has the fourth largest university student population in the U.S.

14. Stanford University Library, California, U.S. 8.2 million. Founded 1892.

15. University of Michigan, Ann Arbor. 8.1 million. Founded 1838.

16. University of California Library, Los Angeles, U.S. Founded 1919. 8 million.

It also has the third largest university student population in the U.S.

17. University of Beijing Library (*Peking Daxue Tushugan*). Founded 1902. 8 million books.

18. Ukrainian National Academy of Sciences, Vernadsky Central Scientific Library, Kiev. 8 million. Founded 1919.

19. University of Calgary Library. Canada. 7.6 million. Founded 1966.

20. St. Petersburg State University Library, Russia. 7.5 million. Founded 1783.

35
Twenty Largest University Libraries in the U.S.

1. Harvard University Library, Cambridge, Massachusetts, U.S. 15 million books. Founded 1636.

2. Yale University Library, New Haven, Connecticut, U.S. 12 million. Founded 1701.

Students arrive for lectures at the University of California, Berkeley, which is the largest and oldest of nine University of California institutions in the state. The combined library collection makes California the state with the largest combined volume of university library books (courtesy of University of California, Berkeley).

3. University of Illinois Library, Urbana-Champaign, U.S. 10.5 million. Founded 1867.

4. University of California Library, Berkeley, U.S. 10 million. Founded 1868.

5. Columbia University Library, New York City. 9.2 million. Founded 1784.

6. University of Texas Library, Austin, U.S. 8.9 million. Founded 1839.

7. Stanford University Library, California, U.S. 8.2 million. Founded 1892.

8. University of Michigan, Ann Arbor. 8.1 million. Founded 1838.

9. University of California Library, Los Angeles, U.S. 8 million. Founded 1919.

10. University of Wisconsin–Madison Library 7.9 million. Founded 1848.

11. Cornell University Library, Ithaca, New York. 7.7 million. Founded 1865.

12. University of Chicago Library, Illinois, 7.4 million. Founded 1892.

13. Indiana University Library 7.2 million, Indianapolis. Founded 1829

14. University of Washington Library 6.9 million. Founded 1862.

The University of Toronto Robarts Library is the largest, most expensive and tallest library building in Canada (courtesy Laura Arsie, University of Toronto Library).

15. University of Minnesota Library, Minneapolis, 6.6 million. Founded 1851.

16. Princeton University Library, New Jersey, 6.5 million. Founded 1746.

17. Ohio State University Library, Columbus. 6 million. Founded 1873.

18. University of Pennsylvania Library, Philadelphia. 5.8 million. Founded 1750.

19. University of North Carolina–Chapel Hill Library, 5.7 million. Founded 1795.

20. Duke University Library, Durham, North Carolina. 5.5 million. Founded 1838.

The 8 universities that make up the Ivy League of prestigious U.S. universities are all in this list of 20 largest U.S. university libraries except Brown University and Dartmouth College. This seems to provide further proof that the best universities in the world tend also to have large libraries (see list 59 for more details). One of the librarians of Columbia University Library, Melvil Dewey, is famous for inventing the popular Dewey Decimal System for classifying books and also founding the first library school in the world. There are so many university libraries in the U.S. with over 3 million volumes that most belong to organizations that help to support these libraries either financially or in a professional capacity to help develop the library. Two major organizations are the Association of Research Libraries and the Association of College and Research Libraries.

36
Ten Largest University Libraries in Europe

1. Russian Academy of Sciences Library. (See list 34.)

2. Romanian Academy Library. (See list 34.)

3. Ukrainian National Academy of Sciences. (See list 34.)

4. Lomonosov Moscow State University Library. (See list 34.)

5. Bodleian Library, Oxford University, U.K. Founded 1602. 9 million books. A new building of the U.K.'s most famous university library, opened in 1946, designed by Giles Scott. The building consists of 11 floors with external walls of Bladon stone and Clipsham dressings.

The main library of U.K.'s largest university, the University of London (excluding the Open University), i.e., the University of London Library at Senate House, had about 2 million books and 98,000 students in 2006 compared to Oxford University's 18,000 students. However, the combined collections of all the London University individual libraries are just slightly smaller than the Bodleian. In 1602 Thomas James became the first full time librarian for Oxford University. By the end of the 17th century most of the books in the Bodleian were in Latin, with only a handful in English. It was not until the

end of the 19th century that the number of books in English exceeded those in Latin.

6. St. Petersburg State University Library (*Biblioteka Universiteta Sankt-Petersburga*). Formerly Zhdanov State University Library, St. Petersburg, Russia. Founded in 1783. It currently has about 7.5 million books.

The university was originally founded in the 18th century. The most memorable moment in the history of the university library occurred during the Second World War. While many of the staff and students had been evacuated, other librarians and university staff stayed on to defend the university against the Nazis during the 900-day siege of St. Petersburg (Leningrad). Ivan Pavlov, who made famous psychological experiments with dogs that earned him a Nobel Prize, was a regular user of the university library, as a student reading chemistry and physiology in the 19th century.

7. The University of Paris Library, France (*Bibliothèque de l'Université Paris*). Has a combined book collection of 7 million books. First university founded 1230.

The University of Paris is made up of 13 separate universities, all given names with Roman numerals I to XIII. For instance the library of the University of Paris V is called Bibliothèque de l'Université Paris

V. The University of Paris also has the 4th largest student population, after the State University of New York, in the U.S., Calcutta (Kolkata) University, in India, and Mexico National Autonomous University, Mexico City. All four universities had over 300,000 students in the year 2005.

8. Berlin Free University Library, Germany (*Bibliothek der Freie Universität Berlin*). Founded 1952. 6.4 million.

It has the second largest university student population in Germany after the Ludwig Maximilians University in Munich. The other and much older Berlin University (called Humboldt University to avoid confusion in names) was founded in 1828. But its allegiance with Communism (since it was in the former East German capital of East Berlin) led several non-communist academics to leave the Humboldt University and found the Berlin Free University in West Berlin. The Library building of the Philiological Department is shaped like a human brain.

9. Cambridge University Library, U.K. 6.4 million. Founded 1347.

Apart from having the U.K.'s second largest university library, Cambridge University is also the richest university in the U.K., worth over $2 billion and with an annual turnover of $300 million.

10. University of London Libraries, U.K. Combined collection of about 5.8 million books. Third largest in the U.K., after Oxford and Cambridge university libraries. First library founded in the early 19th century. The libraries of King's College and University College London (UCL) are the largest.

It has the largest university student population in the U.K.

37
Ten Largest University Libraries in the U.K.

1. Bodleian Library, Oxford University. (See list **36**.)

2. Cambridge University Library. (See list **36**.)

3. University of London Libraries. (See list **36**.)

4. John Rylands University Library, Manchester. 4.8 million books. Founded in 1900.

It also has the second largest university student population in the U.K.

5. University of Birmingham Library. 3 million. Founded 1880.

6. Edinburgh University Library. 2.7 million. Founded 1580.

Charles Darwin, who revolutionized our understanding of evolution, did not have sufficient time to use the library as he spent a little over a year at Edinburgh University studying medicine before dropping out in 1827. Things looked bleak for Darwin until when he went to Cambridge for theological studies, and while there befriended a botany professor. It was this academic who recommended Darwin for the post of naturalist for the exploration of South America by a British navy ship. On his return Darwin would publish a book about his extraordinary voyage and the rest is history.

7. University of Leeds Library, 2.5 million. Founded 1874.

8. University of Glasgow Library, 1.6 million. Founded 1450.

U.K.'s first 24 hour academic library is at Bath University. The round-the-clock library service began in 1996. Bookworms and workaholics will find the service a great way to spend an all-nighter brainstorming. For those who begin to fall asleep in the early hours of the morning, a softbound book will be a good substitute for a pillow.

9. Bristol University Library, 1.5 million. Founded 1909.

10. University of Liverpool Library, 1.4 million. Founded 1881.

SCONUL Research Extra is the largest inter-library borrowing scheme in higher education libraries in the UK. Scholars, university staff and postgrad-

The University of London is made up of 20 institutions, and the combined library collection makes it the third largest in the United Kingdom. A further library is the University of London Senate House Library shown above. The Senate administers all the separate universities.

Kings College Maughan Library is the largest of the 20 University of London libraries. Although the outside has a medieval Gothic look, the inside looks very much 21st century.

The University of Liverpool has the tenth largest university library in the United Kingdom (courtesy of University of Liverpool).

uate students are eligible to borrow books from any participating institutions (including most of the large university libraries listed above) on production of a SCONUL membership card.

38
Ten Largest University Libraries in France

1. The University of Paris Library. (See list **36**.)

2. Strasbourg National University Library (*Bibliothèque Nationale et Universitaire de Strasbourg*). Founded 1540, 5 million books.

   Like the University of Paris, the university is divided into separate universities, each designated with Roman numerals.

3. University of Montpellier Library (*Bibliothèque de l'Université de Montpellier*). Founded 1240. 4.3 million.

   Was divided into three separate universities, each designated with Roman numerals in 1970.

4. University of Lyon Library (*Bibliothèque de l'Université de Lyon*). 3.1 million. Founded 1970.

   Divided into three separate universities.

5. University of Toulouse Library (*Bibliothèque de l'Université de Toulouse*). 2.5 million. Founded 1292.

6. Aix-Marseille University Library (Provence University), Marseille and Aix-en-Provence (*Bibliothèque de l'Université d'Aix-Marseille*). 2.3 million. Founded 1413.

   Has the second largest university student population in France, after the University of Paris. While

Province University in Marseille has the largest university library in the south of France.

the Aix-en-Province campus was founded in 1413, the Marseille campus was founded in 1854.

7. Lille University Library (*Bibliothèque de l'Université de Lille*). 2 million. Founded 1560 (reorganized in 1970).

8. Grenoble University Library (*Bibliothèque de l'Université de Grenoble*). 1.8 million. Founded 1339 (reorganized in 1970).

9. Orléans University Library (*Bibliothèque de l'Université d'Orléans*). 1.6 million. Founded 1306.

10. Bordeaux University Library (*Bibliothèque de l'Université de Bordeaux*). 1.3 million. Founded 1441.

Following the massive 1968 national strike, initiated by the famous student demonstrations at the Latin-Quarter in Paris against the Fifth Republic administration of Charles de Gaulle, many French universities were broken and reorganized between 1969 and 1970, especially with the introduction of Roman numerals designating separate universities, such as those in Paris, Lyon, Strasbourg, Grenoble, Lille and Toulouse. Some adopted theses dates as the new foundation date, rather than the much earlier original foundation date.

39
Ten Largest University Libraries in Germany

1. Berlin Free University Library. (See list **36**.)

2. Hanover Technical University Library (*Bibliothek der Hanover Technische Universität*). 4.8 million books. Founded 1831.

3. University of Leipzig Library (*Universitätbibliothek Leipzig*). 4.8 million. Founded 1409.

Wolfgang von Goethe, the famous German poet, as a student borrowed books from the Leipzig University Library. As it was in former Communist East

Germany, the University of Leipzig was formerly called Karl Marx University before 1990.

4. Martin Luther University Library, Halle-Wittenberg (*Bibliothek der Martin Luther Universität*). Founded in 1502. 4.6 million.

5. George Augustus University Library, Göttingen (*Bibliothek der Georg-August Universität*). 4.1 million. Founded in 1737.

It was founded by King George II of Britain and entrusted with the task to act as the German national library for the eighteenth century. King George II was born in Hanover, Germany, as was his father, King George I (Ernest Augustus). They are among several foreign-born kings of Britain such as King William III of Orange born in the Hague, The Netherlands; King William I "the Conqueror" from Normandy, France, and King Canute from Denmark.

6. Dresden Technical University Library (*Universitätbibliothek Dresden*). 4.6 million. Founded 1828.

7. University of Frankfurt Library (*Universitätbibliothek Frankfurt am Main*). 4.5 million. Founded in 1511.

8. Rupert-Charles University Library, Heidelberg (*Ruprecht-Karls Universitätbibliothek Heidelberg*). 4.3 million. Founded 1386, hence the oldest in Germany.

9. Humboldt University Library, Berlin (*Bibliothek Humboldt Universität zu Berlin*). Founded 1828. 4 million.

10. Ludwig–Maximilians University Library, Munich (*Bibliothek* Ludwig–Maximilians *Universität München*). 3.8 Million. Founded 1472. It has the largest university student population in Germany.

For most of the 1800s, a university library in Germany was run by a university professor, but each was later headed by a full time librarian.

40
Ten Largest University Libraries in Italy

1. University of Florence Library (*Biblioteca Università degli Studi di Firenze*). Founded in 1321. 4 million books.

2. University of Rome Library (*Biblioteca Università degli Studi di Roma "La Sapienza"*). Founded 1304. 2.9 million.

It also has the second largest university student population in Europe, after the University of Paris in France.

3. University of Turin Library (*Biblioteca Università degli Studi di Torino*). 2.6 million. Founded 1404.

4. University of Bologna Library (*Biblioteca Università degli Studi di Bologna*). 1.8 million. Founded 1088.

5. University of Milan (*Biblioteca Università degli Studi di Milano*). 1.3 million. Founded 1923.

6. University of Naples Library (*Biblioteca Università degli Studi di Napoli*). 900,000. Founded 1295.

It also has the second largest university student population in Italy, after Rome University.

7. University of Padua Library (*Biblioteca Università degli Studi di Padova*). 810,000. Founded 1122.

8. University of Pisa Library (*Biblioteca Università degli Studi di Pisa*). 735,000. Founded 1343.

9. University of Siena Library (*Biblioteca Università degli Studi di Siena*). 700,000. Founded 1245.

10. University of Pavia Library (*Biblioteca Università degli Studi di Pavia*). 680,000. Founded 1361.

The largest book-burning ritual in a Western university library in the twentieth century occurred outside Berlin's Humboldt University Library during the Nazi regime in Germany.

41
Ten Largest University Libraries in Austria and Switzerland

1. University of Vienna Library, Austria (*Universitätbibliothek Wien*). 5.8 million books. Founded 1365.

It also has the largest university student population in Austria. The university's Institute of Ethnology Library owns the largest collection of Chinese and Japanese books in Europe.

2. Swiss Federal Institute of Technology Library, Zürich (*Bibliothek Eidgenössiche Technische Hochschule Zürich*). 5.6 million. Founded 1855.

Albert Einstein was the most famous user of the university library, which today has the largest collection of Einstein's original research papers outside the U.S.

3. Innsbruck University Library, Austria (*Universitätbibliothek Innsbruck*). 3.2 million.

Founded 1669. Also called Leopold-Franzens University.

Among the books in the university library is the famous book Man in Ice, *written by the Innsbruck University professor who, as head of the Innsbruck University Institute of Prehistory, led research on the equally famous 5300-year-old Ice Mummy Oetzi, which was discovered in an ice glacier in the Italian Alps in 1991. It was the most famous ancient mummy find since the 3,000-year-old mummy of King Tutankhamun was discovered in Egypt in 1922 by Lord Carnarvon and Howard Carter.*

4. University of Basel Library, Switzerland (*Universitätbibliothek Basel*). 3.1 million. Founded 1460.

5. University of Graz Library, Austria (*Universitätbibliothek Graz*). 3 million. Founded 1586. Also known as Karl-Franzens University.

Vienna University Library in Austria is also the oldest university library in central Europe.

6. University of Bern Library, Switzerland (*Universitätbibliothek Bern*). 2 million. Founded 1528.

7. University of Zürich Library, Switzerland (*Universitätbibliothek Zürich*). 1.9 million. Founded 1523.

It was here in 1905 that Albert Einstein obtained his Ph.D. for the first of several published scientific papers in a German physics journal, which eventually led to the famous paper on the theory of relativity. Einstein had earlier graduated from the Swiss Federal Institute of Technology in 1900.

8. University of Salzburg Library, Austria (*Universitätbibliothek Salzburg*). 2 million. Founded 1623.

9. University of Lausanne Library, Switzerland (*Bibliothèque de l'Université de Lausanne*). 1.8 million. Founded in 1537. It is the largest French-speaking university library in Switzerland.

10. University of Fribourg Library, Switzerland (*Universitätbibliothek Fribourg*). 1.6 million. Founded 1848.

42
Ten Largest University Libraries in Spain and Portugal

1. Complutense University Library, Madrid, Spain (*Biblioteca de la Universidad Complutense de Madrid*). Founded 1293. 2.9 million.

It also has the largest university student population in Spain.

2. Madrid National Autonomous University Library. Spain (*Biblioteca de la Universidad Nacional Autónoma de Madrid*). Founded 1510. 2.7 million books.

3. University of Coimbra Library, Portugal (*Biblioteca Universidade de Coimbra*). Founded 1290. 2 million.

The university was originally founded in Lisbon, before it moved to Coimbra in 1537.

4. University of Saragossa Library, Spain (*Biblioteca de la Universidad de Zaragoza*). Founded 1480. 1.8 million.

5. University of Barcelona Library, Spain (*Biblioteca de la Universitat de Barcelona*). Founded 1430. 1.6 million.

It also has second the largest university student population in Spain.

Joint 6th. Ramon Llull University Library, Barcelona, Spain (*Biblioteca de la Universitat de Ramón Llull*), founded 1980 and Santiago de Compostela University Library, Spain (*Biblioteca de la Universidade de Santiago de Compostela*), founded 1532. Both have 1.5 million books.

7. University of Navarre Library, Pamplona, Spain (*Biblioteca de la Universidad de Navarra*). Founded 1952. 1.3 million.

8. University of Bilbao Library, Spain (*Biblioteca de Universitaria Bilbao*). 910,000. Founded 1886.

9. University of Murcia Library, Spain (*Biblioteca de la Universidad de Murcia*). 730,000,000. Founded in 1915.

10. Oviedo University Library, Spain (*Biblioteca de la Universidad de Oviedo*). 712,000. Founded in 1609.

43
Ten Largest University Libraries in Scandinavia

1. Lund University Library, Sweden (*Bibliotek Lunds Universitet*). 5.3 million. Founded 1671.

2. Uppsala University Library, Sweden (*Bibliotek Uppsala Universitet*). 5.2 million. Founded 1477.

3. University of Copenhagen Library, Denmark (*Bibliotek Københavns Universitet*). 5 million books. Founded 1482.

It is also forms part of the National Library of Denmark. Copenhagen University Library was once open only to professors; students enrolled at the university were only finally allowed to borrow books from 1789. A famous relic at the library is a British cannonball, part of the British bombardment that destroyed parts of the university in 1807, during the war between Denmark and the U.K. Ironically one of the books of the library hit by the cannonball was titled Defender of Peace.

4. University of Oslo Library, Norway (*Universitet Bibliotek i Oslo*). 4.5 million. Founded 1811.

5. University of Helsinki Library, Finland (*Helsingin Yliopiston Kirjasto*). 3.4 million. Founded 1640.

It is also part of the National Library of Finland.

6. Gothenburg University Library, Sweden (*Göteborgs Universitetsbibliotek*). 2.8 million. Founded 1891.

7. University of Stockholm Library, Sweden (*Stockholms Universitetsbibliotek*). 2.5 million. Founded 1878.

8. University of Trondheim Library, Norway (*Universitetsbibliotek i Trondheim*). 2.4 million. Founded 1768.

9. Turku University Library, Finland (*Turun Yliopiston Kirjasto*). 2.3 million. Founded 1922.

10. Abo Academy University Library, Turku, Finland (*Abo Akademi Yliopiston Kirjasto*). 1.9 million. Founded in 1918.

Complutense University Library in Madrid is the largest university library in Spain and the oldest in the city.

44
Ten Largest University Libraries in Belgium and The Netherlands

1. Leuven Catholic University Library (*Katholieke Universiteitbibliotheek Leuven*). Leuven, Belgium. 4 million. Founded 1425.

The above university is in the Flemish (Dutch) speaking part of Belgium. There is another university in the French speaking part of Belgium, called Louvain Catholic University (Université Catholique de Louvain), and located in the city of Louvain-la-Neuve. It has about 2 million books. Both universities were originally one, founded in 1425 by Pope Martin V, but were split up in 1968. The central library was established in 1627. The university has the largest student population in Belgium.

2. University of Utrecht Library, The Netherlands (*Universiteitbibliotheek Utrecht*). 4.6 million. Founded 1584.

3. University of Amsterdam Library, The Netherlands (*Universiteitbibliotheek Amsterdam*). 4.1 million books. Founded 1578.

4. Gent University Library, Belgium (*Universiteitbibliotheek Gent*). 3 million. Founded 1817.

5. Groningen State University Library, The Netherlands (*Bibliotheek der Rijksuniversiteit te Groningen*). 2.9 million. Founded 1615.

6. Leiden University Library, The Netherlands (*Bibliotheek der Rijksuniversiteit de Gronigen*). 2.4 million. Founded 1575.

7. Brussels Free University Library, Belgium (*Bibliothèque de l'Université Libre de Bruxelles/*

Universiteitbibliotheek Vrije Brussels). 1.6 million. Founded 1834.

In 1970 the university was split into Flemish and French universities.

8. University of Liège Library, Belgium (*Bibliothèque de l'Université de Liège*) 2.6. Million. Founded 1816.

9. Nijmegen University Library, The Netherlands (*Universiteitbibliotheek Nijmegen*) 2.1 million. Founded 1923.

10. Erasmus University Library, Rotterdam, The Netherlands (*Universiteitbibliotheek Erasmus*) 1.2 million. Founded 1973.

45
Three Largest University Libraries in Ireland

1. Trinity College, Dublin University Library. 3.8 million books. Founded 1592. The current building was built between 1712 and 1724 and designed by Thomas Burgh. Its Long Room, with arched ceilings, is a famous sight, with books filling the entire length of the room, as well as to the ceiling. The most famous book in the library is the *Book of Kells*, which is the most remarkable artifact of medieval Celtic art.

2. National University of Ireland Library, Dublin, Cork, Maynooth and Galway. 2.5 million. Founded 1840s and 1850s. Maynooth campus was founded in 1795.

In medieval times, Galway was the most important center of learning in Ireland. Trinity College Library receives by law a copy of every book published in the U.K. This began in 1801 (when Ireland was then part of the U.K.) and has continued long after Ireland gained its Independence. The other five legal deposit libraries in the U.K. entitled to receive, free of charge, a copy of every single book produced in the U.K. are: Bodleian Library (Oxford University), Cambridge University Library, the national libraries of Scotland and Wales, and the British Library.

3. University College Library, Dublin, Galway and Cork. 2 million books. Founded 1849.

46
Three Largest University Libraries in the Vatican City

1. Pontifical Gregorian University Library, Rome (*Biblioteca Pontificia Università Gregoriana*). 1.3 million books. Founded 1553.

Because Latin is one of the six languages of instruction, its library has the largest collection of academic books in Latin, after those in the library of St. Thomas Aquinas Pontifical University Library.

2. Pontifical Lateran University Library, Rome (*Biblioteca Pontificia Università Lateranese*). 810,000. Founded 1773.

3. St. Thomas Aquinas Pontifical Library, Rome (*Biblioteca Pontificia Università S. Tommaso D'Aquino*). 570,000. Founded 1580.

47
Five Largest University Libraries in Greece and Turkey

1. Aristotelian University of Thessaloniki Library (*Bibliotheke Aristoteleio Panepistimio Thessalonikus*). 2 million books. Founded 1927.

2. National and Capodistrian University Library. Athens (*Bibliotheke Athinisin Ethnikon*

Kai Kapodistriakon Panepistimio). 1.2 million. Founded 1837.

3. Ankara University Library (*Ankara Üniversitesi Kütüphane*). 750,000. 1946.

Despite being destroyed twice during the two world wars, Leuven Catholic University in Belgium and its library building (the oldest and largest in Belgium) has managed to maintain the same architectural style (photograph © K.U. Leuven).

4. Istanbul (Constantinople) University Library, Turkey (*Istanbul Üniversitesi Kütüphane*). 620,000. Founded 1455.

5. Hacettepe University Library, Ankara and Beytepe, Turkey (*Hacettepe Üniversitesi Kütüphane*). 370,000 books. Founded 1206.

48
Ten Largest University Libraries in Russia

1. Russian Academy of Science, St. Petersburg. (See list **34**.)

2. Lomonosov Moscow State University Library. (See list **34**.)

3. St. Petersburg University Library. (See list **34**.)

4. Kazan State University Library. 4.9 million books. Founded 1804.

V.I. Lenin was a famous user of the library in the late 1880s. He graduated with a first-class degree in law from the university.

5. Irkutsk State University Library. 4.2 million. Founded 1918.

6. Tomsk State University Library. 3.5 million. Founded 1888.

7. State Central Polytechnic Library, Moscow. 3.1 million. Founded 1961.

8. Saratov State University Library. 3 million. Founded 1909.

9. Rostov State University Library. 2.8 million. Founded 1915.

Joint 10th. Voronezh State University Library, founded 1918; and Moscow Technical University Library, founded 1930. Both just over 2.7 million books.

49
Twenty Largest University Libraries in Eastern Europe

N.B. This list excludes libraries in Russia.

1. Ukrainian National Academy of Sciences, Vernadsky Central Scientific Library, Kiev. 8 million. Founded 1919.

2. Lithuanian Technical University Library, Vilnius. 7 million books. Founded 1957.

3. St. Cyril and St. Methodius National Library, Sofia, Bulgaria. 5.4. Founded 1921.

4. University of Vilnius Library, Lithuania (*Biblioteka Universitas Vilnensis*). 5.2 million. Founded 1570.

The library remained closed for almost 100 years, when the university was shut down by the Russian government in 1832.

5. Simferopol State University Library, Ukraine. 4.9 million. Founded 1918.

6. Estonian Academic Library, Tallinn. 4 million. Founded 1946.

7. Jagiellonian University Library, Kraków, Poland (*Biblioteka Universytet Jagielloüski*). 3.9 million. Founded 1364.

The most famous user of the library in the 15th century was Nicolaus Copernicus as a student from 1491. He also studied at Italy's Bologna and Padua universities. His book on astronomy upset many scholars and the Vatican (who banned it). His publishers eventually printed the book, but only after adding a clever preface to exonerate them from criticism.

8. Wroclaw University Library (*Biblioteka Universytet Wroclaw*). Poland. 3.3 million. Founded 1945.

9. Taras Shevchenko University of Kiev Library, Ukraine. 3.6 million. Founded 1834.

Joint 10th. Mickiewicz University Library, Poznan, Poland (*Biblioteka Universytet im Adama Mickiewicza w Poznaniu*), founded 1919; and Cluj-Napoca Lucian Blaga University Central Library, Romania (*Biblioteca Centrala Universitatea Lucian Blaga*), founded 1872. Both have 3.5 million books.

11. Charles University Library, Prague, Czech Republic (*Knihovna Univerzita Karlova v Praze*). 3.4 million. Founded 1348.

12. Odessa University Library, Ukraine. 3.3 million. Founded 1807.

13. St. Clement Ohridski National and University Library, Bitola and Skopje, FYR Macedonia (*Sveti Kliment Ohridski Narodna i Univerzitetska Biblioteka*). 3.2 million. Founded 1944.

The university library is also part of the National Library of FYR Macedonia.

Joint 14th. University of Tartu Library, Estonia, founded in 1802; and Khakiv State University, Ukraine, founded 1805. Both own 3.1 million books.

During the 19th century, students caught stealing books from the library were punished by being locked up in a building at Tartu University that is today called the Student's Lock-Up Museum.

Joint 15th. University of Bucharest Library, Romania (*Biblioteca Universitatea Bucuresti*),

founded 1694; and Ivan Franko State University, Lviv, Ukraine, founded 1661. Both possess 2.5 million books.

16. Warsaw University Library, Poland (*Biblioteka Universytet Warszaawie*). 2.4 million. Founded 1817.

Joint 17. The Marie Curie-Sklodowska University Library of Lublin, Poland (*Biblioteka Universytet Marii Curie-Sklodowskiej w Lublinie*), founded 1944; and the National and University Library, Ljubljana, Slovenia (*Narodna Univerzitetna Knijžnica Ljubljani*) founded in 1595, both have 2.3 million books.

18. Belarus State University, Minsk. 2.2 million. Founded 1921.

Joint 19th. St. Clement Ohridski University, Bulgaria Library, Sofia (*Sofiski Universitet Sveti Kliment Ohridski*), founded 1931; and University of Belgrade Svetozar Markovic Library, Serbia (*Univerzitet u Beograd Biblioteka Svetozar Markovic*), founded in 1863. Both with 2 million books.

Joint 20th. Mikhail Eminescu University Central Library, Iasi, Romania (*Biblioteca Centrala Universitatea Iasi*), founded 1872; and Comenius University of Bratislava Library, Slovakia (*Univerzita Knižnica Komenskeho v Brastislave*), founded in 1465. 2 million books.

50
Ten Largest University Libraries in Canada

1. University of Toronto Robarts Library. 9.5 million books. Founded 1891.

It also has the largest university student population in Canada.

2. University of Calgary Library. 7.6 million. Founded 1966.

3. Laval University Library, Quebec City (*Bibliothèque de l'Université Laval*). 5.3 million. Founded 1663.

4. McGill University Library, Montreal (*Bibliothèque de l'Université de McGill*) 5 million. Founded 1855.

5. University of Alberta Library. Edmonton. 4.8 million. Founded 1906.

6. British Columbia University Library, Vancouver. 4.6 million. Founded 1908.

7. University of Waterloo Library. 4 million. Founded 1961.

The National and University Library of Slovenia is one of three East European universities (in the former Yugoslavia) that combine the function of the national library and university library. The only other European libraries with this sort of arrangement are in Scandinavia (© National & University Library of Slovenia).

8. Montreal University Library (*Bibliothèque de l'Université de Montréal*). 3.1 million. Founded 1878.

9. University of Western Ontario Library, London. 3 million. Founded 1878

10. Saskatchewan University Library, Saskatoon. 3 million. Founded 1907.

51
Five Largest University Libraries in the Caribbean Islands

1. University of the West Indies, founded 1848. Over 2 million books. This university has 14 campuses in several islands in the Caribbean Sea and central America (mostly English-speaking countries). These are in Jamaica, Trinidad & Tobago, Antigua & Barbuda, Belize, the Bahamas, Barbados, British Virgin Islands, Cayman Islands, the Dominican Republic, Grenada, Montserrat, St. Christopher & Nevis, St. Lucia, St. Vincent & the Grenadines. The largest libraries are at the Kingston Campus in Jamaica (over 750,000 books), and the St. Augustine Campus in Trinidad & Tobago (over 430,000 books).

2. Ruben Martinez Villena Library, University of Havana, Cuba. 945,000 books. Founded 1728.

3. University of Puerto Rico Library, San Juan. 520,000 books. Founded 1903.

4. University of Puerto Rico Library, Mayaguez. 410,000 books. Founded 1911.

5. University of Guyana, George Town. 380,000 books. Founded 1963.

52
Ten Largest University Libraries in Japan

1. University of Tokyo Library. (See list **34**.)

2. University of Kyoto Library (*Kyoto Daigaku Toshokan*). 7 million books. Founded 1899.

3. Waseda University Library, Tokyo (*Waseda Daigaku Toshokan*). 5.1 million. Founded 1882.

4. Kansai University Library, Osaka (*Kansai Daigaku Toshokan*). 4.8 million. Founded 1914.

5. Kyushu University of Library, Fukuoku (*Kyushu Daigaku Toshokan*). Founded 1889. 3.6 million.

6. Hokkaido University Library, Sapporo (*Hokkaido Daigaku Toshokan*). 3.3 million. Founded 1876.

Joint 7. University of Kobe Library (*Kobe Daigaku Toshokan*), founded 1949; and Hiroshima University Library (*Hiroshima Daigaku Toshokan*), founded 1949. Both 3.1 million.

More than half of the books at Hiroshima University Library are in foreign languages, notably English. This makes the library the largest with English language books in Japan.

8. Nagoya University Library (*Nagoya Daigaku Toshokan*). 2.9 million. Founded 1939.

9. Ryukoku University Library, Kyoto (*Ryukoku Daigaku Toshokan*). 2.5 million. Founded in 1639 (oldest university in Japan).

10. Hitotsubashi University Library (*Hitotsubashi Daigaku Toshokan*). 2.2 million. Founded 1887.

Tenri Central Library in the city of Tenri has over 2 million books and is part of Tenri University, founded in 1930. The library is also public. The university has a museum (called the Sankokan Museum), open also to the public.

53
Ten Largest University Libraries in China

1. University of Beijing Library (*Peking Daxue Tushugan*). Founded 1902. 8 million books.

The most famous name associated with the library is Mao Zedong (Mao Tse-tung). The Chinese leader was not a student of the university, but an assistant librarian.

2. Chinese Academy of Sciences Library, Beijing. 6.7 million. Founded 1951.

The official name of the library (adopted in 1985) is the Documentation and Information Center of the Chinese Academy of Sciences or DICCAS.

3. University of Nanjing Library (*Nanjing Daxue Tushugan*). 6.3 million. Founded 1908.

4. Fudan University Library, Shanghai (*Futan Daxue Tushugan*). 4.1 million. Founded 1905.

5. Zhengzhou University, Henan (*Zhengzhou Daxue Tushugan*). 3.9 million. Founded 1956.

6. Sichuan Union University Library, Chengdu (*Sichuan Daxue Tushugan*). 3.6 million. Founded 1994. It is the newest university in China.

7. Tsinghua (Qinghua) University Library, Beijing (*Ching-hua Daxue Tushugan*). 3.6 million. Founded 1911.

8. Shandong University Library (*Shandong Daxue Tushugan*). 3.31 million. Founded 1901.

9. Hebei University Library, Baoding *Hebei Daxue Tushugan*. 3.1 million. Founded 1921.

10. Nankai University Library, Tianjin (Tientsin). 3 million. (*Nankai Daxue Tushugan*). Founded 1919.

54
Ten Largest University Libraries in South Korea

1. Seoul National University Library, 3.1 million. Founded 1946.

2. Kaya University Library, Kyungbuk, 2.9 million. Founded 1993.

Joint 3. Yonsei University Library, Seoul, 2.2 million. Founded 1885. It is the second oldest university in South Korea, after Sungkyunkwan University in Seoul, which was founded in 1398. Keimyung University Library, Taegu, 2.2 million. Founded 1954.

4. Ewha Women's University Library, Seoul. 1.7 million. Founded 1886.

South Korea has a number of universities open only to female students. Three other prominent universities in the capital Seoul are Sookmyung Women's University, founded 1906; Seoul Women's University, *founded in 1961; and Duksung Women's University, founded in 1950.*

5. Hong-Ik University Library, Seoul. 1.4 million. Founded 1946.

6. Kyung Hee University Library, Seoul. 1.2 million. Founded 1949.

7. Kyungpook National University Library, Taegu. 720,000. Founded 1946.

8. Pusan National University. 695,000. Founded 1946.

9. Chonnam National University Library, Kwangu. 620,000. Founded 1952.

10. Chosun University Library. 610,000. Founded 1946.

55
Ten Largest University Libraries in Australia and New Zealand

1. University of Sydney Fisher Library. 5.1 million books. Founded 1852.

2. University of Melbourne Library. 3 million. Founded 1855.

3. New South Wales University Library, Sydney. 2.8 million. Founded 1949.

4. Australian National University Librar, Canberra. 2.1 million. Founded 1946.

5. Queensland University Library, Brisbane. 2 million. Founded 1910.

6. University of Adelaide University Library. 2.2 million. Founded 1874.

7. Monash University Library, Clayton. 2 million. Founded 1958.

8. University of Auckland Library, New Zealand. 1.9 million. Founded 1883.

9. University of Canterbury Library, Christchurch, New Zealand. 1.6 million. Founded 1873.

10. Victoria University Library, Wellington, New Zealand. 980,000. Founded 1899.

56
Thirty Largest University Libraries in Africa and the Middle East

1. Hebrew University Library Jerusalem, Israel *(Bet Ha-Sefarim Ha Leummi Weha-Universitai)*. 4.8 million books. Founded 1892.

   Also part of Israel's National Library and the Berman National Medical Library, and is officially called the Jewish National and University Library.

2. Islamic Azad University, Tehran, Iran. 4.3 million. Founded 1982.

3. University of Cairo Library, Egypt. 1.8 million. Founded 1908. It has the largest student population in Africa.

4. University of South Africa Library, Pretoria. 1.7 million books. Founded 1873.

5. University of Haifa Library, Israel. Founded 1963. Founded 1.6 million.

6. Al-Azhar University Library, Cairo, Egypt, founded A.D. 985. Founded 1.6 million.

7. University of Cape Town Library, South Africa. Founded in 1829. 1.5 million.

8. University of Tehran Library, Iran. 1.4 million. Founded 1949.

9. University of Witwatersrand Library, Johannesburg, South Africa. 1.2 million. Founded 1922.

   The most famous student using the library in the 1940s was Nelson Mandela, who studied law.

10. King Saud University Library, Riyadh, Saudi Arabia. 1.2 million. Founded in 1957.

11. University of Pretoria Library, South Africa. 1.1 million. Founded 1908.

12. Israel Institute of Technology Library, Haifa. 960,000. Founded 1912.

13. University of Stellenbosch Library, South Africa. 952,000. Founded in 1895.

14. University of Tel Aviv Library, Israel. 810,000. Founded 1953.

15. Islamic University of Imam Muhammad Ibn Saud Library, Riyadh, Saudi Arabia. 700,000. Founded 1974.

16. University of Algiers Library (*Bibliothèque de l'Université d'Alger*), Algieria. 760,000. Founded 1880.

17. Ben Gurion Negev University Library, Be'ersheva, Israel. 730,000. Founded 1966.

18. American University Library, Beirut, Lebanon. 630,000. Founded in 1866.

   Prior to the 1991 Gulf War, Baghdad University Library, the largest in Iraq, had about 700,000 books, while Mosul University Library had about 660,000 books. Both now have smaller collections of books.

19. University of Natal Library, Pietermaritzburg, South Africa. 645,000. Founded 1909.

20. University of Nigeria Library, Nnsuka. 630,000. Founded 1960.

21. University of Ibadan Kenneth Dike Library, Nigeria. 615,000. Founded 1948.

Joint 22. University of Ghana, Balme Library, Accra, founded 1948; and the University of Dar es Salam Library, Tanzania, founded 1961. Both contain 610,000 books.

23. Jomo Kenyatta Memorial Library, University of Nairobi, Kenya. 600,000. Founded in 1959.

24. American University in Cairo Library, Egypt. 512,000. Founded in 1919.

25. Assiut University Library, Egypt. 501,000. Founded 1957.

26. Obafemi Awolowo University Library, Ife, Nigeria. 479,000. Founded 1961.

27. Helwan University Library, Egypt. 465,000. Founded 1975.

Joint 28th. University of Lagos Library, Nigeria, founded 1962; and Makere University Library, Kampala, Uganda. Both possess 410,000 books.

29. Cheikh Anta Diop University Library, Dakar, Senegal (*Bibliothèque de l'Université Cheikh Anta Diop de Dakar*). 390,000. Founded 1950.

30. University of Khartoum, Sudan. 357,000. Founded 1945.

About a half a dozen more South African academic libraries have large collections with over or approaching 500,000 books, and only the top five largest university libraries in South Africa are listed here. In the first edition of this book, Zimbabwe University Library in Harare (founded in 1955) was listed among the major large university libraries in Africa. But due to the current political and financial problems facing the country, the library's collections have been drastically reduced.

57
Thirty-One Largest University Libraries in Asia

N.B. This list excludes libraries in Australia, China, Japan and South Korea. See lists **52** to **55**.

1. National Science and Technology Library of Kazakhstan, Almaty. 7 million. Founded 1960.

2. Kazakh Academy of Sciences Central Library, Almaty. 6.3 million. Founded 1932.

3. Azerbaijan Scientific and Technical Library, Baku. 6 million. Founded 1928.

The University of Lagos Library, behind the Senate building, is the oldest and largest in Nigeria's largest city and former capital.

4. University of Dhaka Library, Bangladesh. 5.5 million. Founded in 1921.

5. Armenia Scientific and Technical Library, Yerevan. 5.1 million. Founded 1927.

6. National Taiwan University Library, Taipei. 4 million. Founded 1928.

7. Pyongyang Academy of Sciences Library, North Korea. 3.8 million. Founded 1952.

8. Georgian Academy of Sciences Central Library, Tbilisi. 3.4 million. Founded 1941.

9. Soochow University Library, Taipei. 3.3 million. Founded 1900.

10. Tbilisi State University Library, Georgia. 3.2 million. Founded 1918.

11. Central Library of the Armenian Academy of Science, Yerevan. 3.1 million. Founded 1935.

12. Central Library of the Azerbaijan Academy of Science, Baku. 2.5 million. Founded 1925.

13. National Chengchi University, Taipei, Taiwan. 2.3 million. Founded 1927.

14. Malaya University Library, Kuala Lumpur, Malaysia *(Perpustakaan Universiti Malaya)*. 2.2 million. Founded 1957.

15. Baku State University, Azerbaijan. 2.1 million. Founded 1919.

16. University of Hong Kong Library. 2 million. Founded 1911.

17. Chinese University of Hong Kong Library *(Xianggang Zhongwen Daxue Tushugan)*. 1.8 million. Founded 1963.

18. New Delhi University Library, India. 1.6 million. Founded 1922.

The National Taiwan University Library, in the capital of Taipei, is the largest university library in Taiwan (photograph by Liao Yunchi, courtesy of National Taiwan University.)

The National University of Singapore Library's central library is the largest university library building in Asia (courtesy National University of Singapore).

19. Yerevan State University, Armenia. 1.5 million. Founded 1931.

20. Singapore National University Library. 1.36 million. Founded 1946

21. National Cheng Kung University, Tainan, Taiwan. 1.1 million. Founded 1927.

22. University of the Philippines Diliman Library, Quezon City, Metro Manila. 988,000. Founded 1908.

23. Banaras Hindu University Library India, Varanasi. 910,000. 1915.

24. University of Calcutta (Kolkata) Library India. 890,000. Founded 1857.
It has the largest student population in Asia (see list 36).

Joint 25. Tamkang University Library, Taipei, Taiwan, founded 1950; and Chulalongkorn University Library, Bangkok, Thailand, founded 1910. Both contain 840,000 books.

26. Thammasat University Library, Bangkok, Thailand. 822,000. Founded 1934.

27. Vietnam National University, Hanoi and Ho Chi Minh City. 810,000 books. Founded in 1993 by the merger of several universities in Hanoi and Ho Chi Minh City.

28. Penang Science University Library, Malaysia. 743,000. Founded 1969.

29. Panjab University Library, Chandigarh, India. 730,000. Founded 1947.

30. Fu-Jen Catholic University Library, Taipei, Taiwan. 700,000. Founded in 1925 in Beijing and moved to Taipei in 1961.

Joint 31. Jawaharlal Nehru University, New Delhi, founded 1969; and the Chinese Culture University Library, Taipei, Taiwan, founded in 1962. Both contain over 635,000 books.

Several former members of the Soviet Union, such as Armenia, Azerbaijan and Kazakhstan, had very large libraries of academies (as seen in East European countries like Russian, Ukraine and Romania) which they inherited when the USSR was dissolved in 1991. The largest university library in Pakistan is the University of Punjab University in Lahore, with over 480,000 books and founded in 1882.

58
Fifty Largest University Libraries in Latin America

1. Buenos Aires University Library, Argentina (*Biblioteca de la Universidad de Buenos Aires*). 4 million books. Founded 1821.

   It has the second largest student population in Latin America.

2. São Paulo Federal University Library, Brazil (*Biblioteca de la Universidade Federal de São Paulo*). 3.7 million. Founded 1934.

   It has the largest student population in Brazil.

3. Mexico National Autonomous University Library, Mexico City (*Biblioteca de la Universidad Nacional Autónoma de México*). 3.3 million. Founded 1555.

   Also forms part of the National Library of Mexico. It has the largest student population in Latin America.

4. Rio de Janeiro Federal University Library, Brazil (*Biblioteca Universidade de Rio de Janeiro*). 2 million. Founded 1920.

5. University of Guadalajara Library, Mexico (*Biblioteca de la Universidad de Guadalajara*). 1.2 million. Founded 1752.

6. Rio Grande Federal University Library, Porto Alegre, Brazil (*Biblioteca Central de la Universidade Federal de Rio Grande*). 950,000. Founded 1971.

7. La Plata National University Library, Argentina (*Biblioteca de la Nacional Universidade de La Plata*). 810,000. Founded 1905.

8. Tamaulipas Autonomous University Library, Ciudad Victoria, Mexico (*Biblioteca de la Universidad de Tamaulipas*). 710,000. Founded 1956.

9. Puebla Autonomous University Library, Mexico (*Biblioteca de la Universidad de Puebla*). 630,000. Founded 1578.

10. Minas Gerais Federal University Library, Belo Horizonte, Brazil (*Biblioteca Federal de Minas Gerais Universidade*). 630,000. Founded 1927.

11. Pernambuco Federal University Central Library, Recife, Brazil (*Biblioteca Central da Universidade Federal de Pernambuco*). 610,000. Founded 1968.

12. Rio de Janeiro Pontifical Catholic University Library, Brazil (*Biblioteca Pontificia Universidade Católica de Rio Janeiro*). 600,000. Founded 1941.

13. Concepcion University Library, Chile (*Biblioteca Universidad de Concepcion*). 460,000. Founded 1919.

14. Spanish American University Library, Tijuana, Leon and Puebla, Mexico (*Biblioteca Universidad Iberoamericana*). 410,000. Founded 1919.

15. Central Pontifical Catholic University Library, Lima, Peru (*Biblioteca Central de la Pontificia Universidade Católica del Perú*). 402,000. Founded 1917.

The University of Recife library is the largest in Northern Brazil.

59
Largest University Libraries and Top Universities: A Comparison

The epigraph on page 42 for this section ("World Records for University and Academic Libraries") is from U.S. librarian Herman Fussler about large university libraries being among the best. Whether this is true or not is pretty much open to further debate. However, it is possible to match and correlate a proven internationally recognized list of the best universities in the world with the list of largest university libraries given in this chapter, the list of largest special libraries given in the next chapter and at list **381**, which features 345 largest libraries. The best reliable current source for the best universities in the world is the list compiled by both the U.K. newspaper *Times Higher Education Supplement (THES)* and Quacquarelli Symonds (QS), a company with offices in the U.S., Europe and Asia that produces popular guides for students wanting to study in foreign countries, i.e., study abroad. The list produced is called the THES-QS World University Rankings. Below is an interesting selection of univer-sities that appear in both the largest university and specialty libraries list compiled in the 2nd edition of *Library World Records* and the list of 500 best universities compiled in the THES-QS World University Rankings for 2006.

Europe

France: University of Paris; Strasbourg National University; University of Montpel-lier; University of Toulouse; University of Lyon.

Germany: Berlin Free University; Rupert Charles University, Heidelberg; Ludwig Max-imilians University, Munich; Humboldt Uni-versity, Berlin; George Augustus University, Gottingen; University of Frankfurt; Tubingen University.

Italy: University of Rome (*La Sapienza*); Uni-versity of Bologna.

U.K.: Oxford University; Cambridge University; University of London schools and colleges; University of Edinburgh; University of Manchester; University of Glasgow; University of Birmingham; University of Leeds.

Russia: Lomonosov Moscow State University; St. Petersburg University; Tomsk State University; Kazan State University.

Spain: Madrid Autonomous University; Complutense University, Madrid; University of Barcelona; Navarra University, Pamplona; Zaragoza University.

Portugal: University of Coimbra.

Belgium: Louvain (Leuven) Catholic University; Brussels Free University; Liège University.

The Netherlands: University of Amsterdam; Leiden University; Utrecht University.

Ireland: University of Dublin, Trinity College; National University of Ireland, Galway.

Switzerland: Swiss Federal Institute of Technology, Zurich; University of Basel; University of Zurich.

Austria: University of Vienna.

Sweden: Uppsala University and Lund University.

Denmark: University of Copenhagen.

Finland: University of Helsinki.

Norway: University of Oslo.

Greece: Aristotelian University of Thessaloniki; National and Kapodistrian University of Athens.

Czech Republic: Charles University, Prague.

Poland: Jagiellonian University, Kraków.

Americas

Brazil: São Paulo Federal University; Rio de Janeiro Federal University.

Canada: McGill University, Montreal; University of Toronto; University of British Columbia, Vancouver; University of Alberta, Edmonton; University of Waterloo.

Mexico: Mexico National Autonomous University, Mexico City.

U.S.: Harvard University, Massachusetts; Yale University, Connecticut; Stanford University; University of California, Berkeley; Columbia University; University of Michigan, Ann Arbor; University of California, Los Angeles; University of Texas, Austin; University of Illinois, Urbana-Champaign.

Asia

China: Beijing University; Nanjing University; Fudan University, Shanghai; Tsinghua University, Beijing.

Hong Kong: University of Hong Kong.

Japan: University of Tokyo; Kyoto University; Kyushu University, Fukuoku; Hokkaido University; Waseda University, Tokyo; Kobe University.

India: Jawaharlal Nehru University, New Delhi; University of New Delhi.

Malaysia: University of Malaya, Kuala Lumpur.

Singapore: National University of Singapore.

South Korea: Seoul National University; Yonsei University, Seoul; Chonnam National University, Kwangu.

The Philippines : University of the Philippines, Quezon City.

Taiwan: National Taiwan University, Taipei.

Australia: Australian National University, Canberra; Melbourne University Library; University of Sydney; Monash University, Clayton; New South Wales University, Sydney; Queensland University, Brisbane; University of Adelaide.

New Zealand: University of Auckland.

Middle East and Africa

Israel: Ben Gurion University, Negev.

Turkey: University of Istanbul.

Egypt: University of Cairo.

South Africa: University of Cape Town; University of Witwatersrand, Johannesburg; University of Pretoria.

Nigeria: University of Ibadan.

One can't help but notice that at least two or all of the top 5 largest university libraries for each country compiled in Library World Records are also listed in the THES-QS World University Rankings, e.g., the list for universities in the U.K, Germany, China, Japan, Russia and the U.S. to name a few. Not surprisingly the top university listed in the THES-QS World University Rankings is Harvard University, which also has the largest university library in the world. While the list above covers universities worldwide, several countries produce their own rankings of the best universities in their country. For instance the Times Higher Education Supplement also produces the full list for U.K. universities, while in Germany the DAAD (German Academic Exchange Service) produces the full list for German universities. The League of European Research Universities, or LERU, is a partnership of 20 top universities in Europe. All but three of the members of LERU are also listed in Library World Records in the list of largest university libraries. In the United States, 6 of the 8 universities that make up the Ivy League of prestigious U.S. universities are given in this book's list of 20 largest U.S. university libraries. Perhaps after all Herman Fussler's conjecture about the largest university libraries being the best as well was spot on in some ways.

60
Earliest University Libraries in the World

A number of educational institutes that qualify to be called universities predate Al-Qarawiyin University, the oldest existing university today (see list **61**). The very first university in the world was probably the Buddhist Takshila (Takshashila or Taxila) University, established around 600 B.C. in the ancient city of Takshila (capital of the former kingdom of Gandhara) in the northwestern part of the Indian subcontinent. But it vanished centuries later, and very little is known about its library collection today. But some notable relics from the ancient university exist today, such as the Gandharan Buddhist Scrolls (see list **124**) which can be viewed at the British Library and at the Taxila Archeological Library in Pakistan. The second earliest universities to be established in the world after Takshila University are the old Alexandria University in Egypt, and the Academy and Lyceum in ancient Greece, all three having been founded in the 4th century B.C. The only one in existence today is Alexandria University, which was re-founded in 1938.

Gondi Shapur (or Jundi Shapur) University in Iran was founded by Persian King Shapur I of the Sassanian dynasty. It was once a leading medical university in ancient Persia and dates back to the 3rd century A.D. (circa A.D. 270), although it no longer exists. Many of the preserved ancient medical texts from Gondi Shapur university library are good examples of pre–Islamic medical knowledge in the Middle East. The popular university attracted scholars from other regions, particularly from Greece and India, who brought along classical Greek and Indian texts that were subsequently translated into Persian. When the Arabs overran Persia, they made Gondi Shapur University the scholastic center of the Islamic Empire. In this way the Persian translations of classical Greek and Indian texts were now passed on to the Arabs and translated into Arabic. It was during this transition that an advanced Indian numeral system (used for centuries on the Indian subcontinent) was brought to the attention of the Arabs, who made slight modifications of the discovery for their own use. The Arab world thus began to actively use these numerals throughout the Islamic Empire, which included Spain. The Toledo Translation School in Spain around the 12th century (see list **123**) stumbled across these numeral systems and called them Arabic numerals and soon all of Europe replaced their current Roman numeral system with Arabic numerals. The ancient city in which Gondi Shapur University was located is near the city of Ahvaz or Ahwaz in western Iran, where a modern university (founded in 1955) existed under the same name. Around the 5th century A.D., in ancient city of Antioch (today near the Turkish town of Antakya), there existed a religious (Christian) educational institution that had a significant library of Christian manuscripts. Another ancient center of learning in ancient Syria was the School of Nisibis, founded circa A.D. 458. It was based on the earlier School of Edessa (near Urfa in Turkey). The institute also offered courses in Christianity. The most famous book from the library is *Carmina Nisibena*, an important historical manuscript still used by researchers today. The School of Nisibis began to decline in the 11th century. Nalanda University and Vikramshila University, both Buddhist universities, located in what is today the northeastern state of Bihar, in India, were founded circa A.D. 414 and A.D. 760, respectively. They were well known centers of Buddhist education for scholars from all over Asia, and their large library collections contained some of the important Buddhist texts of the day. Both universities are no longer in existence, having been completely destroyed by Muslim armies in the 13th century. In China, there are four famous ancient academies that were important

educational and religious (Confucianism) centers. The oldest is the Bailudong (or Lushan) Academy in the city of Jiujian, founded in A.D. 940, and also known by the name White Deer Cave Academy in later centuries. It was abandoned near the end of the Northern Song dynasty. Next is the Yuelu Academy in the city of Changsha founded in A.D. 976 (which still exists today as Hunan University). The other two ancient Chinese educational institutions are the Suiyang (Songyang) Academy, founded in A.D. 990 and the Shigu Academy founded in A.D. 1031. Finally in Hanoi today, there is a building known as the Temple of Literature, built in A.D. 1076. It is credited as being the first national university of Vietnam and continued to function as a university until 1779. The library contains early Buddhist texts of the period. In 1483 another national university was built. The present National University of Vietnam, which has campuses in both Hanoi and Ho Chi Minh City, was founded in 1993 by an amalgamation of several institutes of higher learning.

*Two further existing educational establishments predate Al-Qarawiyin University. The first is Nanjing University in China. It dates back to A.D. 258 as the Imperial College of Emperor Sun Xiu, during the period in China known as the Three Kingdoms. But the original university no longer exists. Modern Nanjing University was founded in the early 20th century. Istanbul (Constantinople) University Library in Turkey was founded in A.D. 430 and thus founded before Al-Qarawiyin University, so technically should also be called the oldest existing university in the world. However after the Eastern Roman Byzantine Empire and Constantinople fell to the Turkish Ottoman Empire, the university was refounded in 1453. A full list of the 145 oldest university libraries in the world is at list **382**.*

61
Five Oldest University Libraries in the World

The following are the 5 oldest university libraries founded before the start of the 12th century and still in existence today.

1. Al-Qarawiyin University Library, Fez, Morocc (*Bibliothèque de l'Université El-Qaraouiyin*). Founded circa A.D. 859.

This university is not to be confused with Al-Akhawayn University in the city of Ifrane, close to Fez. Fatima Feheri, a wealthy woman who came to Morocco from Tunisia, founded the library as part of the Al-Qarawiyin Mosque. While early universities in Western Europe developed from Christian cathedral schools, early universities in the Arab world

Al-Qarawiyin University in Fez, Morocco, is the oldest existing university in the world (courtesy Moroccan National Tourist Office, London).

developed from Islamic education centers in mosques. It was not uncommon to find a big library in mosques throughout the Islamic world. Mosque libraries are called vakif libraries in Turkey. The most famous scholar to use the library was Arab geographer Leo Africanus, whose notebooks and manuscripts was for over 400 years one of Europe's chief sources of information about Islam.

2. Al-Azhar University Library, Cairo, Egypt. A.D. 970.

This university library also began as a mosque library, and is the largest library in Egypt, after the national library and Cairo University library.

3. Hunan University Library, Changsha, China, A.D. 976.

It began as the Yuelu Academy, one of 4 famous ancient academies in China. Changsha is in Hunan Province. In neighboring Jiangxi Province is another of the ancient academies, called the Bailudong (or Lushan) Academy, founded in A.D. 940 in the city of Jiujian.

4. Al-Nizamiyah University Library, Baghdad, Iraq. A.D. 1070.

The university was one of two universities founded by Vizier Nizam al-Mulk (Vizier of the first Turkish Seljuck sultan, Alp-Arslan). The Turkish Seljuk Empire had earlier captured Bagdad from the Arabs in A.D. 1050. Open to scholars from all over the Muslim world, the university was one of the first prominent Islamic centers of education or colleges also known as madrasahs and masjids. The capture of Baghdad by Hulagu Khan in 1258 following the Mongolian invasion of Arab lands partially destroyed the university library. Tamerlane (Timur "The Lame") later inflicted further devastation on many rebuilt libraries of the Madrasahs and Masjids in Bagdad, when he conquered Baghdad and Damascus in 1392. During the period of the Turkish Ottoman Empire, which overran Iraq and most of the Arab lands from 1517, the concept of madrasahs was continued and many well-stocked libraries were founded in these madrasahs. The first major Turkish Ottoman library of the madrasahs open to the public (with funding from charitable organizations, i.e., a public library) was the Koprulu Library es-

tablished by Grand Vizier Koprulu Ahmet Pasha in Istanbul in 1678. This became the first public library in the Middle East. The madrasahs were officially abolished in Turkey in 1924, but they still exist in several Moslem countries such as Saudi Arabia and Pakistan.

5. Bologna University Library, Italy (*Biblioteca Università degli Studi di Bologna*). A.D. 1088. The university's library in the early days had a large proportion of books only on law, as this course was the main one taught at the university until the 13th century, when other courses were offered and books in other subjects grew in greater numbers. Reliable sources of medieval records in several national archives in Italy seem to indicate that both Parma University and Salerno University were founded before Bologna University, but others (including different official sources) indicate Parma and Salerno universities were founded *after* Bologna University.

62
Earliest Academic Libraries in Europe

Aristotle's Peripatetic School Library in the Lyceum was set circa 335 B.C. in Athens, Greece. Famous Romans such as Marcus Cicero later made use of the library.

Higher education in ancient Greece began in Athens at the Academy, established in about 387 B.C. by Plato, and together with the Lyceum offered advanced study of philosophy. Subsequent schools of philosophy, modeled upon Plato's, were also called academies; this term was eventually used to indicate any institution of higher education or the faculty of such an institution. Plato's Academy remained in existence until A.D. 529 when the Byzantine Emperor Justinian closed it down.

63
Ten Oldest University Libraries in Europe

Aristotle set up the earliest major educational institute in Europe, at the Lyceum in Athens, Greece.

The history of European academic libraries begins with the founding of libraries in monasteries in the Middle Ages. When the Western Roman Empire fell in A.D. 476, much learning and reading was restricted to the libraries in monasteries where monks such as St. Benedict encouraged the importance of reading manuscripts. Examples of these early 6th and 7th century monastic libraries include those of St. Gallen in Switzerland, Jarrow in the U.K., Fulda in Germany, Luxeuil in France, and Monte Cassino in Italy. From the early 11th century libraries in cathedrals began to replace libraries in monasteries as centers for learning. But unlike monastic libraries, the libraries in cathedrals and cathedral schools were designed for educational rather than inspirational and religious reading. Scholars believe universities grew out of cathedral schools. Some well-known cathedral libraries were at York in the U.K., Rouen in France,

Hildesheim in Germany, and Barcelona in Spain.

Coupled with the fact that from the Middle Ages, education was firmly established in monasteries and cathedrals and lectures were theological in content, many pre–Renaissance European university libraries were run by theological librarians such as monks and scribes. It is thus sometimes difficult to differentiate a library set up purely for religious studies and one for academic studies, which included theology. Prior to the 17th century, book and manuscript collecting in Europe was mainly a royal, religious or private pursuit. By the early 17th century many princes, churchmen, and wealthy collectors were organizing their collections with the help of librarians and then opening their collections to the scholarly public. The following are the oldest university libraries in Europe. Córdoba University in Spain was founded in the 10th century A.D. but is not included here. See list **67**.

1. Bologna University Library, Italy (*Biblioteca Università degli Studi di Bologna*). Founded A.D. 1088. See also list **61**.

2. Padua University Library, Italy (*Biblioteca Università degli Studi di Padova*). 1122.
   It has the oldest existing university library building in Italy and in Europe.

3. Modena University Library, Italy (*Biblioteca Università degli Studi di Modena*). 1160.

The famous Cantino World Map, *made by Alberto Cantino in 1502, the most accurate map in the world at that time to include the newly discovered Americas, is housed at Modena University's* Biblioteca Estense. *However Martin Waldemüller's map of 1507 (see list* **6***) at the U.S. Library of Congress in Washington, D.C., also showed the continents of North and South America, but crucially, was the first map to use the word "America."*

4. Vicenza University Library, Italy (*Biblioteca Università degli Studi di Vicenza*). 1204.

5. Palencia University Library, Spain (*Biblioteca de la Universidad de Palencia*). 1210.

6. Salamanca University Library, Spain (*Biblioteca de la Universidade de Salamanca*). 1218.

7. University of Paris Sorbonne Library, France (*Bibliothèque de l'Université de Paris*). 1230. The University of Paris, a leading center of late medieval learning and especially scientific thought, was separated from the cathedral school of Notre Dame.

8. Montpellier University Library, France (*Bibliothèque de l'Université de Montpellier*). 1240.

9. Perugia University Library, Italy (*Biblioteca Università degli Studi di Perugia*). 1243.

10. Siena University Library, Italy (*Biblioteca Università degli Studi di Siena*). 1245.

64
Five Oldest University Libraries in the U.K.

1. Cambridge University Library. Founded 1347. The university was originally founded in the 13th century. Peterhouse College Library was the first in 1302.

2. St. Andrews University Library. 1410.

3. Glasgow University Library. 1451.

4. Aberdeen University Library. 1494.

5. Edinburgh University Library. 1580.

After the establishment of Oxford and Cambridge universities, no more universities were created in England between 1400 and the 1825 (except Scottish universities). Thus a period of 400 years passed before the establishment of University College London in 1826 and King's College London in 1829 (both part of the University of London in 1836). The fifth oldest university in England was the University of Durham in 1832. Further universities in the U.K. were founded from the 1850s, with the

The Sorbonne University of Paris Library is the oldest university library in France. It gets its name from its founder, Robert de Sorbon, chaplain to King Louis IX. The building dates from 1885.

first being the numerous Victorian Red Brick universities. There has been no valid explanation as to why Oxford and Cambridge universities were the sole higher education institutes in England for so long, despite several universities being founded all over Europe during this period.

Oxford University Library was originally founded in 1249 by the Bishop of Worchester, but troops of King Edward VI destroyed the library in 1550. The library was re-founded 1602 by James Bodley and called the Bodleian Library. The library of Eton College, near London, the oldest public school in the U.K. (founded by King Henry VI), dates back to 1440.

65
Five Oldest University Libraries in France

1. University of Paris Library (*Bibliothèque de l'Université de Paris*). Founded 1230.

2. Montpellier University Library (*Bibliothèque de l'Université de Montpellier*). 1240.

3. Toulouse University Library (*Bibliothèque de l'Université de Toulouse*). 1292.

4. Avignon University Library (*Bibliothèque de l'Université d'Avignon*). 1303.

Oxford University's Bodleian Library was founded in the 13th century but was refounded in 1602, hence the title of the United Kingdom's oldest university library goes to the one at Cambridge. This is one of the newer buildings of the library, opened in 1946.

The 14th century university is almost surrounded by 14th century walled gates. This can be explained by the fact that Avignon was once the headquarters of the Vatican when Pope Clement V moved the papacy from Rome to Avignon in 1309. During that period of time several parts of the city were walled and Gothic buildings were built by the Vatican authorities. By the time the papacy returned back to Rome, the Avignon papal library was the largest library in Europe in the 14th century before the start of the Renaissance, when the Vatican Library, university li-

*braries in Italy and Spain, and early national libraries (such as those at Austria and the Czech Republic) began to hold more volumes and surpass the number at Avignon. Before the Avignon Papal Library held the record for Europe's largest library, the record holder between the 8th and 13th centuries was Córdoba University Library in Spain (see list **67**).*

5. Orleans University Library (*Bibliothèque de l'Université d'Orléans*). 1306

66
Five Oldest University Libraries in Germany

1. Rupert-Charles University Library, Heidelberg (*Ruprecht-Karls Universitätbibliothek Heidelberg*). Founded 1386.

In 1623, as an appreciation for financial help given to Maximilian, the Duke of Bavaria, by Pope

Gregory XV, in his religious conflict with Protestants during the Thirty Years' War, a generous gift was sent to the pope. The gift was in the form of 3,000 manuscripts and 4000 books from the Heidelberg University Library (The Palatina Library), which

were donated to the Vatican Library in Rome. About 200 years later some were returned for political reasons.

2. Cologne University Library (*Universitätbibliothek Köln*). 1388.

3. Erfurt University Library (*Universitätbibliothek Erfurt*). 1392.

Martin Luther, who began the Reformation in the Roman Catholic Church, graduated from here in 1505 with a Ph.D. in law

4. Wurzburg University Library (*Universitätbibliothek Würzbur*g). 1402

5. Leipzig University Library (*Universitätbibliothek Leipzig*). 1409.

67
Five Oldest University Libraries in Spain

Córdoba University was founded in the 10th century A.D. (long before Italy's Bologna University). The Moorish Omayyad (Umayyad) Caliphate ruler of the Spain, Al-Hakem, who had established Qurtuba (Córdoba) University, also established its famous library, which became largest library in Europe between the 9th and 13th centuries. Córdoba, as capital of the Umayyad Caliphate in Spain, was the thus first European city in the medieval period to have an Institute of higher education established. The Umayyad dynasty rule of Spain from the 8th to the 13th century A.D. was brought to an end when Córdoba was recaptured by Christian Spanish forces in the 13th century (during the reconquista). Córdoba University was then neglected and a few years later was permanently abandoned. The modern University of Córdoba was re-founded in 1972.

1. Palencia University Library (*Biblioteca de la Universidad de Palencia*). Founded 1210.

Because of a decline of university functions, with staff leaving for the more popular Salamanca Uni-

versity, the entire library collections of Palencia University were transferred to Valladolid and Salamanca university libraries at the end of the 13th century, and the university closed down.

2. Salamanca University Library (*Biblioteca de la Universidad de Salamanca*). 1218.

Christopher Columbus consulted the university library before embarking on his famous voyage in 1492, and on his return gave several lectures here on his discoveries in the Americas (which he mistakenly thought were in Asia).

3. Valladolid University Library (*Biblioteca de la Universidad de Valladolid*). 1290.

4. Complutense University Library, Madrid (*Biblioteca de la Universidad Complutense de Madrid*). 1293.

5. Lleida (Lérida) University Library (*Biblioteca de la Universidad de Lleida*). 1297.

68
Ten Oldest University Libraries in Eastern Europe

1. Charles University Library, Prague (*Knihovna Univerzita Karlova v Praze*). Czech Republic. Founded 1348.

2. Jagiellonian University Library, Kraków (*Biblioteka Universytet Jagielloúski*). Poland. 1364.

Until the end of the 1930s, the main library of the

Opposite, top: Avignon University is the oldest medieval university in the south of France, and the city has many fourteenth century walls and ramparts built by the resident popes who also founded the university. The walls encircle the university and today are part of the entrance gates of the university. **Bottom:** Modern buildings of Cologne University Library, the second oldest in Germany.

The University of Córdoba Rabanales Library in Spain. The university was one of four such institutions (others are at Granada, Cádiz and Seville) founded by the Umayyad Moors, when Spain was under Islamic rule. Córdoba University was refounded in 1972 (photograph by Jose Antonio Perogil, courtesy Cordoba University Library).

Jagiellonian University was situated in the 15th century building known as Collegium Maius. This old library building is today the second oldest surviving university library building in Eastern Europe. Collegium Maius is now part of the Jagiellonian University Archives and Museum. The Jagiellonian University has the largest collection of incunabula in Eastern Europe.

3. Pécs University Library, Hungary *(Könyvtár Pécsi Egyetem)*. 1367.

4. Comenius University of Bratislava Library, Slovakia *(Univerzita Knjižnica Komenskeho v Brastislave)*. 1465.

5. Palacky University Library, Olomouc *(Knihovna Univerzita Palackèho v Olomouchi)*. Czech Republic. 1566

6. Eotvos Lorand University Library *(Könyvtár Eötvös Loránd Egyetem)*. Budapest, Hungary. 1561.

7. Vilnius University Library *(Biblioteka Universitas Vilnensis)*. Lithuania. 1570.

8. Edward Kardelja University Library, Ljubljana *(Edvarda Kardelja Knjižnica Univerza v Ljubljani)*. Slovenia. 1595. It is part of the National and University Library of Slovenia.

9. Ivan Franko State University Library, Lviv, Ukraine. 1661.

10. Zagreb National and University Library *(Nacionalna i Sveučilična Knjižnica u Zagrebu)*. Croatia. 1669.

The old Jagiellonian library building (Collegium Maius) in Krakow, Poland, contains mostly rare manuscripts and incunabula. (The new library building is featured at entry 245.)

Königsberg University was founded in 1544, but it was destroyed in the Second World War. A new university called Kaliningrad University was opened in 1967. Kaliningrad region is a Russian territory (enclave) between Lithuania and Poland; in historic times it was part of the German enclave of East Prussia, and its main city Königsberg is today's Kaliningrad City. The Gdansk Library of the Polish Academy of Sciences was founded in 1596.

69
Fifteen Other Significant Early University Libraries in Western Europe

1. Coimbra University Library, Portugal (*Biblioteca Universidade de Coimbra*). Founded 1290.

2. Lisbon University Library, Portugal (*Biblioteca Universidade de Lisboa*). 1291.

3. University of Vienna Library, Austria (*Universitätbibliothek Wien*). 1365. It is the oldest university in German-speaking parts of Europe (Germany, Austria and Switzerland).

4. Louvain (Leuven) Catholic University Library, Belgium (*Katholieke Universiteitbibliotheek Leuven /Université Catholique de Louvain*). 1425.

New buildings at Lisbon University Library have replaced the old library, the second-oldest university library in Portugal.

5. University of Basel Library, Switzerland (*Universitätbibliothek Basel*). 1460.

6. Uppsala University Library, Sweden (*Bibliotek Uppsala Universitet*). 1477.
   The library is the oldest in Scandinavia and contains the famous 6th century A.D. Codex Argenteus, the oldest surviving fragment from the 4th century A.D. texts of Bishop Ulfilas' translations of the Bible in Latin into the Old German Gothic language.

7. University of Copenhagen Library, Denmark (*Bibliotek Københavns Universitet*). 1482.

8. University of Zürich Library, Switzerland (*Universitätbibliothek Zürich*). 1523.

9. University of Bern Library, Switzerland (*Universitätbibliothek Bern*). 1528.

10. University of Lausanne Library, Switzerland (*Bibliothèque de l'Université de Lausanne*).

1537. It is the oldest and largest French-speaking university library in Switzerland.

11. Pontifical Gregorian University Library, Rome, Vatican City (*Biblioteca Pontifica Università Gregoriana*). 1553.

12. University of Geneva Library, Switzerland (*Bibliothèque de l'Université de Genève*). 1559.

13. Leiden State University Library, The Netherlands (*Universiteitbibliotheek Leiden*). 1575.

14. Amsterdam University Library, The Netherlands (*Universiteitbibliotheek Amsterdam*). 1578.

15. University of Utrecht Library, The Netherlands (*Universiteitbibliotheek Utrecht*). Founded 1584.

70
Ten Oldest University Libraries in Africa

N.B. This list excludes libraries in Morocco and Egypt. See list **73**.

1. Fourah Bay College Library, Free Town (Sierra Leone University). Founded 1828 by the British Church Missionary Society, CMS.

Because of its educational links with Durham University in the U.K., meaning its qualifications were recognized by the U.K. and hence elsewhere in Europe, many leading African academics and politicians who had earned a degree from the middle of the 19th century up to the 1950s were graduates of Fourah Bay College, or to a lesser extent, Monrovia University. Both were the only major educational institutions in the region (with the exception of North and South Africa) at that period of time. Hence Fourah Bay College became one of the four leading centers for intellectual activity in Africa between the 1830s and 1950s (the three others being the universities in Egypt and Morocco and South Africa). From the 1960s, when several Sub-Saharan African countries started to become independent and set up their own universities offering internationally recognized degrees, the link with Durham University was no longer necessary and was finally ended in the late 1960s. The most famous and first graduate was Samuel Ajai Crowther, who went on to become the first African bishop in the 1830s. The second graduate, Henry Carr, became the first African senior civil servant in the colonial administration of Africa from the 1920s.

2. Cape Town University Library, South Africa. 1829.

3. Monrovia University Library, Liberia. 1851.

4. Orange Free State University Library, Bloemfontein, South Africa. 1855.

5. University of South Africa, Pretoria. 1873.

6. University of Algiers Library, Algiers (*Bibliothèque de l'Université d'Alger*). 1880.

7. Orange Free State University Library, Bloemfontein, South Africa. 1855.

8. Gordon Memorial University Library, Khartoum, Sudan. 1901.

9. Rhodes University Library, Grahamstown, South Africa. 1904

Joint 10. University of Natal Library, Pietermaritzburg, South Africa; and the University of Pretoria Library, South Africa. Both founded 1908.

*There were no further universities founded in Sub-Saharan Africa from 1922 (Witwatersrand University, Johannesburg, South Africa) until 1948 (University of Ghana, Accra). Another Sudanese university was founded in 1912 (Omdurman Islamic University), but it only received university status in 1965. The earliest university library founded in Sub-Saharan Africa was probably that of Sankore University in Timbuktu (Tombouctou), in modern day Mali, as part of the Sankore Mosque. It was an Islamic university set up in the 14th century by King Mansa Musa, when Timbuktu, a town originally founded by the Berber Tuaregs from Morocco in the 11th century, was part of the Malian Empire (which flourished between the 10th century and the 1460s). Sankore University was later under the Songhai Empire from the 1460s. The university was destroyed in 1593 by an invasion of Spanish mercenary forces employed by Morocco, and the extensive Arabic manuscripts in the library were transported back to Moroccan libraries in Fez. In 1999 an American scholar, Professor John O. Hunwick, discovered some remnants of manuscripts and other relics that once belonged to Sankore University Library. They had been written by the 16th century academic Mahmoud Kati. His descendants had safely kept the manuscripts from generation to generation. While many of the 600-year-old manuscripts were written in Arabic, some were written in the local Fulani language, using the Arabic script and making them some of the earliest texts in an African language (see the notes on list **137**). There are now ongoing efforts to use modern technology to preserve the manuscripts as so many are rotting away.*

Alongside Sankore University, two other early (but less prominent) universities founded in Timbuktu were Djinguereber (Jingarayber) and Sidi Yahia University, built in the early 15th century. The West

African Berber-founded towns Chinguetii and Quandane, in the Adrar region of Mauritania, were both the sites of 15th century Islamic educational institutions. And they had the second most prominent Islamic libraries in West Africa, after the one at Sankore University. The cultural significance of these ancient libraries as prominent centers of learning in West Africa contributed to Timbuktu, Chinguetii and Quandane being part of the UNESCO World Heritage List.

71
Fifteen Oldest University Libraries in the Americas

1. Santo Domingo Autonomous University Library, Dominican Republic (*Biblioteca de la Universidad Autónoma de Santo Domingo*). Founded in 1538.

   The University was founded by Papal Bull of Pope Paul III. The present library building dates from 1927. Not surprisingly Santo Domingo, founded in 1496, is the oldest city in the Americas founded by European explorers. Its cathedral has the tomb of Christopher Columbus, although the Seville Cathedral in Spain also claims it has the remains of the great explorer.

2. St. Nicholas of Hidalgo Michoacán University Library, Morelia, Mexico (*Biblioteca de la Universidad Michoacana de San Nicolás de Hidalgo*). 1549.

Fourah Bay College in Free Town is the oldest academic institution in Sub-Saharan Africa. This photograph shows one of the buildings (housing the library); it was destroyed in 1997 during the civil war. A new building was constructed a few years later (courtesy L.N. M'jamtu-sie, Fourah Bay College Library).

3. Mexico National Autonomous University Library, Mexico City, Mexico (*Biblioteca de la Universidad Nacional Autónoma de México*). 1551.

Spanish King Charles I (Holy Roman Emperor Charles V) founded the University. It was closed in 1810, during the Mexican War of Independence. Re-opening in 1910, eventually its library becoming part of the National Library of Mexico.

4. St. Mark (San Marcos) National University Library, Lima, Peru (*Biblioteca de la Universidad Nacional Mayor de San Marcos*). 1552.

5. St. Thomas (Santo Tomas) University Library, Bogotá (*Biblioteca Universidad Santo Tomás*). 1580.

6. Ecuador Central University Library, Quito (*Biblioteca Universidad Central del Ecuador*). 1586.

7. Puebla Autonomous University Library, Mexico (*Biblioteca de la Universidad Autónoma de Puebla*). 1598.

Puebla also has the oldest existing non-academic library building in Latin America, founded in 1645 (see World Records for Library Buildings).

8. Córdoba National University Library, Argentina (*Biblioteca de la Universidad Nacional de Córdoba*). 1615.

9. Yucatan Autonomous University Library, Mérida, Mexico (*Biblioteca de la Universidad Autónoma de Yucatan*). 1624.

10. San Francisco Xavier Royal Pontifical University Library, Sucre, Bolivia (*Biblioteca de la Universidad Real y Pontificia de San Francisco Xavier*). 1625.

11. Jesuit College Library, Quebec City, Canada (*Bibliothèque de l'Université Jesuit*). 1635.

Technically Jesuit College is not a full university; the next three oldest universities in Canada are the University of Laval, Quebec City, which was founded in 1663; the University of New Brunswick in Fredericton, founded in 1785; and St. Mary's University in Halifax, which was founded in 1803.

12. Harvard University Library, Cambridge, Massachusetts, U.S. 1636.

13. Rosario University Library, Bogotá, Columbia (*Biblioteca Universidad del Rosario*). 1653.

14. William & Mary College, Williamsburg, Virginia, U.S. 1693.

15. Yale University Library, New Haven, Connecticut. 1701.

Most Brazilian universities were founded in the 20th century, but the oldest university is the Pelotas Federal University in southern Brazil, founded in 1883. The very first academic library to be established in the U.S. was a library set up in 1620, in Henrico, Virginia (just after the Pilgrims on board the ship Mayflower *landed in Plymouth). A gift from Thomas Burgrave, this library was part of an early abortive plan to set up a college in Virginia. See list* **382** *for the list of the 4 oldest U.S. libraries founded in the 1600s.*

72
Ten Oldest Uuniversity Libraries in Asia

1. Hunan University Library, Changsha, China. Founded A.D. 976. The university dates back to time it was known as the Yuelu Academy during the Song dynasty.

Chinese leader Mao Zedong was born in Changsha and was also a student at the university before working as a librarian at Beijing University Library.

2. Sungkyunkwan University Library, Seoul, South Korea, 1398.

3. Pontifical Santo Tomás University Library, Manila, the Philippines. 1611.

Another Filipino university library, San Carlos University Library in Cebu City, was founded in 1595, but it gained university status in 1948, after being closed in 1769 when Jesuits were expelled from the Philippines, and re-opening in 1783.

4. Ryukoku University Library, Kyoto, Japan. 1639.

5. Sydney University Library, Australia. 1850.

Joint 6. Calcutta (Kolkata), Bombay (Mumbai), and Madras (Chennai) university libraries (all in India); and Padjadjaran University Library, Bandung, Indonesia (*Perpustakaan Universitas Padjadjaran*). 1857.

7. Keio University Library, Tokyo, Japan. 1858.

8. Hokkaido University Library, Sapporo, Japan. 1876.

Joint 9. Waseda University Library, Tokyo, Japan; and Punjab University Library, Lahore, Pakistan. Both founded 1882.

10. Yonsei University Library, Seoul, South Korea. 1885

73
Ten Oldest University Libraries in the Middle East

1. Al-Qarawiyin University Library, Fez, Morocco (*Bibliothèque de l'Université El-Qaraouiyin*). Founded circa A.D. 859. See list **61** for more details.

2. Al-Azhar University Library, Cairo, Egypt. A.D. 985. See also list **61**.

3. Al-Nizamiyah University Library, Baghdad, Iraq. A.D. 1070. See also list **61**.

4. Hacettepe University Library, Ankara, Turkey (*Hacettepe Üniversitesi Kütüphane*). 1206.

5. Mustansiriya University Library, Bagdad, Iraq. 1233. Founded by Abbasid Caliph al-Mustansir as a Madrasah.

6. Istanbul (Constantinople) University Library, Turkey (*Istanbul Üniversitesi Kütüphane*). 1455.

The university was believed to have been founded as Constantinople University by Theodosius II, during the time Constantinople was part of the Eastern

Roman Byzantine Empire around A.D. 430, and re-founded after Constantinople fell to the Turkish Ottoman Empire led by Sultan Mehmet in 1453.

7. Istanbul Technical University Library, Turkey (*Istanbul Teknik Üniversitesi Kütüphane*). 1773.

8. Jesuit University of St. Joseph Library, Beirut, Lebanon (*Bibliothèques de l'Université St-Joseph*). 1875

9. American University of Beirut Library, Lebanon (*Bibliothèque de l'Université de Beirut d'Américain*) 1866. Beirut also once had an ancient Byzantine university, founded circa the 5th century A.D.

10. Hebrew University Library, Jerusalem, Israel. 1892.

Although not an educational institute, the Astan Quds Razavi Documentation Center Library in Mashhad, Iran, is the oldest existing reference library in Iran. It was founded in 1460 and is a prominent research library on Islam.

WORLD RECORDS FOR SPECIALTY LIBRARIES AND ARCHIVES

Special libraries are libraries that devote their book collections to one or more specialized subjects such as medicine, law, humanities and business. As such they are more likely to be found in companies, in research institutes or other scholarly bodies, or government-funded libraries. Very few are open to members of the public, as they are primarily for company staff or researchers and members of a research institute. While this section deals with libraries, there is a section dealing with the largest databases in specialized subjects like law and medicine (see lists **290** to **350**). Hence, this book covers, for instance, in the case of medicine, the largest medical libraries and the largest medical databases.

74
Ten Largest Medical and Nursing Libraries

1. National Library of Medicine, Bethesda, Maryland, U.S. Has over 5 million medical books and over 6500 different medical serials. Founded in 1836 as the Library of the Surgeon-General's Office, it is located on the campus of the National Institutes of Health, which has its own medical library. One of the most widely accepted acquisition guides used by medical librarians in the U.S when deciding which medical books to purchase is the Brandon-Hill List, named for the list's compilers Alfred N. Brandon and Dorothy R. Hill. It is approved by the U.S. Medical Library Association.

2. Russian State Medical Library, Moscow. 3.9 million. Founded in 1923.

3. German National Library for Medicine, Cologne (*Deutsche Zentralbibliothek für Medizin*). 1.3 million. Founded in 1908.

4. Harvard University Medical School Library, Cambridge, Massachusetts, U.S. Also known as Francis Countway Medical Library. 1.1 million. It was founded in 1960.

5. New York Academy of Medicine Library, U.S. 810,200. Founded in 1847.

It is the largest public medical library in the world.

6. National Academy of Medicine Library, Paris, France (*Bibliothèque de l'Academie National de Médicine*). 530,000 books. Founded 1762.

7. Yale University Medical School Library, New Haven, Connecticut, U.S. 430,000. Also known as the Harvey Cushing/John Whitney Medical Library.

8. Royal Society of Medicine Library, London, U.K. 413,000 books. Founded 1805. It is the largest postgraduate biomedical lending library in the U.K.

The German National Library for Medicine, based in Cologne, is Europe's largest medical library and the third largest in the world.

9. Karolinska Institute Library (*Karolinska Institutet Bibliotek*), Stockholm, Sweden. It contains more than 360,000 medical books and about 900 medical serials, and is involved in awarding the famous annual Nobel Prize in Physiology & Medicine. Largest medical library in Scandinavia.

10. National Medical Library, Prague, Czech Republic, Narodni lekarska Knihovna. 115,000 books. Founded in 1949.

There are also other several large national medical libraries in Europe (which are distinct from the main national library). The Russian Central Epidemiology Institute, in Moscow, has over 4 million volumes but this figure may include not just books, but also medical reports, microforms, manuscripts and other publications.

The five largest medical libraries in the U.K. are: Royal College of Surgeons Libraries, London and Edinburgh (founded 1505); the Royal College of Physicians Libraries, London and Edinburgh (founded 1518); the Royal Society of Medicine Library, London, founded 1805; the National Institute of Medical Research Library, London, founded 1920; and the British Medical Association Nuffield Library, London, founded in 1832. The combined library collection of these five libraries is over 2 million medical books and over 7000 different medical serials.

The U.K. Royal College of Nursing Library is the largest in Europe, with over 60,000 books.

75
Largest Medical Library in Asia

The Chinese Academy of Medical Sciences Library, based in Beijing, has over 2.8 million books. It was founded in 1917.

76
Largest Medical Library in Latin America

The Pan American Health Organization (*Organizacao Pan-Americana da Saude*) runs the Latin-American Health Sciences Information Center, or BIREME, in São Paulo, Brazil. Founded in 1967, it has over 175,000 books and 3,500 biomedical journals. Library membership is open to all medical researchers and doctors from Latin America.

77
Largest Biomedical and Scientific Periodicals Library

The Canada Institute for Scientific and Technical Information (or CISTI), founded in 1924 in Ottawa, has a huge serial collection of over 16,000 journals and more than 2 million technical reports. It functions as a Canada's national science library and also has about 4.3 million books on science, technology and allied subjects. It is also Canada's foremost publisher of scientific journals and books through the NRC Research Press, its publishing arm, and also operates a huge international electronic journal service called the CISTI catalog.

78
Oldest Dental and Medical School Libraries

The University of Maryland Dental School Library in Baltimore, U.S., was founded in 1842 and is the oldest in the world.

The world's largest dental library is the American Dental Association Library in Chicago, Illinois, U.S. It was founded in 1859 and has over 40,000 books on dentistry and 16,000 dental and medical journals. The British Dental Association Library in London is the largest dental library in Europe, with over 12,000 books.

The two oldest medical school libraries in the world are Florence Medical School Library, in Italy (*Biblioteca Scuola Medica Firenze*) founded in 1287, and the Salerno Medical School Library, also in Italy (*Biblioteca Scuola Medica Salernitana*), was established in 13th century. In France, Montpellier University Medical School Library was set up in the 14th century. Pennsylvania University Medical School Library, Philadelphia, U.S., was opened in 1775, and in 1788, the library of the College of Physicians of Philadelphia (CPP) was founded. They are both the oldest medical school libraries in the Americas. The two oldest medical school libraries in Asia are Calcutta (Kalkota) Medical College Library, India, founded in 1835, and Panaji Medical School Library, set up in Goa in 1845 (a Portuguese colony until 1961 and now a state in India). Today it is part of Goa University. In the U.K., the London Hospital Medical Library was founded in 1786. It is now part of London University Queen Mary's School of Medicine and Dentistry Library in London. The Royal College of Surgeons Library in Edinburgh was founded in 1505, and the Royal

College of Physicians Library in London was founded in 1518. However, both these colleges are not exactly medical schools, but institutes for qualified surgeons and physicians. Nevertheless, both have the oldest medical libraries in the U.K.

79
Largest Pharmaceutical Libraries

Based in New York, Pfizer, the world's largest pharmaceutical company (known for the drug Viagra) also has the largest pharmaceutical library with over 130,000 titles on subjects such as pharmacy, biochemistry, organic chemistry and pharmacology. In the U.K., Boots Pharmaceutical Research Library in Nottingham has over 70,000 books, while books in GlaxoSmithKline libraries in the U.K. and overseas total over 95,000.

80
Largest International Health Library

The library of the World Health Organization Library in Geneva, Switzerland, has a collection of over 150,000 medical books and is open to medical researchers and academics from around the world.

81
Largest Library in Europe on Deafness and Hearing Loss

The Royal National Institute for the Deaf Library in London, U.K., which is part of the University College Library, also in London, stocks more than 10,000 books devoted to deafness, hard of hearing and electronic gadgets to improve hearing.

82
Largest Economics Library

The German National Library of Economics in Kiel (*Deutsche Zentralbibliothek für Wirtschaftswissenschaften*) is the largest in the world with over 3 million books and over 10,000 periodicals on all aspects of economics. It was once a part of the Kiel Institute of World Economics, at the Kiel University in Germany, but both are now two separate entities. The library of the London School of Economics and Political Science (part of London University), the second largest in Europe, currently has more than 1 million books and some 28,000 journals. Sidney Webb founded the library in 1896 as the British Library of Political and Economic Science. The library is the editorial office of the International Bibliography of the Social Sciences, and also has extensive archives on world economics dating from the 19th century. The Stockholm School of Economics Library in Sweden, founded in 1909, with over 250,000 books, is the largest in Scandinavia.

The German National Library of Economics, based in the seaside resort of Kiel, is the largest economics Library in the world (courtesy Lukas Roth, Cologne / German National Library of Economics, Kiel, Germany).

83
Largest Geography and Geology Libraries

The American Geographical Society Library has over 130,000 books. It is based at the University of Wisconsin–Milwaukee Golda Meir Library. Its library holdings extend back as far as second generation vellum copies of the famous 15th century Rome edition of Greek genius Claudius Ptolemy's eight-volume atlas *Geographia*. This manuscript had been originally completed in A.D. 150 at the Alexandria Library in Egypt. The oldest original map in the collection is a world map dating from 1452 and compiled in Italian by the Venetian cartographer Giovanni Leardo. The Russian Geological Library in St. Petersburg, founded in 1880, contains 320,000 books.

In Asia the Chinese Institute of Geography Library in Beijing owns 95,000 books on all aspects of geography, the largest such library in Asia. Also in China is the Institute of Oceanology in Qingdao with 110,000 books.

The Geographia *(also known as* Cosmographia*) was the explorer's bible for more than 1000 years after it was completed. Famous 15th and 16th century sailors such as Christopher Columbus, Vasco da Gama and Ferdinand Magellan used the book as a* guide for planning their overseas explorations. A mistake in Ptolemy's geographic calculations on the size of the oceans contributed to Columbus' believing he was in Asia when in fact he was in the Americas. See list **211** for details on how the Geographia was rediscovered in the 15th century. The Arabs probably were the first to use knowledge gained from the Geographia, to explore the New World. A Chinese manuscript known as the Sung Document (so called because it was written during the time of the Chinese Sung dynasty between A.D. 960 and 1279) provides fascinating details of a voyage made in 1178 by Arab sailors from the Philippines to the Americas. This was more than 300 years before the voyage of Christopher Columbus. The Arab sailors traveled from southern Philippines across the Pacific Ocean and landed on the coast of what is now California, a land the Chinese called Mu-Lan-Pi, then made a return journey to the Philippines. Some of the Chinese sailors in the Philippines who were lucky enough to travel with the Arab sailors to Mu-Lan-Pi sent word of the feat back to Canton (Guangzhou) the same year, where the Sung Document originated. Canton (Guangzhou) at that time had a large population of Arab and Asian Muslim explorers and scholars, and the very first mosque in China (Huaisheng) was built there in A.D. 670. The problem was the Arab sailors made no further voyages to follow up the 1178 voyage, nor did Chinese sailors. And when the Portuguese and Prince Henry "the Navigator" began the Iberian age of overseas explorations in the 15th century that eventually lead to the voyage of Columbus, none of them had ever heard of the Sung Document. Hence, like the insignificance of Leif Erikson and the Norwegian Viking landings in the Americas (Newfoundland) around A.D. 1000, Columbus remains the official discoverer of the New World in 1492. And credit to the crossing of the huge Pacific Ocean, starting from either east of Asia or west of the Americas, goes to Ferdinand Magellan's three-month voyage of 1521. Marco Polo, the Italian traveler, visited extensively China in the 13th century, but there is no mention of the Sung Document in his famous story about his travels (see list **201**). Had Columbus or any other European explorers known about the Sung Document, the history of the Americas would have been very different. The whereabouts of the Sung Document today are unknown as it may exist under a Chinese title. Efforts by the author (during research work for this book in 2006) to see if the manuscript is in the National Library of China, via emails, drew a blank. However, the author was referred to an English book about Chinese explorers. This 2002 book, titled 1421: The Year China Discovered America by Gavin Menzies provides documentary evidence to suggest that in the 15th century Chinese explorer Zheng He circumnavigated the world before Magellan's 1521 voyage. Zheng He also reached the Americas before Columbus did in 1492, starting from the Chinese coast and traveling eastwards to the coasts of California (shipwrecks of 15th Chinese vessels have been found in Sacramento, California). The Sung Document could have been one of the numerous sources of data used by the Chinese explorers during the planning of the 1421 voyage. But we can never be certain about this. But Menzies' book does mention three manuscripts written in 1178, 1225 and 1349 by Chinese scholars, using data obtained from Chinese explorers of the day, about the geography of the world. The manuscript written in 1225 (i.e., during the Sung dynasty) was titled Zhu Fan Zhi by Zhao Rru Kua. The book has information on the discovery of foreign-looking peoples (not Europeans) on lands in waters east of China. Could these foreign-looking peoples be the first evidence of American Indians living in what is today the California coast or perhaps first evidence of Pacific Ocean islanders? Could this book written in 1225 be related to the Sung Document? Is it the Sung Document? Documentary evidence of the Moslems being first to use knowledge gained from the Geographia also exists. For instance, in 1340, Persian writer Hamdollah Mostowfi produced a world map based solely on Claudius Ptolemy's atlas.

84
Largest Library in the Middle East Devoted to Oil Exploration

With the Middle East having very large petroleum deposits, many libraries there have important book collections on oil exploration, refining and petrochemical engineering. The King Fahd University of Petroleum and Minerals Library in Dhahran, Saudi Arabia (founded 1963), is the largest of its kind in the Middle East and currently has over 380,000 books covering chemical engineering and petroleum production among others.

The university was established by the well-known former Saudi Oil Minister Sheik Ahmed Yamani with the help of the Massachusetts Institute of Technology, Princeton University and the American University in Beirut, Lebanon.

85
Largest Engineering Libraries

The Department of Electrical and Computer Engineering library at the University of Illinois in the U.S. (Grainger Engineering Library Information Center) has the largest university engineering library in the Americas. There are currently over 300,000 books. The university also has the largest chemistry library in the world. The largest mechanical engineering library in the world is the library of the American Society for Mechanical Engineers or ASME (founded 1880 in New York), with about 200,000 books. The largest electrical engineering library in the world belongs to the IEEE (Institute of Electrical and Electronic Engineering). Set up in 1884, it has over 220,000 books. The IEEE, based in Piscataway, New Jersey, in the U.S., also publishes about 35 percent of the total books in the world on electronics and electrical and computer engineering. Based close to the Sorbonne University of Paris in France, the École Polytechnique Library has the second largest collection of general engineering books in Europe, with over 133,000 books. It was founded in 1796. Established in 1820, the Institution of Civil Engineers Library in London, U.K., has the largest library for civil and structural engineers in Europe, housing some 100,000 titles. In Asia, the largest collection of books on engineering is at the Chinese Academy of Sciences Library in Beijing.

The libraries of the five major engineering societies in the world (outside Europe) comprising the IEEE, the ASME, the ASCE (American Society for Civil Engineers), the AIME (American Institute for Mechanical engineers) and the AIChE (American Institute for Chemical Engineers) founded the Engineering Societies Library or ESL in 1915. The combined collections of the ESL, which has been based at the Linda Hall Library in Kansas City since 1995, number over 600,000 volumes. This makes the Linda Hall Library the largest (privately-funded) engineering and technology library in the world.

86
Largest Genealogy Library

The Family History Library in Salt Lake City, Utah, U.S., is the largest in the world. Part of the Mormon Church of Jesus Christ of Latter-day Saints, it has over 300,000 books, 2.4 million rolls of microfilm and over 2 billion names in its databases. It was founded in 1894 as part of the library of the Genealogical Society of Utah.

87
Largest Music Library

U.S. Library of Congress Music Division, Washington, D.C., founded in 1897, has about 1.4 million books all on all aspects of music. It also has the largest collection of sound recordings in the world. The Eastman School of Music at the University of Rochester in New York has the largest music library in an academic library. Its Sibley Music Library has over 750,000 books and other items. The William and Gayle Cook Music Library, Indiana University, Bloomington, has over 500,000 books.

88
Largest Poetry Library

Founded in 1953, the Poetry Library based at the Royal Festival Hall in London, U.K., is the largest of its kind in the world devoted to modern poetry, with over 95,000 books.

89
Largest Film and Television Library in Europe

The British Film Institute Library in London provides access to over 40,000 books on film and television in English and fifteen or more other languages. In addition it holds 5000 periodical titles, dating back to the earliest years of cinema in the 19th century. The British Broadcasting Corporation (BBC) Library in London has the largest audio-visual library collection in Europe.

*The University of California, Los Angeles, has the largest collection of film and television programs in a university (the earliest is from the year 1890). This is not surprising as the university is close to Hollywood. The world's largest collection of U.S. and foreign produced films are in the U.S. Library of Congress. It includes the oldest existing motion picture, made by Thomas Edison in the 1890s. While libraries are busy replacing acid-based books with alkaline-based books (see list **142**), audio-visual libraries are also busy replacing their old nitrate-based films with acetate-based films because nitrate-based films deteriorate quicker. Films made before the 1950s were mostly nitrate-based.*

90
Largest Sound Archives

The British Library's National Sound Archive has over 1 million disks and over 150,000 tape recordings of sounds. This is the largest such collection in Europe.

91
Largest Agriculture Libraries

The U.S. National Agricultural Library, in Washington, D.C., which is part of the agricultural research service of the U.S. Department of Agriculture, has more than 3.5 million books. It was founded in 1862. The Russian Academy of Agricultural Sciences Library, in Moscow (*Rossiskaya Akademiya Selskokhozyaistvennyjk Nauk*) has over 3 million books and periodicals. It was founded in 1930. The largest agricultural library in Western Europe is the David Lubin Memorial Library, which is based at the headquarters of the UN Food and Agricultural Organization (FAO) in Rome, Italy. The library currently has over 1.2 million books and was founded in 1952. The largest agricultural libraries in Asia are the library of the Chinese Academy of Agricultural Science (CAAD), established in 1957 in Beijing, with over 690,000 books; the Japanese Ministry of Agriculture, Forestry and Fisheries Library (*Norin Suisansho Toshokan*) with over 310,000 books; and the Chinese Institute of Soil Science Library in Beijing with 115,000 books.

92
Largest Botany and Zoology Library

The Zoological Society of London Library in the U.K. has over 200,000 books and is the largest of its kind in the world. This is also the largest library in a zoo, as the Zoological Society of London Library is based in the famous London Zoo. The largest library on aquatic sciences and fisheries in Europe is the National Marine Biological Library, in Plymouth, U.K. Founded 1887, the library has over 14,000 books. In Asia, the Kunming Institute of Zoology Library in China is the largest zoology library, with about 150,000 books. The Chinese Institute of History of Natural Sciences Library contains over 113,000 books.

The library of the New York Botanical Gardens in the U.S. (called the LuEsther T. Mertz Library) possesses more than 300,000 books, making it the largest botany library. The largest botany library in Europe is at Berlin Free University in Germany. It Botanical Museum Library has 120,000 books. The largest library on plant and horticulture in the Europe is the Royal Botanical Gardens Library, Kew, London, U.K. The library contains over as about 75,000 books and 4,000 periodicals. It was set up in 1852.

93
Largest Science Library

The German National Library of Science and Technology (*Die Technische Informationsbibliothek* or TIB) is a specialist library for all areas of technology and its fundamental sciences, especially chemistry, computer science, mathematics and physics. It is the world's largest specialist library in science. The holdings of the joint German National Library of Science and Technology and University Library Hannover comprise a total of 8.2 million volumes, microforms and CD-ROMs as well as subscriptions to 21,000 general and specialist journals. Of these, approximately 18,000 are technical and scientific journals. There are also 1.2 million media units as well as 3,000 journals concerning the arts and social sciences. The holdings also contain conference reports, research reports, patent specifications, norms, standards, dissertations as well as Eastern European and East Asian specialist literature.

94
Largest Military Libraries

The largest military libraries tend to be either those administered by government departments, or the military libraries attached to military colleges or academies. The 5 largest government department libraries, or nonacademic military libraries, are:

1. Library of the Central House of the Russian Army, Moscow, Russia (*Biblioteka tsentral'nogo doma Rossiiskoi Armii*). 5.6 million books. Formerly called Library of the Central House of the Soviet Army (up to 1991).

2. British Ministry of Defense Library, Whitehall, London. 750,000 books. Founded in 1964. The extensive collection includes books from the ministry's famous predecessor, the former War Office Library (1684 to 1963).

3. Pentagon Library, Department of Defense, Washington, D.C. 155,000 books. Founded in 1944. The Defense Department's more expensive library is at the National Security Agency (see list **112**).

4. French Defense Ministry Library, Paris(*Bibliothèque Ministrie de la Défense*), dates back to the 16th century. 186,000 books.

5. German Federal Defense Ministry Library, Bonn (*Bibliothek Bundesministerium der Verteidigung*), founded in 1955. 130,000 books.

The two largest military libraries in Latin America are the Central Library of the Navy (*Biblioteca Central de la Armada*) in Buenos Aires, Argentina, founded in 1914, with over 110,000 books, and the Brazilian Army Library (*Biblioteca do Exercito*) in Rio Janeiro, founded in 1881, with just over 91,000 books.

The five largest academic or military college libraries in the world are:

1. The combined collections of the three U.S. military academies at West Point in New York, Annapolis in Maryland (Naval Academy) and Colorado Springs in Colorado (Air Force Academy). 3.2 million.

2. Air University Library, Maxwell Air Force Base, Alabama, U.S. 2.6 million. Founded in 1946.

3. National Defense University Library, Fort McNair, Washington, D.C. 500,000. Founded in 1982.

4. Royal Military Academy, Sandhurst, Library, Camberley, U.K. 321,000.

The Royal Military Academy, Sandhurst, was formed in 1947 as the successor to the Royal Military Academy, Woolwich, founded in 1741, and the Royal Military College, Sandhurst, founded in 1801. Established in 1875, the Institution of Royal Engineering Library in Brompton Barracks, Chatham, has over 40,000 books on military engineering. The Joint Services Command and Staff College Library in Shrivenham is the second largest military library in the U.K.

5. Royal Military College Library (*Bibliothèque Ecole Militaire*), Paris, France. 180,000. Founded in 1751.

Napoleon Bonaparte made good use of books at the library of the Royal Military College Library in Paris while he was a student there. He completed his military training in 1784, and was commissioned as a second lieutenant.

95
Largest Prison Libraries

According to the U.S. Justice Department, Bureau of Justice Statistics, the largest prison libraries for the 2.5 million inmates in the U.S. in 2006 are at Cook County Jail in Chicago (Illinois) and Los Angeles County Jail (California). The three largest prison libraries in the U.K. are at Wandsworth (*largest*), Liverpool and Brixton prisons. A library is a legal statu-

tory requirement in the U.K.'s 139 prisons. The Prison Service College Library in Wakefield has over 210,000 books on penology, criminology, etc. The library also holds official prison reports for the U.K. going back to 1835. See list **201** for details of famous and infamous people who wrote bestsellers while serving a prison sentence.

Bibliothèque Ecole Militaire in Paris, France's largest military library, was founded by King Louis XV.

96
Largest Law Libraries

Harvard University Law Library was founded in 1817, the same year as the law school. It is the world's largest law library, with about 2.5 million law books, manuscripts and other library items such as legal gazettes and periodicals, and is also the oldest university law library in the U.S.

The U.S. Library of Congress in Washington, D.C., is the second largest law library in the world, as it has more than 2 million law books. Columbia University Law Library is the third largest in the U.S with approximately 800,000 volumes, followed by New York University Law Library with 710,000 books (5th largest in the world). The largest law library on the Internet is www.lawresearch.com, which has over 1 million legal Internet resources. The largest law library in Canada is York University's Osgoode Hall Law School Library in Toronto. It was founded in 1889 and its collections total over 400,000 books. This also makes it the largest law library of the Commonwealth countries.

The largest law library in Europe is the Cujas Library (*Bibliothèque Cujas*) which is part of the Sorbonne University of Paris, France. There are over 130,000 books in the library.

In the U.K. apart from the British Library's law collection, the 15th century Lincoln's Inn law library in London (oldest of the four Inns of Court law libraries for U.K. lawyers), has about 180,200 law books. Oxford University Bodleian Law Library has the largest collection of academic law books in the U.K. (200,000 titles).

The Inns of Court law libraries in the United Kingdom was once the largest chained law library in the world.

The largest law library in Asia is China's Tsing Hua University Law School Library in Beijing. It currently holds just over 110,000 books

So valuable were the majority of law books in Lincoln's Inn Law Library that they were all secured by chains in the library until 1771.

97
Largest Art Library

Based in New York, the Avery Architectural and Fine Arts Library is the largest in the world with more than 250,000 books and about 1,300 periodicals. Established in 1890, its book collection is diverse, encompassing architecture, art history, painting, sculpture, graphic arts, and archaeology. The National Art Library in London is the largest in Europe with over 170,000 books and manuscripts. At the Smithsonian Institution of Archives of American Art in San Marino, California, the Huntington Library has the largest collection of books about the history of visual arts. It was founded in 1954. The Russian State Art Library in Moscow is the second largest in Europe with over 100,000 books.

98

Largest Libraries in Europe with Specialized Collections of Books on Africa

1. London University School of African and Oriental Studies or SOAS, U.K. Founded in 1920, its library has over 850,000 books and 4,500 periodicals, as well as extensive collections of archives and manuscripts written in African and Asian languages.

2. Belgian Ministry of Foreign Affairs African Library (*Bibliothèque Africaine*), Brussels. It has over 480,000 books, and was developed from a collection started by King Leopold II in the 1860s.

99

Largest Astronomy Library

The United States Naval Observatory in Washington, D.C., has over 100,000 books on all topics of astronomy including space exploration and astrophysics. It was established in 1830.

100

Largest Libraries in Europe Specializing in Education

Comenius Library (*Comenius-Bücherei*), founded 1871 in Leipzig, Germany, has over 460,000 books on education and teaching on all levels. Founded in 1902, the Institute of Education Library (part of London University) has over 300,000 books and more than 2000 periodicals. The largest government library devoted to education is the U.S. National Library of Education in Washington, D.C. It was founded in 1878.

101

Largest Social Sciences Library

The Russian Academy of Sciences Institute for Scientific Information on Social Sciences Library in Moscow, better known by the acronym INION (Insitut Nauchnoi Informatsii po Obshchestvennym Naukam) has over 12.8 million books. It was founded in 1969.

The London School of Economics and Political Science has the second largest collection of books on social sciences in Europe. The largest history library is at the Russian State Public History Library in Moscow, stocking 3.6 million books. It was founded in 1938. The largest collection of archeological books in a European museum is in the Ashmolean Museum Library in Oxford, founded in 1683 with over 180,000 books. The Oriental History Library in Tokyo (Toyo Bunko) has over 950,000 books, including rare Chinese and Japanese manuscripts, and Western books on Asia.

The Ashmolean Museum Library in Oxford, United Kingdom, has the largest collection of archaeological books in a European museum.

102
Largest Religious Libraries

Christianity: Established in 1969, the Flora Lamson Hewlett Library in Berkeley, California, has over 500,000 books on Christianity. It is part of the Graduate Theological Union. Based in New York, the American Bible Association presently has about 44,000 books, including the largest collection of ancient and modern copies of the Bible in several languages. The largest Christian library in Europe is in the St. Gallen Monastery in eastern Switzerland. The library, called *Stiftsbibliothek*, contains over 150,000 books and the monastery, which dates back to the A.D. 719, is the premiere tourist attraction in the city of St. Gallen and a UNESCO Heritage site.

The largest publisher of books on Christianity in the world is Thomas Nelson, based in Nashville, Tennessee, U.S. The largest Christian library in Latin America is the St. Benedict Monastery Library *(Biblioteca do Mosteiro de S. Bento) in Rio Janeiro. Founded in 1600, it has over 95,000 books.*

Islam: The largest non-academic Islamic libraries are in the Al-Mutawakki Mosque, Samarra, Iraq; Shah Faisal Mosque in Islamabad, Pakistan; and the Suleymaniye Mosque in Istanbul, Turkey. Hartford Seminary Library, founded in 1834, probably has the largest Islamic library in the U.S. The collections (totaling over 75,000 volumes) include hundreds of rare Arabic and Islamic manuscripts and a collection of thousands of books and other materials from the personal library of D. B. Macdonald, at one time the premier Arabist in the U.S. The Hartford Seminary is also one of the largest official U.S. repositories for all materials published in the Middle East. The library of the Institute for Advanced Studies of World Religions, founded in 1972, in Carmel, New

The London School of Economics and Political Science has the largest social science library in Western Europe.

York, has over 70,000 books on the five major religions in Asia.

Buddhism: The library of the Sakya Buddhist Monastery in Shigate, Tibet, is the largest in the world with over 46,000 books, including thousands of *sutras* (teachings and discourses of the Buddha). The monastery itself was originally founded in A.D. 1073 by Khon Konchog Gyalpo. Shigate is the seat of the Panchen Lama, the highest spiritual Buddhist authority below the rank of the Dalai Lama. The largest Buddhist library outside Tibet is the Tawang Buddhist Monastery Library in Tawang, Arunachal Pradesh, in India. It is over 300 years old.

Buddhist libraries in Thailand (which are the largest in numbers, outside China and Japan) are called ho trai.

Judaism: The largest Jewish libraries in the world are the Hebrew University Library, Jerusalem, Israel; the Jewish Theological Seminary of America Library in New York; the *Bibliothèque de l'Alliance Israélite Universelle,* Paris, France; and the Budapest Synagogue Library in Hungary.

Hinduism: The largest Hinduism libraries are at the Pashupatinath Temple in Kathmandu, Nepal, and the Tirupati-Tirumala Temple of Sri Venkateswara (Balaji), Andhra Pradesh, India.

103
Largest Library in the U.K. Devoted to Women and Children

The Women's Library, with over 60,000 volumes, based in London's Whitechapel, was founded in 1927, when it was located in London Guildhall University. The library collection includes books on past and present famous women who have made important contributions to U.K. society, and is the most extensive of such a collection in the U.K. Incidentally, the only women's lending library in the U.K. is the Glasgow Women's Library. In Russia, the St. Petersburg Children's Library is the largest of its kind in the world. It opened in 1982.

104
Largest Collection of Shakespeare's Printed Works

The Folger Shakespeare Library, founded in 1930 in Washington, D.C., has more than 300,000 books. Henry Clay Folger, who had an intellectual passion for buying rare books on Shakespeare, founded the library.

105
Oldest and Largest National Archives

The growth of archives for the preservation of state and commercial documents started in Europe during the late Renaissance period. The Vatican Archives in Rome (*Archivio Segreto*

The Women's Library in London is devoted only to issues facing women in U.K. society and includes books on the most famous women in the United Kingdom over the last few centuries.

Vaticano) dates back to 1611 (some archives however date further back to the 4th century A.D. collections of Pope Damascus), while the Swedish Chancery Archives was set up in 1618. However, Europe's first modern state archives was the French National Archives (*Archives Nationales de France*), established in 1789. It was also the first to use microfilm to archive documents. The largest modern archives is the U.S. National Archives in Washington, D.C. Europe's two largest archives are the Vatican Archives in Rome and the General Archives of Simancas in Spain.

In 2004, Canada broke library tradition by merging its National Library with its National Archives. Most countries normally have these two institutions as separate entities. One of the holdings in the Vatican Archives most sought after by scholars are the files pertaining to the Inquisition, which were not available for research until 1998, when the Vatican Archives permitted limited access to the Inquisition files.

106
Oldest National Archives in the Americas

The National Archives of Argentina was set up in Buenos Aires in 1821.

The National Archives of Mexico dates back to 1790, but was not officially opened until 1900.

The first modern archives are the French National Archives in Paris.

107
Oldest National Archives in the Middle East

The National Archives of Egypt has been in existence since 1828.

108
Oldest National Archives in Asia

The National Archives of India was set up in 1891 in Calcutta (Kolkata). It moved to Delhi in 1911.

109
Oldest National Archives in Africa

This appears to be the National Archives of Angola, set up by the Portuguese colonial government in 1654 (an earlier smaller archive had been founded in 1603, but was destroyed by the Dutch in 1641). In the 1970s a new archive was established after Angola gained independence.

MISCELLANEOUS WORLD RECORDS FOR LIBRARIES

110
Twenty-Three Major Libraries That Have Suffered Devastating Fires or Natural Disasters

1. Alexandria Library, Egypt. The collection of 750,000 parchment and papyrus scrolls of the greatest library of the ancient world was destroyed with fire by an Arab army led by Arab general Amr Ibn-al-As in A.D. 638 on the orders of Caliph Omar I in Mecca, after surviving two earlier devastating fires. Caliph Omar was said to have justified the burning of the library by quoting the famous words, *if the writings of the Greeks in the library agree with the Koran they are unnecessary and need not be preserved, but if they disagree they are blasphemy and will be destroyed....* So either way the Alexandria Library lost out and was thus destroyed. One of two other earlier fires to devastate the library was started by Julius Caesar in 47 B.C., when he got involved in a political struggle between Queen Cleopatra and her younger brother Ptolemy XIII. A brand new Alexandria library was opened in 2002.

2. Harvard University Library, Cambridge, Massachusetts. It suffered a devastating fire in 1764, which destroyed over 90 percent of its collection of books (it was the largest library in the original 13 colonies in the 17th and 18th century at that time). Luckily donations rebuilt the library to its original size in just two years. The British, in charge of the colonies, did not start the fire, as it would be another 12 years before the American Revolution. Today Harvard University Library is the largest university library in the world.

3. U.S. Library of Congress, Washington, D.C. It was burnt down in 1814 by British forces during a brief war between the U.S. and the U.K. over Canada and the sea trade. And in 1851, another fire caused by a faulty chimney flue destroyed over 30,000 books.

4. Lomonosov Moscow State University Library, Russia. In 1812 as the invading army of Napoleon Bonaparte from France marched onto Moscow, locals there set fire to the city, and in the ensuing inferno the university library was among the buildings obliterated. Even when the library was rebuilt, it was further damaged during the Second World War. But its collections were again rapidly rebuilt at such a pace that today it is the largest university library in Europe.

5. Russian Academy of Sciences Library, St. Petersburg, Russia. The largest fire to damage a major library in the 20th century happened here in February 1988. Nearly 2 million books were destroyed as well as a third of the newspaper holdings.

6. National library of Finland, Helsinki. When this library was based in the old Finnish capi-

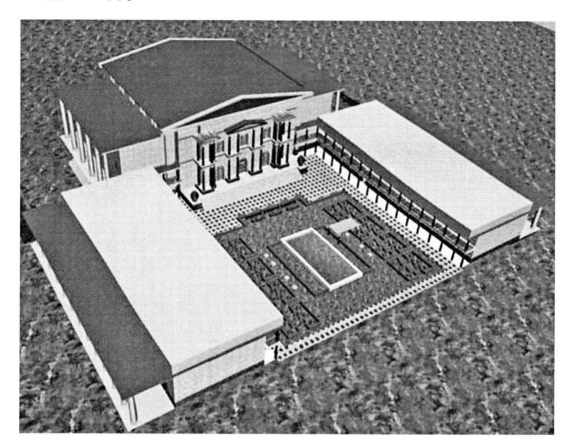

The ancient Greek Alexandria Library in Egypt, before it was destroyed by fire in A.D. 638 (courtesy UNESCO).

tal of Turku (Åbo), as the Helsinki University Library, much of it was destroyed by fire in 1827. The library was moved to Helsinki in 1828 and rebuilt from scratch.

7. British Library, London. Over 250,000 books were lost in 1941 during the Second World War, when German incendiary bombs started fires that forced the library to close until 1946.

8. Belize libraries. In 1931 an unnamed hurricane wreaked devastating havoc by destroying all libraries in this Central American state.

9. Louvain (Leuven) Catholic University Library, Belgium. The library was destroyed completely twice as a result of the two World Wars, first in 1915, and the second time in 1940, in both instances due to invasion by the German army. As a result the university library had to be rebuilt twice.

10. National Library of Algeria, Algiers. It was rebuilt in 1962, after a huge fire set by French colonial troops destroyed the library.

11. Hamburg University Speersort Library, Germany. Totally destroyed during the Second World War, it was one of several large German libraries to suffer devastation in the war, which included the Berlin State Library and the Bavarian State Library in Munich.

12. Copenhagen University Library, Denmark. It was rebuilt from scratch, when its entire collection was destroyed in the fire of 1728 in Copenhagen.

13. National Library of Bosnia and Herzegovina, Sarajevo. The library (which dates back to the time Sarajevo was part of the Austria-Hungarian Empire) was razed to the ground by Bosnian-Serb forces during the 1992–1995 civil

war, which forces also destroyed the library of the Oriental Institute containing irreplaceable rare manuscripts.

14. National Library of Cambodia, Phnom Penh. Troops of Pol Pot's Khmer Rouge forces wrecked the library in 1975, forcing it to close until 1980, when Vietnamese troops (who invaded Cambodia in 1978) drove the Khmer Rouge out of the country's urban areas.

15. Ambrosian Library, Milan, Italy. During the liberation of Italy by Allied forces during the Second World War, the library was severely damaged by fire, and a large number of rare manuscripts were lost forever.

16. Chicago Public Library, U.S. In 1871 the Great Chicago Fire destroyed what was the predecessor of the Chicago Public Library, a subscription library. This older Chicago library was not huge (its total book collections was under 50,000 at the time). But the destruction of the library was what gave rise to the founding of the Chicago Public Library in 1873. Because appeals for donation of books by descendants of Chicagoans living in Europe, who heard news about the fire, caused so many donated books to be sent to Chicago, legislators in the city had to pass an Act to establishing the Chicago Public Library.

17. Bucharest University Library, Romania. During the 1989 Romanian revolution, the central library was completely destroyed. Following the overthrow of the communist regime, the library was later rebuilt.

18. Heidelberg University Library was Germany's oldest university library, containing some of the most treasured manuscripts outside of Italy during the Renaissance. The library was totally destroyed during the War of the Palatine Succession in 1693.

19. The famous Duchess Anna Amalia Library in Weimar, Germany (a UNESCO World Heritage site), famous for many medieval manuscripts, was burnt down accidentally by sparks from a faulty cable in 2004. Over 50,000 books were destroyed outright (many found later to be rare and irreplaceable). A further 60,000 books were severely damaged with water used to douse the fire. A $20 million restoration project was completed in 2007.

20. In 2003, the Iraqi National Library in Baghdad was burnt down, and in the process priceless 16th to 18th century Turkish Ottoman manuscripts (dating from the time Bagdad was an important city of the Ottoman Empire), as well as Sumerian and Babylonian cuneiforms, were lost.

21. Tokyo University Library was destroyed during a massive earthquake in 1923 and later rebuilt, only to be destroyed again during the Second World War. It was rebuilt again after the war ended.

22. Fourah Bay College Library in Free Town, Sierra Leone, is part of the oldest academic institution in Sub-Saharan Africa, as it was founded in 1828. It was thus one of the few most important educational institutes in Africa for many decades. It was obliterated during the civil war of the early 1990s. It has since been rebuilt.

23. During the 2004 Asian tsunami, several public, college and school libraries were ruined in Sri Lanka and Indonesia. After the natural disaster, task forces were set up with the help of UNESCO and Western governments to rebuild the libraries.

Libraries in the U.S. granted landmark status by local or state government review boards have legal protection against demolition. A remarkable incident occurred near the end of the Second World War with the Berlin State Library in Germany in flames. A young Russian soldier, Yuri Knorosov, risked serious burning to randomly snatch two books from the burning library. After the war Knorosov became a Mayan language scholar after reading and discovering that one of books he had saved at the Berlin library was actually the only surviving copy of the Madrid Codex *in Germany. After university training, Knorosov published a number of research papers on deciphering Mayan cuneiforms and they were translated from Russian by other scholars who realized Knorosov's work was essential to the understand-*

ing of Mayan inscriptions. During the Sino-Japanese wars of the 1930s, over 500 libraries were ruined in China. When the Second World War broke out, the National Library of China in Beijing shipped its most rare and irreplaceable books and manuscripts to the U.S. Library of Congress for safekeeping. After the war, China reclaimed them. Taking a cue from this, the Library of Congress transferred the Declaration of Independence manuscript to Fort Knox for security reasons, in case the war spread to the U.S. After the war, it was transferred to the National Archives. Today libraries destroyed by natural disasters (or accidentally or deliberately such as in times of war) can get extra help in reconstruction with generous funds made available from both UNESCO and the World Bank. See also list **213** on book-burning rituals.

111
Library with the Most Branches Worldwide

The British Council, the U.K.'s international organization for educational and cultural relations, has over 1441 libraries and information centers in 110 countries. The largest library is in Bombay (Mumbai) in India. In Moscow, Russia, there exists the M. I. Rudomini State Library for Foreign Literature founded in 1922. In this case, instead of having branches all over the world, this library has exchange agreements with over 2000 libraries worldwide in 98 countries for continuous annual supply of a selection of important books published in each country. It thus has over 4.8 million books, making it the library with the largest collection of foreign language books. The library also occupies the same buildings housing several large international libraries, such as the American Cultural Center, the British Council and the French Cultural Center libraries. It is thus a popular destination for foreign tourists in Moscow wanting to keep up-to-date with news from home.

Several countries around the world have similar organizations for promoting educational and cultural activities in foreign countries. Most notable are the Institut Français (or Alliance Français) of France, which has over 150 branches in more than 50 countries, and the Goethe-Institut of Germany, which has over 128 branches in 76 countries. Both have over 600 libraries attached to these organizations. The Spanish equivalent of the above cultural institutions is the Instituto Cervantes, based in Madrid, with branches worldwide.

112
Most Expensive Library

The U.S. National Security Agency (NSA) library based at Fort George Mead in Maryland is believed to be more secure than the CIA, Israeli Mossad, British MI6, French DGSE, and former Russian KGB libraries in terms of the huge cost of implementing high-tech security devices and computer systems. These include the world's most sophisticated voice recognition systems, as well as retinal and finger print digital scanners, in addition to body heat, body movement, and sound digital sensors (as seen in the spy films Sneakers, Enemy of the State and Mission Impossible). The NSA Library collections include several PC terminals linking to a Cray supercomputer system (used especially for code breaking work), extremely sensitive and classified intelligence publications as well as the best books written on cryptology (cryptography and cryptoanalysis), bugging devices and eavesdropping. The huge audio-visual collection includes hundreds of dossiers with (National Reconnaissance Office) Keyhole KH-12, and Lacrosse-3 spy satellite photographs and 3-dimensional imagery. The library budget has been estimated at over a billion dollars per annum (based on a 1997 Freedom of Information Act law suit filed by Steven Aftergood, director of the Federation of American Scientists Project on U.S. Government Secrecy). This is the largest annual library budget anywhere in

The British Council Library branch in Recife, Brazil. The "circles in a square arrangement" is the easily recognized logo of the British Council.

the world (and is larger than the annual budgets of many third world countries in Africa and the Caribbean). The second largest annual library budget in the world is that of the U.S. Library of Congress, at $462 million per annum.

Among university libraries, Harvard has the largest annual budget, with over $200 million. New York Public Library has an annual budget of over $100 million. For more library budgets see also list **380**.

113
Oldest and Largest Major Private Libraries

The Boston Athenaeum was set up in 1807, from a need for a library to store the collections of the Anthology Society. Its huge collection of books (today, over a half a million) made it the largest private library in the U.S. It is now a subscription library, and yearly membership is available to members of the public.

In Europe private libraries were already well established from the Middle Ages, and most had religious books, such as the large 14th century library of Richard de Bury, Bishop of Durham in the U.K.

114
Largest Chained Libraries

The use of chains in libraries to prevent theft began at the Sorbonne Library at University of Paris, France, in the early 13th century. The largest chained library in the world today can be found in the Hereford Cathedral library in the U.K. When it was built circa A.D. 1079, it did not employ chains; they were installed in the late 14th century. The chained library contains just over 1,500 books, both handwritten and printed. Each book is attached to an oak bookcase with a chain. Another famous large chained library in the U.K. is the Francis Trigge Library in Grantham, founded in 1598. The most famous chained library in Italy was the Laurentian Library in Florence. Manuscripts were chained to the reading desk up till the early 20th century. So valuable were the majority of law books in the U.K.'s Lincoln's Inn law library that they were all secured by chains in the library until 1771, despite the fact that the law students had difficulty trying to study with the books. In fact, before the use of electronic tags hidden in books to prevent their being stolen from libraries and bookstores, several major European university libraries such as the Leiden State University in The Netherlands used chains fastened to their books, as this was the only serious option available. The problem with chained libraries is that you could not take a book and read it in your "favorite corner" in the library.

The Hereford Cathedral library's 700-year-old Mappa Mundi *is the largest complete medieval map in Europe today. Luckily it is not chained to the bookshelf.*

This monument to the era of chained books at an entrance of a U.K. library is a relic reminding visitors about the limited technology of days long gone that protect books from being stolen. Today libraries have many choices, including closed-circuit television cameras and electronic tags.

115
Eight Unusual Things That Happened at Libraries

1. In 2005 it was reported in New York newspapers that a poor and homeless creative writing student at New York University (name withheld) had lived in the university's Bobst Library for over 8 months without the university authorities knowing about it. This may not be surprising since the library is open 24 hours a day. He kept his belongings in the library's lockers and washed in the bathroom. His plight was only found out when the student's dramatic website recounting his quest to earn a decent education in New York was spotted. Known now as the "Bobst Boy," he was promptly given a free room in the residence hall to complete his studies.

2. Thousands of books were destroyed at the Loreto College Library in Darjeeling, India, in 2001, by dozens of hungry langur monkeys, who were after the food in the student's lunch boxes. Local wildlife officials' hands were tied as they said they could not capture the monkeys without upsetting the worshippers at the nearby Hindu Mahakal Temple, who love feeding the monkeys, and see them as sacred and as having a symbolic relationship with the temple. Over the last decade, there had been similar periodic raids by the monkeys (who are no longer afraid of humans due to the constant caring attention given to them by the temple worshippers) on the long suffering Loreto College. The 2001 attack was one of the largest, and the international media picked up the story. Some exaggerated headlines read "Monkeys chew up college library."

3. In 1999, staff repairing bookshelves at the rare book section of the National Library of Italy in Florence stumbled across the "lost" remains of Dante, Italy's greatest poet, in a sack with a letter indicating it was the remains of Dante. It has been investigated and the conclusion is that the remains had been mislaid by staff in the library 70 years ago. Back in 1865 on the 600th anniversary of his birth, scientists opened Dante's tomb and donated a small

quantity of his remains to the library. The remains were last seen in 1929, when librarians at a world congress in the library exhibited them to visitors. Staff at the library described the find as very emotional, saying it was the only remnant of Dante in Florence. The remains have since been stored in a secret location in the library.

4. In 2007, Barbican Public Library in London celebrated its 25th anniversary with a strange treasure hunt. Photographs were hidden randomly in books and users given clues on the library's website so they could track down the books with hidden photographs and locate prizes.

5. For many years the Central Bank of Nicaragua building in Managua was also the location for the National Library of Nicaragua. This odd combination began in 1964. It is not known if the secure bank vault was inside the library.

6. The National Institute of Studies and Research Library in the capital of Guinea-Bissau was turned into a military garrison by soldiers in 1998. But first they had to destroy several thousand books to make way for military equipment and sleeping quarters.

7. The Kukes Public Library in Kosovo, Albania, was turned into a bar in 1995. It was later used to house hundreds of refugees when Albania was occupied by the Yugoslav army.

8. In 2003, two FBI agents visited College of Santa Fe's Fogelson Library to pick up an unusual item a librarian had kept waiting for them: an envelope containing a smallpox sample and possibly the deadly smallpox virus. The story of how this sample ended up in the library began when a librarian reading through an 1888 book on Civil War medicine came across a small yellow envelope which was tucked tightly between pages. After removing the envelope from the book, the librarian noticed that the

top of the envelope had the words: "scabs from vaccination of W.B. Yarrington's children." Below the words was the signature "Dr. W.D. Kelly," the book's author. After some Google research, the librarian decided not to open the envelope but email details of the discovery to the National Museum of Civil War Medicine in Fort Frederick. The staff at the museum got very excited about the envelope and passed on details of the find to Washington's Walter Reed Army Medical Center, which in turn contacted the Centers for Disease Control and Prevention (CDC) in Atlanta. The CDC replied they would like to see it. When the FBI arrived, they collected the envelope and gave it to New Mexico Department of Health, which then finally passed it on to the CDC in a triple-bagged, overnight mail package. At the CDC the envelope was stored in a deep freezer to undergo a battery of tests in hope that the envelope could shed light on the development of American smallpox vaccines. As for the librarian who found the envelope and did the smart thing not to open it, instant one-day stardom beckoned, as the media got hold of the story and ran it on the front pages.

116
First Outer Space Library

The libraries on board the former space stations Skylab (U.S.), Mir and Salyut 6 and 7 (USSR/Russia) were the first ever permanent space libraries. (The book collection at Skylab was a bit smaller as the space station had room for only three people at one time.) Due to zero gravity and security risk of floating books, the books had specific standard weights and were fastened to the shelves (reminiscent of the famous medieval chained libraries at list **114**). The current space lab, the International Space Station orbiting the earth, has a small library in the Russian-built Zvezda service module unit. There is no space for libraries on board the U.S. space shuttles and the Russian Soyuz space crafts, save for space for a bookshelf for storing the operating manuals.

117
Largest Floating Library

Built in 2004, by Alstom Marine's Chantiers de l'Atlantique of France, and some 800 companies, mostly French, the *Queen Mary 2,* or *QM2,* is the world's second largest passenger ship at 1,138 feet long and 238 feet high, tall as a 21-story building. It is also the most expensive, costing $800 million to build. The ship features a planetarium, 22 elevators and the world's largest floating library. Because the size of the ship meant there is lots of room, and because of the longer time for a standard cruise, a well stocked library was included. The ship is operated by the British Cunard Lines and is owned by Miami-based Carnival Corp. Built in 2006, Royal Caribbean International's passenger ship *Freedom of the Seas* is larger than the *QM2,* but its library collection is smaller.

118
Largest Mobile Library

The first modern mobile libraries (horse drawn carriages) in Europe were set up in Scotland in 1810. In the Middle East the camel is synonymous with travelling in the deserts. However, another use for the camel was soon found, with camels being employed on caravans to carry library books starting in the ninth century. Soon this new use of the camel became widespread. When Muslim forces defeated the Byzantine Emperor Michael III, he was ordered by the victors to send to Bagdad a camel caravan with books from Constantinople's important libraries. An extreme example of camels being used to transport books can be seen in the case of the 10th century Grand Vizier of Persia (now Iran), known as Abdul Kassem Ismael. He was such a prolific bookworm that he took his entire library collection of over 100,000 books (volume total probably exaggerated) wherever he went with him, employing over 500 camels, that carried the books in alphabetical order. Camel-drawn libraries can still be found today in many remote parts of the world, such as in some Kenyan villages.

119
Fifty Exciting Films That Featured Libraries

Hollywood and other national film industries around the world, such as Bollywood in India, are not exactly obsessed with making a blockbuster movie featuring lots of interesting library scenes, but many libraries did get to star in major films! Here are 50 of them that should be part of a real librarian's DVD collection.

The Day of the Jackal (1973). Edward Fox (as Jackal, an assassin hired by a French paramilitary organization) pays a visit to the newspaper section of the British Library in London, looking for information as part of his plot to assassinate Charles de Gaulle. Based on a novel by British author Fredrick Forsyth.

All the President's Men (1976). The U.S. Library of Congress has starred in many films in the 20th century, and this film is one of most popular due the fact the film is based on political facts of the 1970s. Dustin Hoffman and Robert Redford play the famous journalists who uncovered the Watergate bugging scandal. In the film, Hoffman and Redford do some detective work at the library trying to figure out the confidential borrowing activities of a particular user of the library who happens to work for the White House and the CIA. Actor James Murtaugh also plays the role of a Library of Congress staff member assisting the two men in their quest. However, in the 1970s, real librarians did not give access to confidential borrowing activities of library users because it was illegal. But today this is legit as it comes under the 2001 Patriot Act (see also list **23**). The library at the White House is also featured in the film.

Carrie (1976). Sissy Spacek is shown in a high school library searching for books on paranormal telekinetic powers, which she possesses. Based on a novel by U.S. author Stephen King.

Il Casanova di Federico Fellini (1976). Donald Sutherland plays Casanova in this Italian film about the real-life Casanova who, apart from his famous antics as a womanizer, also worked "seriously" as a librarian in the Czech Republic.

Escape from Alcatraz (1979). Clint Eastwood (incarcerated in the notorious Alcatraz Island Prison) is seen very busy each day at the impregnable island's prison library.

War Games (1983). California State Library books on computers interests Matthew Broderick (a teenage computer whiz kid), who almost starts the Third World War after hacking into the Pentagon computer systems.

Ghostbusters (1984). Los Angeles Public Library gets an unscheduled visit by a bunch of scary ghosts, and all hell is let loose as the ghosts run amok. Who ya gonna call?

Wings of Desire (1987). This German film features Bruno Graz and Peter Falk at the giant Berlin State Library in Germany.

Fatal Attraction (1987). A passionate but deadly love affair is confessed quietly by Michael Douglas to his lawyer in a law firm's library (the worst possible place to make such a confession); it is hoped no one overheard him.

Indiana Jones and the Last Crusade (1989). Harrison Ford, as Indiana Jones, the world's greatest archaeologist, digs a big hole in a library in Venice, Italy (making a lot of noise in the process), to reveal a secret passage underneath and some ancient secrets about the Knights Templar and the Holy Grail.

Operation Condor (1991). From Hong Kong comes this sequel to an earlier film called *Amour of God*. Jackie Chan, as secret agent Asian Hawk, and his beautiful female sidekick plan his imminent Sahara Desert mission at the stunning 18th Royal Library in Madrid (*Real Biblioteca*), Spain, that looks very much like the Vatican Library interior.

The Pelican Brief (1993). A law library is used by Julia Roberts in her efforts to solve a high level conspiracy against judges.

The Shawshank Redemption (1994). Tim Robbins, a jailed bank executive, performs a miracle when he becomes an amateur librarian overnight and almost single-handedly transforms the small Shawshank State Prison library in Maine into a well stocked library that would rival a public library. Money to improve the library came from Robbins' rather persistent letters for financial help sent to the Maine Senate. Could this be a tip some public libraries with budget problems could learn from? Based on a Stephen King novella.

Goldeneye (1995). Trigger-happy KGB guards in a Russian military library shoot at Pierce Brosnan and a beautiful girl, and in the ensuing armed confrontation, many books get destroyed. Based on the James Bond novel by British writer Ian Fleming.

Party Girl (1995). Parker Posey works as a temporary librarian in New York City to earn money to pay back a fine for hosting an illegal party. She soon masters several library skills such as using the complex Dewey Decimal Classification and ends up a professional librarian to the amazement of her work colleagues. An entertaining movie for library school students.

Hak hap, or Black Mask (1996). Jet Li plays a librarian in Hong Kong who metamorphoses into a masked martial arts superhero to help cops fight mysterious superhumans.

City of Angels (1998). The movie shows scenes in the San Francisco Public Library, with Nicholas Cage in a rendezvous with angels.

Mercury Rising (1998). FBI agent Bruce Willis uses a public library computer to locate the whereabouts of e-mails that seem to come from the super secret National Security Agency.

Most Wanted (1999). Framed for murdering the first lady, Gulf War veteran Keenen Ivory Wayans and doctor Jill Hennessy, who unwittingly filmed the shooter, visit a public library in Los Angeles to search Westlaw databases while on the run, trying to find out who set up Wayans. While in the library, a silly security guard recognizes Wayans from TV reports, but instead of capturing him and dialing 911, he asks Wayans for his autograph, then lets him leave.

The Ninth Gate (1999). Johnny Depp (a rare book expert) is seen visiting private libraries in Europe looking for follow-ups and leads to locating copies of a rare book about occultism and demons. During his visits, he has several mysterious close shaves such as escaping with a few scorches from a burning library in Paris and dodging falling scaffoldings at a rare bookstore in Portugal.

The Mummy (1999). Rachel Weisz, an Egyptologist at the library of the Museum of Antiquities in Cairo, demonstrates the complex technique "how to shelve a single book on a high bookshelf while standing and balancing perilously on a tall ladder." What at first seems like a simple task ends up in a debacle as all the bookshelves (set in a circular arrangement) fall like dominoes, leaving all the books scattered all over the library. To rub salt into the injury, her boss orders her to tidy up the library by herself or else.

A Murder of Crows (1999). Disbarred lawyer Cuba Gooding, Jr., desperately searches a public library in Louisiana in effort to identify a writer who framed him for murder. The mysterious writer had unwittingly given him an unpublished manuscript, which Gooding later takes credit for when the manuscript becomes a bestseller, and earns him a period of fame.

Beautiful Life (2000). This is a Japanese movie about a librarian and a hairdresser who meet by chance in a car accident and later meet regularly in a Tokyo library to develop their blossoming friendship.

Harry Potter and the Philosopher's Stone (2001). David Radcliffe (the orphaned son of wizards) is shown looking for information in Oxford University's Bodleian Library. Based on

J.K. Rowling's popular children's story books. The film was released in the U.S. as *Harry Potter and the Sorcerer's Stone.*

Revelation (2001). While searching for clues about an ancient relic called the Loculus of the Knights Templar in a race against time to prevent the immortal Grand Master from recovering the relic, billionaire's son James D'Arcy and alchemist Natasha Wightman visit the rare books section at Cambridge University Trinity College library in the U.K. for some research. The librarian (played by Derek Jacobi) allows them to view a rare parchment manuscript as long as they wear plastic gloves to keep human stains at bay. Before leaving the library, D'Arcy ties up the librarian after discovering he somehow works for the Grand Master, and asks him if they could photocopy parts of the manuscript. When the librarian ignores the question, D'Arcy improvises by simply tearing off the part of the rare manuscript he wanted to photocopy.

Read or Die: OVA (2001). A colorful Japanese manga adventure film about the British Library (portrayed as an intelligence agency) and secret agent Yomiko Readman, aka "The Paper," who works at the fictitious Special Operations Division of the British Library. The job of agent Yomiko is to obtain rare manuscripts and books for libraries around the world and engage in defeating the bag guys who either dislike books or love to steal or destroy books. The anime film is a hilarious look at world of libraries and books and had a 2003 sequel called *Read or Die: The TV.*

Ballistic— Ecks vs. Sever (2003). The magnificent Vancouver Public Library in Canada takes repeated direct hits from heavy artillery, machine guns and RPGs as FBI agent Antonio Banderas and a SWAT team try to capture a top female assassin, played by Lucy Liu. Luckily a lot of CGIs were used in the film, and today a visit to the Vancouver Public Library shows no scars of the deadly ground assault by the SWAT team.

Last Life in the Universe (2003). An intriguing Thai and Australian production about a Japanese librarian (played by Japanese superstar Tadanobu Asano) in Bangkok, Thailand, on the run from the Japanese Mafia, the Yakuza.

The Devil's Library (2003). This is an interesting New Zealand horror film. Swiss actress Nadine Bernecker, as Amy, is among a dozen people who accept an invitation to have dinner with Richard Thompson, not knowing he is the devil. While at the dinner table, Amy spots a large private library and as she browses through the many subjects, Thompson informs her that his library contains every book burnt by man since time immemorial. Amy is not sure whether to believe this but soon discovers from the books' contents that the library must belong to someone very sinister. By the time Amy and the other guests figure out who their host really is, it is too late.

The League of Extraordinary Gentlemen (2003). Sean Connery as Allan Quatermain and the rest of the extraordinary gentlemen face a Mexican standoff with the henchmen of a masked bad guy known as the Fantom in a Victorian era library. When the henchmen open fire and the extraordinary gentlemen return fire, what happens to the library and its books after the shooting ends is anyone's guess.

The Librarian: Quest for the Spear (2004). Noah Wyle, as a new librarian for the Metropolitan Library, soon discovers his job is much more than being a librarian. Part of his duties include protecting incredible relics and artifacts not normally found in a library, such as Pandora's Box and the Ark of the Covenant. He soon becomes involved in a quest to recover the biblical Spear of Destiny stolen from the library that takes him to exotic places such as the Amazon forest in Brazil and the Himalayas.

National Treasure (2004). Lovely views of both the U.S. Library of Congress and the National Archives in Washington, D.C, are part of the scenes. While in the library, Nicolas Cage and Justin Bartha debate the pros and cons of stealing the Declaration of Independence from the National Archives to save it from being stolen by a former friend played by Sean Bean.

The Manchurian Candidate (2004). Denzel Washington plays a Gulf War veteran and has to rely on several important resources of the New York Public Library such as the audiovisual room and the microfilm room to help him make sense of alleged Pentagon and CIA mind control experiments.

Day After Tomorrow (2004). Jake Gyllenhaal and his friends take refuge at the New York Public Library after the city (as well as parts of the library) gets hit by tsunami-size tidal waves caused by a global warming event. Not content with the safe haven provided by the library, and as soon as snowstorms start to get worse, Jake and his buddies proceed to burn priceless books to keep warm in the freezing temperatures. At one point there is a debate as to whether it is OK to burn a book by the renowned philosopher Friedrich Wilhelm Nietzsche. But no debate ensues when a voluminous collection of "boring" books on U.S. taxes is discovered. At least Jake can be forgiven for his dreadful act of destroying public property, since he was given the go-ahead to burn the books, over the phone by his parents.

The Librarian: Return to King Solomon's Mines (2006). Noah Wyle returns as Flynn Carsen in this sequel to the 2004 movie. Wyle (part librarian, part Indiana Jones) finds himself in Africa on the way to the fabled King Solomon's mines. He encounters many tribulations such as attacks by a hippopotamus. A third film, *The Librarian: Curse of the Judas Chalice*, was released in 2007 (see below).

National Treasure: Book of Secrets (2007). A sequel to the 2004 film *National Treasure*. The Library of Congress once again plays host to Nicolas Cage and Justin Bartha, this time helping Cage solve riddles and puzzles related to U.S presidents from Abraham Lincoln and a supersecret book the FBI wants badly. Several different angles of the library were shot, including a scene where Cage is on top of the Thomas Jefferson Building. The other significant library scene was filmed at the University of Maryland and its Theodore R. McKeldin Library, where extras used in the scene were students from the university as well as staff librarians.

The Librarian: Curse of the Judas Chalice (2007). Noah Wyle returns in this third exciting installment about a librarian turned bounty hunter and adventurer. Wyle, as Flynn Carsen, is on a well-deserved vacation from his perilous day job in the library. However, déjà vu strikes, and he soon ends up on a quest to find a rare scroll that has the secrets to resurrect the vampire Count Dracula in Romania.

The Hollywood Librarian: A Look at Librarians Through Film (2007). Ann Seidl (a real librarian from Denver, Colorado, in the U.S.) made this movie as a rather amusing and enjoyable tale of the way librarians have been portrayed on cinema over the decades. The movie scores good points on such topics such as book censorship and privacy laws. A must-see-it-now movie by a librarian for librarians.

The rest of the exciting films with some scenes of libraries are: *You're a Big Boy Now* (1966), New York Public Library; *The Graduate* (1967), University of Southern California's Doheny Library; *Foul Play* (1978), Pasadena Public Library; *Sakara no Sono* (a.k.a. *The Cherry Orchard*, 1981), Fukagawa Library, Tokyo; *Twelve Monkeys* (1995), Philadelphia Public Library, Ridgeway branch; *Robo Cop* (1997), Dallas Public Library; *Mr. Magoo* (1997), Vancouver Public Library, Canada; *Double Jeopardy* (1999), Vancouver Public Library, Canada; *Charlie's Angels* (2000), Huntington Library, San Marino, California; *Cadaverous* (2000), New York University's Bobst Library; *Sweetest Thing* (2002), Huntington Library, San Marino, California; *The Crimson Rivers* (2000) Guernon University Library; and *Red Dragon* (2002), the Library of Congress, Washington D.C.

A lot of the libraries mentioned above play the role of offering the stars of the film a place to search for reliable information. This turns out to be a beneficial way to encourage millions of viewers of the film to use their local libraries more often. For some reason the Vatican Library and King's College Library (part of London University) were not featured in the Da Vinci Code *(2006), even though Dan Brown's book (from which the film was adapted) does mention Professor Langdon and police inspector Neveu visiting these libraries. However, the film does show Langdon, played by Tom Hanks, and Neveu, played by Audrey Tautou, on their way to Chelsea Public Library in London (not mentioned in Dan Brown's novel), only to use a cell phone while on the bus, to go online and search for information via Google and ultimately skip visiting the library. Not everything we see in cinemas or on television that depicts libraries or librarians has a happy ending. Back in the summer of 1996, a new advertisement for Packard Bell computers in the U.S. caused an outrage among librarians. Designed by*

Saatchi and Saatchi, the advertisement seemed to portray libraries as scary dark places with spiders creeping out of dusty books and a skinhead as a librarian uttering the dreaded "keep quiet" sound, "shhh..." It suggested that those looking for information were better off using a Packard Bell computer to access information sources at home, such as via the Internet, than visiting their local library. The slogan for the advertisement was, "Wouldn't you rather be at home?" After a couple of runs, the advertisement was eventually withdrawn to the relief of librarians, who no doubt saw it as the worst advertisement made depicting libraries. In October 2007, several U.K. county public libraries, such as Kent County Libraries in Bromley, initiated advertising inside library books. The scheme, run by a direct marketing company, involved inserting over 500,000 cards into books. Companies wanting to advertise their goods or services would pay a fee which will be shared in a percentage agreed by the host library and the direct marketing company. If the scheme is successful it is expected to cover all public libraries in the middle of 2008 with around 3 million insets made available per month. Whether this scheme will have a positive response from users of the library remains to be seen.

There are several stories about the origin for the Oscar statuette. But the official version is that in 1934, an Academy librarian named Margaret Herrick remarked excitedly that the statue looked like her uncle Oscar. The name stuck, and the Academy staff began referring to the statuette as "Oscar." The Academy officially adopted it in 1939. Before 1939, the award, a ten-inch gold-plated bronze statue of a man with his arms in front of him resting on the handle of a sword, was known only as "the statuette." Mrs. Herrick, who later became executive director of the Academy, came to regret the remark that she made in a mad moment of whimsy. The Oscar, which weighs 8.5 pounds, is carefully cast in a metal alloy called britannium, and plated with 24 carat gold. It depicts a crusader knight, grasping a sword. The knight stands on a film reel, with five spokes that represent the five original branches of the Academy: directors, actors/actresses, writers, producers and technicians.

120
Some Notable People Who Have Worked in Libraries or as Librarians

Over the centuries, hundreds of famous people, and some infamous, have been involved in library work or worked for a while as librarians. Below are some.

Jalal ud-Din Akbar. Mogul emperor of north India organized a rather meticulous Islamic library in 1605. Among other things he helped catalog all the books in his library and stored them in arrangements, such as by author or calligrapher, and by language, such as Hindi, Greek, Arabic and Persian.

Al-Khwarizmi. This 9th century Arabic mathematician, who invented *Al-Jabr* (Algebra), worked as a librarian in the famous library of Abbasid Caliph Al-Mamun, in Baghdad, also known as the House of Wisdom. Latinization of Al-Khwarizmi was the origin for the word algorithm.

Allesandi Arturo, Chilean president, worked at the National Library of Chile in the 1940s.

Ashurbanipal (Assurbanipal), Assyrian king, helped developed the famous Nineveh library in the 600s B.C. He was also involved in organizing the library's catalog in Sumerian cuneiform script.

Avicenna. This well known Persian physician, also known as Ibn Sina, classified medical books in a Baghdad library in the 11th century A.D., making them easier to find by the Arab doctors of the day who used the library.

Alfredo Baquerizo worked at a public library in Ecuador, and later became president of the country in the early 1900s.

Baybars I. This famous Mamluk sultan of Egypt and Syria established the Al-Zahiriyah Library in Damascus in 1277.

Karl Ernst von Baer, Estonian zoology professor and a founding father of developmental biology, was appointed librarian of the Russian Academy of Sciences library, St. Petersburg, in 1843.

John Billings was the U.S. surgeon instrumental in the development of the U.S. National

Library of Medicine's *Index Medicus* medical journal abstracting services, which evolved into today's MEDLINE database.

St. Benedict. This Italian monk was also a librarian for the Monte Cassino monastery, near Rome, from A.D. 510. He was famous for his *Benedictine Rules,* which stipulate that everyone should have time to study in a library. (A translation of the rules by Dom Justin Mc-Cann in 1961 was the winner of an award for best English language translation.)

Hector Berlioz, French composer, was employed as librarian at the Paris Conservatoire (a school of music) in 1838.

Cardinal Bessanone of Venice, Italy, began the famous Marciana National Library, which is today the oldest of Italy's ten national libraries, and the third largest.

Simón Bolívar, Latin American hero and soldier. Founded the National Free University (*Universidad Nacional de la Libertad*) in Trujillo, Peru, in 1824, the same year after helping Peru gain its hard fought independence from Spain. Bolívar was also involved in helping to set up the university's first library.

Jorge Luis Borges, Argentine author, was a librarian at the National Library of Argentina in the 1940s.

Federico Borromeo, Bishop of Milan. He founded the Ambrosian Library in Milan around 1609. It later became Italy's first public library.

Laura Bush. The current U.S. first lady, who has a master of library science degree from the University of Texas, worked as a librarian at Houston Public Library, Dawson Elementary School Library and Dallas Public Library.

Jimmy Carter, the former president of the U.S., once was a member of the board of the University of Georgia Library, before becoming governor in the state of Georgia.

Giovanni Casanova. This Italian adventurer in 1785 began a 13-year career as a librarian for Count von Waldstein in the chateau of Dux in Bohemia, Czech Republic.

Charlemagne. Also known as Charles the Great, this French king and first Holy Roman Emperor set up in A.D. 800 the Aachen palace library (near the German border with France

today) and helped expand it into a major library of the time.

Mikhail Eminescu. This famous Romanian poet worked in the 1870s as a librarian at the Iasi (Jassy) University Library. The University is today named after him.

Fredrich Engels, German philosopher, was appointed librarian at the Schiller-Anstalt library in the late 19th century.

Eratosthenes. This prominent ancient Greek geographer was a chief librarian at the Alexandria Library in ancient Egypt, around the 2nd century B.C. Significantly, all the librarians at the Alexandria Library were scholars, such as poets, critics, and grammarians. They included Zenodotus, the writer; Aristophanes, the grammarian who invented several punctuation marks used today such as the asterisk and circumflex marks; Callimachus, the poet who wrote the 120 volumes of Greek bibliography (a famous catalog of the library called *Pinakes*); and the only female librarian, the Platonist philosopher named Hypatia (see below).

Abigail Powers Fillmore, first wife of Millard Fillmore, president of the United States from 1850 to 1853, established the first White House Library.

U.S. presidents since Rutherford B. Hayes have had libraries named after them. These presidential libraries are more museums and archives than libraries because they mostly contain official documents related to the president's term in office. They are administered by the U.S. National Archives and Records Administration. Before Rutherford B. Hayes, outgoing presidents took their official papers with them, and some ended up in university or state libraries.

Benjamin Franklin, U.S. politician and inventor, helped set up the first subscription library and library serial in the U.S., in the 1730s. He was librarian of the Library Company of Philadelphia for a brief period. Franklin famously called his subscription library founded in 1731 "the mother of all North American subscription libraries."

Johann Wolfgang von Goethe, German poet, supervised the Jena University library in Germany between 1817 and 1832.

Another famous name associated with Jena University is Karl Marx, who received his Ph.D. in 1841.

Latin American revolutionary Simón Bolívar helped set up the National Free University and its library in Trujillo, Peru.

Bishop Borromeo founded the first public library in Italy in 1609. His statue can be seen in front of the Ambrosian Library in Milan.

But he wrote the first volume of the classic book Das Kapital *(known as the Bible of the working classes) in London in 1867, making use of the British Library for much of his research.*

King Hammurabi, Babylonian king and the sixth ruler of the first dynasty of Babylon. While he is famous for putting together the *Code of Laws,* he is equally famous for setting up the second most important major library in ancient times, after the libraries founded by the Sumerians in Mesopotamia. Among the books in the library, of course, was his *Code of Laws.*

J. Edgar Hoover. This U.S. law enforcement officer, lawyer and first FBI director worked as a cataloger at the U.S. Library of Congress.

J. Edgar Hoover once ordered the FBI to carry out clandestine surveillance on many writers suspected of "un–American activities." Those targeted included Ernest Hemingway, for whom the FBI had a huge dossier, Sinclair Lewis, James Baldwin, W.E.B Dubois, Alfred Kinsey and Allen Ginsberg.

David Hume, Scottish philosopher and historian, worked as a librarian at the Library of the Faculty of Advocates Edinburgh (National Library of Scotland) from 1757.

Hypatia. She was a well-known ancient Greek philosopher and mathematician alongside Plato and Plotinus. She worked for some time as a librarian at the Alexandria Library in ancient Egypt.

Immanuel Kant, German philosopher, in the middle 1700s was assistant librarian at Königsberg Castle library (now in modern day Kaliningrad).

Stephen King, the famous horror fiction writer, worked as a library assistant at the University of Maine Folger Library while a student in the late 1960s.

Nadezhda Krupskaya, the famous former Russian first lady, was a cultural crusader and the librarian wife of Lenin, who founded the USSR. She became a prime figure in the movement to centralize Soviet library services and helped her husband set up 50,000 public libraries throughout the USSR. Following the Russian Revolution, many women were recruited into librarianship and a rapid feminization of the profession occurred.

Lao-Tzu, Chinese philosopher and founder of Taoism, was a librarian in a Henan province library in the 6th century B.C., perhaps the first official librarian in China. He was in charge of the library, which housed original government records during the Zhou dynasty.

Philip Larkin, British poet, was also a librarian at Hull University Library, U.K.

Gottfried von Leibniz. This German philosopher and mathematician worked as a librarian in the law courts of Hanover from 1676 and later as a librarian of the duke of Braunschweig-Lüneburg. He is often considered the greatest librarian of his generation, even though he was a scientist and not a librarian.

Archibold Macleish, poet and assistant U.S. Secretary of State, was employed as head librarian at the U.S. Library of Congress between 1939 and 1944, an appointment that did not meet the approval of the American Library Association because he lacked the appropriate graduate degree.

Mahmud I, Turkish Ottoman sultan, founded many libraries in the 18th century, such as the Faith Library, and the Ayasofya Library built in Ayasofya Mosque in St. Sophia (Hagia Sophia), which is a masterpiece of Ottoman architecture.

During the Ottoman era, several other sultans founded libraries in Constantinople (Istanbul), such as Sultan Ahmet and Sultan Süleyman the Magnificent, who set up the famous library of the Süleymaniye Mosque, the largest mosque in Istanbul. Most of these libraries were situated among a collection of buildings composed of a mosque, a medrese (high school of theological studies), a primary school, a hospital, and a kitchen for the poor. The mosque libraries were also called vakif libraries and the very first official vakif library in Istanbul was set up in 1459. In Istanbul today, the Topkapi Museum Library contains many Islamic manuscripts collected by sultans, generals, and other officials of the Ottoman Empire since 1452.

Mohamed Khatami, former Iranian president, was former head of the National Library of Iran in Tehran.

Jules Mazarin, French cardinal and a first minister to Louis XIII, founded the Mazarin Library in Paris in 1643. He employed French physician Gabriel Naudé as its first librarian. The Library was originally set up in the Hôtel Tubeuf in Paris, eventual home for the French National Library. Gabriel Naudé studied medicine at Paris and Padua. In 1629 he became librarian to Cardinal Bagni, and in 1641 was librarian to Cardinal Barberini, both Vatican cardinals.

Ulrike Meinhof, the infamous German radical leftist terrorist, started out as a journalist and librarian. She was one of the founders of the Red Army Faction in Germany.

Golda Meir. The former prime minister of Israel had earlier worked as a public librarian in the U.S. city of Milwaukee, Wisconsin. She became prime minster in 1969.

Gabriel Naudé, French doctor. See details on Mazarin.

Pope Nicholas V. A former librarian to Cosimo de' Medici (involved in setting up Italy's famous Laurentian Library), he began to build up the Vatican Library in the Vatican City in 1451.

Frank O'Connor. This famous Irish writer and director of Dublin's Abbey Theatre once worked as a librarian at Trinity College Library.

Christopher Okigbo, the Nigerian poet, was acting librarian at the University of Nigeria in Nsukka, where he helped to found the African Authors Association. He was killed while fighting as a soldier during the Biafran war.

Antonio Panizzi. This famous Italian lawyer and politician worked at the British library in the 19th century.

Pierre Pasquier. The French governor general of Indochina (French colonies of Vietnam, Laos and Cambodia) helped organize the *Bibliothèque Pasquier*, which later became the National Library of Vietnam.

Philip II, king of Spain (Felipe II), in 1563 set up the famous San Lorenzo de El Escorial Monastic Library northwest of Madrid, which today has one of the best collections of Arabic manuscripts in Europe. The contents of the library (rare manuscripts and incunabula) and the way the library's interior was designed (painted ceilings, etc.) makes it stand alongside the greatest and most beautiful sixteenth and seventeenth century non-academic library buildings, including the Mazarin Library in Paris, the Vatican Library in Rome, the Laurentian Library in Venice and the Ambrosian Library in Milan.

Among the rare Arabic manuscripts in the library is the oldest handwritten book on paper in Europe, dating from A.D. 1009. The El Escorial Monastic Library owns some of its rare Arabic books to the lucky chance interception by Spanish ships of a small vessel in the Mediterranean Sea carrying the entire private library of important handwritten books belonging to Sharif Zaydan, sultan of Morocco. He was fleeing Spain, after Spanish Christians were gradually recapturing many cities ruled by the Moors.

Pope Pius XI. Before becoming pope in 1922, he worked for many years in the Ambrosian Library in Milan, Italy, as chief librarian. He also helped to reorganize the Vatican Library collections in Rome. Several other popes have worked in the Vatican Library or in other libraries such as those in monasteries.

Joseph Priestley. This British chemist, who isolated many gases, including oxygen, worked as a librarian for the 2nd Earl of Shelburne, William Petty Fitzmaurice (British statesman and prime minister), in 1772.

Ptolemy I, Greek Macedonian general and king of Egypt, founded the famous Alexandria Library.

Henry Pu Yi. This last Chinese emperor of the Qing dynasty in the 1960s worked as a librarian in Beijing. The story of his life was made into a successful film *The Last Emperor* in 1988.

Rama V of Chakri (Chulalongkorn), king of Thailand, founded the National Library of Thailand in 1905. His palace was the first home for the library. In 1834, his predecessor Rama IV made a chance rediscovery of the long forgotten oldest inscription of the Thai script by

Spanish king Charles II went the extra mile in planning the El Escorial Monastic Library he founded in 1563. Today, it is not only a stunning library to visit, it is Spain's most famous sixteenth century library.

its inventor, the king of Sukhothai (Rama Khamheng or Ramkhamhaeng), in A.D. 1292 (see list **136**).

Giuseppe Ripamonti, an Italian historian, worked at the Ambrosian Library in Milan.

Count Nikolai Rumyantsev. This Russian politician's library became part of the Russian State Library, Europe's largest library.

Robert de Sobon was the French theologian who, as chaplain to French king Louis IX, founded the Sorbonne University Library in Paris in the 13th century. It still bears his name.

Alexander Solzhenitsyn, Russian novelist, dramatist and poet, became a prison librarian in the infamous gulag run by Joseph Stalin.

Ainsworth Spofford, U.S. journalist, author and co-founded of UNESCO, helped develop the U.S. Library of Congress in the early 20th century.

John Strindberg, Swedish playwright and novelist, was a library assistant at the Royal Library in Stockholm, Sweden, in the late 1870s.

Marcus Trajan, Roman emperor in A.D. 98–117, founded the largest library in the Roman Empire. It was patronized by the leading philosophers, scientists, astronomers and politicians of the day.

Mao Tse-tung (Mao Zedong), Chinese leader, worked at the Beijing University Library from 1918 as an assistant to the chief librarian, who happened to be Li Ta-chao, founder of the Chinese Communist Party.

Alexandre Vattemare, French ventriloquist, was a famous nineteenth century vocal lobbyist for free public library access and free exchange of books between Europe and North

Marcus Trajan, one of Rome's most popular emperors, ordered the construction of the largest and most popular library in the empire.

America. His efforts helped with making the Boston Public Library in Massachusetts the first real tax-supported public library.

Oscar Wilde. During his time spent in Reading Prison, this British writer looked after the prison library. Among his responsibilities was taking books to other prisoners and repairing books damaged by them.

121
Fifty Translations of the Word "Library"

Latin	*Libraria*	German	*Bibliothek*
*Greek	*Bibliotheke*	Dutch	*Bibliotheek*
Esperanto	*Biblioteko / Librejo*	Flemish	*Bibliotheek*
English	*Library*	Swedish	*Bibliotek*
Spanish	*Biblioteca*	Icelandic	*Bibliotek*
Italian	*Biblioteca*	Norwegian	*Bibliotek*
Portuguese	*Biblioteca*	Danish	*Bibliotek*
Romanian	*Biblioteca*	Macedonian	*Biblioteka*
French	*Bibliothèque*	Faeroese	*Bokasavnid*

*Hebrew	*Bibliotek*	Igbo	*Ulo Akwukwo*	
Polish	*Biblioteka*	Afrikaans	*Bibliotheek*	
*Russian	*Biblioteka*	*Berber	*Maktaba*	
*Ukrainian	*Biblioteka*			
*Serbian	*Biblioteka*			
*Bulgarian	*Biblioteka*			
Irish	*Leabharlanna*			
Finnish	*Kirjasto*			
Hungarian	*Könyvtár*			
Turkish	*Kütüphane*			
Czech	*Knihovna*			
Slovakian	*Knižnica*			
Slovenian	*Knjižnica*			
Croatian	*Knjižnica*			
*Farsi	*Ketab-khaneh*			
*Arabic	*Maktaba*			
*Urdu	*Qutab-khana*			
*Hindi	*Pustakalaya*			
*Bengali	*Granthagar*			
*Japanese	*Toshokan*			
*Chinese	*Tushugan*			
*Korean	*Tosogwan*			
*Thai	*Hongsamud*			
Maori	*Matauranga*			
Malaysian	*Perpustakaan*			
Indonesian	*Perpustakaan*			
Filipino	*Aklatan*			
Vietnamese	*Thu viên*			
Swahili	*Maktaba*			

*Indicates transliteration from non–Roman alphabets such as Cyrillic and Devanagari. The most common word for a library in Europe is derived from the Greek word for library, but apparently English is the only major language that uses the Latin word. In Arabic a bookstore is also called Maktaba and a library can also be called *Dâr al-Kutub* or "house of books." Finnish is the only Scandinavian language that is not an Indo-European language, hence the difference in the word for library. Irish, Hungarian and the languages of several former Yugoslav republics have been less influenced by Greek and Latin, so the word for library is very different compared to the rest of Europe. Vietnamese, Malaysian, Filipino and Indonesian are the only major Asian languages that use the Latin alphabet.

The French word for library is bibliothèque, but the French word for bookstore is librairie. So it can sometimes cause confusion to an English-speaking tourist who mistakenly reads the sign on a bookstore to mean a public library. The Spanish word for bookstore is librería, but it can also be spelled as libería, which in English can be confused for Liberia, an African country.

122
UNESCO World Heritage List and Libraries

The first important connection between UNESCO and libraries is the generous funding from UNESCO for establishing new libraries (such as the new Alexandria Library in Egypt), maintaining existing libraries (in many developing countries) or repairing libraries hit by natural disasters or man-made events such as military conflicts. The library at UNESCO contains the latest information on the World Heritage List. This list is produced annually and for 2007 there are 851 sites on the list from over 115 countries across the world that are considered to be an essential part of the world's cultural and natural heritage.

Some of the oldest and most significant libraries in this book are on the list, including those of Sankore University and related areas in Timbuktu (Tombouctou) in Mali; the University in Caracas Library in Venezuela; the Alcala de Henares University Library in Spain; the St. Gallen Monastic Library called *Stiftsbibliothek* in Switzerland; the famous Duchess Anna Amalia Library in Weimar, Germany; the Chinguetii and Quandane libraries and surrounding areas in Mauritania; the Haeinsa Temple and its library in South Korea; and the San Lorenzo de El Escorial Monastic Library and surrounding environs, in Spain.

The UNESCO Memory of the World Register was set up in the early 1990s to preserve valuable library books, manuscripts and archive collections and ensure their dissemination worldwide. Some of the oldest and most significant texts in the world are listed, including the *Vedas* from India (see list **124**); the *Codex of Suprasl* (see list **135**); the remaining books of the old Malatesta Library in Italy (see list **236**); the *Mushaf of Othman* (the oldest Koran in the world) in Uzbekistan (see list **127**); Martin Waldsemüller's map of 1507 in the U.S. Library of Congress (see list **6**); the *Mappa Mundi* from the U.K. (see list **114**); the Gutenberg Bible; and *Jikji Simgyeong,* a Korean book which UNESCO accepts is the oldest evidence of movable metal type. The book was printed in 1377 so is older than the Gutenberg Bible (see list **143**). In the Americas, the oldest library whose books are on the register is the Palafox Library in Puebla, Mexico, which was founded in 1645 (see list **236**). Every two years since 2004, UNESCO awards the UNESCO/Jikji Memory of the World Prize to in-

dividuals or institutions that have made significant contributions to the preservation and accessibility of documentary heritage, and it is named after *Jikji Simgyeong.* One particular library collection on the list worth mentioning is the Corvinian Library *Bibliotheca Corviniana* in Hungary. This library was founded in 1460 and was the second greatest collection of books in a library in Europe in the Renaissance period, after those of the Vatican Library. *Bibliotheca Corviniana* was wrecked when the Turkish Ottoman Empire overran Hungary in the 1526 Battle of Mohács. Today the surviving collections of the library are well preserved all over Europe in libraries in Austria (largest, since Hungary was once part of the Austria-Hungary Empire), France, Italy, Germany, Belgium, Turkey, and in the U.K. and the U.S.

123
Earliest Libraries

Necessity, they say, is the mother of invention. It was the invention of writing that led to the need to store written documents for later use and research by others. Thus the credit to starting up the first library goes to the ancient Sumerians, who lived in the southern part of ancient Mesopotamia, now in modern-day Iraq, notably at the town of Warka where the first clay tablets have been uncovered. They devised an early form of writing, the cuneiform system, around 3500 B.C. The Sumerians began to store and organize collections of their written documents (clay tablets), as "libraries" around 2700 B.C. Some of the clay tablets in these 4300 year old libraries were small enough to be held in the hand.

Libraries were also set up in several other ancient civilizations apart from the Sumerians. The following are some of the other early significant libraries of the world that were founded before A.D. 1000. Almost all of them no longer exist, except for some preserved ruins.

Babylonia. Borsippa Library was founded 1700 B.C. by King Hammurabi. It is probably

the second earliest significant library to be founded in ancient times after the ones set up by the Sumerians. The most important and famous book (clay tablet) was King Hammurabi's *Code of Laws,* and it is now preserved at the Louvre Museum in Paris, France.

Ancient Egypt. The most important library established by the pharaohs was the Ramses II library, in Thebes. It was founded circa 1250 B.C., and its collections were composed entirely of papyrus scrolls, inscribed with hieroglyphics and hieratic script.

Assyria. The Nineveh library (near modern day Mosul in northern Iraq), originally started by King Sennacherib, was developed fully around 650 B.C. by King Ashurbanipal (Assurbanipal). The library had over 20,000 clay tablets and was the greatest library in Assyria. The Nineveh library was first discovered by British and French archaeologists in the 19th century. Remnants of the library can be seen today at the British Museum in London, and the Louvre Museum in Paris.

Ancient China. Several major ancient libraries were in existence in China from 500

UNESCO, based in Paris, France, has several schemes, projects, and initiatives for looking after libraries and books and disseminating their rich cultural legacy to the rest of the world. Programs include the World Heritage List and the Memory of the World Register.

B.C. The first known Chinese librarian was the philosopher Lao-Tzu, who was appointed keeper of the royal historical records (written on silk, bamboo and wood) of the libraries of the Zhous (Chou) dynasty rulers, in about 550 B.C. The libraries were situated in the modern day Chinese province of Henan. The most famed library of China's numerous dynasties is the Wenyuange Imperial Library of the Qing (Manchu) dynasty, which began in 1644. Based in Beijing, its numerous books and manuscripts, some dating back 1000 years to the Song dynasty (A.D. 960–1279), had been deemed very valuable and well preserved over the centuries. When the Qing dynasty ended in 1911 and revolution broke out in China, the recently founded National Library of China made it a top priority to obtain the entire collection of the Wenyuange Imperial Library.

Ancient Greece. The three earliest and greatest libraries of the ancient Greek world were among the world's best. The Alexandria Library was founded 305 B.C. by King Ptolemy I Soter (after Greek Macedonian King Alexander the Great conquered Egypt). The Serapeum or Serapieion Library was founded 230 B.C. in the temple of Serapis (near the Italian port of Pozzuoli, then an ancient Greece town), while the Pergamum Library near present-day Smyrna (Izmir), in Turkey, was founded 175 B.C. by Attalus I and Eumenes II.

The ancient Greek scribes obtained their papyrus from Alexandria, the principal market for buying and selling papyrus, via the port of Byblos (which gave its name to the Bible). Following an embargo on the export of papyrus from ancient Egypt by King Ptolemy Philadelphus, the price of papyrus became expensive. So starting from about 6 B.C. the use of parchment, made typically from the skin of calf, goat, and sheep (which had been used in insignificant amounts since 300 B.C. alongside papyrus), in manuscript production was encouraged at the Pergamum Library and elsewhere in ancient Greece. Later on, vellum (which was made from specially prepared calf skin) was introduced. However, several Greek scholars still made papyrus rolls until the 14th century A.D. During the French Revolution of the 18th century, the skins of some of the aristocrats executed with the guillotine were used by a bookbinder in Meudon, France, to produce a copy of the new Constitution of 1791 drafted by the Constituent Assem-

Ramses II, who built the two famous rock temples at Abu Simbel, also set up the largest library in ancient Egypt.

bly. The Pergamum Library was actually used as a romantic gift. Although the romance between Roman general Marc Anthony (Marcus Antonius) and Queen Cleopatra ended in tragedy, as William Shakespeare reminds us, the romance did involve one of the most expensive romantic gifts ever given for centuries before the fall of the Roman Empire, when Marc Anthony raided the Pergamum Library and gave Cleopatra its entire contents of over 200,000 parchment and papyrus scrolls. Since this library was the main rival to the greatest library in existence then, the equally famous Alexandria Library in Egypt, the Pergamum Library collections was probably worth a huge amount in today's money. Sadly the library was completely destroyed in the 3rd century A.D.

Western Roman Empire. When ancient Greece became part of the expanding infant Roman Empire around 146 B.C., all of its important libraries became Roman libraries. The most important library was the Ulpian Library, founded by Marcus Trajan in A.D. 114 in Rome. Among the important manuscripts stored in

Assyrian King Assurbanipal developed the Nineveh Library into one of the greatest libraries in the ancient Middle East.

Roman libraries are the *Rylands Papyrus* and the *Codex Vaticanus*. The only Roman library that has survived the ages is the Piso Library, set up by Lucius Calpunrius circa A.D. 20 in the ancient city of Herculaneum, close to Pompeii. Although the eruption of the volcano Mount Vesuvius in A.D. 79 destroyed the library, it was discovered among the volcanic ash ruins of Herculaneum in 1754. Hundreds of preserved Piso Library papyrus and parchment scrolls, some just lumps of charcoal, can be seen today at the National Archaeological Museum in Naples, Italy. Since the Coptic Egyptian Church (1st century A.D.) is much older than the Roman Catholic Church (4th century A.D.), the first Christian libraries were Coptic Church libraries, founded when St. Mark was in Egypt. The important Christian library in the Middle East is believed to be the one founded in Jerusalem by Bishop Alexander in A.D. 250. The earliest Christian libraries in Rome was founded by Pope Damascus (bishop of Rome, in the 4th century A.D.) and Pope Agapetus (6th century A.D.).

Eastern Roman Empire. The Eastern Roman (Byzantine) Empire was carved out of the Roman Empire in A.D. 285 by Emperor Diocletian. Emperor Constantine the Great (who converted to Christianity in A.D. 311), founded the Byzantium Imperial Library in A.D. 332 in Constantinople (which he founded in A.D. 330, now called Istanbul). The library rose to contain some of the most important Christian manuscripts (in parchment, vellum and papyrus) of the day, with many written in Greek, the official language of the Byzantine Empire. Much of the collection of Christian manuscripts was made possible from the late 4th century A.D. when Theodosius I the Great encouraged Christianity as a state religion of the Roman Empire, and put an end to pagan worship. The Byzantium Imperial Library was destroyed in the 13th century, when the armies of the 4th Crusade invaded Constantinople. With the fragmentation of the Western Roman Empire, the Benedictines and friars in monastic libraries preserved the collections of these Christian libraries across the whole of Europe. Today many of these manuscripts are preserved in the Vatican Library.

Islamic Empire. The earliest significant Islamic libraries were founded during the time of the Abbasid Caliphate in Baghdad from about A.D. 750, when the first mosques were built. Some important manuscripts of these libraries (usually situated in a building in a mosque) included Arabic translations of important Indian texts such as *Panchatantra* and *Siddhanta*. During the ninth century, the famous library of Abbasid Caliph Al-Mamun, in Baghdad, also known as the House of Wisdom or *Bayt al-Hikmah*, had important translation departments. Here language scholars such as Hunayn ibn Ishaq translated texts dating from the civilizations of the Assyrians and Babylonians to those in Greek, Persian and Sanskrit, into Arabic. Donations from Byzantine Emperor Leo III were among the many sources for classical Greek texts. Another important source for the House of Wisdom was Gondi Shapur University Library in Persia (see list **60**). Most of the Abbasid Caliphate was destroyed later in the 1258 Mongolian invasion. The Moorish Omayyad (Umayyad dynasty) Caliphate based in Córdoba, Spain, from the 8th to 12th century A.D. was another important Islamic caliphate that had extensive holdings. The library of Caliph Al-Hakem II in Córdoba was the largest library in Islamic Spain, with over 500,000 manuscripts, and became the largest library in Europe during the caliphate's existence. The library was part of the Córdoba University library which the Omayyad Moors established in Spain in the 10th century. Other important Islamic libraries were founded in later caliphates, such as those of the Fatimids in Cairo (famous for the Caliph Al-Hakim bi Amar Library in 1004), and the 12th century Ayyubid Caliphate of Saladin (Salah al-Din Yusuf ibn Ayyub). This later caliphate, which deposed the Fatimid dynasty in 1171, was involved in the 3rd Crusade battle with Richard the Lionheart of England (featured in the film *Kingdom of Heaven*). A number of religious libraries were founded in Jerusalem. The last major Arab kingdom in the Middle East to establish Islamic libraries before the Middle East was conquered in 1517 by the Turkish Ottoman Empire was the Egyptian Mamluk (Mameluke) dynasty.

When the Moorish city of Toledo in Spain was captured by Christian Europe in 1085, its libraries, which contained many important scientific and medical texts of the Greek and Roman era as well as Arabic translations, changed hands. Using Jews in Spain as translators for the Arabic texts (because both Arabic and Hebrew languages have similar origins as well as scripts), all of the manuscripts in the libraries were translated into Latin at what was the famous Toledo Translation School. Many indigenous Arabic texts, as well as those originally translated from classical Greek texts, were then translated into Latin. A lot of these texts were copies originally from the 3rd century Persian Gondi Shapur University (see list **60**) and the House of Wisdom (see above). As every city and town of Islamic Spain was retaken, their library collection was translated into Latin, and this continued until 1492 when Granada, the last Moorish state, was captured, thus ending over 700 years of Arab colonization that began in A.D.

711. It is believed that the fall of Toledo and the opening of its many libraries to European scholars of the day was one of the contributing factors (along with the knowledge gained from manuscripts written during the Greek and Roman periods which were brought back by the crusaders from Byzantium in the 13th century) to the revival of intellectual learning in Christian Europe prior to the Renaissance. Among the many benefits introduced by the work of the translation school at Toledo was the adoption of Arabic numerals and the symbol zero, an Arabic word. One of the translations of the text of famous Persian mathematician Al-Khwarizmi at the Toledo Translation School was by English monk Adelard of Bath and written in the 12th century. The translation went on to become a major mathematics textbook in Medieval Europe.

For a list of the oldest existing libraries today see list **382**.

The Toledo Translation School near Madrid, Spain, played an important part in the revival of Western intellectual learning before the start of the Renaissance.

WORLD RECORDS FOR BOOKS, PERIODICALS AND BOOKSTORES

Evidence suggests that early humans such as Neanderthals 170,000 years ago probably could not speak, or at least not as modern humans do, because the arrangement of their larynxes prevented full vocalization. Communication no doubt took place by other means such as gestures and grunts and shouts. Modern humans (*Homo sapiens sapiens*), who appeared about 120,000 years ago (first in Africa, then later in the Asia-Pacific region, Europe and the Americas), fared much better. Their larynxes were well developed for speech. Hence the earliest forms of modern human language probably began about 90,000 years ago, but it would almost certainly have been many thousands of years later before humans attempted any form of writing.

Before humans invented writing, they first drew pictures on objects such as stone and wood and in caves. The oldest radiocarbon-dated cave paintings in the world go back to 50,000 B.C., such as the one discovered in France and Spain in the 19th century. Sumerian was the language of perhaps the first civilization in the world (based in what is now modern day Iraq), and it was spoken extensively around 6000 B.C. Then from about 3500 B.C., or over 5000 years ago, people finally began writing.

Prior to the invention of paper, clay tablets were used as writing materials in ancient Sumer, Babylonia and Assyria and the later civilizations that overran these. While the ancient Egyptians, Greeks and Romans used papyrus in addition to clay, later on, parchment and vellum were the chief materials used in Europe and the Middle East, replacing papyrus. In some instances tablets dipped in wax were used as well. Silk, bamboo, bones, bronze and linen were the main writing materials in China, Korea, and many other East Asian cultures that had written forms of their languages before the arrival of paper. On the Indian subcontinent and in Southeast Asia, lontar leaves, tree barks such as birch bark, palm leaves as well as bamboo were used as writing materials. Across the Atlantic in the Americas, before the arrival of Columbus, for ancient civilizations such as the Maya, Moche, and Aztec, the chief materials for writing were stone, wood, and deerskin. The change from papyrus to more long-lasting parchment for the production of books in large quantities in Europe began circa 6 B.C. at the Pergamum Library in ancient Greece (although the earliest use of parchment as a writing material dates back to 300 B.C., long before the Pergamum Library was founded). Early books made from parchment had a problem though, because text could only be written on one side and it is difficult to refer to a particular part of the book (e.g. as locating words from the index page today). This problem was solved with the introduction of the parchment codex. The change from parchment rolls to parchment codex began about 1st century A.D. in the Roman Empire and was used extensively in Christian book makers from the time the Roman Catholic Church was founded in 4th century A.D.

Following the invention of writing, three writing systems or scripts were eventually developed over the centuries:

1. Alphabetic writing systems were used for languages such as Arabic, Latin, English, Greek, Russian, Hebrew, Malay, and Korean.

2. Syllabic writing systems (known as syllabaries or pseudo-alphabets) were used on the Indian subcontinent and in East Asia (Indic writing systems) for languages such as Hindi, Khmer, Bengali, Burmese, Javanese (Indonesia), Thai, Tibetan, and Tamil and Sinhalese (Sri Lanka), as well as some non–Asian languages such as Amharic.

3. Pictographic, logographic and ideographic writing systems were first used for Sumerian cuneiforms and ancient Egyptian and Mayan hieroglyphics, and ideograms are used today in China and Japan.

Today there are more than fifty scripts. The Khmer (Cambodian) script is the largest with 74 letters, 39 vowels, 10 digits, and 14 other punctuation marks. One of the Melanesian languages of Papua New Guinea in the Pacific Ocean called Rotokas has the shortest alphabet, with only 11 letters. Modern Chinese script commonly uses just over 8,000 ideograms (but the total number of ideograms in existence are between 40,000 and 50,000). A Japanese child must learn about 2,000 Chinese ideograms, or *Kanji*, as well as two Japanese phonetic scripts, *Hiragana* and *Katakana*, both with about 45 symbols. All three make up the Japanese script. A Roman alphabet (for use in transliteration of ideograms) was introduced in Japan in 1981 and called *Romanjii*, and another in 1958 for the Chinese, called *Pinyin*. The Korean script is not an ideographic one but a full alphabet using modified symbols adapted from Chinese script. Korean script has two Roman alphabetic systems, the McCune-Reischauer System and the Korean Ministry of Education System. So complex are Japanese and Chinese scripts that it takes a child several years longer to master the script than compared to a child learning how to use the Roman script.

In March 2001, an international forum was hosted in Baghdad by the Iraqi government to celebrate the 5000th birthday of the invention of writing. Out of the perhaps 53 alphabets and scripts in use today for over 6000 language, both the Roman and the Arabic scripts are the most commonly used international alphabets, as they are used as official orthography by several countries on more than two continents. The Roman or Latin script is used for about 110 languages mostly in Europe, Sub-Saharan Africa and the Americas. The Arabic script is used in 20 languages such as much of the Middle East with Arabic populations; Berber language (Morocco, Mauritania and Algeria); Farsi (Iran); Urdu (Pakistan); Pashto (Afghanistan); Azeri (Azerbaijan) and Malay (Brunei, Indonesia and Malaysia). Countries that have used two or more scripts officially for the national language include Turkey (Roman and Arabic script); Romania (Roman and Cyrillic script); Indonesia (Roman and Arabic script); Azerbaijan (Arabic, Cyrillic and Roman script) and Uzbekistan (Arabic, Cyrillic and Roman script.) For most languages around the world today, writing is horizontally from left to right, so a book is opened on the right-hand side. There are, however, some exceptions. Arabic and Hebrew documents are both written horizontally from right to left (as they were both strongly influenced by Aramaic, which was written from right to left), so a book is opened from the left-hand side. While both Chinese and Japanese can typically be written in vertical columns from right to left or horizontally from left to right, or from right to left.

124
Ten Oldest Existing Written Works

The following are ten major groups of inscriptions, manuscripts and text fragments from around the world. Most date from well before A.D. 1, and are thus thousands of years old. Since radiocarbon dating and other scientific criteria for determining age cannot always guarantee precise dates, approximations or rough estimates are a way to get round this.

1. Sumer, Babylonia and Assyria. Clay tablets from Sumer (in southern Mesopotamia, near the Tigris and Euphrates valley of present-day Iraq), inscribed in Sumerian cuneiform writing, are dated from circa 3500 B.C., and are thus about 5500 years old. Some of these tablets were discovered by French archaeologists in 1877 at the ancient town of Lagash

(now Telloh in southern Iraq). Many museums around the world, such as the Louvre in Paris, display many fragments from these ancient clay tablets, including the oldest storybooks such as *The Epic of Gilgamesh* and *The Lord of Aratta*. A number of scripts based on the Sumerian cuneiform appeared later on, notably the Elamite script. Fragments of clay tablets found at Suse (Susa), the capital of the ancient kingdom of Elam in south-western modern Iran, were dated at 2900 B.C. When the Sumer civilization declined, it was taken over by the civilizations of Babylonia and Assyria. Several 4200-year-old cuneiform clay tablets inscribed in Akkadian, the language of ancient Babylonia and Assyria dating from about 2650 B.C., have been uncovered. Like the clay tablets from Sumer, museums today also display many fragments of these ancient clay tablets from Babylonia and Assyria. Later on in time, the Hittites, (originally from parts of what is today modern Turkey), who overran the Babylonian Empire, began inscribing hieroglyphic and cuneiform writings on clay and stone around 1400 B.C. Some were written in Akkadian cuneiform, the rest in Hittite hieroglyphics. In 1906 German archaeologists discovered thousands of Hittite clay tablets from the ruins of the ancient Hittite capital Hattusas (near the modern Turkish town of Boghazköy, east of Ankara).

There also exist stone fragments of archaic pre-cuneiform inscriptions (known as the early Uruk period inscriptions of Sumer) that are older than the Lagash tablets. Three such examples are the Hoffman Tablet, preserved at the General Theological Seminary in New York, and another stone tablet at the Pennsylvania University Museum of Archaeology and Anthropology in Philadelphia; both date from 5100 B.C. The other pre-cuneiform relic is known as the Monuments Blau (or Blue Monuments), and are pieces of greenish stone housed at the Ashmolean Museum and the British Museum in the U.K. and dated at 4800 B.C. All 7000-year-old fragments were retrieved from the royal tombs in the city of Ur (the biblical birthplace of Abraham) in the 1920s. Even though these are not regarded as full-length examples of human writing, as they are merely short inscriptions and often numerical, nevertheless they are the oldest surviving samples of any form of primitive human writing today. Another empire close to Babylonia worth mentioning, the Persian

Empire (occupying parts of modern-day Iran), also produced many ancient texts. At the city of Persepolis founded by Darius I, near today's Shiraz, several cuneiform inscriptions on clay tablets in Old Persian have been found dating back to 560 B.C. These tablets were related to the administration of Darius I. But they were not in significant numbers as they were eclipsed by the number inscriptions in Elamite and Aramaic languages also found in Persepolis, one reason being that not much of the population in Persia was fluent in Old Persian. Modern Persian is called Farsi.

2. Egypt. Before the ancient Egyptians began using papyrus to write on, inscriptions were made on stone (clay was not available in the Nile Valley). The earliest simple hieroglyphics were in use around 5000 B.C. (predynastic Egypt, or before Menes, the founding king of the 1st Egyptian dynasty). The oldest known hieroglyphic inscriptions today are those of the Naqada culture, dating back to 4000 B.C. and preserved at the Ashmolean Museum in Oxford, U.K. Some of the inscriptions depict the work of Shera, the priest of Send, and hence the stone is known as the *Send Inscription*. The ancient Egyptians first used papyrus reeds, from the plant *Cyperus papyrus* (which gave rise to the word paper), for writing around 3400 B.C. The *Prisse Papyrus* made in ancient Egypt around 2300 B.C. is the oldest existing written work on papyrus. It was named after Prisse d'Avennes, the French Egyptologist, and the contents of the papyrus, written in hieratic script, are based on the teachings of Ptah-Hotep, Grand Vizier under the 5th Egyptian dynasty Pharaoh Isesi (Izezi). The National Library of France now houses the 4000 year old papyrus. The *Book of the Dead*, another ancient Egyptian papyrus scroll, dates from 1800 B.C. Discovered in Egypt in 1799 by a French archaeologist, the *Rosetta Stone*, dating from 195 B.C., was used as a dictionary to translate the first Egyptian hieroglyphics.

Today the ancient Egyptian language has evolved into the Coptic language, which is still used by minority Christians in Egypt who belong to the Coptic Egyptian Church, founded when St. Mark introduced Christianity to Egypt during the reign of Emperor Nero in A.D. 37–68. The Coptic Church (also practiced in ancient Ethiopia and Sudan) is thus much older than the Roman Catholic Church,

Because Egyptian hieroglyphics were time-consuming to read and write, the Egyptians from 2000 B.C. mostly used hieroglyphics on tombs.

This papyrus contains the text of

Samples of the hieratic script on papyrus introduced to replace hieroglyphics and thus simplify ancient Egyptian writing on papyrus.

circa 1000 B.C. in ancient China by the Naxi Dongba people (Yao Xie) of the Yunnan, Sichuan and Xizang provinces, in southwestern China. It is much harder to learn than standard Chinese ideographs, so the Naxi people today use it instead for reading and writing. Today scholars from both China and more than ten countries are still trying to systematically translate and transliterate the 300 year old Naxi Dongba ideographic script.

The Chinese script is the oldest existing script in the world today, and after more than 4000 years it has not changed much in structure, apart from a reduction in the number of characters. Two Chinese words that have made its way into English are tea and tycoon.

4. India, Pakistan and Sri Lanka. The ancient Indus Valley civilization occupied parts of the Indian subcontinent such as Harappa and Mo-henjo-daro in present-day Pakistan, and several areas in the modern Indian states of Rajasthan and Gujarat. The civilization produced ideographic inscriptions (in a partially deciphered Indus Valley script adopted from Sumerian pictograms) on faience and ivory which have been dated to around 2100 B.C. The most significant ancient language used on the subcontinent was Sanskrit, from which such languages as Hindi, Urdu and Bengali were derived. Sanskrit is one of the two main classical Indo-European languages used on the subcontinent, the other being Pali. Some of the oldest Sanskrit texts (written originally on palm leaves in the Sanskrit script) from the region are the *Vedas*, epic religious poems that form the basis of Hinduism, the oldest religion in the world. The *Rig Veda* or *Ṛg Veda,* the oldest of the *Vedas,* dates from 1710 B.C. Those that are extant are not in their original form, hav-

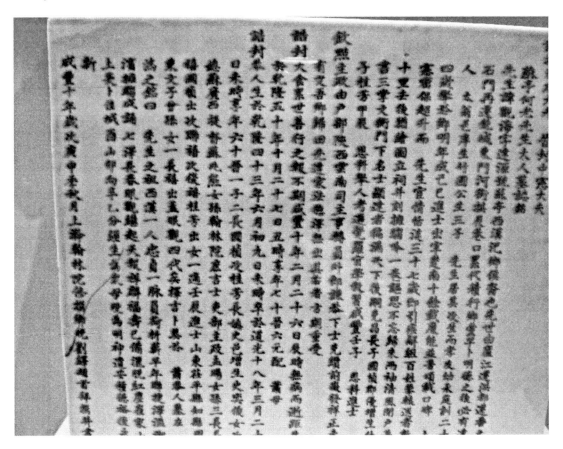

The Chinese script used today is more than 4000 years old, and apart from forming part of the existing Japanese script, it has also been used in Vietnam and Korea as the official scripts.

ing been expanded by generations of several authors.

Today the only place to view the *Rig Veda* is the Bhandarkar Institute Library in Pune (Poona) southeast of Mumbai (Bombay). The *Vedas* are so valuable to worldwide historical scholars that they are part of the UNESCO Memory of the World Register. After the Indus Valley script and the Sanskrit script declined in use, the next important script to evolve on the Indian subcontinent was the Brahmi script. Written works in Brahmi script (from which all scripts used on the Indian subcontinent developed), were in existence from 650 B.C. The Brahmi script itself developed from the Aramaic script (see section below on Syria and Palestine). Fragments of Tamil (in Sri Lanka) texts are the oldest of the Brahmi-derived texts in the southern parts of the Indian subcontinent, as the earliest Tamil texts date from 600

B.C., making Tamil the India's oldest living language and script. The oldest existing complete Sanskrit manuscripts written in the Brahmi script are the work of the Indian grammarian Panini circa 400 B.C. The laws of King Asoka (Ashoka) (who once ruled a large portion of modern day India and is now immortalized on the Indian national flag), written in Brahmi and inscribed on monumental columns and pillars, notably at Buddhist Sarnath Shrine, east of Varanasi, mostly date from 290 B.C. The oldest extant Buddhist texts from the Indian subcontinent not inscribed on stone are the 2000-year-old Gandharan Buddhist Scrolls (preserved at the British Library). The scrolls, which date from about A.D. 1 and were written in Kharosthi script, were discovered in Peshawar, Pakistan, once the capital of the ancient kingdom of Gandhara, famous for the ancient Takshashila University (see list **60**). This Kharosthi script, which is based on the Aramaic script like the Brahmi script, was in use from about 300 B.C. when the northwestern India subcontinent was ruled by the Persian Achaemenid empire.

Today Hindi, the most widely used language on the Indian subcontinent, is written in the Brahmi script known as Devanagari. Modifications of Devanagari are also used in other separate northern and central Indian scripts such as those used for Bengali, Telegu and Guajarati. But Urdu (spoken in Pakistan), which is related to Hindi (as speakers in both languages understand each other most of the time), but strongly influenced by Arabic and Persian, is written in the Arabic script. Hindi and Urdu were better known as Hindustani. Meanwhile, Tamil and several southern Indian Dravidian languages such as Kannada (whose written records all date from the 5th to 9th century A.D.) are all written in a unique Brahmi script, the Dravidian script. Sinhalese (used in Sri Lanka) is written in the script used for writing Pali texts such as Theravada Buddhism texts

The Buddha, Siddhartha Gautama, forbade the use of Sanskrit for his religion and encouraged the use of Pali; hence, all Asian texts in Theravada Buddhism are written only in Pali.

(see below), and the oldest texts date from the 4th century A.D., which are thus not as old as Tamil texts from Sri Lanka.

Buddhism (the third oldest religion in the world, after Hinduism and Judaism) originally began in India from the 6th century B.C., and several of the oldest Buddhists texts came from India. However over the centuries starting from about the 4th century A.D., during the Gupta dynasty, Hinduism was revived and began to overshadow Buddhism, of which there are today only about 6 million followers on the Indian subcontinent, mostly in Sri Lanka. Hinduism is the major religion in India, with over 800 million adherents. Worldwide there are over 500 million followers of Buddhism in southeast Asia, e.g., Sri Lanka, Burma and Thailand (Theravada Buddhism); east Asia, e.g., China and Korea (Mahayana Buddhism); Lamaism (Tibet and Mongolia) and Zen Buddhism (Japan and Korea). Many important ancient Buddhist documents were not written in Sanskrit because the Buddha, teaching in India, was opposed to the use of Sanskrit for reading and writing his sermons. Hence, as a substitute, Pali, a classical ancient Indo-European language related to Sanskrit and used in Sri Lanka, was used as the classical language of Buddhism, its script used for writing the earliest Buddhist scriptures. The Tripitaka Canon *(the holy book of Theravada Buddhism) is written entirely in Pali. In Sri Lanka, where Pali was first used to record the earliest teachings of the Buddha in the main language Sinhalese, the majority religion is Theravada Buddhism, although the Tamils in Sri Lanka practice Hinduism.*

5. Crete. Clay tablets discovered in Knossos in Crete (Europe's earliest civilization) by British archaeologist Arthur Evans date from the Minoan civilization circa 2000 B.C. They were written in what is called the Linear A script and some in the Linear B script, and both are the earliest texts found in Europe (alongside the Hittite cuneiforms from Turkey). Unlike the more robust Linear B, used in the later Mycenaean civilization, which is more widely understood by scholars and is an early form of ancient Greek, Linear A is currently not completely deciphered.

The *Oera Linda Boek* is a manuscript from the Frisian Islands in the North Sea, allegedly written in an ancient Celtic alphabet, and believed to be the oldest written manuscript in

The 2000-year-old Gandharan Buddhist Scrolls from the ancient Kingdom of Gandhara based near Peshawar, Pakistan. These are the oldest examples of Buddhist texts from the Indian sub-continent not inscribed on stone (by permission of The British Library, Or 4915.3:I.3).

Europe. It has been controversially dated to 2100 B.C. (older than the Linear A script above and around the time of the Celts built the later parts of Stonehenge in Bath, U.K.). There is still a big debate as to the origins and authenticity of the manuscript, but the Celts certainly were able to read and write. The oldest surviving Celtic language, Irish Gaelic, goes back to 500 B.C., and the first Celtic script, the Ogham alphabet, only dates from the 3rd century A.D. (see list **132**). So based on this sort of authenticated timeframe, it is no surprise the date of *Oera Linda Boek* baffles scholars. Most scholars put the starting date of Celtic languages at around 2000 B.C. And the Celts' first known territory was in central Europe about 1200 B.C. So if the *Oera Linda Boek* is not Celtic then it has to be in another language and script. There are two candidates: the Beaker culture from Iberia, which spread to Ireland and the U.K. and central and Western Europe from the 3rd millennium B.C. (circa 2800 B.C.). Although the people were skilled in arts such as metalworking (they have been associated with the early construction of Stonehenge), not much is known about the Beaker language or script. In the book *Origins of the British: A Genetic De-*

tective by Stephen Oppenheimer published in 2006, he theorizes that most modern-day people of Ireland, Wales, and Cornwall were descended not from Celts, but from Iberians from Spain and Portugal who did not speak a Celtic language but spoke Germanic languages. He based his theory on genetics, linguistics, archaeology and historical record. He emphasizes that the Celts and Celtic languages only arrived later. So the *Oera Linda Boek* may be from two languages which predate the Celtic language; the Beaker culture language or the Germanic language mentioned by Oppenheimer.

6. Syria and Palestine. The Semites who lived in parts of ancient Syria (Aram) and Palestine (Canaan) created the first known crude alphabetic system (the Semitic alphabet) around 1800 B.C. or about 3800 years ago. It was an improvement on the ancient Egyptian hieroglyphics and Sumerian cuneiform, but was not a picture-based writing. The oldest known Semitic alphabetic inscriptions were found on clay tablets in Syria in 1929 at Ras Shamra (near the ancient city of Ugarit), and also close to the Sinai Peninsula in 1904 by British Egyptologist

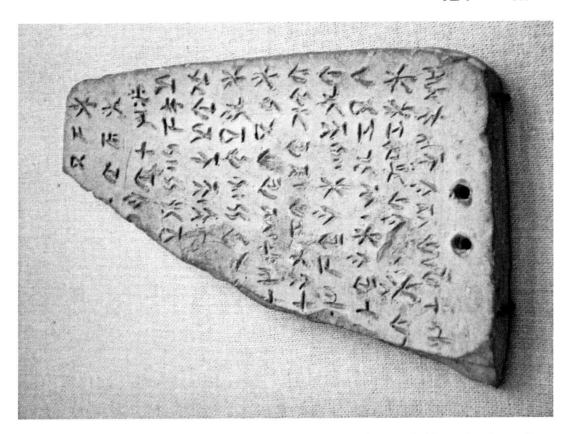

These Linear B inscriptions from Crete, dating from 600 B.C., are the second oldest scripts invented in Europe. The oldest are the Turkish Hittite cuneiforms.

Flinders Petrie, both dating from 1600 B.C. Scholars and academics mostly agree that the Semitic alphabet is the origin of all other alphabets in the world, as the three main branches (North Semitic, South Semitic and Greek) are the ancestors of today's modern alphabets. The letter "O" is said by some to be the oldest letter of the alphabet, as it has remained virtually unchanged since the Semites first used it. The Semitic language spoken in ancient Syria, known as Aramaic, became the lingua franca of the ancient Middle East for many centuries. And the Aramaic script gave rise to a number of Middle Eastern and Asian scripts such as Arabic (via the Nabatean script), Hebrew, and the Brahmi scripts.

7. Phoenicia. The Phoenicians living along the coast of the Mediterranean Sea corresponding to modern day Lebanon and Syria, especially at Byblos (near present-day Beirut) as well as in parts of modern day Tunisia, developed an alphabetic system related to the Semitic alphabet for their language, called Punic. Phoenician clay tablets such as the one discovered by a French archaeological team in 1923 belonging to a Phoenician King of Byblos called Ahiram, known as the *Ahiram Inscriptions*, have been dated to about 1260 B.C., but the alphabet was created much earlier. The Greek script (ancestor to all European scripts), the Brahmi script (ancestor to most Asian scripts), as well as the Arabic and Hebrew alphabets were all influenced by the Phoenician alphabet. The most famous of all Phoenician inscriptions is King Mesha's *Moabite stone*, parts of it written in Aramaic, and dating from 880 B.C. and containing biblical stories found in the Old Testament of the Hebrew Bible. Discovered at Dibon, Jordan, it is preserved at the Louvre Museum in Paris.

8. Israel. The oldest surviving example of Old Hebrew writing (which developed directly from Aramaic script) were discovered in the 1930s at the Lachish Palace, south-east of Jerusalem in Israel, dating from 700 B.C. But the earliest Old Hebrew documents are believed to date from 1400 B.C. The Dead Sea Scrolls discovered in 1947 are among the oldest existing extensive papyrus manuscripts in Old Hebrew. The oldest of the scrolls, know as the *Isaiah* scroll, contains parts of the Jewish Old Testament and date from 300 B.C. Fragments of the Dead Sea Scrolls are now housed in a building called The Shrine of the Book, in the Israel Museum in Jerusalem.

By the time Roman Emperor Titus and the Roman army put down the first Jewish Revolt in Roman Palestine in A.D. 70 with the capture and destruction of Jerusalem, the Dead Sea Scrolls had been safely hidden in secret caves, to be discovered in 1947. Had Titus known about the scrolls, he would have ordered their destruction, meaning the scrolls and the important historical contents revered by scholars today would have been lost forever.

The *Nash Papyrus* preserved at the Cambridge University Library in the U.K. dates from 100 B.C. and is written in Old Hebrew. It contains the biblical text of the 10 Commandments. The first five, and oldest books of the Jewish Old Testament (Genesis, Exodus, Leviticus, Numbers and Deuteronomy) are known as the Torah or Pentateuch and are traditionally said to have been written by Moses. The following are a selection of the oldest books of the Hebrew Old Testament and the approximate first year of events mentioned in the books: Book of Exodus, 1300 B.C.; Samuel, 1020 B.C.; David, 980 B.C.; Solomon, 960 B.C.; Elijah, 850 B.C.; Psalms, 700 B.C.; Ezekiel, 597 B.C. Some scholars say that the oldest book in the Bible is Job because the script, in which some sections of the book was written on clay tablets, is an archaic form of early Aramaic script dating before 1000 B.C. and Job also makes references to the great flood. But parts of Genesis, the first book of the Jewish Old Testament, which includes the stories taken from the Sumerian *Epic of Gilgamesh* about Noah and the great flood, are believed to have been originally recorded on clay tablets around 2900

B.C. Despite these few ancient clay texts, biblical stories were not recorded in detail in the early days of Judaism but passed from generation to generation orally. Some early biblical stories managed to be inscribed in detail on stone or clay tablets such as the Sumerian clay tablets described above and the *Moabite stone* (880 B.C.); clay and stone inscriptions at the Assyrian Palace of Sargon II (circa 700 B.C.), which mention biblical stories found in Isaiah; and the clay *Cyrus Cylinder* (545 B.C.), whose Persian cuneiform inscriptions mention biblical stories found in Chronicles and Ezra.

The date at which the biblical stories of the Jewish Old Testament were probably first extensively written on papyrus (and then later on parchment) by Jewish scribes in Babylon was circa 586 B.C. Around this time armies of Nebuchadnezzar had destroyed Jerusalem and took the people of Judah (the Israelites) into captivity. Eventually over the centuries, before the birth of Jesus, other stories of the Jewish Old Testament were written and added

One of the earliest successful elaborate plans to protect ancient manuscripts occurred during the first Jewish Revolt in A.D. 66 to 70, when the Dead Sea Scrolls were cleverly hidden in caves from Roman Emperor Titus (pictured here).

to existing texts. The various books of the Bible existed separately for a while, before they were put together to become the complete Bible as we know it today. Most of the older texts of the Bible (Old Testament) were written in Aramaic (almost extinct today, such as the *Moabite stone*), then translated into Old Hebrew (which is now extinct). Old Hebrew was also used to write other parts of the Old Testament, such as the oldest of the Dead Sea Scrolls, i.e., 300 B.C.) and later translated into Greek (such as the *Codex Vaticanus*) and Modern Hebrew. Most books in the Christian New Testament from the gospels to the Book of Revelation were originally mostly written in Greek such as the *Codex Sinaiticus*, even though Jesus spoke only Aramaic; they were completed between A.D. 45 and 110. To some extent, a great deal of the books in the New Testament was believed to have been written by the Apostle Paul.

The entire Bible (Old Testament in Hebrew and New Testament in Greek) was first translated into Latin accurately circa A.D. 384 by St. Jerome as the vulgate Bible. St. Jerome is believed to have consulted a manuscript called the *Hexapla* (no longer existing), compiled in the 3rd century A.D. by Greek scholar Origen, for his translation work. Original Latin versions of the Bible dating from the 4th century A.D. exist today in the *Harley Latin Gospels* and the *Codex Vercelli* (see below at section on the Roman Empire). The Bible (written over a period of 2500 years), is thus one of the oldest existing compiled works in the world. Today the Bible contains 24 books (Jewish Bible) or 66 to 73 books (Christian Bible). The Bible was also the very first major book to be printed in Europe (by Gutenberg, see list **144**).

The Bible is not only an interesting book to read. It has also been used for other purposes. For instance the founder of modern Ethiopia, Emperor Menelik II, a deeply religious leader, is said to have eaten some pages of the Bible each time he felt ill because somehow he felt better the next day. He once ate all of the pages of the Book of Kings, as part of a massive cure for flu. The Bible was also subjected to severe translation restrictions during the time of the Vatican Inquisition. In 1536 in Belgium, William Tyndale, who had earlier painstakingly translated the Latin Bible into English, was strangled and burned at the stake for his efforts. "All" copies of his translation had been burnt in 1530 in London.

9. Greece. The Greeks created the first true alphabetic system, by using symbols not just for consonants but also for vowels. The first two letters of the Greek alphabet, alpha and beta, was adopted to form the word "alphabet." The earliest Greek text, in the form of Mycenaean Linear B tablets, dates from 1100 B.C. The oldest works of classical Greek literature are those of Homer, who completed his epic poems *The Odyssey* and *The Iliad* around 810 B.C., and Hesiod (*Theogony* and *Works and Days*) around 700 B.C. Laws written by the statesman Dracon in Athens (the very first in Greece) date from 620 B.C. The oldest extant papyrus fragments written in Greek make up the *Persae of Timotheus*, written in about 320 B.C. *Papyrus 53*, or *P53*, is the oldest existing biblical text written in Greek on papyrus, as it dates from the middle 2nd century A.D. It is part of the collection of ancient biblical papyri fragments at the John Rylands University Library in Manchester, U.K. The oldest extant and complete parchment manuscript from Europe is the *Codex Vaticanus*, a Greek Bible dating from A.D. 300 which is now housed in the Vatican Library; it is also the oldest complete Bible in existence in the world (as it is older than St. Jerome's original Latin Vulgate Bible of A.D. 384). The second oldest parchment Bible in existence is the copy of the *Yonan Codex* which dates from A.D. 355 in the U.S. Library of Congress. It belonged to the Malek-Yonan Family (near Lake Urmia in Azerbaijan) for centuries before being loaned to the Library of Congress. President Eisenhower was photographed with it the White House. The *Codex Sinaiticus* (preserved in the British Library), dating from A.D. 350, is the oldest known vellum manuscript of the New Testament in Greek. It was originally discovered by German scholar named Count Konstantin von Tischendorf at a Greek Orthodox St. Catherine's monastery at the foot of Mt. Sinai. The *Codex Alexandrinus* (housed in the British Library) is a 5th century Greek Bible on vellum containing parts of the New and Old Testament. Together with the *Codex Sinaiticus*

and the *Codex Vaticanus*, the three texts are the most valuable Greek manuscripts today.

The Codex Vaticanus was so tightly guarded by the Vatican Library that it was not available to scholars until 1889, after more than 400 years of secrecy. It had been found by librarians by accident in 1481 in a section of the Vatican library.

10. Roman Empire. Written texts in Latin (Roman script) first began to appear around 600 B.C. when Rome existed as a republic, the earliest known surviving example being a golden fibula, or cloak pin, with Latin inscriptions discovered in the ancient Roman city of Praeneste (today the city of Palestrina, not far from Rome, in the Italian region of Latium or Lazio). The cloak pin is now preserved in a museum in Rome. However, the first major authors in Latin were Livius Andronicus around 300 B.C. and Ennius circa 210 B.C. The Latin alphabet was developed from the alphabet of early settlers in what is now Tuscany, Italy, called the Etruscans, who in turn had copied their own Etruscan alphabet from the Greek alphabet (around 800 B.C.). The word "Latin" is the equivalent of the word "south" because it was the people living south of the Etruscans who began writing in a modified form of the Etruscan alphabet (a precursor to the Latin script).

The best known inscription in the Etruscan alphabet is the *Marsiliana Tablet*, discovered in the valley of the Albegna River and dating from 700 B.C. and preserved today at a museum in Florence.

The first Christians in Rome spoke Greek, before Latin became the dominant language for Christianity. Christian manuscripts are also the oldest existing types of major documents in Latin, on parchment, surviving today. The four of the oldest extant manuscripts of the New Testament gospels in Latin before the 5th century A.D. are as follows: the *Harley Latin Gospels*, which dates from the 4th century A.D. It can be seen in the British Library. The *Codex Vercelli* also dates from the 4th century A.D. It is preserved at a cathedral library in Vercelli, Italy, and was written by St. Eusebius, Bishop of Caesarea (modern Qisarya in Israel) and author of a history of the Christian church to A.D. 324. The third example of old Latin gospels surviving today is safeguarded in the national library in Turin, Italy. Some are charred pieces of a manuscript cataloged as *Codex G.VII.1.5* dating from the late 4th century A.D. Curiously, biblical scholars have discovered that no original copies of St. Jerome's 4th century A.D. Latin manuscripts exist today. St Jerome was the most prolific early translator of the Bible from Greek and

The Greek script was the first true alphabet in the world; virtually every single script used in Europe today descended from the Greek alphabet.

Hebrew to Latin. However, at the St. Gallen monastic library *(Stiftsbibliothek)* is *Codex 1395*, written in the early 5th century A.D. and believed to be annotated by St. Jerome.

The earliest and most popular guide to the Latin language throughout the Middle Ages was written by Aelius Donatus in the 4th century A.D. Several other early Latin versions of parts of the Bible dating from the 5th century A.D. onwards exist today in places such as the Abrosian Library in Milan, the Vatican Library in Rome, the Ashmolean Museum Library in Oxford, the British Library, the National Library of France and John Rylands University Library in Manchester, the U.K. Although Latin is now used officially only in the Vatican City, the Roman script (with modifications) is used in most European languages, as well as widely outside Europe. The other main scripts used today in Europe are the Cyrillic and Greek alphabets.

One living organism has existed for thousands of years around the time most of these 10 categories of ancient texts was written. It is, however, a plant called Bristlecone pine tree (Pinus langueva), which first appeared around 6200 B.C. One specimen still alive today, and identified in 1957, is called Methuselah (named in the Bible as the oldest man who ever lived). Methuselah seeded around 2766 B.C. and is thus more than 4700 years old. Methuselah, which botanists believe will live for another 400 years, exists among the White Mountains of California in the U.S. From A.D. 3, parchment and later vellum was preferred over papyrus by Roman scholars for writing manuscripts. By A.D. 400 parchment had displayed papyrus as the chief material for manuscript production in Europe, until the introduction of paper in the 12th century. The basic structure of a modern book today with pages bound on the left side (right side for books published in Hebrew and Arabic), to allow pages to be opened easily, was developed from the Roman parchment codex. This was a major deviation from the papyrus or parchment scroll, which had to be wound and rewound after use. However, both forms of manuscripts, i.e., roll or codex form, were used simultaneously until the introduction of printing with moveable type in the 15th century, which saw the ascendance of the codex form

The first major Greek writer was Homer, famous for his narrative epics the *Iliad* and the *Odyssey*. Both were derived from oral tradition, as the ancient Greeks did not write a lot before the time of Homer.

over the roll form. Christian libraries in Medieval Europe after the fall of the Western Roman Empire were the first to employ the codex form extensively for manuscripts. Some of these early collections survive today in libraries such as Dublin's Chester Beatty Library in the Irish Republic and the Vatican Library. The Latin script in many codices tended to be mostly in capital letters, or majuscule (and had various forms such as uncials, square and rustic capitals). But from the 8th century, during the time of Charlemagne, Latin manuscripts with a combination of both capitals and small letters (or minuscule) were used.

The Etruscan alphabet was the script derived from the Greek alphabet used in Italy before the Roman Republic was established.

125
Earliest Written Works in German

The German monk Ulfilas (a bishop of the West Goths and the religious leader of the Visigoths) produced several works including translations of the Bible from Latin and Greek to German in A.D. 320. Parchment fragments from his works appear in religious manuscripts, which date from the 5th to 6th century A.D., such as the famous *Codex Argenteus* preserved at Sweden's Uppsala University Library. Two of the oldest extant non-religious texts in German (Old High German to be precise) are *Hildebrandslied*, a ballad written circa 9th century A.D. and the 8th century A.D. *Abrogans* Latin-German dictionary. The earliest significant Middle High German from the 12th century is *Nibelungenlied*, written in A.D. 1210. Modern German spoken today in Germany, Austria and Switzerland developed from Middle High German. Apart from ancient Runic inscriptions discovered in Germany dating from A.D. 200 and carved on wood and stone, Ulfilas' work is the oldest surviving German literary text, although it was written in Old German or Gothic using the Gothic alphabet devised by Ulfilas. N.B.: The Gothic alphabet (now extinct) is very different from the Gothic script, a form of writing using the Latin alphabet.

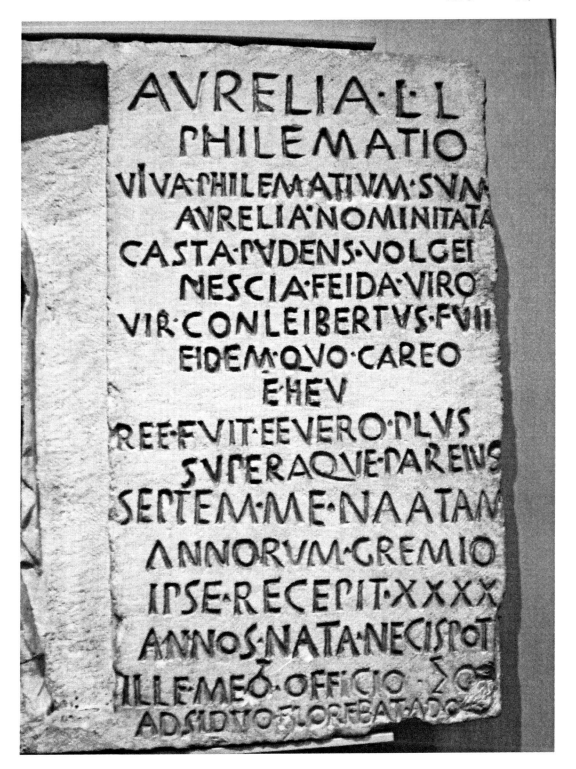

The Latin alphabet, the most used alphabet in the world, was derived from the Etruscan alphabet. These majuscule Latin inscriptions date from 80 B.C.

126
Earliest Written Works in Mayan

Popol Vuh is a Mayan hieroglyphic inscription on stone stelae, describing the creation of the world. It dates from A.D. 200. Today the ancient Mayan language is still spoken in parts of southern Mexico, such as Yucatan State, and Central America, such as Guatemala.

The Olmec civilization, the first developed civilization in the Americas (and located in the Mexican states of Veracruz and Tabasco), invented a hieroglyphic writing system around 1200 B.C., and influenced the later development of the Mayan, Toltec and Aztec hieroglyphic system. Scholars have been very eager to accurately decipher Mayan inscriptions in Mexico. One of two of the early aids to do this was the so called Madrid Codex. *The age of this manuscript is still in dispute. There is no con-sensus as to whether the* Madrid Codex *was written before or after Spanish explorer Hernán Cortes reached Mexico in the 1520s. The* Madrid Codex *is most important of four surviving Mayan codices, the others being the* Dresden Codex *(in Germany's Dresden State Library),* Grolier Codex *(in a Mexican Government vault), and the* Paris Codex *(at the National Library of France). These codices are the only materials for reading original Mayan writing, as most surviving Mayan writings are on stones. Most other non-stone examples of Mayan hieroglyphics were destroyed in the middle 1550s by Spanish conquistadors. Delicate infrared, ultraviolet, and X-ray photography of the* Madrid Codex *is ongoing at the manuscript's location in the Museo de América de Madrid in Spain to discover its real age. The other important deciphering aid is the Yuri Knorosov research papers (see list* **110***).*

127
Earliest Written Works in Arabic and Farsi (Persian)

The earliest important texts in Arabic (which developed from the ancient Aramaic-based Nabatean script of northern Arabia) date from about A.D. 400. Islam dates from the time Muhammed fled to Medina from Mecca, circa A.D. 622. The standard text of the original Koran, or *Quran* (which has 114 chapters or *Suras),* was completed between A.D. 650 and 651. It was written for Othman, the 3rd Caliph, who was the first to order that the various separate writings of Muhammed be combined together into a single book. This Koran, called the *Mushaf of Othman,* is preserved and on display today in a library in Tashkent, Uzbekistan. It is on the UNESCO Memory of the World Register (see list **122**). The second oldest existing version of the Koran (attributed to Imam Al-Hasan al-Basri) dates back to A.D. 697. Both books are not complete, with several pages lost in time. See list **207** for details on the oldest surviving complete copy of the Koran. The oldest existing non–Islamic Arabic manuscript is the *Mount Sinai Arabic Codex 151* (an Arabic translation of the Bible), written in A.D. 867.

The oldest surviving Koran in Europe is an 11th century Koran preserved at Ireland's Chester Beatty Library in Dublin. Arabic is spoken in different dialects, e.g., the Arabic generally spoken in Morocco is different from the one spoken in Iraq, and the same goes with the Arabic script used in these two countries. The universal solution is the use of classical Arabic and its script, which are both widely understood in the Arab world. Classical Arabic is based on the original the way the Koran was first written and spoken in the 7th century A.D. Maltese text is a form of Arabic written in the Roman script. The Maltese language itself is a unique dialect of the Arabic language.

Before Old Persian became the dominant language in Persia, the oldest written documents from what is today modern Iran were Elamite language inscriptions written in Elamite cuneiforms from ancient kingdom of Elam, based at Suse (Susa), near Dezful, southwest of Iran. The cuneiform clay tablets are dated circa 2900 B.C. The earliest Old Persian cuneiform texts date from the time of the

Mayan hieroglyphic inscriptions on stone from Mexico.

Achaemenid Persian Empire founded by Cyrus circa 550 B.C. The most significant surviving texts are those discovered in the ruined city of Persepolis from the time of King Darius I, which date from the late 5th century B.C. On Mount Behistun (Bisitun or Bisotun), King Daruius I also had a description of his reign between 512 and 486 B.C. inscribed on the mountain in three languages: Old Persian, Babylonian and Elamite cuneiform. It was this famous trilingual rock inscription that Henry Rawlinson, a British diplomat in Persia, in the 1840s and other scholars in the 1850s and onwards used to decipher and translate more accurately all major cuneiform inscription, notably Sumerian and Assyrian cuneiform (see also the *Rosetta Stone* in list **124**). A notable word passed from Old Persian to English is the word paradise. From about 100 B.C. Old Persian was written in a new script called the Pahlavi, based on the Semitic alphabet invented in ancient Syria (i.e., the Aramaic script) (see list **124**). Before Persia adopted Islam and the Arabic script, the major religion in Persia was Zoroastrianism, founded in the 6th century B.C. by Persian prophet Zoroaster. Sacred texts (the *Avesta*) in Zoroastrianism were written in an alphabetic script called Zend-Avestan, derived from Old Persian Pahlavi script. Both Zend-Avestan and the Pahlavi scripts were in use in Persia for writing documents up to A.D. 637 when the Persian Sassanian Empire was overthrown by Muslim Arabs at the Battle of Qadisiya and Islam replaced Zoroastrianism. The earliest medieval Persian (Farsi) documents based on the Arabic script (used today for writing Farsi or Modern Persian) thus date from the 7th century A.D. The greatest writer in Persian is the poet Ferdowsi, who wrote the classic Persian epic *Bayasanghori Shâhnâmeh* in the 10th century.

Deciphering the Old Persian cuneiform script in the 1840s made it possible to accurately re-decipher earlier cuneiform texts such as those used by the Sumerians, Babylonians, Assyrians and Hittites.

128
Earliest Written Works in Japanese and Korean

Although Japan is situated close to China (which has written works over 4000 years old), Japan had no written language until Korean scholars in A.D. 405 introduced Chinese (*Kanji*) script for writing documents in Japanese. Later on in the 9th century A.D., the phonetic syllabary *Kana* (invented by Kukai, a Japanese Shingon Buddhist priest and saint) helped to simplify writing in Japanese. Two of the oldest existing manuscripts written in Japanese are *Kojiki* (A.D. 681) and *Nihon Shoki* (A.D. 720). Both of them detail the ancient history of Japan and are preserved at the National Library of Japan in Tokyo. Today Japan is probably the only country that uses three different scripts concurrently. While Chinese ideographic scripts or *Kanji* represents ideas, and objects, the phonetic *Kana* scripts *Hiragana* and *Katakana* represent sounds only.

On the Korean peninsula (comprising today of North and South Korea), the Chinese script was also used for writing books and other documents in the Korean language for many centuries from the 2nd century A.D., until King Sejong of the Chosun (Choson) dynasty invented the current Korean alphabet called *Hangul* (*Hankul*) in A.D. 1446. The Korean alphabet is mainly different from the Chinese script in that characters (letters) in *Hangul* also represent sound (a requirement for a script to be classified as alphabetic), whereas Chinese script does not represent sounds. The sounds produced when reading a Chinese script depend on which Chinese language or dialect is being used to read the script (there are more than 20 different main Chinese languages). This explains why the Chinese script is easily suitable and adaptable for use in all the different Chinese languages. See list **203** for more details. Unlike China, there is only one major Japanese language (as in Korea), and although *Katakana* was added to Japanese script to cater for sounds (just like in the Korean script), the main portion of the Japanese script is *Kanji*. Hence, like the Chinese script, the Japanese script is not classified as an alphabet.

Before A.D. 400, text did exist covering Japan, its people, its culture and customs, but all these manuscripts were written either by Chinese scholars in Japan and China, or travelers returning to China from visits to Japan. The diary belonging to Kino Tsurayuki, a prominent Japanese poet and governor of Tosa Province, known as Tosa Nikki *or* The Tosa Diary, *is the oldest existing one in the world. It records his travels in Kyoto, Japan, and was written in Kana in A.D. 935.*

129
Earliest Written Works in Italian

The early Italian texts were very closely related to Latin texts in grammar and pronunciation, and as such, texts in vernacular Italian only became clearly distinguishable linguistically from texts in Latin from the 13th century A.D. By this time texts in other Romance languages (which had descended from Latin) such as Spanish, French and Portuguese had already been around for at least 200 years. The earliest

Opposite: **Japanese script is made up of three further different scripts: Kanji, Katakana and Hiragana. Only Kanji script is Chinese in origin.**

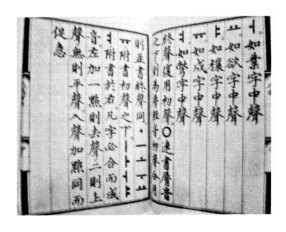

Italian texts from the 13th century had many French words and grammar and were known as Franco-Venetian texts. One of the earliest notable such texts was Tesoretto (*Li Livres dou Tresor*) by Brunetto Latini in 1266. The most famous early Italian writer is undoubtedly Dante. His book *Il Convivio*, finished in 1308, is said to be the first major work of its kind to be written in Italian rather than in Latin.

130
Earliest Written Works in French

One of the earliest written major texts in French is the *Strasbourg Oath (Serments de Strasbourg)* written on parchment in A.D. 842. It is an Old French version (Western Franks) of an oath sworn by two of Charlemagne's sons, Frankish kings Charles the Bald and Louis the German. The oldest extant epic is *La Chanson de Roland*, an Anglo-Norman poem which dates from the early 11th century. The main public library in the northern French town of Valenciennes is famous for housing some of the very first texts written in the French language, most dating from the 9th to 10th century A.D.

131
Earliest Written Works in Spanish and Portuguese

Two versions of Spanish exist today in Spain, Catalan and Castilian Spanish. The former is spoken in areas of Spain known as Catalonia, the Balearic Islands and in Andorra, while the latter is the official language of Spain. Manuscripts found near the Liga region in Spain, and written in Castilian Spanish, date from the 10th century A.D. The best known earliest extant epic is probably the 11th century *Poema del Cid* (Poem of the Cid), about a military commander Rodrigo Diáz de Vivar (called El Cid by the Moors) who fought against the Arab occupation of Valencia. The first major Spanish writer was the 14th-century satirist Juan Ruiz. Poems written by King Sancho I of Portugal (second King of Portugal) in the 12th century are among the oldest existing Portuguese texts today.

The Basque language (known locally as Euskara), spoken in the Basque Provinces of Spain, is more than 2000 years old (much older than Spanish), as it is one of the few surviving languages in Europe that existed before Latin became the dominant language. The oldest existing documents in Basque date from the 8th century A.D. Basque has contributed just a handful of words to European languages; one such is "bizarre." The oldest extant text in Catalan Spanish (found in Barcelona) dates from the 12th century. On April 23 of each year, which is St. George's Day in Spain (known as Festa de Sant Jordi in Catalan Spanish, after the patron saint of Catalonia who famously killed a dragon), people present each other with books and red roses in a massive celebration of reading. While the celebrations, dubbed as "a gigantic literary orgy" by the Spanish press, are going on, Gambetta Square in Barcelona is the big meeting place for authors and publishers. Armies of booksellers also take possession of roads such as the famous La Rambla, for the whole day. On April 23, 1996, UNESCO launched the United Nations World International Book Day based on St. George's Day in Spain. Hence April 23 is a big day for books in Spain and the international community.

132
Earliest Written Works in English, Welsh, Irish, and Scottish

The oldest comprehensive Old English (or Anglo-Saxon) texts date from about A.D. 680. *Beowulf*, a fascinating poem of a Danish warrior, was written around A.D. 885, at a time when armed Danish (Viking) raids into what is now the U.K. were common. It is the oldest surviving Old English manuscript and is now housed in the British Library. The 9th century *Anglo-Saxon Chronicles*, written around the time of King Alfred, is the oldest extant historical document in Old English. The oldest comprehensive legal document in English (Middle English) is the *Magna Carta,* which dates from 1215, during the time of King John I, and describes terms of agreement between the king and the barons on issues such as taxes. Another significant existing manuscript written in Middle English is the *Provisions of Oxford* of King Henry III, written in 1258. This was a governmental reform document (written on parchment) forced upon the king by the leader of the barons, Simon de Montfort, limiting the power of the king. Although papermills were not set up in the U.K. until 1494, paper made outside the U.K. was imported. The oldest extant major document written in Middle English on paper was a letter written to King Henry III by the son of the duke of Navarre, Spain in 1275.

Most of the earliest surviving religious manuscripts written before the 10th century in the U.K. are not in Old English but in Latin, because most of the earliest religious documents in Europe were written either in Greek or Latin. The most ancient religious documents were written in Hebrew and Aramaic. Christianity itself reached England in A.D. 596 with the arrival of St. Augustine of Canterbury, who was sent by the Pope. There are three important Latin texts written in the U.K. The Lindisfarne Gospels *were written and illustrated in A.D. 698 by the monk Eadfrith on the English Island of Lindisfarne. The* Historia Ecclesiastica Gentis Anglorum *(Ecclesiastical History of the English People), finished in 731 by the Venerable Bede, a monk in Jarrow, is the earliest text on the early days of Christianity in the U.K. and is preserved at the British Library. Incidentally King Alfred and his staff did manage to translate Bede's work from Latin into Old English about 150 years later. The* Domesday Book *is not a religious book but a sort of official record of landholdings in the U.K. Its compilation began in 1085 during the reign of William the Conqueror.*

The oldest examples of Welsh texts are the four ancient books the *Black Book of Carmarthen*, the *Book of Taliesin*, the *Book of Aneirin*, and the *Red Book of Hergest* dating

from the 6th century A.D. The oldest texts in Irish (Gaelic) existing today in Roman script date from A.D. 650. But Irish as a spoken language dates much further back, having been introduced into Ireland by the Celts around 500 B.C. This makes Irish Gaelic, alongside Latin, Basque and Greek, one of the four oldest vernacular languages today in Europe. The Irish alphabet was first written in the ancient Celtic Ogham alphabet and the oldest extant texts today are inscriptions that date back to the 4th century A.D. After St. Patrick arrived in Ireland (to help in the spread of Christianity) in 432 A.D., the Roman script was used to write Irish texts. A form of Celtic Gaelic was introduced in Scotland (Scottish Gaelic) in the 5th century A.D. The earliest major examples of Scottish Gaelic in the Latin script date back to the 12th century A.D. The two most notable texts are the history of the MacDonalds in the *Red and Black Books of Clanranald* and *the Fer-*

One of the main reasons for the major difference between English and Scottish texts was the dividing wall ordered by Roman Emperor Hadrian in second century A.D.

naig manuscript, both written in the 1600s. The most famous Scottish Gaelic word passed to English is the word trousers, although Scotland is more well-known for the Scottish kilt.

The Celts also inhabited the British Isles from around 200 B.C., before the Romans led by Julius Caesar invaded in 55 B.C. But the lands ruled by the Romans did not include Ireland and much of Scot-

land (divided from England by Hadrian's Wall). This meant the influence of Latin on the development of Gaelic happened much later, compared to English, the reason why Irish and Scottish Gaelic have fewer words originating from Latin. See list **124** *section on Crete for details on the oldest Celtic alphabet.*

133
Earliest Written Works in Dutch

The manuscript called *Wachtendonk Psalm*, fragments which survive today, were written around A.D. 910, and are the oldest of several religious manuscript fragments from 10th century Netherlands. The earliest major writer in Dutch was Heinrich (Heindrik) van Veldeke in the 12th century A.D. Because Dutch and German both originated from the West Germanic language group, Veldeke also wrote of the several earliest texts in Middle High German (German language used in the 12th century).

134
Earliest Written Works from Scandinavia

Early languages from Scandinavia and Iceland (such as Old Norse, with the exception of Finnish), all date from the 10th century A.D. The oldest extant Scandinavian manuscript is the *Necrologium Lunense*, written in A.D. 1123. Due to historical and political reasons, Swedish was the language of education and literature in Finland for many centuries up to the 19th century. Thus the earliest major Finnish text is the *Kalevala*, a national epic poem in 1835. But the first recorded Finnish text was the translation of the New Testament by Michael Agricola in 1548. Today Finland uses two official languages, Finnish and Swedish.

135
Earliest Written Works from Turkey and Eastern Europe

In the western or European part of modern Turkey, centered around Constantinople (Istanbul), which was formerly part of the Byzantine Empire, the key script used up to A.D. 1453 was Greek. In the Asian part of modern Turkey (known as Asia Minor or today Anatolia), which was also formerly part of the Byzantine Empire, the Greek script was used until A.D. 1071, when Seljuk Turks, led by sultan Alp-Arslan (of the Turkoman from Moslem Turkistan), captured much of Asia Minor from the Byzantines and introduced the Arabic script. Anatolia became known as the Seljuk Sultanate of Rum in A.D. 1077, with its capital at Nicaea (modern Iznik or Kocaeli). This sultanate was the earliest forerunner of modern Turkey and from which the Turkish language evolved in Anatolia. Hence the earliest documents in Turkish from Anatolia in the Arabic script date from the 11th century. However, the earliest prolific Turkish writer was Yunus Emre in the 1200s. Literature written in Turkish (during the reign of the Seljuk dynasty) was based on Persian models for many centuries until Suleiman the Great became Turkish sultan in 1494 and Turkish texts became more homegrown. Consequently, many Turkish texts of the 11th to late 14th century are based on Persian culture and language. When the Ottoman Turks (who had displaced the Seljuk Turks in Anatolia in 1243 as rulers) captured Constantinople in 1453, the Arabic script replaced the Greek script in the western part of modern Turkey. Turkey continued to use the Arabic script until 1928 when it adopted the Roman script. Two common words in English from Turkish are coffee and yogurt.

Most east European languages belong to the Slavic language family, but two different scripts have been used to write texts: the Cyrillic and Roman scripts. The Cyrillic alphabet, which is somewhat related to the Glagolitic alphabet, dates back to the 9th century A.D. It was developed from the Greek alphabet by Greek monks Saint Cyril and his brother Saint Methodius for use in writing Greek Orthodox Church manuscripts in the Slavic languages. Early major Slavic Cyrillic texts in Russian and Ukrainian such as the *Tale of the Armament of Igor* date from the 10th century A.D. But scholars agree that the oldest example of early Slavic writing is the 10th century *Codex of Suprasl*, written in a monastery near the ancient Bulgarian town of Preslaw. The national libraries of Poland and Slovenia share possession of this ancient relic. Other earliest dates for Slavic languages using the Cyrillic script are: Bulgarian (10th century) and Belarusian (11th century). Serbo-Croat, used in Serbia and Croatia, are very similar languages, except that while Serbian uses the Cyrillic alphabet and most people practice Greek Orthodox Christianity, Croatian uses the Roman alphabet and the people are primarily Roman Catholic. The earliest Serbo-Croat text dates from the 12th century A.D. The most famous early Serbian text is the *Miroslav Gospel* manuscript, dating from 1180. The earliest dates for texts in Slavic East European languages written in the Roman script are: Czech (13th century); Polish (12th century);

Slovenian (14th century); and Macedonian (11th century). Some East European languages are not Slavic in origin. The earliest dates for texts in non–Slavic East European languages written in the Roman alphabet are: Hungarian (13th century); the Baltic states (Estonian, 14th century; Lithuanian, 16th century; Latvian, 14th century); and Albanian (5th century, the most famous Albanian text is the 6th century Christian Codex *Purpureus Beratinus*). Moldovan spoken in nearby Moldova is related to Romanian but uses the Cyrillic script, while Romania also used the Cyrillic script from the 16th century until the 19th century, when it adapted the Roman script.

Before the Greek script was used in Anatolia, the Hittites who inhabited Anatolia from the 2nd millennium B.C. (circa 1900 B.C.) used hieroglyphics and later cuneiform for writing documents. The capital of the Hittite Empire was based at the ancient city of Hattusas (modern Boghazköy, east of Ankara). The Greeks began to establish colonies all along the western (Aegean) and southern (Mediterranean) coasts of Anatolia from around 900 B.C., including Lydia. Although Anatolia was part of the Roman Empire between the 2nd century B.C. and the 2nd century A.D., the Greek script prevailed over the Latin script. In the 4th century A.D., Anatolia developed into the Byzantine Empire before falling to the Turkish Seljuk dynasty. Turkistan is a region in central Asia (east of the Caspian Sea) encompassing modern day Kazakhstan, Uzbekistan, Turkmenistan, Kyrgyzstan, Tajikistan, Siberia, Mongolia and western China. The Orkhon Inscriptions (see below), which describe the ancient history of the Turks and the Tartar khans of Mongolia, provide evidence that Turkish, before it was written in the Arabic script, was written in an unusual non–Aramaic script widespread in western Turkistan. The Tartar tribe of the Turkoman (Turkmen), whose later generations adopted Islam and the Arabic script in the 8th century A.D. and went onto Anatolia to establish what evolved into today's modern Turkey, originally came from western Turkistan.

136
Earliest Written Works from the Asia-Pacific Region

This section excludes texts used from China, the Indian subcontinent, Korea and Japan. Almost all east Asian scripts, except Vietnamese, Malaysian, Filipino and Indonesian, developed from the Brahmi script (see list **124**). The earliest dates of the first Asian texts are: Tibetan script (7th century A.D.); Javanese script (used in Indonesia, and introduced in the 8th century A.D. by Buddhist monks from India); Burmese (11th century); Khmer script (used in Cambodia, 12th century); Laotian script (14th century); and Thai script (13th century, the first major writer was the King of Sukhothai, ruler of the forerunner of Thailand, in 1292, who invented it).

The earliest of several scripts used for early Mongolian texts date back to the 8th century A.D. The oldest extant texts are the *Orkhon Inscriptions*, discovered near a valley in the Orkhon River in northern Mongolia in 1889. Danish philologist Vilhelm Thomsen, who deciphered the inscriptions, noted that they were an early form of a script once used in large areas of ancient Turkistan, before Islam and the Arabic script was introduced. The *Orkhon Inscriptions* are also related to the Turkish alphabet (used before the arrival of Islam), and the Uyghur alphabet used in the eastern Chinese province of Xinjiang, whose descendants, the Uyghurs, are related to the Turkish. The Mongolian language began using the Cyrillic script from 1937 when it was part of the Soviet Union.

Filipino (Tagalog), Vietnamese, Malaysian, and Indonesian texts are all written today in the Roman script, although the last two (technically the same Malay language) were once written in the Arabic script, before European colonialism. The oldest Malay texts date from the 7th century. Some ancient 7th century Malay texts were written in a south Indian Brahmi script called Pallava, based on the script used in the southeastern Indian Pallava dynasty. Sea traders from the region had been venturing from the Bay of Bengal to the west coast of the Malay peninsula and brought along the script. Today the most famous Malay word in English is ketchup. Vietnamese texts were previously written in the Chinese script (when Vietnam was under Chinese rule between 110 B.C. and 939 A.D.), until the 17th century, with the arrival of French missionaries and European traders. Filipino (Tagalog) texts first appeared in the 12th century A.D.

In central Asia, the majority of the earliest texts are as follows: Armenian (5th century A.D., using a unique indigenous Armenian script, based on the Old Persian Pahlavi alphabet); Azerbaijan, 10th century A.D., using the Arabic script. Azeri was also written in the Cyrillic script and most recently in 1992, in the Roman script; Georgian, 5th century A.D., using two Georgian scripts adapted from the Greek script called Khutsuri and Mkhedruli. Georgia and Armenia are the only two central Asian countries still using their own indigenous scripts today (as can be seen in their official government websites). In Kazakhstan, Uzbekistan, and Kyrgyzstan the earliest texts in the Arabic script all date from the late 8th century A.D. In Tajikistan, where Tajik is similar to Farsi, the earliest written documents date back to late 7th century A.D. Written texts in Turkoman (or Turkmen), which is spoken in Turkmenistan and is closely related to the Turkish, are in the Arabic script and date from the early 8th century A.D. In Afghanistan the earliest Pashto or Pushtu (related to Farsi) texts written in the Arabic text date from the 13th century. The Kurdish language (also related to Farsi) used in parts of Turkey, Iran and Iraq, uses three alphabets: Arabic, Roman and Cyrillic. The oldest texts date from the 9th century A.D.

The Pacific Islands can be divided into Melanesia, covering islands east of Indonesia (e.g. the Solomon Islands, Fiji, Vanuatu and Papua New Guinea); Micronesia (covering islands north of Melanesia and west of Polynesia, e.g., Caroline and Marshall Islands, Kiribati and Guam); and Polynesia (covering islands east of Melanesia and Micronesia, e.g., Samoa, Tonga and Tahiti). During human evolution, the first human settlement in the Pacific Ocean occurred first in Melanesia, circa 50,000 years ago before migrating eastwards. Hence the first evidence of human languages occurred in the Melanesian parts of the Pacific Ocean, notably in Papua New Guinea and Fiji. More than 900 Melanesian languages exist, with most spoken in Papua New Guinea. The earliest evidence of writing in the Pacific Ocean is associated with the ancient Lapita culture between 1600 and 500 B.C. Crude examples of petroglyphs or inscriptions on a rock are among relics of the Lapita culture discovered in Papua New Guinea and New Caledonia. The next scientifically authenticated script to originate from the Pacific Islands is the fascinating but mysterious Rongorongo script of the Polynesian Easter Island. Fragments of wooden tablets with the script were discovered in 1868 by Bishop Jaussen of Tahiti and are now preserved in Rome, Italy. They have been dated from the late 1400s. Since Ferdinand Magellan was the first to cross the Pacific Ocean in 1521 and Easter Island was not discovered by Europeans until visited by Dutch explorer Roggeveen in 1722, the Rongorongo script was definitely not influenced by the Roman script. The Lapita culture and the Rongorongo script remain the only major evidence of early major human inscriptions found in the Pacific Ocean islands until the arrival of the first European explorers to major islands of the Pacific Ocean, mostly from Spain, particularly Álvaro Mendaña de Neira, traveling from Peru in 1567, who brought along European languages, the Roman script, and thus literacy to the islands.

137
Earliest Written Works from Africa

Outside Egypt, the African languages (totaling more than 2000 at the last count) with the oldest indigenous alphabets are Ge'ez, Amharic, Old Nubian and Berber (not surprisingly the areas where three of the languages, with Africa's first indigenous alphabets, are spoken are all within close proximity to ancient Egypt). The earliest inscriptions on granite stelae in ancient Ge'ez script used in ancient Ethiopia (the kingdom of Aksum) date from A.D. 190. Ge'ez as a language dates back to the 1st century B.C. when the language and its script was first used in the Sebaean Kingdom in southern parts of the Arabian Peninsula (modern-day Yemen and southern Saudi Arabia). Today Ge'ez is still written in the original Sebaean script. However, it is not an official language in Ethiopia anymore, having been superseded by a later version of the language called Amharic, but Ge'ez is still used today as a liturgical language in the Ethiopian Coptic Church. The oldest extant Ge'ez text in parchment are 4th century A.D. religious texts, most notably the Coptic Christian works of St. Frumentius (Abba Salama), the first bishop of Ethiopia. Coptic Christianity first reached Ethiopia (the second country to adopt the religion in Africa after Egypt) in A.D. 350; the nation managed to hang onto this religious faith while most of its neighbors adopted Islam. Old Nubian was spoken in parts of northern Sudan (known also as Kush or Nubia in ancient times, with its capital at Meroe near modern-day Khartoum) before Arabic was introduced. It has written text,

based on both Egyptian hieroglyphics and the Coptic script. In its earliest form, Old Nubian was first written in what was called the Meroitic script (based on Egyptian hieroglyphics, due to its proximity with ancient Egypt), which dates from about 400 B.C. Later, around the 8th century A.D., Old Nubian adopted the Coptic script (which is based on a pre-Islamic script used in Christian parts of Egypt before it was Arabized). One of the oldest written works in Coptic Old Nubian script is *The Old Nubian Miracle of Saint Menas*, written on parchment circa A.D. 900, and now housed in the British Museum. A Coptic Psalter found in 1984 in Beni Suef, south of Cairo, Egypt, and dating from A.D. 300, is the oldest existing complete handwritten book (in an alphabetical script) in Africa. This Coptic book of Psalms is on display at the Coptic Museum in Cairo, Egypt. But today modern Nubian (Nile Nubian) is hardly in written form, although some modern texts have been written in Arabic script. The Berbers were the original inhabitants of northwestern Africa (Morocco, Algeria, Tunisia and western Libya), before the Arabs invaded North Africa from the 7th century A.D. One group of Berbers, called the Tuaregs, speak a dialect called Tamashek which had been in a written form long before the introduction of Arabic. The indigenous alphabet of Tamashek, which is related to the Phoenician script, is called Tifnagh. Tamashek is also written in the Arabic script. In South Africa, Afrikaans, which originated from Dutch in the 17th century, only became a written language in the late 19th century. The oldest stone inscriptions in Sub-Saharan Africa in a European language are the Portuguese inscriptions chiseled on rocks left on the banks of the Congo River in Africa. They are known today as the *Yelala Inscriptions* and date back to the 1480s. It is believed that Portuguese explorer Diogo Cão made them, during his voyage up the Congo River in 1485. On his return in 1486 (or at least before August 1487) he appears to have re-entered the Congo River, ascending it as far as the Yelala Falls, where an inscription records the names of Diogo Cão, Pedro Annes and Pedro da Costa.

Even though the Ethiopians had written versions of their Amharic language since the 3rd century A.D., *neighboring Somalia had no written version of the Somali language until 1972. However, in nearby Tigre and Eritrea, there were some early 12th century texts. The earliest written example of Tigrinya*

(spoken in Tigre) is a text of local laws found in the district of Logosarda, southern Eritrea, which date from the 13th century. Not counting Arabic, used officially in many parts of Africa where Islam is the official or majority religion, most of Sub-Saharan Africa today did not have any indigenous texts until the arrival of the Arabs for the first time in the 9th century A.D., *mostly in the areas south of the Sahara (e.g., Timbuktu in Mali) and the northeastern coast of Africa, (e.g., Mombasa in Kenya). Two reasons for this were the presence of a strong oral tradition going back for centuries, and the crucial fact that only northern and northeastern portion of Africa was directly exposed to the civilizations of ancient Egypt, the Roman Empire and the Fertile Crescent, the cradle of early civilizations. The huge Sahara Desert and the tropical rainforests formed some natural barriers preventing direct exposure of the early civilizations to other parts of Africa. In the Middle Ages, when Islam managed to penetrate the Sahara Desert, reliable early texts about African arts, customs and*

The Meroitic script was used around 400 B.C. in Sudan for the Old Nubian language. In the eighth century A.D., Old Nubian abandoned the Meroitic script for the Coptic script before northern parts of Sudan fell to Arab invaders and introduced Arabic.

An Ethiopian Ge'ez parchment document dating to A.D. 190. Ethiopia has the oldest existing script in Sub-Saharan Africa.

culture were written mainly by Arabic writers, such as Ibn Battutah in A.D. *1352, who lived and traveled extensively in parts of central and eastern Africa, visiting places such as Timbuktu and Mombasa (both cites were founded by Moslems and soon became Islamic cultural centers). Not surprisingly, many of the these places visited frequently by Battutah and others developed into renowned centers for reading and writing, especially with the establishment of the first Sub-Saharan university, Sankore University in Timbuktu. The manuscripts, produced in these places, although not indigenous, and written in Arabic, were the only comprehensive texts about Africa until the arrival of the European explorers, in the 15th century. One of the earliest such Europeans was Alvise da Cadamosto, an Italian explorer from Venice, in the service of Portugal, who wrote one of the most authentic firsthand written accounts about the West African way of life, in Portuguese, during his voyages there in 1450s. Cadamosto's book, published in 1507 in Vicenza, Italy, by Montalboddo and Rumusio, was also frequently reprinted and translated from Italian into Latin, French and German, as it was one of the first of its kind to appear in Europe. In the 1500s, several attempts were made to document some of the several languages spoken in Europe's first major African colony, Angola, most notably the works of Italian scientist Fillppo Pigafetta in 1591. The first African language to be translated into a European language, to enable written texts (in Roman script) of the African language to be produced, was the transla-*

tion of Kongo, the Bantu language spoken in the ancient kingdom of Kongo (in modern day Angola), into Portuguese in 1624 by Jesuit priests in the kingdom, with help from natives who had learned to speak Portuguese. This book (published in Lisbon) is thus the first extant non-Arabic book written in an African language south of the Sahara (excluding Ethiopia and Sudan). Later, Italian Franciscan friar Giacinto Brusciotto produced a Kongo dictionary with Portuguese, Latin and Italian translations in 1650. Brusciotto also produced several further books on the Kongo language, published in Rome in the middle 1650s. Kongo thus became the first Sub-Saharan African language to be widely documented by European scholars. The first major Sub-Saharan African language to adopt the Arabic script was Hausa (spoken in the northern parts of Nigeria and in southern Niger), in the 16th century. But the Roman script was taken up for writing Hausa in the 19th century, when British explorers arrived. Finally the majority of history books today agree that the Portuguese were the first to explore the African coast from the early 1430s via Prince Henry the Navigator. However, the Laurentian Library in Florence, Italy, contains the oldest accurate map of Africa, Portolano Laurenziano Gaddiano, made circa 1351 by Genoese cartographers based on information from 13th century Genoese and Venetian sailors (notably the Vivaldo brothers and Tedisio Doria from Genoa who all reached the Senegalese coast in 1291). This has undoubtedly left historians baffled about who were the actually first explorers of the African coast.

138
Oldest Existing Papyrus Manuscript

The oldest surviving papyrus document is the *Prisse Papyrus*, preserved at the National Library of France. It dates back to 2300 B.C. and was written in ancient Egyptian hieroglyphics (see list **124** for more details) The national library of Austria (Department of Papyri) holds the biggest papyrus collection in Europe and the second largest collection after the one at the Egyptian Museum in Cairo.

The ancient Egyptian city of Oxyrhynchus, south of Cairo, has been the source of numerous Latin, Greek and Arabic papyrus manuscripts, discovered by British archeologists Grenfell and Hunt in the late 1890s. Most have been preserved British and U.S. locations, notably the Ashmolean Museum in the U.K. (see list **100***) and Princeton Theological Seminary in New Jersey, the U.S. Collectively the collection is called the* Oxyrhynchus Papyri.

139
Oldest Existing Parchment Manuscript

The Vatican Library is home to the oldest surviving fine parchment manuscript, the *Codex Vaticanus*. The Greek Bible dates back to A.D. 300. (See list **124** for more details.)

140
Oldest Existing Vellum Manuscript

The British Library is home to the oldest surviving vellum manuscript, the *Codex Sinaiticus*. The Greek Bible (New Testament only) dates back to A.D. 350. (See list **124** for more background details.)

141
Oldest Written Works by Subject

It is now obvious that some of the earliest and oldest extant texts around the world in the regions so far discussed in this chapter are either religious or political documents, or literature such as poetry and prose. But early documents on subjects such as law, medicine and science did eventually appear. The following are selections of the earliest and oldest most comprehensive extant texts in a variety of subjects (excluding religion, politics and literature).

Medicine

1. Ancient Egyptian papyri. About 9 important ancient Egyptian medical papyri exist today, preserved in Europe and the U.S. They all date from 1900 to 1600 B.C., and include the *Ebers Papyrus, Ramesseum Papyrus, Berlin Papyrus, Leiden Papyrus* and *Kahoun Papyrus.* The oldest of these papyri is the *Ebers Paypyrus.* It was discovered by German Egyptologist George Maurice Ebers at Thebes in 1873. Dated to 1900 B.C., it is the oldest medical work known, containing hundreds of folk remedies for various diseases.

2. *Atreya Sumhita.* India. Originally written on leaves around 800 B.C., it is part of the ancient Sanskrit *Veda* texts called *Atharva or Atharvaveda.*

3. *Neijing* or *Yellow Emperor's Classic of Internal Medicine.* Written on bones in China, circa 770 B.C., and copied onto paper, when it was invented 400 years later.

4. *Corpus of Simples* is a 12th century Arabic manuscript made in Malaga during the Umayyad Caliphate of Islamic Spain. It was also a very important pharmacological manuscript as it described over 1000 drugs from plants.

Mathematics

1. Euclid's *Stoicheia* (a book composed of 13 separate volumes) was the first major work on mathematics. The Greek mathematician completed the text, circa 300 B.C. His work formed the basis for teaching mathematics in academies and universities for the next 2,000 years. It was translated first into Arabic when the Arabs overran ancient Egypt in the 8th century A.D. and came across several classical Greek texts of famous scientists at Alexandria (where Euclid had earlier set up his school of mathematics) and taken then to Baghdad, the capital of the ruling Abbasid caliphate. Next it was translated from Arabic into Latin at the Toledo Translation School in Spain in the 11th century A.D. (see list **123**) before being translated later into other European languages. It was not until the 19th century that several scientists, such as

German mathematician Georg Riemann, began to reject some parts of Euclid's main theories, especially on geometry, and developed what is called non–Euclidean mathematics. Einstein's famous Theory of Relativity is based on non–Euclidean mathematics. Nevertheless, for 2000 years Euclid's texts remained excellent examples of classical Greek knowledge in the development of mathematics.

2. The first major non–Greek text on mathematics in the medieval period were those written by Indian mathematicians notably Aryabhata and Yativrsabha in the 6th century A.D., and by Arab mathematician Muhammad Bin Musa Al-Khwarizmi in the 9th century A.D. He invented *Al-Jabr* (algebra). Al-Khwarizmi also worked in Bagdad as Abbasid Caliph Al-Mamun's librarian. His texts, based on the earlier Euclidian theories and Indian mathematics, were also later translated into Latin at the Toledo Translation School. One of the translations of Al-Khwarizmi's work at Toledo by English monk Adelard of Bath, written in the 12th century, was a major mathematics textbook in the Middle Ages. (See the notes at list **123**.)

Law

Babylonian King Hammurabi published the *Code of Laws*, circa 1700 B.C. The oldest comprehensive legal texts or statutes are the ancient Greek Draco Laws compiled in Athens circa 620 B.C. Before ancient Rome became an empire, it existed as a republic from 510 B.C. to 30 B.C. The famous 12 bronze tablets of Roman Republic codified laws (*Lex XII Tabularum*) were completed in 450 B.C. They were then publicly displayed in the Forums.

Military Science

The *Art of War* by Sun-Tzu is oldest existing military treatise, written in 475 B.C. during the Chinese Warring State Period.

Astronomy

The oldest astronomy manuscript is the 7th century A.D. *Dun Huang scroll.* It is a Chinese astronomical chart and contained the most accurate measurements showing the locations of stars and other space bodies better than ancient Greek and Arabic texts until appearance of Renaissance astronomers like Galileo and Copernicus.

Sports

The first football book was made in Florence in 1580, and was titled *Discorso sopra il gioco del Calcio Fiorentino* by Giovanni de Bardi. It explains the rules of 16th century Italian football.

142
Oldest Existing Books Made from Paper

Two documents are the oldest existing paper manuscripts in the world. The first is the *Dharani Sutra*, made in South Korea in A.D. 704. It is about 21 feet long and is stored at the Seoul National Museum. The second is the *Diamond Sutra* (*Chin-kang Ching* or *Jin gang Jing*) which was made in China circa A.D. 868 by Wang Chieh (Jie). A seven-page scroll printed with wood blocks on paper and measuring 1 foot wide by 17 feet long, first of a series of books on Buddhist incantations ordered by Japanese Empress Shotoku. Discovered in the early 20th century by Aurel Stein, a British archaeologist, the document is now housed in the British Library. Sutras are teachings and discourses of the Buddha. Because Buddhism was a major religion in China in the 8th century A.D., and books on religious topics were the most important kinds of early books produced in many parts of the world at that time, it is not surprising that the two manuscripts described above are both Buddhist manuscripts. The first major book printed in Europe was another religious book, the Bible (the Gutenberg Bible).

The earliest use of paper in Europe dates back to A.D. 950 in southern Spain, notably Islamic Mur-

Ruins of the Forum in Rome, Italy. Forums were public meeting places in ancient Roman towns and were the ideal place for the first statutes in the Roman Republic, the *Lex XII Tabularum*, to be put on display for citizens to read and obey.

cia, Granada and Córdoba, where the large Arab communities (Moors) used it for administrative purposes. The art of making paper from wood fiber first reached Spain around A.D. 1098 when Arab traders from Fez, in Morocco, took paper making techniques with them to the Spanish towns of Játiva (formerly called Xativa) and Capellades, both of which had the earliest papermills in Europe. Not surprisingly, the oldest paper manuscript in Europe preserved at the El-Escorial Monastic Library in Spain dates back to A.D. 1009. The third oldest extant manuscript made from paper in Europe is the Spanish *Silos Missal*, a prayer book used by Spanish Catholic priests in Burgos, which dates back to A.D. 1110. After Spain, paper was later introduced into central Europe through the Italian ports at Genoa, Venice and Palermo from 1258 (the second oldest document on paper in Europe is a deed of King Roger I of Palermo, Sicily, written in Greek and Arabic in A.D. 1102). In these Italian ports commerce had long existed between the Italians and Arabs from faraway Baghdad, Damascus, and Cairo. In these Arabic cities, paper was already in use and manufactured in papermills in the 8th and 9th century

A.D. But paper had remained unknown outside China for over 600 years, having been invented by Ts'ai Lun (Ts'ai Louen) in Lei-yang earlier in A.D. 105, when he used vegetable fibers to make the very first paper from pulp and told Emperor Ho Ti, who decided to keep it intentionally secret from the outside world. From China, the first countries to learn about paper production were Korea in A.D. 602 and Japan in A.D. 610. The Arabs were said to have discovered how to manufacture paper soon after the A.D. 751 Battle of Talas River, near the city of Samarkand (the famous center of the Chinese silk trade route now in modern-day Uzbekistan). This battle between Arab Muslim forces led by Ziyad bin Salih and a Chinese army led by Kao-Hsien-Chih, during the Chinese Tang dynasty (618–907), was the only major conflict between Arabs and the army of the Chinese Empire. After Samarkand was captured by the Arabs, the few papermakers among the Chinese prisoners taken in the battle passed on the secret of making paper to the victorious Arabs. The technique of making paper then reached Mecca, then Baghdad in A.D. 793 and other Arabic cities such as Damascus, and they became the largest supplier of *paper and market in the world in 9th and 12th centuries. Chinese religious libraries were the first libraries in the world to stock manuscripts made from paper, and the earliest such libraries included those of the Han dynasty, which ruled China when paper was invented. Islamic libraries were the next libraries to have book collections made from paper. After the introduction of books made with paper at the Spanish university libraries of Palencia and Salamanca, the first European academic libraries to stock books made with paper were Italian university libraries such as those at Bologna and Padua. The Italian papermills at Fabriano and Amalfi were set up around 1276 A.D. From Italy and Spain, the art of paper making and the setting up of papermills spread to other European countries such as France (1348, in the Saint-Julien region near Troyes); Germany (1390, in Nuremberg); Poland (1491 in Kraków); the U.K. (1494, in Stevenage, Hertfordshire); and Sweden (in 1690 in Uppsala). It is worth mentioning that paper imported from Arab papermills was used in significant quantities in some parts of Europe well before papermills were set up. Outside Europe, and the Middle East, in places such as the Americas, papermills were set up, first in Mexico by Spanish colonists in 1575, and then in 1690*

A Chinese block printed book.

The Dharani Sutra is the oldest block printed manuscript and the oldest manuscript printed on paper.

in the American English colonies and a few years later in the French colony of Quebec. Elsewhere in central Asia, friendship between Arab merchants from Samarkand and Asian leaders such as King Zanulabin Budshah of Kashmir bought paper production knowledge to the Indian subcontinent from 1420. Until the onset of the industrial revolution in the 19th century, most paper production was a manual process. The use of machines in paper production was not widespread in India during the colonial times and today India has the largest population of hand papermakers in the world. Paper production itself around the world has been so similar that a problem of paper decay was not treated seriously until the middle of the 20th century. In research carried out in 1980, the New York Public Library in the U.S. estimated that over 98 percent of books published between 1900 and 1937 would disintegrate completely in 30 to 50 years' time because of the amount of acid in the paper on which the book is printed. In 2003, French newspaper Le Monde *reported that nearly 65 percent of books and manuscript published between 1975 and 1960 stored at the National Library of Paris would disintegrate. The only way to ensure that the books' contents survive is to microfilm them or digitize them. Some libraries decided on mass deacidification projects in which they deacidify old books with a chemical treatment such as magnesium oxide (MgO) to neutralize acid in the paper. At the National Library of Paris about 20,000 books are deacidified yearly at a cost of $7 to $8 per book. Today alkaline-based paper is used in book production, as the paper lasts longer. International Paper, based in Stamford, Connecticut, in the U.S., is the largest manufacturer of paper in the world, with sales of over $22 billion in 2006.*

143
First Block Printed Books

Before the advent of printing in the 15th century, production and copying of text around the world was done manually. The Chinese and Koreans were the first to break this tradition by experimenting with block-printing in 6th century A.D. (long after paper was invented in 105 A.D.). Both the 8th century A.D. *Dharani Sutra* and the 9th century A.D. *Diamond Sutra* (both discussed earlier) are the two oldest surviving block-printed manuscripts today. The largest voluminous block printed book with the most pages is a 13th century book preserved at the Haeinsa Temple on Mount Kaya, in South Korea. Block printing was used for many centuries in China, Korea and later Japan until the 9th and 10th centuries A.D. when crude forms of movable type (typographic printing) were invented and experimented with, using clay, wood, bronze and iron. However, the complexity of the Chinese ideographic scripts (used also in Korea) discouraged further development of printing with movable type, and block printing remained the de facto way of printing books in China, Korea and Japan until the late 1500s. But a Chinese book was successfully printed with movable type in A.D. 1050 by Pi Sheng (Bi Sheng). The world would have to wait a little over 400 years before a better form of movable type printing was invented by Gutenberg. Meanwhile UNESCO actually recognizes a Korean book as the oldest evidence of movable metal type. The book titled *Jikji Simgyeong*, printed in 1377 in Chongju, is a collection of texts on Zen Buddhism compiled by a Korean Buddhist priest named Baegun, and is today preserved at the National Library of France. *Jikji Simgyeong* has been included in UNESCO's Memory of the World Register (see list **122**). Although block-printing was invented in China in the 6th century A.D., it was unknown in Europe until after paper was introduced into Europe in the 12th century A.D. Marco Polo also wrote about block-printing activities when he returned to Italy from his extensive travels to China in the 13th century. The three oldest extant block printed books in Europe are: *Biblia Pauperum,* a 14th century German block-printed Bible and today the most expensive block-printed book in the world (see list **207** on the most expensive manuscripts); *St. Christopher,* printed circa 1423, discovered in the library of the Carthusian monastery in Buxheim, Germany; and the *Apocalypse of St. John,* printed in 1450.

144
First Book Printed with Movable Type

Whether Johann Gutenberg, who invented an improved method of movable type printing, knew about similar early crude movable type devices used in China (described by Marco Polo) and Korea is open to debate. Gutenberg, in Mainz, Germany, printed the 42-line Gutenberg Bible in 1455. This was the first successful attempt to make multiple copies of any manuscript very quickly, without the need to reproduce them by handwriting, which was slow and frequently inaccurate or with the slower painstaking method of block-printing. In many parts of Europe there were some form of block-printing activity before Gutenberg's invention finally gathered pace. Two original editions of the Gutenberg Bible exist today. One is housed in a museum of printing in Mainz, while the other made its way to the Mazarin Library in Paris, France. The Gutenberg Bible was printed in Latin, not German. About 46 paper and vellum 1st edition copies are still in existence in places such as the British Library, the U.S. Library of Congress, the National Library of France, the New York Public Library, and the libraries at Harvard and Yale universities in the United States. The first books printed in German were later editions of the Bible by Gutenberg and others in the late 15th century such as *Biblia*, printed in 1466 by Johann Mentelin. With the overall popularity of Gutenberg's printing device widespread, no further European block-printing books were printed after the early 16th century. Once a book has been printed, it has to be bound, usually at a printer or a separate bindery. The world's oldest existing book bindery is based at the Sorbonne University of Paris, in France, which has been printing and binding books since about A.D. 1470.

Apart from UNESCO's recognition of Jikji Simgyeong printed in 1377 (see list **143** *above), there is only one other authenticated book with movable type before Gutenberg. That was printed by Laurens Janszoon Coster from Haarlem in The Netherlands. Coster demonstrated movable type printing in 1423. And in the 1430s several types of what has been called*

metallographic printing were widespread in The Netherlands. In fact, Gutenberg had actually practiced metallographic printing in Strasbourg, France, in 1439 before he set up his printing press in Mainz. The Arabs (who themselves had passed on the secrets of making paper to the Europeans), were interested only in the hand-copying of books, as they felt nothing else could replace the fine handwritings of Arabic calligraphers. This dislike of movable type printing explains why throughout the Arab world the Koran was only hand-copied until 1825, when the first official copies of the Koran were printed with movable type. While paper found its way from China to Europe, it was Gutenberg's method of movable type that was finally adopted in China as the de facto method of printing books, when Jesuit priests introduced it there in 1589. From Mainz, printing presses were established in Basel, Switzerland (1466); Subiaco, Italy (1465); Utrecht, The Netherlands (1470); London, U.K. (1475); Valencia, Spain (1473); Paris, France (1480); Lisbon, Portugal (1487); St. Petersburg, Russia (1562); Mexico City, Mexico (1533); and Cambridge, Massachusetts (U.S.) (1638). The use of paper in medieval Europe did run into early problems. Around the time paper was introduced in medieval Europe, there was a very lucrative market for parchment and vellum in the 13th century. And the fact that paper was introduced into Europe by Arabs was enough for the Holy Roman Emperor Frederick II (who led the 6th Crusade) to issue an edict in A.D. 1221 that any official or legal document written on paper was invalid. However when Gutenberg printed the first book and printing presses began to appear all over Europe in the 15th century, the dislike for paper in Europe was soon forgotten. Following the invention of printing with movable type, the first attempt to speed up printing, i.e., mechanically with a machine, was the invention of the linotype machine by Otto Mergenthaler in Germany in 1884, which worked on the principles of the modern typewriter. Full integration of computers with printing began with the invention of Desk Top Publishing or DTP in 1985 with the introduction of Aldus PageMaker version 1 for the Apple Macintosh, by Paul Brainerd, founder of Aldus (now part of Adobe). Later on, QuarkXPress version 1 was introduction in 1987. The next revolution in printing and publishing books was the introduction of CD-ROM-based books in the middle 1980s, and the ad-

An early Victorian printing press based on the Gutenberg model of the 1450s. Even though Gutenberg's invention allowed books to reproduced quickly, doing away with hand copying, the printing press was still manually operated until it was speeded up with Mergenthaler's linotype machine of 1884.

vent of the Internet and publishing on the web, which became feasible when Netscape Navigator version 1 (based on the 1993 Mosaic web browser) was released in October 1994. The latest innovation in the production of books is the electronic book or e-book, which can either be available on a CD-ROM or can be downloaded from the Internet onto laptops or hand-held PDAs (Personal Digital Assistants). These devices, such as the Ipaq Pocket PC, use the Windows Mobile operating systems. Software for reading e-books includes Microsoft Reader, and Adobe Acrobat. E-Books began to make a major impact from early 1999 with publishers such as Oxford University Press releasing e-book simultaneously with printed books. In 2000 horror fiction writer Stephen King invited his readers to pay $2.50 to download from the Internet an e-book version of his novella Riding the Bullet. In this way his readers bypassed his publishers, who were shocked at the development. Since then more than 600,000 downloads have been made. Aside from books, journals and newspapers are also now widespread in electronic form alongside print form, and are mostly in HTML or PDF format for access and downloading via the Internet. A list of services that offer access to thousands of e-books and electronic journals and newspapers can be seen at list **283**.

145
First Books Printed in English and Scottish

Recuyell of the Histories of Troye was printed by William Caxton on 1474 in Belgium. It was written by Raoul Lefèvre. The first printed book in Scottish Gaelic was a translation of Knox's *Prayer Book* in 1567.

146
First Books Printed in English in the U.K.

William Caxton printed *Dictes and Sayings of the Philosophres* in 1475 at his printing press in Westminster, London, when he returned there from Belgium. *The Canterbury Tales* was printed by Caxton in 1477 in London. These printed Caxton works and others are preserved at the British Library.

147
First Books Printed in English in the U.S. and Canada

Massachusetts Bay Colony: Oath of a Free Man was printed in 1638 in Cambridge, Massachusetts. Stephen Daye printed the *Bay Psalm Book* in 1640 in Cambridge, Massachusetts. In January 1947, Yale University Library bought the last copy up for sale.

Before New Mexico became a state in the U.S. following the 1846 Mexican-American War, it was part of independent Mexico from 1821. Going back further in time, New Mexico was part of the Spanish colony of Neuva España or New Spain. During this time the Spanish Governor Gasparde Villagra had a book he wrote on the history of Mexico, printed in 1610 in Santa Fe, thus this book (although written in Spanish) was the first to be printed in the U.S. In 1765, Joseph Briand's book Catechism, *printed Quebec, was the first in Canada*

148
First Books Printed in French

Recueil des histories de Troyes by Raoul Lefèvre was printed in 1466. *Éditions de Luxe* was printed by French publisher and businessman Jean Dupré in Paris in 1481.

149
First Book Printed in Italian

German monks Arnold Pannartz and Konrad Sweinheim printed *De Oratore* in Subiaco (east of Rome) in 1465. The production of the book, written by Marcus Cicero, took place at the Benedictine monastery of Subiaco, which was the cradle of Italian printing.

150
First Books Printed in Spanish, Portuguese and Basque

Fernando de Córdoba and Lamberto Palmart printed *Les obres o trobes dauall scrites les quals tracten dela sacratissima verge Maria* in Valencia in 1475. The first book in the Basque language (used officially alongside Spanish in the Basque Provinces of northern Spain) was printed in 1545. Samuel Gacon printed the first book in Portuguese, *Pentateuco*, in 1487 in Faro, Portugal. *Sacramental* by Clemente Sánchez de Vercial was printed in 1488.

151
First Books Printed in Russian and Eastern European Languages

Ivan Fedorov printed the first book, a Russian translation of a Latin Bible, *Apostol,* in 1564 in Lvov (Lviv) in Ukraine, where he was in exile. But copies of his book found their way to Russia. He also produced the first book in Ukrainian. Early in 1520 Fedorov published the first handwritten book in Russia, on the Bible's New Testament. It is known as the Russian Gutenberg.

In Eastern Europe, the years in which the first books were printed are as follow: Czech, 1468; Croatian, 1483; Serbian, 1494; Ukrainian, 1494; Polish, 1513; Lithuanian, 1521; Hungarian, 1533; Latvian 1585; Romanian (Deacon Coresi printed Romanian translations of the *Acts of the Apostles* in 1563. In 1508, a book had been printed in Romania, but not in Romanian.)

152
First Books Printed in Scandinavia

Johan Snell printed *Dialogus Creatururum Moralizatus* in Stockholm, Sweden, in 1483. Gotfried van Os (Gotfred of Ghemen) printed several books including *Den danske rimkrønike* in Copenhagen, Denmark, in 1489. Bartholemeus Ghota's *Missale Aboense* was printed in Turku, Finland, in 1488.

153
First Book Printed in Irish

In 1571, John Ussher's *An Irish Alphabet and Catechism* was the first book printed in Irish, while Humphrey Powell's *Book of Common Prayer*, printed in 1551 in English, was the first book printed in Ireland.

Although made before printing was invented, the 7th century Book of Kells, *has been described as the most beautiful book in the world. It is an ancient manuscript from medieval Celtic Ireland and is preserved at Trinity College, Dublin University Library.*

The book, produced in St. Columba's monastery of Iona, contains the four gospels of the Bible in Latin. Some parts of the book at the beginning and at the end have been lost in time.

154
First Book Printed in Arabic

Samuel Nedivot's *Abudarham* was printed in Arabic in Fez, Morocco, in 1516.

155
First Books Printed in Turkish and Greek

David and Samuel Ibn Nahmias printed *Arba'ah Turim* (*The Four Rows*) in 1493 in Istanbul. Constantine Lascaris printed the first Greek book in Milan, Italy, in 1476.

The book was printed in Arabic script because Turkish was not written in Roman script until 1928. During the time the Turkish Ottoman Empire ruled Greece following the capture of Athens in 1456, there was a total ban on the printing of books. As such, Greece had no printing press until 1921, when by that time it was already independent. Books in Greek before then had to be imported from Milan, Venice, Italy, and from other European countries.

156
First Book Printed in Farsi

Iran (formerly called Persia), like most other Moslem countries, did not adopt printing with movable type till the early 19th century, hence the first book printed in Iran was an Armenian translation of the Bible, printed in 1638 in New Julfa by Armenian Primate Khach'atur. Located near the border with Azerbaijan, New Julfa at that time was part of the Persian Safavid dynasty of Shah Abas I.

The Armenians, who were Christians, had adopted movable type printing way back in 1512 when the first Armenian book was printed in Italy.

Throughout the Arab world, the Koran was only hand-copied from the 8th century A.D. until 1825, when the first official copies of the Koran were printed. The reason for this was that the style of the calligrapher's fine handwritings made the Koran look better.

157
First Book Printed in Hebrew

Arba'ah Turim (*The Four Rows*) by Jacob Ben Asher was printed in Sefed in 1475. Sefed, also known as Safed, was part of the Turkish Ottoman Empire. It is now the Jewish holy city Tzfat. However the first book printed anywhere in Hebrew was a work by Rashi on the *Torah* that was printed in Rome in 1470.

158
First Books Printed in Hindi

The first major book printed in India was Portuguese book *Coloquios dos Simples e drogas he da India*, by Garcia D'Orta in 1563 in Goa, then a Portuguese colony. The first book written in Hindi was printed in 1670 by Bhimjee Parikh in Bombay (Mumbai), who had a book printing business. The first book to be printed in an Indian language was *Thambiran va Nakkam*, which was printed in Tamil in 1578 by Portuguese Jesuit missionary Henrique Henriques in Goa.

159
First Book Printed in Australia

The first book printed in Australia was Raffaello Carbini's *New South Wales General Standing Orders*, in 1802.

160
First Book Printed in Chinese

The Chinese produced their first printed book (based on Gutenberg's model) in 1589. But a Chinese book was successfully printed with movable type in A.D. 1050 by Pi Sheng (Bi Sheng). See list **143**.

161
First Books Printed in Japanese and Korean

The first book printed with movable type in Japan was in 1596 (based on Gutenberg's model).

Jikji Simgyeong was printed in 1377 in Seoul, South Korea, by a Korean Buddhist priest named Baegun. See list **143**.

162
First Book Printed in Southeast Asia

A Spanish colonialist in Manila in the Philippines printed *Doctrina Christiana* in 1593.

163
First Book Printed in Latin America

Bishop Juan de Zumarraga printed, in Mexico City in 1536, the first book that is still extant. But Juan Pablos in Mexico City had printed a much earlier book in 1534, but no copies exist today.

164
First Book Printed in Africa

Samuel Nedivot's *Abudarham* was printed in Arabic in Fez, Morocco, in 1516.

In 1513, a book of Psalms was printed in the ancient Ethiopian language of Ge'ez by a German printer with the help of Ethiopian monk Abba Tesfatsion, but it was printed in Rome. However, after Dutch settlers set up a printing press in South Africa in the late 18th century, Ethiopia set up the second oldest printing press in non–Muslim Africa in the 1863 in Massawa. Ethiopia adopted Christianity in the 4th century A.D., making it the earliest African country after Egypt to do so. It also has the second oldest civilization in Africa after that of Egypt; it is more than 2000 years old. These two facts give some credence to the mysterious link between the Ark of the Covenant, as described in the Bible, and Ethiopia. According to ancient Ethiopian tradition and backed up by stone inscriptions in Ge'ez, going back to the time Ethiopia was part of the kingdom of Aksum, Menelik I, the first emperor of Ethiopia, was a son of the biblical King Solomon and the Queen of Sheba. The young Menelik I grew up in Ethiopia and at some point in his adult life was able to travel to Jerusalem around the 6th century B.C. during the reign of King Manasseh. When he was about to return home, Menelik I and his entourage removed the original Ark of the Covenant from King Solomon's temple and took it back to Ethiopia. It was then stored in the Church of St. Mary Zion. Inside this religious artifact is believed to be Tablets of the Law that were given to Moses on Mount Sinai circa 1400 B.C. This stone tablet, written in ancient Hebrew, contained inscriptions found today in the five oldest books of the Jewish Old Testament or the Torah, most notably the 10 Commandments. The location of the Ark of the Covenant today is unknown. It may still be in Ethiopia, but the 1981 film Raiders of the Lost Ark *depicts the Ark of the Covenant as being in Egypt. Some say it rests beneath the Temple Mount in Israel. Western journalists have spent years researching in libraries trying to find the location of the original Ark of the Covenant. If it is ever found again, the Tablets of the Law will probably be the most important religious text discovered since the Dead Sea Scrolls in 1947.*

165
Largest Collection of Books Printed Before 1501

The Bavarian State Library located in the German city of Munich, has the most extensive collection of incunabula, or books printed before 1501, in the world. The library, founded in 1558, has been actively collecting 15th and 16th century books dating from the time of Gutenberg. It now has over 10,000 incunabula.

The Library of Congress in Washington, D.C., the British and French national libraries, the Vatican Library in Rome, the El-Escorial Library in Spain, the Mazarin Library in Paris, France, the Ambrosian Library in Milan, and the Laurentian Library in Florence (both in Italy) all own the next largest and rarest collections of books and manuscripts dating before the 16th century. Another notable rich collection can be found in Biblioteca Comunale dell'Archiginnasio in Bologna, Italy. Its incunabula are so rare that the library attracts an endless stream of scholars and prominent figures from all over the world. The library was established in 1801 to gather the book material of the religious orders dispersed by Napoleon Bonaparte and it now has over 750,000 books among which are 3,500 incunabula and 15,000 rare 16th century books.

166
Oldest Book Museum

For almost 100 years, the German Book and Writing Museum (*Deutsches Buch- und Schriftmuseum*) in Leipzig has been collecting, preserving and indexing documents about the

Top: Incunabula section at the Vatican Library in Rome (© Biblioteca Apostolica Vaticana). *Bottom:* Incunabula section at the British Library in London.

history and development of books from 5000 year old ancient clay tablets to the electronic book (e-book) of the third millennium. The museum also holds the world's largest collection of watermarks. The largest museum library in Europe is the German Museum of Science and Technology Library (Deutsches Museum Bib-

liothek), based in Munich and Bonn. Founded in 1903, its library has over 860,500 books and 20,000 journals relating to the history of science and technology. The largest museum library in the U.S. is at the Smithsonian Institution in Washington, D.C.

167
Six Earliest Dates in Copyright

Once paper production was common in Europe and moveable type printing invented, it began to occur to many that there was a need to protect books from piracy, since mass production of them was now possible. Following are six significant dates that played a major role in the development of copyright as we know it today.

1. 15th century. Venetian government in Venice, Italy, introduces the *Privilegii,* a series of privileges pertaining to the protection of printed works in the republic. These were the forerunners to modern copyright.

2. The first copyrights under the *Privilegii* rules are granted to John de Speyer (1469), Marc An-

Apart from displaying cultural heritage relics, museums also have libraries. The German Museum of Science and Technology in Munich is the largest museum library in Europe.

tonio Sabellico (1486), Bernadinus de Choris (1491), and the famous Aldus Manutius (1496), who gave us *italic* type.

In comparison, the first recorded patent for an industrial invention was granted to Italian Filippo Brunelleschi in 1421.

3. Thomas Godfry is granted the first British copyright in 1510 for his book *The History of King Boccus*. This is the first English book to be given a copyright. The second was granted to Henry VIII's printer Richard Pynson in 1518.

The copyrights were issued before the 1710 Statute of Anne, which is the basis for modern copyright in the U.K.

4. In 1514, Thomas Murner, a famous German satirist who wrote *Geuchmatt,* was the first author to be paid royalties for a published work.

5. The world's first copyright law was legalized in the Venetian Republic in 1533, replacing the *Privilegii.* The first comprehensive statutory copyright law was the British Copyright Act of 1710, also known as the Statute of Anne. After this, several other nations introduced similar statutory copyright laws, such as the U.S. in 1790, France in 1793 and Germany in 1839.

6. In 1537, the National Library of France ordered that all French printing presses to deliver a copy of every copyrighted book they had printed to the royal library (which later became the present National Library of France). Thus the French national library was the first to make this a legal requirement, and it is now a standard practice for nearly all national libraries today. But not all such libraries follow this rule; for instance, in China there is no legal deposit law (although such laws do exist in Hong Kong and Macau).

Denmark was the first to introduce international copyright in 1828. This was a reciprocal agreement in which foreign authors in Denmark would receive the same protection of their work as Danish authors. The Bern Convention of 1886 legalized the standard

The government of the Venetian Republic (today's Venice, Italy) was the first to introduce some sort of legislation to protect books from unauthorized copying.

for international copyright. With the explosion of electronic versions of books, such as encyclopedias on the web or on CD-ROM, copyright laws have been drafted to protect such new digital formats. An international digital copyright treaty put forward in December 1996 by the Geneva-based World Intellectual Property Organization (the Internet Treaties) covers international protection of copyright on the Internet and other digital media such as CD-ROM books and DVDs. A number of countries around the world have already ratified the treaty. The 1998 Digital Millennium Copyright Act, passed by the U.S. Congress, is concerned with, among other things, the application of copyright law to digital formats such as e-books, computer games and websites.

168
First Autobiography

The earliest major autobiography was written 397 A.D. by Roman Bishop and prolific writer St. Aurelius Augustine of Hippo, one of the earliest Christian leaders in Rome, just after Christianity was adopted as the state religion in the Roman Empire in the 4th century A.D. The title of the autobiography was *Confessions*.

169
First Book to Use Page Numbers

In 1470 in Cologne, Germany, printers of the book *Sermo Populam* by Werner Rolewinck added page numbers for the first time in a printed book.

170
First Book with Illustrations (Not Photographs)

The first printer to add illustrations to his books was Albrecht Pfister of Bamberg, Germany. Pfister began printing around 1460 when he bought the press from Gutenberg. By adding pictures he helped explain the text, a concept soon copied by other printers. In 1476 a book titled *De Casibus Illustrium Virorum* written by Baccaccio was printed in Belgium, with illustrations drawn by artists.

171
First Book to Use Photographs

Three books appeared in the 1840s with black and white photographs for the first time. In 1842 photographs were included in a printed book titled *Excursions Daguerriennes* by Lerebours. *Photographs of British Algae, Cyanotype Impressions, 1843–53*, by Anna Atkin, was the first book to use photographic illustrations. The book was auctioned in 2004 at Christie's. In 1844, William Talbot, an early pioneer in the development of cameras, provided several photographs he took for use in a book he wrote titled *Pencil of Nature*.

172
First Book Printed in Color

Color printing arrived in 1456 with the production of the *Mainz Psalter* by German printers Peter Schoffer and Johann Fust. This book was also the first to give the date and place of printing and the printer's names. Schoffer also assisted Johannes Gutenberg.

173
First Book to Be Published on Tape (Talking Book)

In 1957 an entire book on cassette tape was produced for sale in bookstores. The book published by *Tape Recording* magazine was appropriately titled *All About Tape on Tape.*

174
First Regular Newspapers

Nieuwe Tijdingen, produced in Antwerp, Belgium, in 1605, was the first printed modern newspaper in the world. A 1621 edition of the newspaper still exists today at the Belgian national library. The first English newspaper was the *Corante*, a translation of a Dutch newspaper which was published in London in 1621. The first daily newspaper was the German *Einkommende Zeitung* in 1650. Austria's *Wiener Zeitung* is the oldest continuously published newspaper, having begun in 1703 in Vienna. Here are the years in which the first modern newspapers were printed in other continents: North America (the U.S. in 1689, the first official newspaper was the *Boston News* in 1704); South America (Peru in 1744); Africa (South Africa in 1800); Caribbean Islands (Dominican Republic in 1804); Asia-Pacific region (the Philippines in 1811; in Japan, during the Tokugawa period, there were earlier regular news reports called yomiuri); the Middle East (Turkey in 1831).

*The largest daily circulation of newspapers in the world by continent are: Europe (*Bild-Zeitung, *Germany); North America (*Wall Street Journal, *U.S.), South America (*O Estado de São Paulo, *Brazil); Asia-Pacific region (*Yomiuri Shimbun, *Japan); and Africa (*The Star, *South Africa). For information on the largest edition of a newspaper see list* **192**.

175
First Printed Magazines

Erbauliche Monaths-Unterredungen (*Edifying Monthly Discussions*) was published in Berlin, Germany, in 1664. *Mercure Galant* was published in Paris, France, in 1672. The first English language magazine was *The Gentleman's Magazine,* published in London in 1708.

176
First Scholarly or Academic Journal

Philosophical Transactions was first published in 1665 by the Royal Society in London. It is also the oldest continuously published periodical in any subject in the world today.

177
First Law Journals

Journal du Palais was published in Paris, France, in 1673.

178
First Medical Journals

Miscellanea Curiosa Medico-Physico Academiae Naturae Curiosorum Sive Ephemerides Germanicae was published in Leipzig, Germany, in 1670. The oldest continuously published medical journal is the *New England Journal of Medicine*, first published in Massachusetts, U.S., in 1812.

179
First Weekly Business Journals

The *Denver Business Journal* is the oldest weekly business journal in the U.S., first published in 1949.

180
First Library Journals

Library Journal, published in the U.S. by Reed Business Information, is the oldest independent national library publication. Begun in 1876, it is the "Bible" of the library world and each issue is read by probably over 100,000 people. Benjamin Franklin and friends began the first library serial in the U.S. in the middle 1700s.

181
First Paperbacks

Crude versions of what we call paperbacks (pocketbooks), first appeared in Florence, Italy, in the 16th century. In 1932 Albatross Books appeared in Paris and Milan bookstores. The first mass-produced paperbacks were Penguin Books founded in 1935 by Allen Lane in Bristol, U.K. His revolutionary paperback allowing the mass production of copies of cheaper smaller book versions of original expensive hardback titles. The first three Penguin titles were *Ariel* by André Maurois, *A Farewell to Arms* by Ernest Hemingway and *Poet's Pub* by Eric Linklater. The first mass-produced paperbacks in the Americas were issued by Pocket Books, founded in 1939.

182
Earliest Professional Handbooks for Librarians

1. Gabriel Naudé's *Advis pour dresser une bibliothèque* published in 1627.

2. John Durie's *The Reformed Librarie-Keeper* published in 1650.

Frenchman Gabriel Naudé was the first librarian for the famous Mazarin Library, in Paris, France (which owns the first copy of the original Gutenberg Bible). John Durie was a Scottish cleric and librarian who later became a librarian for the British royal *family. George Eberhart's Whole Library Handbook, published by the American Library Association, is read by more librarians than any other handbook today.*

183
Largest General Reference Book in English

The first printed edition of *Encyclopædia Britannica* (originally a 3-volume book, and today in 32 volumes comprising 65,000 articles) was first published in 1768 in Edinburgh, Scotland. Today the CD-ROM version, first released in early 1994, sells more than the printed version. In 1997 an Internet version was released, and in 1999 the DVD version was made available. *Encyclopædia Britannica* is now published in the U.S. The main general reference books in the U.S. are *Encyclopedia Americana*, first published in 1829, and today by Grolier. The other is *Collier's Encyclopedia*, first published in 1950.

The largest online reference work is Wikipedia. *Set up in 2001 by Jimmy Wales and Larry Sanger, it has over 2.5 million articles and is available in over 189 languages. The English language version reached 100,000 articles in 2003, growing at a rate of 3000 articles per day. In 2006 it reached 2 million articles. This can be compared with the 2007 edition of* Encyclopædia Britannica *Ultimate DVD*

(the largest of the several commercial categories of the encyclopedia on electronic media) which has just over 100,000 articles, but it is better in quality than Wikipedia, since all the articles are peer-reviewed and written solely by experts in their fields. Greek scholar Speusippus wrote the first known encyclopedia around 350 B.C. *The first modern encyclopedia was Kitab Uyun al–Akhbar written in Arabic by Ibn Qutaybah, an Arabic writer in* A.D. *800. Its style in organizing the contents was adopted by all later encyclopedias around the world. The first publications to use the title "encyclopaedia" were Paul Scalich's book published in Basel, Switzerland, in 1559 and Johann Alsted's book published in Switzerland in 1631. The oldest extant encyclopaedia is the one written by Pliny the Elder (a Roman scientific encyclopedist and historian) called* Historia Naturulis *in* A.D. *77. The largest encyclopedia is undoubtedly the one commissioned by Emperor Yung Lo in the 15th century, made up of over 11,000 volumes comprising 22,800 chapters. It was titled* Yongluo Dadien.

184
Largest General Reference Book in French

The largest main French encyclopedia is *Encyclopédie Français* published in Paris. It was initiated by French historian Lucien Febvre in 1935. Pierre Larousse, a French grammarian and lexicographer, is the creator of the famous French encyclopedic dictionary, *Grand dictionnaire universel du XIXème siècle* (*Great Universal 19th-Century Dictionary*), issued 1865–1876. The voluminous book is still published today as the *Larousse Encyclopedia* and is a popular reference book among scholars in France. The other popular general reference in France is the *Encyclopédie Universalis*.

185
Largest General Reference Book in German

In Germany, the largest main encyclopedia is *Brockhaus Enzyklopadie*. It was first published in 1796 in Wiesbaden.

186
Largest General Reference Book in Chinese

Zhongguo Dabaikequanshu is a 74-volume Chinese encyclopedia, with 78,000 main entries. It is the largest general reference book in China. An other notable Chinese encyclopedias is *Hanyu fangyan dacidian*, 41 volumes and 320,000 main entries. The main Chinese dictionary is the 4-volume *Zhonghua zihai* (the equivalent of the *English Oxford Dictionary*).

187
Largest General Reference Book in Japanese

Buritanika Kokusai Daihyakka jiten was first published in 1972 in Tokyo, based on *Encyclopædia Britannica*. A larger reference book is the *Encyclopedia Nipponica* (*Nihon Daihyakka zensho*), a 30-volume book, available online, first published in 1984. The largest English language general reference in Japan is the *Kodansha Encyclopedia of Japan*, first published in 1983. Many of the articles in the encyclopedia are actually English translations from several multidisciplinary Japanese encyclopedias. *Kodansha Encyclopedia* and *Encyclopedia Nipponica* can also be accessed electronically in libraries in Japan and overseas, via a database called JapanKnowledge. The largest Japanese dictionaries are *Nihonkokugo daijiten* and *Daikanwa jiten*.

188
Largest General Reference Book in Arabic

Dairat Al-maarif was first published in 1876 in the Lebanese capital, Beirut.

189
Largest General Reference Book in Other Languages

In The Netherlands, the largest standard encyclopedia is the 25-volume *Grote Winkler Prins Encyclopedie* published by the major publisher Elsevier in Amsterdam. It was first published in 1870. The major Italian encyclopedia is the *Enciclopedia italiana di scienze, lettere ed arti*, first published in 1925 in Milan. During the time the Soviet Union existed, the main encyclopedia was *Bolshaya Sovetskaya Entsiklopediya*, first published in 1926. An English translation appeared in 1970s. The largest Spanish and Latin American encyclopedia is *Enciclopedia universal ilustrada europeoamericana*, published since 1905 in Madrid, Spain. Another major Spanish encyclopedia is the *Enciclopedia hispánica*. The major Portuguese encyclopedia is *Enciclopédia Barsa*; it is also popular in Brazil, alongside Brazil's major encyclopedia *Enciclopédia Mirador Internacional*. In Turkey, the major reference book is *Türk ansiklopedisi*. The first major southeast Asian encyclopedia was Indonesia *Ensiklopedia Indonesia*, published in 1953 in Jakarta, Indonesia.

The first dictionary in the world is believed to be a Chinese work written in 1150 B.C. The first edition of the famous Oxford English Dictionary *was completed in 1860. The five earliest writers of English dictionaries are Robert Cawdrey (published in 1604), Henry Cockeram (1626), John Kersey (1700), Nathaniel Bailey (1721) and Samuel Johnson (1755). Samuel Johnson's dictionary was the first comprehensive and authoritative English dictionary. The earliest U.S. English dictionaries were those written by Samuel Johnson junior, published in 1798, and*

Noah Webster, published in 1828, both in New York. The largest dictionary is the 33 volume German dictionary Deutsches Wörterbuch that was started by Wilhelm Grimm in 1854 and finished in 1971.

190
Biggest, Heaviest and Smallest Books

For those used to metric units, 12 inches (i.e., 1 foot) are equal to 304 millimeters or 30.4 centimeters, 3 feet is approximately 1 meter, and 1 kilogram is about 2.2 pounds.

Biggest Books. In 2004 in Tokyo, Japanese car maker Mazda Motor Corporation unveiled a book measuring 10 feet (wide) by 11 feet (high). The book contained numerous large photographs of Mazda's new compact car, the *Verisa*. It took four people, two on opposite sides of the book, to open the pages of the book for visitors at the Mazda gallery. *The Super Book*, a huge visitor's book, produced in Denver, Colorado, U.S., in the 1970s is the largest existing book in the Americas. It measures 9 feet by 10 feet, and contains 300 pages and weighs just over 555 pounds. *Bhutan: A Visual Odyssey Across the Last Himalayan Kingdom* is the same size as the dimensions of a table-tennis table, i.e., 5 feet by 7 feet. See list **207** for more details. A selection of books over 2 feet wide or high are: John J. Audubon's 19th century *Birds of America*, 3.5 feet high and 2.5 feet wide; *Modern Art: Revolution and Painting*, 3 feet by 1.6 feet; *Sumo* by Helmut Newton, 2.6 by 2.4 feet.

Heaviest Books. The heaviest book published in existence today is the *Arabic Legislation Encyclopedia*, printed in Libya and written by Mohammed Ben Younis. It weighs in at over 881 pounds, but is made up of 200 separate volumes, totaling over 164,000 pages. The *Super Book* noted above is 555 pounds. *Bhutan: A Visual Odyssey Across the Last Himalayan Kingdom*, by Massachusetts Institute of Technology professor Michael Holey, weighs 132 pounds and has 112 pages. *Modern Art: Revolution and Painting* weighs 77 pounds, has 544 pages and was published in 2003 by ArtMedia. The book covers the past 200 years of painting, with 265 works by Cézanne, Matisse, Monet, Picasso, Rivera, van Gogh and others. Boxer Muhammed Ali's biography published in 2004 is 72 pounds and has 800 pages and 3000 photographs. The heaviest photographer's book published is Helmut Newton's *Sumo*, which weighs in at 66 pounds. See list **207** on most expensive books for more details on *Sumo*. The list of heaviest periodicals is at list **192**.

Smallest Books. Because it is not very easy to rate and accurately measure contenders for the title of the world's smallest book, a shortlist of five contenders are given below and the claimed dimensions. All of them, however, need both a needle to turn the pages and a powerful magnifying glass to read it properly.

1. *Chekhov's Chameleon*, a Russian book, owned by head librarian for the College-Conservatory of Music Library in the U.S., measures just 0.03 inches by 0.03 inches, and has 30 pages.

2. *Old King Cole* measures approximately 0.04 inches by 0.04 inches. It is part of the U.S. Library of Congress book collections.

3. *Kobzar of Taras Shevchenko* is about 0.11 inches by 0.11 inches. It was published in Ukraine in 1840.

4. A book appropriately titled *The World's Smallest Book* measures 0.12 inches by 0.13 inches. It was produced in Germany in 2001.

5. Published in Germany in 1958, *The Lord's Prayer* or *Het Onze Vader* is 0.22 inches by 0.22 inches.

To understand what these measurements mean, half an inch or 0.5 inches is 12.7 millimeters, 0.25 inches is equal to 6.3 millimeters, and 0.12 inches is approximately 3.1 millimeters. A comparative object is the size of a match head, which is roughly 0.23 inches in diameter. Any one of these four books would comfortably sit on a match head — while opened!

The miniaturization of books did occur around the time of Gutenberg. The oldest authenticated smallest book is Diurnale Maguritinum *printed in 1468. It measures 2.5 by 3.7 inches (this small size is obviously no match for the four pint-sized books above). John Hopkins University Library Baltimore, Maryland, U.S., owns a copy of the smallest book ever printed with movable type. The book, written by Galileo, was printed in 1897. Miniature books are painstakingly difficult to make via moveable type, so the 1897 book is a remarkable feat illustrating the art of bookmaking on a minuscule scale. The biggest book in the U.S. Library of Congress in Washington, D.C., is John James Audubon's* Birds of America, *measuring over 3 feet high because it contains life-size pictures of birds. In 1660, Dutch merchants from Amsterdam presented the English King Charles II with a 6 feet by 3 feet high world atlas (*Klencke Atlas*). The atlas, which is now housed in the British Library, is the biggest book in existence in Europe. The second largest is* Berline Kurfursten Atlas, *measuring 5 feet by 1 feet. The third largest book published in Europe is probably* Carte Topographique de l'Egypte. *It was printed in France in 1809 for Napoleon Bonaparte and is was almost 4 feet high and 2.5 feet wide. Before the invention of printing several gigantic manuscripts over 2 feet in height were produced, notably* Gigas Librorum, *a huge bible made from parchment and preserved in a Swedish library in Stockholm. In the port of Mandalay, Burma, the Kuthodaw Pagodas, built in 1868 by King Mindon, contains over 700 marble slabs joined together and inscribed with the* Tripitaka Canon *(the holy book of Theravada Buddhism). It is written in Pali, an ancient Indo-European language of northern India, related to Sanskrit, and a classical language of Buddhism, in which Buddhist scriptures were written. Building the huge marble inscription was a massive feat that took more than 2,500 Buddhist monks years to build and is often symbolically called the "biggest book in the world." The ancient Egyptian* Harris Papyrus *(dating from 1200* B.C. *and now in the British Library in London) is the longest existing papyrus. It is over 140 feet long and has to be kept in dozens of separate frames.*

191
Books with the Most Pages

The *Tripitaka Canon* in Chinese script was completed on paper in China in A.D. 972, and is composed of over 120,000 printed pages. This makes it the book with the largest number of pages in the world. The English language book with the largest number of pages was the 1988 edition of Victor Hugo's *Les Misérables*, which has over 1,400 pages. Between 1980 and 1992, French author George-Jean Arnaud completed his 62-volume novel *La Campagne des Glaces*. It is the longest novel in the world with over 11,000 pages. Other books with a large number of pages are the 33-volume German dictionary *Deutsches Wörterbuch* by Wilhelm Grimm and the 200-volume *Arabic Legislation Encyclopedia*, by Libyan writer Mohammed Ben Younis, with 164,000 pages. These last two books are described in lists **189** and **190**.

There is a limit to the number of volumes of a major work that can be available in print format. Going beyond 250 volumes is enormous and for practical reasons is best made as an online database. The 300-volume academic reference collection from Blackwell Publishing is the largest modern voluminous book and is available only as a database. See list **329**. However, there is one record holder for the most voluminous book. *Yongluo Dadien* (*Yung Lo Ta Tien*), a Chinese encyclopedia, had over 11,000 volumes when it was published in the 15th century for Emperor Yung Lo. It also has about 22,800 chapters. An abridged 100-volume edition was published in 1962 on the orders of Chairman Mao, the Chinese leader, as the 15th century book does not exist intact today.

192
Biggest and Heaviest Periodical

The heaviest and biggest edition of a newspaper was the Sunday, September 14, 1987, issue of the *New York Times*. It had 1,612 pages and weighed 11 pounds. The heaviest magazine published to date was the September 1989 edition of *Vogue*, the fashion magazine. This particular edition had 808 pages and was almost 3 pounds in weight. The biggest and smallest books are entered on list **190**.

In 1980, mathematicians worldwide completed the classification of all finite and simple groups. The enormous and difficult undertaking took over 100 mathematicians more than 35 years to complete. The results of the task took up more than 14,000 pages in many mathematical journals of the day.

193
Most Popular Author Among Library Users

In 2007, J.K. Rowling's final book about a boy wizard, *Harry Potter and the Deathly Hallows,* created the longest waiting list for a reserved book in public libraries in the several English speaking countries, including the U.K. and the U.S. The Public Lending Right in the U.K. noted that the waiting list was several weeks long, making the book the most borrowed book to date in the U.K. See list **216** for Harry Potter facts.

Before Harry Potter mania was well established, according to figures published by the U.K. Public Lending Right in 2001, for the 15th year, books by Catherine Cookson *were the most popular. Between July 1999 and June 2000 she came in at the top of a list of 12 authors who saw their books borrowed on more than a million occasions, beating the likes of William Shakespeare and Jane Austen. Danielle Steel's novels are the next most borrowed books in public library. But the two most published authors in the U.K. are William Shakespeare and Charles Dickens. Some British authors earn an extra income from the U.K. Public Lending Right, on top of their royalties, whenever their books are lent out in libraries, hence the more books borrowed, the more they earn.*

194
Most Widely Read Magazine

The *Reader's Digest* is the most widely read magazine in the world. It has a devoted following of 100 million readers across the globe today.

195
First Book Blessed by the Pope

Lew Wallace's book, *Ben-Hur*, was the first piece of fiction ever to be blessed by a pope. Pope Leo XII blessed the book in the 1880s.

196
Best Selling Books of All Time

The Bible is the best-selling book of all time. In the whole of the 20th century, over 4 billion copies were printed around the world in over 1000 languages. The bestselling non-religious book is Mao Zedong's *Little Red Book* (containing quotations and summaries of his work with the Chinese Communist Party). Over 900 million copies were published to meet the demands of China's huge population. Today just two other books have broken the 100 million barrier, the *Guinness Book of World Records* and the Koran.

The Chinese dictionary, Xinhu Zidan (Zonghua Zihai), first published in 1953, has sold more than 400 million copies by 2006, making it the best selling dictionary.

197
Most Translated Books

The Bible is the most translated non-fiction book in the world, available in more than 1000 languages. *Don Quixote*, by Miguel de Cervantes in 1605, has been translated into more languages than any book outside of the Bible. He wrote the parts of the bestseller while a prisoner of the Barbary pirates in Algiers, Algeria.

198
First and Most Prolific Novelist

Between 1986 and 1996, Brazilian author Jose Carlos Ryoki de Alpoim Inoue had a massive 1,058 novels published. He writes westerns, science fiction and thrillers. The first novel has been credited to the one written by Japanese author Murasaki Shikibus in A.D. 1005, titled *The Tale of Genji*.

199
First Author to Use a Typewriter

Mark Twain was the first writer ever to submit a typewritten manuscript to a publisher. The name of the his book was *The Adventures of Tom Sawyer*. Mark Twain used a Remington typewriter in 1875. The typewriter had been patented and marketed by Christopher Sholes in 1874. Russian writer Leo Tolstoy was unfortunate not to invest in a typewriter. Between 1865 and 1869, he worked on a voluminous novel called *Voyna i mir,* or *War and Peace,* and his wife had to copy his long manuscript by hand seven times.

Authors and journalists began to substitute typing their manuscripts on an electric typewriter (e.g., IBM Selectric typewriter of the 1960s) with computerized typewriters in the 1970s. The Wang 2200 Word Processor was the first in 1972, followed by the Wang WPS Word Processor in 1976 (complete with display monitor, keyboard, printer and storage device on cassette). Similar products such as the IBM Displaywriter followed (1980). Desktop computer software for word processing arrived with the introduction of MultiMate and Word Star word processors for CP/M computers in 1979. When MS-DOS computers arrived in 1981 (IBM 5150), the popular word processor was IBM's DisplayWrite software. The first version of Microsoft Word for MS-DOS computers was in 1983.

200
First Major Computer Software for Book Publishing

The release of Aldus PageMaker in 1985 and QuarkXPress in 1987 revolutionized the way final manuscripts from writers reached the printing stage. These two packages, known as DTP or Desk Top Publishing software, allowed publishers and editors to create the layout and arrangement of texts and illustrations in the manuscript before sending the finished proofs to the printers, which tended to be not part of the publishing company. Before DTP arrived, the printers also handled preparing the proofs, which had to be sent back to the publishers for approval before being printed. In other words DTP speeded up the time taken for a book to be published.

The first books to be published with DTP were in fact the manuals and user guides that accompanied PageMaker version 1 and QuarkXPress version 1 when both were released.

201
Famous and Infamous People Who Wrote Bestselling Books in Prison

Marco Polo (Italian), Miguel de Cervantes (Spanish), Wole Soyinka (Nigerian), Walter Raleigh (British), Alexander Solzhenitsyn (Russian), Daniel Defoe (British), Jawaharlal Nehru (Indian), Oscar Wilde (British), Jack Unterweger (Austrian) and Adolf Hitler (German) are among famous and infamous people who made good use of prison libraries in their countries to write bestsellers while incarcerated. Here is a brief look at Marco Polo's fantastic book: Marco Polo was the famous Italian traveler who took 24 years visiting Asia and meeting rulers such as the Mongol leader Kublai Khan. He was probably the first European to witness block-printing of documents on paper during his travels to China in the 13th century. Having invented paper, the Chinese took the first step in inventing printing by developing what is called block-printing in the 6th century (the precursor to the printing technique invented by Gutenberg in the 15th century). At this time block-printing was unknown in Europe, even when the secrets of making paper finally reached Europe late in the 12th century. Among other "firsts" attributable to Marco Polo are that he was the first European to see paper money (the first European paper money was issued in Sweden in 1661), paper playing cards, and libraries with books made from paper. After his travels in Asia, he returned to Venice and dictated the story of his travels while a prisoner in Genoa to a fellow inmate who was a writer. His book, *The Travels of Marco Polo*, became a best-seller in medieval Europe, but there were some people who were skeptical and called him "Marco Milione," and his book *Il Milione* or *The Million Lies*, because the story of his travels was too fantastic to be true. To his skeptics, Marco Polo said the memorable words, "I have only told half of what I saw."

202
Most Severe Punishments Suffered by a Writer

In 1643 a book by English writer William Prynne caused so much contention he was accused of libel. As punishment, he was set in the pillory, had his ears cut off, was fined the equivalent of $9,000 today and imprisoned. He continued writing while in the Tower of London prison and in 1647 was brought to back to court and punished again. This time he was branded on his cheeks with the words "Seditious Libeller" (sic) and fined another $9,000. Today there are good libel laws to ensure a person is not slandered, and the punishment is usually fines. English translator William Tyndale did not fare better than Prynne. Due to restrictions imposed on the production of religious books, notably the Bible, during the Vatican Inquisition, it was deadly to publish a book judged as heretical by the Vatican or a senior bishop. In 1536 in Belgium, William Tyndale paid the ultimate price for ignoring this. His translated versions of the Latin Bible into English, caused a big remonstration, and he was strangled and burnt at the stake as a heretic for his books. Some of the words in Tyndale's Bible (that were not in the Latin version he used for translations) that caused so much resentment were "filthy lucre" and "God forbid." See also list **213**, first major book-burning rituals, and list **214**, famous government-sanctioned book bans.

203
Countries with the Largest Number of Books Published in More Than 10 Major Languages

Among the 20 major languages in the world with the largest number of native speakers, India is home to 11 major languages with more than 30 million speakers each. These are *Hindi, Bengali, Gujarati, Telugu, Bihari, Maharati, Tamil, Malayalam, Kannada, Punjabi* and *Oriya*. Annual production of books, magazines and newspapers and other publications in all 11 of these languages in India for the masses is thus staggering. China has 8 major languages with more than 30 million speakers each. These are *Mandarin (Han)*, by far the largest, *Cantonese (Yue), Min, Jinya, Min Nan, Xiang, Hakka* and *Wu*. Because of the size of its population, China produces the largest number of books in the world, while UNESCO has calculated that Iceland publishes the most books per capita in the world.

Chinese languages, with millions of speakers each, vary greatly in their spoken versions. But the Chinese script (which thankfully is not alphabetic) makes it possible for a speaker of Mandarin Chinese living in Beijing to visit a bookstore in Hong Kong or Macao and read books written by an author fluent in Cantonese Chinese. The same situation does not exist in India, where several separate scripts exist— e.g., for Hindi, Bengali, Gujarati and Tamil, even though they all descend from the same ancient Brahmi script. However, it should be noted that the different Chinese languages are in fact different dialects, which adopted a single Chinese script. For instance Mandarin is a dialect that originated in Beijing, Cantonese originated from Canton (Guangzou), Min and Xiang originated from Fujian and Wu originated from Shanghai.

204
Largest National Book Expenditure

According to the 2006 OCLC report *Libraries: How They Stack Up*, the annual expenditure of books for all libraries in the United States is about $14 billion.

205
Most Expensive Book Project

The 60-volume *Oxford Dictionary of National Biography* published in 2004 cost over $45 million (£25 million) to produce. The book project took over 12 years to conclude and profiles about 55,000 people who have made a major impact on British society. The complete set cost $13,000 (£7,500) to purchase and takes up to 12 feet of bookshelf space. The budget for the book project for first edition of the book published in 1882 cost less than $100.

206
Biggest Book Launches

According to Scholastic, the biggest one day sale of a fiction book was *Harry Potter and the Order of the Phoenix* by J.K. Rowling, which sold 5 million copies in the first 24 hours in 2003. *Publishers Weekly* noted that the biggest one day sale of a non-fiction book was *My Life*, the autobiography of former U.S. President Bill Clinton. It sold 400,000 copies on the first day it was published in 2004.

According to the publishers Bloomsbury in the U.K. and Scholastic in the U.S., *Harry Potter* advanced sales were higher than for any other book in history. In the U.K. orders exceeded 1 million, and over 7.5 million copies in the U.S. were printed before publication. Amazon handled orders for *Harry Potter and the Order of the Phoenix* online and said it was its fastest-selling novel in 2003. It broke Internet sales records when Amazon received more than 2 million advance orders to become the biggest distribution of any single item in e-commerce history. For her work in writing the book J.K. Rowling received about $55 million and was reported to have filed a £100 million lawsuit against the *New York Times* for publishing details about the plot in her book before it was officially released. To date over 200 million copies of Harry Potter books have been sold worldwide in 55 languages including Latin and ancient Greek. The 7 books in the series are: 1. 1997, *Harry Potter and the Philosopher's Stone* (500 copies printed in the first run); 2. 1998, *Harry Potter and the Chambers of Secrets*; 3. 1999, *Harry Potter and the Prisoner of Azkaban* (best seller); 4. 2000, *Harry Potter and the Goblet of Fire* (best seller); 5. 2003, *Harry Potter and the Order of the Phoenix*; 6. 2005, *Harry Potter and the Half Blood Prince*; 7. 2007, *Harry Potter and the Deathly Hallows*. The last book in the series created the longest waiting list for a reserved book in a library, see list **193.**

In March 2004, Jacqueline Wilson set a British record of the longest book signing in the U.K. The children's author began signing at 3 P.M. and finished just after midnight at a Bournemouth bookstore.

207
Fifteen Most Expensive Books and Manuscripts

There are two kinds of expensive books, those bought from auction houses such as Sotheby's and those bought from bookstores or from the publisher. Naturally books sold by the former are several times more expensive than the latter, because they are often rare, very old and collector's items. The following are the most expensive books and manuscripts auctioned by winter 2007.

1. The Estelle Doheny Collection (rare book collections of U.S. millionaire Estelle Doheny). Six-part book sale bonanza, sold in total for $38 million at Christie's, New York, in 1987. The collection included 12th century manuscripts to 19th and 20th century American literature.

2. Leonardo da Vinci's notebook *The Codex Hammer* (16th century Latin manuscript). Sold for $29 million at Christie's, New York, in 1994. Microsoft's Bill Gates was the proud buyer of the manuscript. In a 1980 auction, it had fetched $6 million.

3. The *Rothschild Prayer Book* (16th century illuminated manuscript). Sold for £8.5 million (about $12.5 million) at Christie's, London, in

1999. The book was sold by the famous German Rothschild banking dynasty.

4. The Duke of Saxony's manuscript *The Gospels of Henry the Lion* (12th century German illuminated manuscript). Sold for £8 million (about $11.8 million) at Sotheby's, London, in 1983.

5. John James Audubon's book *The Birds of America* (1827). Sold for $8 million at Christie's New York in 2000.

6. Geoffrey Chaucer's *The Canterbury Tales* (15th century English manuscript). It was printed by the famous London-based William Caxton and sold for £4.5 million (about $7 million) at Christie's, London, in 1998 to Paul Getty.

7. A manuscript by William Shakespeare dated 1623 was sold for £4.1 million ($6.2 million) in 2001 at Christie's, London.

8. The Gutenberg Bible (1455). Sold for $5.3 million at Christie's, New York, in 1987.

9. *The Burdett Psalter and Hours* (13th century French illuminated manuscript), sold for £2.3 million ($4.6 million) at Sotheby's, London in 1998. The manuscript remained a secret to scholars and art historians until a descendant of Jane Burdett (who first bought it in 1634) took it to the British Library in 1978 in an effort to have it evaluated.

10. *The Northumberland Bestiary* (13th century English illuminated manuscript). Sold for £2.8 million (about $4.1 million) at Sotheby's, London, in 1990.

11. *The Cornaro Missal* (16th century Italian illuminated manuscript). Sold for £2.5 million (about $3.7 million) at Christie's, London, in 1999. The famous German Rothschild banking dynasty sold the book.

12. Hebrew Bible (6th century A.D.). Sold for £1.7 million (about $2.5 million) at Sotheby's, London, in 1989.

13. *Biblia Pauperum* (14th century German block-printed Bible). Sold for $2.2 million at Christie's, New York, in 1987. It is older than the Gutenberg Bible by almost 100 years.

14. *The Psalter and Hours of Elizabeth de Bohun* (14th century English illuminated manuscript). Sold for £1.4 million (about $2.1 million) at Sotheby's, London, in 1988.

15. The Koran (1203). Sold for £1.2 million ($2 million) at Christie's, London, in 2007. It is the earliest-known complete Koran and is transcribed in gold. At the same auction an incomplete 10th century Koran sold for £916,500 ($1.7 million).

The only online database on auction records in existence providing information to auction sales catalogs from all major North American and European auction houses as well as many private sales is the SCIPIO database produced by OCLC in Dublin, Ohio. At the time this book was going into print, Sotheby's in New York had began preparing the sale of a rare copy of the *Magna Carta* (13th century English manuscript). It had been bought by Ross Perot in 1984 and is expected to fetch at least $20 million or more, propelling it third on the rich list. Many books and manuscripts in this list are record holders in their own right; e.g., John James Audubon's book *The Birds of America* is the most valuable, or at least the most expensive modern book ever sold. Leonardo Da Vinci's notebook *The Codex Hammer* is the most valuable manuscript in the world. *The Rothschild Prayer Book* is the most expensive illuminated manuscript. The 13th century Koran (15th on the list) is the most expensive Islamic holy book sold. Meanwhile Geoffrey Chaucer's *Canterbury Tales,* the *Biblia Pauperum* and the Gutenberg Bible (one of Johannes Gutenberg's original copies) are the three most valuable incunabula in the world. The Duke of Saxony's manuscript, the 12th century *Gospels of Henry the Lion,* is the oldest expensive item in the list. Around the second quarter of the 13th century there began to appear, both in France and in Britain, specialized religious manuscripts covering prayers and the biblical Psalms known as psalter-hours. *The Rothschild Prayer Book* is the most expensive of the three psalter-hours, listed above. A rare first edition of *Alice's Adventures in Wonderland* by Lewis Carroll raised $1.5 million at auction in New York in 1995, making this the most valuable children's book ever sold. The book was Carroll's own working copy that he used to prepare the text for a simplified version for younger children. Only 22 copies of the 1865 first edition are known to exist today, 17 of which are in libraries and five, including the copy sold, are in private hands.

Sotheby's was founded in 1774 and is the largest auction house in the world. It auctioned only books from the start, until 1780 when it began to auction other items such as paintings and sculptures. The second of the famous two auction houses, Christie's, is slightly older, having been founded in 1766. In many countries, the export of valuable rare books and manuscripts over a country's borders can be prohibited by law, even if bought legitimately from an auction house like Sotheby's or private sale, if government appointed experts deem it to be of national or cultural importance to stay in the country. In Britain, the decisive factors which determine whether valuable rare books and manuscripts can be taken out of the country or not is listed in a set of strict guidelines called the Waverley criteria. The first recorded major public auction of rare books and manuscripts occurred in 1599 (about 145 years after Gutenberg printed the first book), with the sale of the contents of Philip Van Marnix's library in Amsterdam, The Netherlands. *The Sherborne Missal, a 15th century English illuminated manuscript bought by the British Library and valued at $21 million, is better seen as a fine example of medieval art than an illuminated manuscript and so does not make the most expensive list. The Estelle Doheny Collection is still a lot cheaper than the one world's most expensive painting, Vincent Van Gogh's* Portrait of Doctor Gachet, *which was sold at Christie's, New York, in 1990 for approximately $81 million. When Microsoft's Bill Gates purchased the* Codex Hammer *in 1994 he displayed a rare modesty. Bill Gates chose not to name the manuscript after himself, i.e., call it* Codex Gates, *as previous owners of the Leonardo da Vinci's notebook had done in the past, when they named the manuscript after themselves. The* Codex Hammer, *also known as* Codex Leicester, *is named after its previous owners.*

208
Six Most Expensive Books That Could Be Bought from Bookstores

Six of the most expensive books that could be purchased from a bookstore or the publisher by winter 2007 are:

Bhutan: A Visual Odyssey Across the Last Himalayan Kingdom by Michael Holey. It cost $110,000 per copy when it was first published in 2003. It was not published in the conventional way, as Professor Holey made the book himself with an advanced digital printer. Holey says the book costs $2,000 to produce, and Amazon is charging $10,000 for the book. Because the book is only produced on demand, it does not topple the world record for the most expensive published book on sale in the conventional sense, but Holey's book is currently the most expensive book advertised by Amazon and also now the heaviest book on sale in the world.

Oxford Dictionary of National Biography. This 60-volume reference book published in 2004 cost $13,000 for the complete set. See list **205** for more details.

Modern Art: Revolution and Painting published in 2003 retails for $6000.

A Muhammad Ali biography published in 2004 cost $3500. Only 10,000 were produced, and sold exclusively by Amazon.

Construction Law Reports 1985–1997 edited by M.P. Furmston and V. Powell-Smith (Editor), $2500, published in 1993. It was the first book to be sold for more than $2000 by Amazon.

Sumo by Helmut Newton. Published in January 2000 by Taschen, it had a price tag of $2,400. The book was about the controversial career of German erotic photographer Helmut Newton and has over 450 photographs in over 500 pages. The mammoth book project that produced *Sumo* took more than three years with more than 50 people working with the author.

The final cost of the book production was estimated at $5 million. *Sumo* is available in English, German and French. It also comes complete with it own coffee table. Anyone wanting to buy a copy of the book may be out of luck, as only a limited edition of 10,000 hand-bound copies was printed. In 2001 a film about the book was made in Germany. Some of these books are very large and heavy, which make them record holders in other categories. See list **190** for more details.

209
Most Overdue Library Book

In 1667 Robert Walpole borrowed a book from the library of Sidney Sussex College (one of the 31 colleges of Cambridge University). The book, titled *Scriptores Rerum Germani-carum Septentrionalium*, was published in Germany in 1609. A direct descendant of Robert Walpole returned the book 289 years later in 1956. (However, no fine was charged.)

210
Biggest Book Fines

In 2002, a student from the University of Iowa in the U.S. was jailed for not returning books he had borrowed from the Iowa City Public Library. His charge was fourth-degree theft. His overdue fines for the books from the library were almost $450, which he had not yet paid before he was jailed. In 2003, bookworm teacher Emily Cannellos-Simms faced $345 in overdue book fines. In 1999 a library user at Prairie Creek Library, in Dwight, Illinois, paid $292 in fines for returning a book 40 years overdue. Mildred Pugmire, a library user at Salt Lake City public library, returned a book 76 years overdue and faced a possible fine of $5000, which was waived.

211
Five Famous Stolen Books and Manuscripts

1. The *Geographia (Cosmographia)*. During the Middle Ages while Europe was fighting with the Arabs in the Crusades, people began looking for the *Geographia* when it suddenly disappeared and seemed lost forever. But all along the Arabs had been quietly looking after the *Geographia* after it had apparently been stolen during the Crusades by persons unknown. Europe was able to recover a copy of the original *Geographia* when a member of the Italian nobility (the Strozzi family of Florence) obtained a perfect copy in Constantinople (Istanbul) in 1407. Taken back to Italy it caused a sensation, and to ensure it was not lost again, several further copies of the recovered copy of the *Geographia* were made and promptly translated from Greek into Latin and several other languages for scholars and university libraries all over Europe. The first copy was made in Genoa by Jacobis Angelus in 1409. Some of the earliest copies after 1409 were obtained by the Vatican Library in Rome in 1478 and are on display today, but the copy at the Nancy City Library in France dates from 1427 (hence hand-copied and not produced with Gutenberg's printer) and is the oldest surviving copy today. In 2007, a former employee of the National Library of Spain who stole the cream of the library's collection of rare cartographic manuscripts negotiated their return to the library staff while on the run in Buenos Aires, Argentina. Among items eventually returned, to the astonishment of the Spanish library staff, was a very rare 1482 edition of the

Geographia belonging the library and worth over $100,000.

2. *The Rothschild Prayer Book.* This manuscript, originally printed in the 16th century, was among the numerous items looted from the palace of Baron Louis de Rothschild in Vienna in 1938 after the Nazis annexed Austria. After the end of the Second World War, the manuscript remained the property of the Austrian government, which placed restrictions on the manuscript's movements, until 1999, when it was finally returned to the Rothschild family following lengthy negotiations between them and the Austrian government.

3. Harvard University Library was the victim of the theft of $3 million worth of cartographic manuscripts by map dealer E. Forbes Smiley III, who was arrested in 2005.

4. In 2003, rare books worth over $50 million were recovered after Danish police arrested four suspects who had stolen over 4000 rare books belonging to the National Library of Denmark

in the 1960s and 1970s. Items stolen included manuscripts by Martin Luther and first editions by Immanuel Kant, Thomas More and John Milton. The thieves were caught when they foolishly tried to sell a rare 500-year-old book at the London auction house Christie's, not realizing it was the only copy existing in the world and hence had only one legitimate owner: it was registered as belonging to the National Library of Denmark. When police raided the suspects' home, they found the stolen rare books. Danish police soon identified the inside man: an employee of the library's oriental department. Before being caught, the thieves did mange to sell books between 1998 and 2002, worth some $2 million, at various auctions.

5. In 1990, the FBI charged a man from Minnesota with the theft of over 30,000 books from 140 university libraries in the U.S. When the FBI raided his home, they were shocked to find that the haul of stolen books had filled 14 rooms, resembling a large legitimate private library.

212
Most Famous Persons Barred from Borrowing Books from a Famous Library

When the Bodleian Library at Oxford University was refounded in 1602 after being destroyed by troops of King Edward VI, the library took drastic measures to protect its growing collection.

In 1645, the library refused to allow English King Charles I to borrow books from the library, despite the fact Charles I was the reigning English monarch. When King Charles I was executed and England became a republic, the

library also refused to allow Oliver Cromwell to borrow any books in 1654. At that time Cromwell was the military ruler of England. The reason for the refusal was the fact that by the 17th century, one of the statutes of the new Bodleian Library specifically banned the loan of books from the library as it was only a reference library. And there was no exception to the rule whatsoever, even if the borrower was the king of England.

213
First Major Book-Burning Ritual

Right up to the 20th century, major book-burning ceremonies have been carried out in various countries by their governments or

rulers. These rituals were mostly for religious, political, or ideological reasons. Medieval Europe witnessed several huge religious book-burning ceremonies, such as the famous "Bonfire of the Vanities" in Florence, Italy, in the 15th century, when books by authors such as Dante, Plato, Boccaccio and Ovid were destroyed in public for being "anti–Christian." The first major book-burning event on a very large scale probably occurred with the complete destruction, which took 7 months to complete, of the huge collections of the Alexandria library in Egypt in the 7th century A.D., by Arab invaders. The reason given for the book-burning was *to destroy the books of the infidels.* With Egypt about to be completely Islamized, the Arabs felt the contents of the papyrus and parchment books in the library went against the principles and teachings of Islam.

The largest recorded mass burning of books in the 20th century occurred in Germany and parts of occupied Europe during the Nazi regime in the 1930s and 1940s, such as the May 1933 burning of over 30,000 books at Berlin's Humboldt University. This was part of the policy of Gleichschaltung (synchronization) to control library collections. Joseph Goebbels, Hitler's propaganda minister, conducted many of the public book-burning ceremonies. During the Qing dynasty (1644–1911) in China, for almost 10 years there were big book-burning ceremonies, due to the Qing rulers' concerns about the activities of intellectual Chinese scholars, which it felt could destabilize the government. Going back earlier in time, the first Chinese Emperor Qin Shih Huang (Ch'in Shih Huang) of the Qin dynasty was known to have carried out a massive book-burning exercise around 213 B.C. To suppress the spread of classical Chinese literature, he issued an edict for the destruction of books, especially those of Lao-Tzu, Confucius and Mencius. The emperor also went a step further by carrying out executions of several scholars alongside the book-burning rituals. Scholars believe that in ancient Greece and the Roman Empires, in an effort to prevent unexpected destruction by fire, several important books were written deliberately on vellum and not on parchment or papyrus. This was because vellum does not burn as easily as the other two. An alternative to book-burning is banning books from reaching the public. This is the more civilized method used today by governments.

214
Famous Government-Sanctioned Book Bans

The earliest instance of banning books from the general public occurred when Roman Emperor Caligula simply banned Homer's *Odyssey* from libraries in the entire Roman Empire rather than destroy them with fire. Some famous government-sanctioned book bans include that of Russian dictator Josef Stalin who banned both the Bible and the Koran in the former USSR. Iran's Ayatollah Khomeini banned Salman Rushdie's *The Satanic Verses* and issued a fatwa (or death sentence) against him, and Augusto Pinochet disallowed the sale of *Don Quixote* in Chile in the 1970s. The longest list of major government sanctioned banned books started around the time of the infamous 16th century era of the Inquisition. In 1559 the Vatican and Pope Paul IV published the first edition of a book listing over 4,000 published works that were censored and banned in Roman Catholic countries because they contained opinions that were considered to be heretical or anti–Christian. During the time this ban was in force, there were of course several book-burning events. Over the years, among the famous books on the Vatican's banned list, known as the *Index Libroram Prohibitorum* (Index of Prohibited Books), have been those written by such novelists, scientists, philosophers and astronomers as Victor Hugo, Francis Bacon, René Descartes, Emmanuel Swedenborg, Blaise Pascal, Nicolaus Copernicus, Giovanni Casanova, Galileo Galilei and Jean-Paul Sartre. During periods of book banning, there have been efforts on the other side to protect books, especially those in university libraries. In the mid–1700s, Pope Benedict XIV issued a papal bull which in effect punished anyone caught stealing or destroying books in universities or public libraries. The banned list was discontinued in 1966, after more than 400 years, although the Inquisition (instituted in 1542) officially ended much earlier, in 1820.

Turkey once banned the sale of the complete set of *Encyclopædia Britannica* in the 1980s because they felt it was "too politically incorrect" and thus a bad influence on its younger generation. Not only was the book forbidden in Turkey, all existing copies were destroyed and recycled to make more acceptable Turkish publications. In the middle 1980s, the British government banned the publication of a book by former MI6 secret agent Peter Wright. The book, titled *Spy Catcher*, had theorized who the 5th man was. The ban was related to a KGB spy ring in the U.K. of 5 British MI6 double agents working for the KGB, some recruited as students from Cambridge University in the 1930s including Kim Philby and Anthony Blunt. The spy ring was gradually unmasked in the 1960s and 1980s, but only 4 of the 5 MI6 agents were positively identified up to the time *Spy Catcher* was eventually published in Australia in 1987. In the 1990s the 5th man was positively identified as John Caincross, which was not the name revealed in the book. In Israel, it was a custom not to throw away or burn religious texts but to store or bury them in a synagogue's *Genizah*.

215
Oldest Bookstores

Today the oldest existing bookstore in the world is Libreria Editrice, founded in 1587 by Pope Sixtus V. It also publishes and prints books for the Vatican. Livraria Bertrand in Lisbon, Portugal, has been selling books since 1732. The oldest English bookstore was John Smith & Sons Bookshop in Glasgow, Scotland, which had been booksellers since 1751. Sadly, in November 2000 it closed for the last time, a victim of the phenomenal growth of the online bookstore revolution. Popular poet Robert Burns was a regular customer of the bookstore. WHSmith, a large bookseller in the U.K., was formed in 1792, but it originally sold only newspapers for a number of years before branching into selling books as well. The oldest university bookstore, including those which are part of a university press, is Cambridge University Press in the U.K. (the oldest publisher of books in the world, see list **229**), which has been selling its own books since 1590. The oldest bookstore in the world specializing in only antiquarian books is the one owned by Henry Sotheran, founded in York, Britain, in 1761.

The renowned U.S. collector of Shakespeare, Henry Clay Folger (who founded the Folger Library), acquired much of his collection, including the Halliwell-Phillips library, through the Sotheran bookstore.

216
Oldest Existing Bookstore in the Americas

The Moravian Bookstore has been in existence in the quiet town of Bethlehem, Pennsylvania, U.S., since 1745.

The origin of the Moravian bookstore dates back to 17th of November 1745 when Bishop Augustus Spangenberg, the leader of the Bethlehem Moravian Congregation in the U.S., suggested to Samuel Powell, keeper of the Bethlehem Inn, the possibility of importing and distributing books in Bethlehem. Aware of the importance of a well-organized commerce in books for Bethlehem (then a new settlement), with its missionary and educational activities, Powell began to buy and sell books, initially religious books, but later books on other subjects as well.

217
Oldest Existing Bookstores in Asia

Higginbotham's, Madras (Chennai), was founded in 1844. Maruzen bookstore in Tokyo, Japan, was founded in 1869.

218
Oldest Existing Bookstores in Africa and the Middle East

Juta Bookshop, Cape Town, South Africa, was founded in 1923. Steimatzky's Bookstore, Tel Aviv, Israel, was established in 1925.

219
First and Largest Book Clubs

Swiss Co-operative Movement of Switzerland was founded in 1900. The largest book clubs in Europe are probably the Book Club Associates or BCA. It is jointly owned by Germany's Bertelsmann and the Anglo-Dutch Group Reed Elsevier and is based in London, U.K. The other big European book club is France Loisirs, which is also the world's largest book club, with over 6 million members in France, Belgium, Switzerland and Canada (Quebec) combined. The two largest book clubs in the United States are Book-of-the-Month Club and Doubleday Direct. Oprah Winfrey's Book Club is the world's most popular book club, and one of the best places to promote a new book on contemporary issues.

220
Largest Online Bookstore

Amazon was founded in 1995 by Jeff Bezos and based in Seattle in the U.S. In the financial year 2006 it had over 10 million titles and annual sales average $9.2 billion. Online advertising is very important to online bookstores. According to Thomson Intermedia, a leading advertising monitor, Amazon is also the largest online advertising spender in the U.K., with more than 90 percent of its total advertising budget of over $22 million going towards web and WAP advertising. Although Amazon started the online bookstore revolution a decade ago, today all major bookstores and book publishers also have websites to enable readers to browse and purchase books. Bookfinder.com is the largest book search engine, searching over 30,000 bookstores and online bookstores including Amazon. It currently has over 40 million new, used, rare, and out of print titles.

The largest online bookseller of used, rare, second hand, out-of-print and antiquarian books is 21 North Main. The company has more than 11 million books available from more than 2,800 rare book dealers.

Opposite, top: Bertrand bookstore in Portugal, opened in 1732, is the second oldest bookstore in the world. This is the Lisbon branch. *Bottom:* The Moravian Book Shop, in Bethlehem, Pennsylvania, which opened in 1745, is the oldest in the United States (courtesy Moravian Book Shop).

221
Largest Online Bookstore in Europe

The Internet Bookshop, which is a division of the book and magazine retailer WH-Smith (Swindon, U.K.), currently has a stock of over 4 million titles. It was set up in 1994, and is probably the oldest online bookstore, as it was set up before Amazon.

222
Largest Online Bookstore in Asia

Xinhua, with offices located in Beijing, China, has a collection of over 6 million titles on the web.

223
Largest Online Bookstore in Latin America

Brazil's Livraria Cultura has over 2 million titles. The online bookstore is based in São Paulo.

224
Largest Online Bookstore in Africa

Exclusive Books, located in Johannesburg, South Africa, has over 100,000 titles.

225
Largest Online Bookstore in the Middle East

Based in Beirut (Lebanon), Nile & Euphrates offers more than 50,000 Arabic books on the Internet. The second largest online bookstore in the Middle East, Almaktabah, is also located in Beirut.

226
Largest and Tallest Bookstores

Barnes & Noble Bookstore, with its headquarters in New York City, is the largest in the world in both volume and total floor space. Currently the bookstore has a stock of over 4.5 million titles. The largest bookstores in the U.S. are in Manhattan and Queens. Barnes & Noble operates over 800 bookstores in the U.S. The tallest bookstore is the 27-floor Shanghai Book City in China at 427 feet. Donner Boekhandel, Rotterdam, The Netherlands, is the tallest bookstore building in Europe, with 11 floors, at 126 feet.

227
Largest Bookstores Around the World

I found it hard to compile an accurate list of the largest bookstores in the world because bookstores acquire new books faster than libraries. So I have decided instead to provide a list of the largest bookstores from a selection of countries. Most of these bookstores now have online versions similar to Amazon, but as always Amazon is "unique" in that it has no physical branch you can visit, you can only browse or buy books online. Some bookstores aided me by sending in current total number of books, but this may not represent the actual total by the time this book went into print. Unless otherwise noted, each bookstore listed here represents all the branches of that particular bookstore in the same city.

Argentina

1. Librería ABC, Buenos Aires.

2. El Ateneo, Buenos Aires. Largest bookstore chain in South America.

3. Grupo ILHSA, Buenos Aires.
   The Spanish word for bookstore is Librería.

Australia

1. Angus & Robertson Bookshop, Sydney.

2. Australian National University, Co-op, Canberra.

3. Dymocks, Sydney.

4. Birchalls Bookshop, Launceston, Tasmania. Founded in 1844, it is the oldest bookstore in Australia.

Austria

1. Buchhandlung Lektüre, Vienna

2. Buchhandlung Hollrigl, Salzburg. Also oldest in Austria.

Belgium

1. Standard Boekhandel, Brussels.

2. Belgique Loisirs, Brussels.

3. Club, Brussels.
   Belgium is bilingual, so names of bookstores are in French (Librairie) and Flemish (Boekhandel), depending on location. The largest online bookstore in Belgium is Brussels-based Proxis.

Brazil

1. Livraria Siciliano, São Paulo.

2. Livraria Nobel, São Paulo.

3. Livraria La Selva, São Paulo.

4. Livraria Lojas Saraiva, Rio de Janeiro. Largest bookstore chain.

5. Livraria Vozes, Belo Horizonte.
   The Portuguese Brazilian word for bookstore is Livraria.

Canada

1. Chapters Bookstore, Toronto. Largest Canadian bookstore.

2. WBB or World's Biggest Bookstore, Toronto. Stocking over 1 million titles.

3. McNally Robinson Bookstore, Toronto.

4. Librairie Gallimard, Montreal.

5. Indigo, Toronto.
   The French word for bookstore is Librairie.

China

1. Xinhua, Beijing.

2. Shanghai Book City, Shanghai. The building is massive: 27 floors. Possibly the largest

bookstore in China, and tallest book store in the world. with over 500,000 books.

3. Wang Fu Jing, Beijing.

4. Beijing Tushu Daxia (aka Beijing Book Building), the biggest bookstore in Beijing.

5. Xi Shu, Shanghai (largest bookstore chain in China).

The Chinese word for bookstore is Shu-Dian.

Denmark

1. Arnold Busck, Copenhagen.

2. Politikens Boghallen, Copenhagen.

3. GEC GAD, Copenhagen. The bookstore was founded in 1855 and is the oldest in Denmark.

The Danish word for bookstore is Boghandel.

Dominican Republic

Cuesta, Santo Domingo.

Egypt

Madbouli's Bookstore, Cairo.

The Arabic word for bookstore is Maktaba.

Finland

1. Akateeminen Kirjakauppa, Helsinki. Founded in 1893, oldest in Finland.

2. Suomalainen Kirjakauppa, Helsinki. Largest bookstore chain.

The Finnish word for bookstore is Kirjakauppa.

France

1. Librairie FNAC, Paris.

2. Librairie le Furet du Nord, Lillie. Its 10 floors of books make it a leading contender for the largest bookstore in Europe.

The Politiken bookstore in Copenhagen is the largest in Denmark.

The FNAC is the largest chain of bookstores in France. This store is in Lyon.

3. Librairie Mollat, Bordeaux. Oldest bookstore in France, as it was founded in 1896.

4. Librairie Decitre, Paris.

5. Librairie la Procure, Paris.

The French word for bookstore is Librairie, which is also used in the French speaking parts of Belgium, Switzerland and Canada.

Germany

1. Thalia, Hamburg.

2. Buchhandlung Kiepert, Berlin.

3. Kulturkaufhaus Dussmann Buchhandlung, Berlin.

4. J.F. Lehmanns Fachbuchhandlung, Berlin.

5. Hugendubel Buchhandlung, Munich.

6. Phönix-Montanus Buchhandlung, Berlin.

The German word for bookstore is Buchhandlung, used also in Austria and Switzerland.

Greece

1. Eleftheroudakis, Athens.

2. Mihalopoulos, Thessaloniki.

India

1. Metropolitan Bookshop, New Delhi.

2. Higginbotham's, Madras (Chennai). It claims to be the largest bookstore in India. It is India's oldest booksellers, founded in 1844.

3. Flora Fountain Bookshop, Mumbai (Bombay) and College Street Bookshop, Calcutta (Kolkata). Both have over two kilometers of books in open space, meaning that you can "window shop" for hours on what are the world's largest outdoor book markets. Over 500,000 books available to buy on a single day.

4. Gangaram, Bangalore.

New Delhi–based Firstandsecond.com, with over 1 million titles, is the largest online bookstore in India.

Indonesia

Gramedia, Jakarta.

Ireland

1. Eason and Sons Bookshop, Dublin.

2. Hodges Figgis Bookshop, Dublin.

3. O'Mahony's, Limerick.

Israel

Steimatzky's Bookstore. Tel Aviv. It is also the oldest in Israel, having been established in 1925.

Italy

1. Libreria Marzocco, Florence.

2. Libreria Feltrinelli, Milan.

3. Libreria Rizzoli, Rome.

4. Libreria Flaccovio, Palermo.
The Italian word for bookstore is Libreria.

Japan

1. Kinokuniya, Tokyo. 3 million titles.

2. Maruzen, Tokyo. 2.5 million tiles. It is the oldest existing bookstore in Japan, originally founded in 1869.

3. Kanda Book Town, Tokyo. 2 million titles.

4. Junkudo, Tokyo. 1.5 million titles.

5. Sanseido, Tokyo.

6. Yaesu Book Center, Tokyo. Japan's 2nd biggest bookstore after Kinokuniya.

The Japanese word for bookstore is Hon-ya. The largest bookstore district in Japan is Tokyo's Kanda-Jimbocho in the Chiyoda-Ku section of the city.

Hugendubel is the largest chain of bookstores in Germany. This store in Munich is one of the busiest.

It's past 9 P.M. at Berlin's Hugendubel, and a lot of customers are still busy in the bookstore.

Korea

1. Kyobo, Seoul. 1.4 million titles.

2. Yeongpung (Youngpoong), Seoul.

3. Bandi & Luni's, Seoul. With an area of 60,385 square feet, Bandi & Luni's is the biggest bookstore in Asia and stocks 2 million volumes.

4. Chongno, Pusan.

5. Jongro, Seoul.
    The Korean word for bookstore is Seo-Jeom.

Kuwait

Al Muthanna, Kuwait City.

Latvia

Jina Rozes, Riga. It is the largest bookstore in the Baltic States.
The Latvian word for bookstore is Libro.

Malaysia

1. Kinokuniya, Kuala Lumpur.

2. MPH, Kuala Lumpur.

3. Reader's World (Plaza Kotaraya), Kuala Lumpur.

Mexico

1. Librería de Cristal. Mexico City.

2. Librería Gandhi, Mexico City.

3. Librería Porrúa, Mexico City.
    The Spanish word for bookstore is Librería. The largest online bookstore in Mexico is Librería Jovellanos.

The Netherlands

1. Scheltema Holkema Vermeulen Boekhandel, Amsterdam.

2. Donner Boekhandel, Rotterdam. The tallest bookstore building in Europe, with 11 floors. May have more books than Waterstone's Bookshop in London.

3. Athenaeum Boekhandel, Amsterdam.

4. De Slegte Boekhandel, Amsterdam.

5. Bruna Boekhandel, Rotterdam.
The Dutch word for bookstore is Boekhandel, which is also used in the Flemish speaking parts of Belgium.

New Zealand

Whitcoullis and Bennetts, Auckland.

Nigeria

1. CMS Bookshop, Lagos.

2. Abiola Bookshops, Lagos.

Norway

1. Tanum Bokhandel, Oslo.

2. Bokkilden Bokhandel, Oslo

3. Olaf Norlis Bokhandel, Oslo.
The Norwegian word for bookstore is Bokhandel.

The Philippines

1. Goodwill Bookstore, Manila.

2. National Bookstore, Manila.

Poland

Empik, Warsaw.

Portugal

1. Livraria Bertrand, Lisbon.

2. Livraria Barata, Lisbon.

3. Livraria Portugal.
The Portuguese word for bookstore is Livraria. The second oldest bookstore in the world is Livraria Bertrand, set up in 1732.

Russia

1. Biblio-Globus, Moscow.

2. Book House (Moskovsky Dom Knigi), St. Petersburg.

3. Molodaya Gvardia, Moscow.

4. Moskva, Moscow.

5. Presstorg, Moscow.
The Russian word for book store is Knizhniy Magazine.

Saudi Arabia

1. Jareer, Riyadh.

2. Obeikan, Riyadh.
The Arabic word for bookstore is Maktaba which is also used as the word for library.

Singapore

1. Kinokuniya. Claims to be the largest bookstore in southeast Asia.

2. Popular Bookshop.

Slovenia

Mladinska Knjiga, Ljubljana.

South Africa

1. Juta Bookshop, Cape Town. It is the oldest bookstore in South Africa, founded in 1923.

2. Juta Bookhop, Johannesburg.

3. Exclusive Books, Johannesburg.

Spain

1. Diaz de Santos, Madrid.

2. Casa de Libro, Barcelona.
The Spanish word for bookstore is Librería.

Sweden

1. Akademibokhandeln, Stockholm.

2. Bokhandeln Nyströms, Stockholm.

3. Bokhandeln Bokia, Stockholm.

The Swedish word for bookstore is Bokhandeln. Bokus.com is the largest online bookstore in Scandinavia, and the third largest in Europe; over 1.5 million titles are available.

Switzerland

1. Buchhandlung Orelli Fuessli, Zürich.

2. Buchhandlung Stauffacher, Zürich.

3. Buchhandlung Luthy, Zürich.

4. Buchhandlung Jaeggi, Basel.

Taiwan

1. Eslite Books (Xin Yi), Taipei.

2. Hess Bookstore, Taipei.

Eslite Books is a 24 hour bookstore, one of the few bookstores with round-the-clock opening hours in the world. Timeasia magazine voted the 8-story building the best bookstore in Asia in 2004. With large readers lounges in the aisles, a restaurant, over 3000 magazines, a million books, and a steady stream of classical music played in the background, it is hard to fall asleep in the early hours of the morning, let alone get bored, in this fascinating bookstore.

Thailand

1. Asia Books, Bangkok.

2. DK Books, Bangkok.

3. SE Education, Bangkok. Largest bookstore chain.

The Thai word for bookstore is Rarn-Khai-Nang-Seur.

Turkey

1. Enderun Kitabevi, Istanbul.

2. Dünya Aktüel Kitabevi, Istanbul. Turkey's largest bookstore chain.

3. Bilgi, Istanbul.

The Turkish word for bookstore is Kitabevi.

U.K.

1. Waterstone's Bookshop. London. Many branches were formerly known under the name Dillons. The Piccadilly Circus branch of Waterstone's is the largest single bookstore in Europe, with a stock of 3 million titles, covering 7 floors. The Glasgow branch of Waterstone's is the third largest bookstore in the U.K.

2. Foyles Bookshop, London. Most probably the second largest single bookstore in Europe, with a stock of about 2 million titles.

3. Blackwell's Bookshop, London.

4. Books etc, London.

5. Borders Bookshop, London.

6. WHSmith, London. It is also the largest seller of magazines and newspapers in the U.K.

7. Grant & Cutter, London. Largest foreign bookseller in the U.K.

United States

1. Barnes & Noble Bookstore New York City. Largest bookstore in the world. Over 4.5 million titles to choose from. There are over 800 bookstores.

2. Borders Bookstore, New York City. 2 million titles.

3. Powell's Bookstore, Portland, Oregon. More than 1.5 million books.

4. Waldenbooks Bookstore, headquartered in Ann Arbor, Michigan. It runs the largest mall-based bookseller in the U.S. with over 900 bookstores.

5. Lectorum Bookstore (Librería Lectorum), New York City. It is the largest bookstore in the U.S., stocking books in Spanish for the Hispanic community.

Waterstone's Bookshop near London's Piccadilly Circus is still the largest single bookshop in Europe.

The U.S. Government Printing Office, better known as the GPO, is the largest publisher of government documents, reports and books in the world, with over 30,000 publications issued each day. The GPO, which began printing in 1861, also operates about 25 bookstores around the U.S. that sell its publications. The largest private distributor of U.S. government publications as well as intergovernmental agency publications such as those from the World Bank and the OECD is Bernan, based in Lanham, Maryland.

Vatican City

Libreria Editrice Vaticana, Rome.

It is also the oldest bookstore in the world having been founded in 1587. See also list **215**. *The Latin word for bookstore is Libreria.*

Venezuela

Librería Lectura, Caracas.

Vietnam

1. Fahasa, Ho Chi Minh City.

2. Xuan Thu, Hanoi and Ho Chi Minh City.

The Vietnamese word for bookstore is Dan Thu (the world for library is Thu vien).

Yugoslavia (Serbia)

1. Nolit, Belgrade.

2. Prosveta, Belgrade.

3. Narodna Knjiga, Belgrade.

Powell's bookstore in Portland, Oregon (courtesy Powell's Bookstore).

228
Largest Publishers of Books

Here are lists of some of the largest publishers around the world, publishing in the official language. Some are government owned, others are private or partially privatized. N.B. many of these publishers, such as Harper-Collins, have numerous imprints or brand names, depending on the subject or category of the books being published.

Australia: Collins (imprint of Harper-Collins).

Bangladesh: UPL.

Canada: Harlequin; University of Toronto Press.

China: China Publishing Group.

Denmark: Gyldendal.

Egypt: Dar Al Ma'aref.

Finland: Werner Soderstrom Oyi (WSOY); Otava.

France: Havas; Lagardère; Hachette (the largest French publishing house, also largest magazine publisher in Europe); Groupe de la Cité, France's second-largest book publisher; La Martinière; Vivendi.

Germany: Bertelsmann (largest book publisher); Axel Springer (Ullstein Heynelist); Holtzbrinck; Weltbild.

Indonesia: Gramedia.

Israel: Stemzky.

Italy: Arnoldo Mondadori; Feltrineli De Agostini; Garzanti.

Japan: Kodansha.

Mexico: Oceano de Mexico, Although part of the Oceano group based in Spain, an imprint is the largest publisher in Mexico.

Malaysia: Dewan Bahasa dan Pustaka (DBP).

Norway: Cappelen.

The Netherlands: Elsevier (largest scientific, technical and medical publisher).

Poland: Wsip (Wydawnictwa Szkolne Pedagogiczne).

Russia: Adolf Marx.

South Africa: Nasional Pers.

Spain: Planeta Actimedia; Santillana (the largest book publisher in the Spanish-speaking world, and smaller advertising agencies and printing companies into the group).

Sweden: Bonnier Group (Arnold Bonnier, AB).

Switzerland: Edipresse.

Sri Lanka: M.D. Gunasena.

Taiwan: Cite.

U.K.: Oxford University Press; Hodder Headline; Pearson (world's largest education publisher; Cambridge University Press.

U.S.: Random House (largest English language book publisher in the world, part of Germany's Bertelsmann); Wiley-Blackwell (2nd largest scientific, technical and medical publisher). Time Warner Books (2nd largest English language book publisher); Penguin Putnam; IDG Scholastic (largest publisher of children's books in the U.S.); Macmillan Computer Publishing (largest computer book publisher); HarperCollins.

Yugoslavia (Serbia): Narodna Knjiga, Belgrade.

The largest publisher of magazines is IDG, based Boston, Massachusetts, with branches worldwide.

229
Oldest Publishers of Books

Cambridge University Press is the oldest publisher in the world, having been continuously publishing books since 1584. The Vatican's publishing house, Libreria Editrice, was founded in 1587 by Pope Sixtus V, when he set up the Holy See's printing press. Libreria Editrice is also a major bookstore in the Vatican. Oxford University Press dates back to the late 1590s. The earliest book publisher in Europe was the one set up in Milan, Italy, in 1472, but it no longer exists today. In the Americas, the earliest publisher was the one established by Mathew Carey in 1785 in Philadelphia. The oldest continuously operated university press in the U.S. is the Johns Hopkins University Press, founded in 1878. The oldest continuous publisher of commercial journals is Taylor & Francis, founded in London in 1798. Its journals are also available via Informaworld (see list **283**).

230
Largest Annual Book Fair

The biggest book fairs are measured in the number of exhibitors and not number of visitors. Reed Exhibitions (part of Reed Elsevier) organizes several of the largest book fairs in the world, including the London Book Fair, the Tokyo Book Fair in Japan and the Book Expo America in several U.S. cities. The Frankfurt International Book Fair in Germany is the largest in the world. In 2007 there were 7272 exhibitors from over 113 countries and 57,000 visitors each day. It is also the oldest-continuously hosted book fair, as it was first held in 1534 (the modern event, however, began in 1950). The event is held annually at magnificent Messe Trade Center in Frankfurt, since 2002 in October, along with the event an annual fair for online databases and services for libraries called InfoBase (see list **342**). The other main book fair event in Germany is the Leipzig Book Fair, which first began in 1991. The London Book Fair, which began in 1972, had 1510 exhibitors in 2007 from 45 countries. The third largest book fair in Europe is the Moscow International Book Fair, which was set up in 1977 and features 719 exhibitors for the 5 day event. The largest children's book fair is the Bologna Children's Book Fair in Italy (founded in 1962). In 2006 11,000 daily visitors came to the fair, with

Each year the Frankfurt International Book Fair, the world's largest, is held at the Messe Trade Center in Frankfurt, Germany.

over 1200 children books exhibitors from 63 countries. The largest book fair in France is Salon du Livre held every year in Paris. The second largest book fair in Eastern Europe is Poland's Warsaw International Book Fair.

231
Largest Annual Book Fairs in the U.S. and Canada

First held in 1983, about 2565 exhibitors came to the week-long Miami Book Fair International in Florida in 2006.

The same year, the Book Expo America (first expo in 1985), held in Chicago, Los Angeles and San Francisco, all had more than 2100 exhibitors from 48 countries and over 95,000 daily visitors each. In Canada, the 2007 Salon du Livre Montreal book fair (founded in 1978) had 875 exhibitors and 20,500 daily visitors. The 2007 American Library Association annual conference was attended by over 28,000 visitors with over 950 exhibiting companies.

232
Largest Annual Book Fairs in Asia

Six countries vie for the largest annual fairs in Asia. The 2007 Tokyo International Book Fair Japan had 55,943 daily visitors and 712 exhibitors in 51 countries. The Taipei International Book Exhibition in Taiwan (first held in 1991) for 2007 had 73,000 daily visitors with

545 exhibitors from 42 countries. The Beijing Book Fair, which started in 1993, had 1501 exhibitors in 48 countries and 51,00 daily visitors. The 2007 Hong Kong Book Fair, established in 1990, attracted 98,084 daily visitors, with more than 480 exhibitors from over 45 countries. The Seoul International Book Fair in South Korea had over 462 exhibitors from 52 countries and 46,000 visitors. The World Book Fair in New Delhi, India (founded in 1989), in 2007 had 125,000 daily visitors and 400 exhibitors. Mumbai (Bombay) International Book Fair and the Calcutta (Kolkata) Book Fair both in India averaged about 250 exhibitors and 15,000 visitors over the last few years. The Bangkok International Book Fair does not have more exhibitors than any of the 6 fairs listed above, but it has the largest attendance of a book fair in the world, with over 130,000 daily visitors in 2007 for the 12 day event.

233
Largest Annual Book Fairs in Latin America

The largest book fair in South America is the Buenos Aires Book Fair (first held in 1975). In 2007 the 19 day event attracted 1325 exhibitors and 52,000 daily visitors. It is the oldest book event in the Spanish-speaking world. Guadalajara International Book Fair in Mexico had more than 2001 exhibitors in 2005. It is the biggest book fair in Latin America. The 11 day Rio de Janeiro Book 2007 Fair in Brazil (founded in 1983) had 57,272 daily visitors and 525 exhibitors.

234
Largest Annual Book Fairs in the Middle East

The 20th annual Tehran International Book Fair in Iran in 2007 and the 2007 Istanbul Book Fair in Turkey were both the largest in the Middle East. Both averaged just over 382 exhibitors and 31,000 daily visitors.

235
Largest Annual Book Fairs in Africa

The annual Cape Town Book Fair in 2007 had 16,000 visitors and 170 exhibitors. It is not a big event as it only began in 2004, but is growing steadily. The Zimbabwe International Book Fair, held each year in the capital, Harare, was once the largest in African, and attracted over 200 exhibitors before 2002, but has since been scaled back over the last few years. The oldest book fair in Africa is the Cairo International Book Fair in Egypt, which began in 1969. For 2007, it had 136 exhibitors and 49,000 daily visitors. It is a 60 day event, the longest in any book fair.

WORLD RECORDS FOR LIBRARY BUILDINGS

236
Oldest Existing Library Buildings

The famous Indian librarian Shiyali Ramamrita Ranganathan once remarked in his equally famous "five laws of library science" that "a library is a growing organism." Very true, as today's libraries see their book collections grow in size at a faster rate than decades before. The U.S. Library of Congress in 1979 had about 16 million books, but today that figure is over 25 million. While Harvard University had 901,000 books in 1900, today that figure is over 13 million. As libraries acquire more books, naturally more space is needed, meaning expanding an existing library building or constructing a new library building with bigger space from scratch. Listing the oldest library building proved a bit difficult to research. Should the list include library buildings renovated but with several parts of the original buildings intact?

The earliest library buildings were those built by the Sumerians (part clay and part stone) to store collections of their written documents in the form of clay tablets, around 2700 B.C. These libraries do not exist intact anymore. The ancient Egyptians were the first to build library buildings made entirely of stone. But the oldest existing stone building in ancient Egypt and indeed the world is not a library building but Imhotep's Step Pyramid of Djoser, in what is now Saqqara (Sakkara). It was completed in Third Egyptian dynasty (circa 2800 B.C.) for King Zoser.

Library buildings built with concrete (pozzolana) first appeared in the Roman Empire about 180 B.C. Many of the libraries in the oldest universities in the world (see lists **61** and **63**), were actually part of the university buildings themselves and so cannot count as separate buildings. But it is worth mentioning that universities in existence before the first half of the 13th century — i.e., before A.D. 1250 (see list **382**) — and still existing today have some surviving buildings with some parts devoted to a library, some of which have now been replaced with modern buildings. These libraries include the universities of Bologna, Padua, Modena, Parma, Piacenza, Vicenza, Perugia and Sienna in Italy; Salamanca University in Spain; Paris and Montpellier universities in France; Oxford and Cambridge universities in the U.K.; Hacettepe University in Ankara, Turkey; Al-Azhar University in Cairo, Egypt, and Al-Qarawiyin University in Fez, Morocco. Padua University in Italy possibly has the oldest existing university library building in Europe.

The following are some of the oldest library buildings in the world (with the exception of national and university library buildings).

Asia-Pacific region (excluding the Middle East): The Tianyi Ge Library building in the Chinese coastal city of Ningbo (Ningpo or Ninghsien) on the Yong River was built in 1516, during the Ming dynasty. It also houses some

The entrance to Parma University Library in Italy reveals curved walls and arched ceilings. A standard architectural style is still present on some old university buildings (courtesy Parma University).

of the oldest and rarest Chinese manuscripts to be found outside the national library in Beijing. It is the oldest library building in Asia, outside the Middle East.

The four major religions of Asia, Hinduism, Buddhism, Islam and Christianity all had some of the earliest buildings for storing sacred manuscripts and books. The oldest religion, Hinduism, had temple buildings housing libraries that date back to the first millennium B.C., but few exist today. Some of the few surviving library buildings of Buddhist monasteries

(or Vihar) date from the 7th century B.C. in India. The Huaisheng Mosque in Canton (Guangzhou), China, built in the 7th century A.D., also included an Islamic library.

Europe: The monastic Malatesta Library building (*Biblioteca Comunale Malatestiana*) was constructed between 1447 and 1452 in Cesena, northern Italy, and is probably the oldest surviving original library building in the world today. Prince Novello Malatesta founded the library and the architect was Matteo Nutti.

Today most of the rare books of the library are in the Laurentian Library in Florence, but it still has over 400,000 books, which are on the UNESCO Memory of the World Register. The building of the Laurentian Library itself is old as well. Construction of the Laurentian Library began in 1524, and it was opened to the public in 1571. The present Vatican Library building dates back to 1588, when Pope Sixtus V asked Domenico Fontana to design a new library building. The other early monasteries that still exist today (but with renovated buildings) had some form of libraries inside, and they included the 4th century A.D. St. Maurice Monastery of Switzerland, the 5th century A.D. St. Honorat island monastery of France, and the 12th century Poblet Monastery in Spain. There are many existing cathedral buildings with libraries in Europe, some dating back to the Middle Ages such as the Canterbury Cathedral in U.K., Notre Dame Cathedral in France, and the Toledo Cathedral in Spain.

The St. Gallen Monastery building in Switzerland dates back to the 7th century A.D., but has since been renovated externally while retaining the gothic architectural style. It was one of Europe's greatest centers of learning. Its famous library, Stiftsbibliothek, is the largest of the oldest existing monastic libraries today, with over 100,000 books.

Latin America: The oldest existing non-academic library building in Latin America is the Palafox Library (*Biblioteca Palafoxiana*), in the Palafox Cathedral, Puebla, Mexico (rich in the oldest Spanish colonial buildings in Mexico). The building dates back to 1645 and also the first public library in the Americas. The oldest book in its collection, brought from Spain, was printed in 1493, a year after Christopher Columbus discovered the Americas. The library was founded by bishop Juan de Palafox y Mendoza, and is housed in the Archdiocese Palace, south of the early baroque style cathedral, which has the highest towers in Mexico. The original building of the Mexico National Autonomous University and the library dates back to 1584, but it was demolished in 1910 to make way for a new building.

The Palafox Library is not older than the oldest university library in the Americas, Santo Domingo University Library, in the Dominican Republic, which dates back to 1538.

Middle East: The mosque libraries are undoubtedly the oldest kinds of libraries in the Middle East. It was common in the early days of Islam for libraries to be built in the same compound as mosques. Some mosque libraries were later part of a university library, such as Morocco's 9th century Al-Qarawiyin University library in Fez. Most mosque libraries were used for storing and consulting sacred Islamic manuscripts and books such as the Koran. Among the oldest existing mosque buildings dating from the 7th century A.D. (when the first mosques in the world were built) are the Umayyad Mosque in Damascus, Syria; the Amr Mosque in Cairo, Egypt (containing the oldest building housing a library in Africa); and the Al-Aqsa Mosque in Jerusalem, Israel (then under Arab rule). The mosque and the Dome of the Rock shrine (built in the 7th century A.D.) are both located on the Temple Mount.

United States: In the U.S., the oldest existing library building is the Sturgis Library in Barnstable, Massachusetts, built in 1644. It is listed in the U.S. National Register of Historic Places. The building is also one of the oldest houses remaining on Cape Cod. And the oldest structure still standing in America where religious services were regularly held.

The oldest continuously-operated university library building in the U.S. is the South Carolina University Library in Columbia. It dates back to 1840 and is also called the South Carolinian Library. This library building made the University of South Carolina the first university in the U.S. to have a separate building for the library.

Africa: In Sub-Saharan Africa, as in the Middle East, mosque libraries were the oldest types of libraries. Three of the oldest mosques in the region are Djinguereber (Jingarayber), Sankore, and Sidi Yahia mosques, built in the 14th and early 15th centuries and all based in Timbuktu, Mali. Sankore mosque is also famous for the Sankore University, the oldest in Sub-Saharan Africa.

Sturgis Library in Barnstable, Massachusetts, is the oldest library building in the United States today. It has existed since 1644 and is protected by the U.S. National Register of Historic Places (courtesy Sturgis Library).

237
First Library Building to Use Extensive Electrical Lighting

The most important invention used in library buildings in the 19th century, with the industrial revolution in full swing, was that of harnessing electric power to illuminate the library. One can imagine how hazardous it was in those days to have lamps in big libraries, with the possibility of books catching fire or arson being encouraged. The British Library in 1879 (then part of the British Museum Library) was the first major library in the world to have permanent electric light bulbs in its reading rooms. At first electric Jablochtoff arc lamps were used, then carbon filament lights. In the 1890s electricity was fully installed in the Reading Room.

The electric power was achieved with two pairs of dynamos driven by two steam engines.

British public libraries were the first public libraries to use electricity. Thomas Edison's Electric Light Company opened the first public power station in London on January 12, 1882, based on direct current technology. It was later replaced with technology based on George Westinghouse's use of alternating current. The provision of general public electricity was a first in the U.K., due to the fact that it was the most industrialized country in the world, and reliable sources of electricity were essential to power the industrial machines.

The British Museum Library in London was the first library in the world to use permanent electric lights, starting in 1879.

238
Ten Tallest Library Buildings

1. Shanghai Library, China. Architect(s): Zhang Jie Zheng, et al. The new public library building has two towers: the tallest is 348 feet tall with 24 floors, while the other tower has 190 feet tall with 11 floors. It employs an elaborate retrieval system of "little trains" to transport books throughout the tall building. It is still quite shorter than Malaysia's Petronas Twin Towers in Kuala Lumpur, which is over 1,400 feet tall (the Eiffel Tower is 986 feet tall). The city of Shanghai also features the tallest bookstore in the world (and the second tallest building housing books, after Shanghai Library); see notes section below.

2. University of Massachusetts, W.E.B. Du Bois Library, Amherst, U.S., opened in 1973 and has 28 floors, scaling over 295 feet from the base. Architect: C.E. Macguire.

3. The new National Library of France building in Paris has of 4 glass towers each shaped like an opened book. The architect was Dominique Perrault. Each of the 4 glass towers housing the books is 293 feet tall, making them the tallest library buildings in Europe and the tallest national library in the world. Its foundation was originally supposed to handle the building being 328 feet (100 meters) tall, but the designers settled for 293 feet (90 meters) after taking account several factors such as the fact that as the national library book collection would grow substantially fast, making the towers heavy.

4. Notre Dame University, Hesburgh Library. Notre Dame, Indiana, U.S., is 215 feet tall with 13 floors. Completed in 1963. Architect(s): Doug Marsh, et al.

5. Toronto University, Robarts Library, Canada. It is the largest university library in Canada, and is 182 feet tall with 13 floors. Built in 1964 and opened in 1973. Architect(s): Mathers and Haldenby, et al.

6. Calgary University, MacKimmie Library Tower, Canada. It has 12 floors and is 167 feet tall. Constructed in 1975. It is also the home of the Canadian Architectural Archives. The library is the sixth largest university library in Canada.

7. Los Angeles (California) Central Public Library, U.S., measures about 160 feet. It is made up of 12 floors. Architect(s): Bertram Goodhue.

8. New York University, Bobst Library, in New York City, scales 151 feet and has 12 floors. Architect(s): Johnson and Foster.

9. University of Memphis Library, John Wilder Tower, U.S, is about 120 feet in height, with 12 floors.

10. Seattle Public Library Central Library measures 11 stories from the ground and is 113 feet in height.

The tallest bookstore in the world is the 27 floor Shanghai Book City in China and is 327 feet. The tallest bookstore in Europe is Donner Boekhandel, in Rotterdam, The Netherlands. The 11 floor building is 110 feet and has 27,000 square feet. Lomonosov Moscow State University, located on Moscow Lenin Hills, Russia, is the tallest and largest university building in world. The building, opened in 1953, has 32 floors, and over 40,000 rooms and is 787 feet tall and 6 million square feet in area. The University of Pittsburgh's Cathedral of Learning building, completed in 1956, in the U.S., is a 42-story building. At 535 feet, it is the second tallest university building in the world. Germany's Leipzig University has a famous tall tower building built in 1971 scaling 502 feet in height, making it the second tallest and largest university building in Europe. The tall tower has 34 floors and is called the "wisdom tooth" in German. In Asia the three tallest university buildings are: Kogakuin University Shinjuku campus in Tokyo, Japan, with 29 floors at 436 feet; Hosei University Boissonade Tower in Tokyo, Japan,

The University of Massachusetts' W.E.B. Du Bois Library, in the city of Amherst, is the second tallest library building in the world (courtesy UMass Amherst Facilities and Campus Planning).

at 400 feet and 27 floors; while Kogakuin University STEC building in Tokyo, Japan, is 405 feet tall. In South America, the tallest university is Bolivia's University of San Anders, which stands 326 feet. "Library Tower," opened in 1990 and located in Los Angeles, California, has 75 floors and is 1018 feet tall. But its name is misleading; it is actually an office building not a library building. São Paulo Municipal Library (Mario de Andrade Library), Brazil, is the tallest library building in Latin America. The library, which was opened in 1938, has 7 floors and is 106 feet tall.

239
Six Largest Library Buildings

For those used to metric units, one square meter is about 10.76 square feet and 43,560 square feet roughly equals about 1 acre.

1. The U.S. Library of Congress in Washington, D.C., has three buildings. The main building, or Jefferson Building, was completed in 1897; the adjacent Adams Building was completed in 1939; and the Madison Building was completed in 1981. All three of the library buildings are close together and are the world's largest group of library buildings occupying an overall space of 2.5 million square feet. The largest of the three buildings is the Madison Building. The architects were John L. Smithmeyer and Paul J. Pelz.

2. While the British and French national libraries relocated to a new site in the city to build a brand new library building from scratch, the Russian State Library in Moscow, like the U.S. Library of Congress, decided to remain on the original site and expand the building. The total area of the library building is now 2.2 million square feet. The original building, built in the 1930s, was immense, with 18 floors.

3. The National Library of Japan, Tokyo. The two buildings that make up the National Diet Library measure 1.8 million square feet in total area.

4. The National Library of China, Beijing. The main building, which opened in 1987 is the largest single library building in the world, giving about 1.5 million square feet of floor space. It occupies 22 floors, allowing for 33-odd reading rooms with more than 3,000 seats.

5. The British Library, London. The new building, which opened to the public in 1998, is about 1.2 million square feet in area. In addition there are four levels of storage basements for books, which go down as deep as the London Underground tunnels. It costs $843 million to build. The project for the new library building began way back in 1975, and only opened its doors to the public in December 1997. There is one nostalgic part of the British Library that is absent to anyone who has used the British Museum Library before it became separate from the British Museum in 1973: the famous Round Reading Room. This spectacular domed reading room has been used by the likes of Vladimir Lenin, Charles Dickens and Karl Marx. But the new British library does have its own spectacular features, most notably the King's Library tower inside.

6. The new National Library of France building in Paris, which cost between $750 million and $970 million, takes up 980,000 square feet. The new building, opened officially to the public in December 1996, is composed of 4 glass towers each shaped like an opened book and arranged in a square formation, with a big garden in the center. Architect: Dominique Perrault. The height of the glass towers makes it the tallest library building in Europe.

The largest national library building in the Middle East is the National Library of Turkey building in Ankara, which occupies 419,640 square feet. The largest national library building in the Baltic states is the National Library of Estonia.

The new British Library building in London is the fifth largest library building in the world.

240
Six Largest University Library Buildings

1. Toronto University, Robarts Library, Canada, roughly measures about 1 million square feet. Architects were Mathers and Haldenby, et al. It costs a reported $50 million to build and is Canada's most expensive library building.

2. Brigham Young University, Harold B. Lee Library, Provo, Utah, U.S. The massive building occupies 665,000 square feet. The five-story building has comfortable seating capacity for 4,600 people. Completed in 2000, it is the largest university library building in the U.S.

3. University of Chicago, Regenstein Library, U.S., has 577,085 square feet. Architect(s):

Skidmore, Owings and Merrill. Completed in 1970.

4. Indiana University, Central Library, Bloomington, U.S., has just over 378,420 square feet, and was opened in 1969. Architect(s): David Meeker (James Associates).

5. University of Tennessee Hodges Library, 350,000 square feet. Has 6 floors and 3,000 seats.

6. Nova Southern University Library, Fort Lauderdale, Florida. 325,000 square feet

*The National University of Singapore Library Central Library occupies about 316,000 square of space and is the largest single university library building in Asia. See photograph at list **57**.*

The University of Toronto Robarts Library in Canada is the world's largest university library building (courtesy Laura Arsie, University of Toronto Library).

241
Six Largest Public Library Buildings

1. Shanghai Library, China. Architect(s): Zhang Jie Zheng, et al. The two present buildings that make up the library occupy 902,300 square feet. Its massive size and height (it is the largest and tallest public library in the world) alone makes it stand out along the busiest shopping street in downtown Shanghai, the fifth largest city in the world. Known locally as Shanghai Tushugan, its merging with the Shanghai Institute of Scientific and Technical Information has meant it has international connections and foreign librarians and information professionals visiting China almost certainly pencil-in a visit to the library in their diary if possible. Construction of the new building of Shanghai Library started in early 1993 and it was officially opened in 1997. Among decorations inside the library building is the statue of Chinese philosopher Confucius, and multilingual versions of the slogan "Knowledge Is Power."

2. Harold Washington Library Center, Chicago, U.S., has 756,640 square feet. It is Chicago's central public library and opened in 1991. It has 9 floors and is neo-classical in design with stunning red brick walls forming columns and arches.

Architects Hammond Beeby & Babka won an international competition to design the building, and spent $195 million to carry out the massive project.

3. Cincinnati & Hamilton County (Ohio) Public Library, U.S. The new building, completed in 1997 occupies 542,527 square feet. Architect(s): Abott Design and Shepley Richardson.

4. San Antonio (Texas) Central Public Library, U.S., measures 240,000 square feet, which includes a 1,300-seat auditorium. It opened in 1995 at a cost of $28 million.

5. Vancouver Public Library, Canada. This library measure 378,360 square feet. It is easily recognized for its fascinating shape.

6. Malmö Public Library, Sweden. It measures 164,000. square feet and is 60 feet tall. It is the largest single public library in Europe. The building, which opened in 1997, was designed by the Danish architect Henning Larsen. Branches of the Malmö City Library include a hospital library and a mobile library. Photographs of the library are at list **15**.

242
Largest Scientific and Technical Library Building

Grainger Engineering Library Information Center, University of Illinois, Urbana-Champaign, U.S. The library building which opened in 1994 is about 130,000 square feet. Architect(s): Evans Woollen.

243
Most Fascinating Library Buildings

As we may appreciate, library buildings are nowadays as fascinating as their book collections. Often the appearance of a building outside gives us some insight of what to expect inside. What really makes a library building fascinating? The size of the building, the shape of the building, the age of the building? Perhaps the architecture of the building is groundbreaking, or perhaps it is simply a very expensive building!

Shanghai Library in China is the world's largest and tallest public library building (courtesy Ben Gu, National Library of China).

Vancouver Public Library is Canada's largest public library building (courtesy Diana Thompson and Oi-Lun Kwan).

During the summer and autumn in 2006, during research work for the second edition, the author sent out e-mails to several Internet based bulletin boards for librarians around the world, asking for a vote on the most fascinating library buildings in the world they had visited or seen. The categories voted for were:

1. 10 most fascinating national library buildings.

2. 10 most fascinating university library buildings.

3. 10 most fascinating public library buildings.

Back in 2001, the author carried out a similar survey on the above mentioned categories. The results of that survey, with photographs of some winners of the votes, can be seen in the first edition of the book published in 2004. Voters were made aware of this, and if a library voted in 2006 was also voted in 2001, it will not be included, but a very brief list of winners of the vote for 2001 is included in this edition.

Each respondent voted for one or more of the three categories. Here are the results of all the votes.

244
Ten Most Fascinating National Library Buildings

1. Marciana National Library. Based in Venice, Italy, it is the oldest of Italy's ten national libraries and the third largest. The library was founded in 1468 by Cardinal Bessarione and is inside the San Marco Museum, at the famous Piazzetta San Marco (St. Marks Square). A voter commented that the library building has undergone several refurbishments over the centuries. The library is home to the most important book collections, manuscripts and miniatures in Venice. There are also many works of art by renowned Venetian artists including sculptures which have been inspired by classic mythology. The exhibits are arranged on two floors and these are linked by a magnificent staircase similar to the Golden Staircase in the Ducal Palace in Venice.

2. National Library of Scotland. It is the U.K.'s third largest library, located in Edinburgh, Scotland. It was formerly part of the Library of the Faculty of Advocates, which is still in existence, but now as a law library. The photograph of the building shown is the new building of the national library; the older library building at George IV bridge can be seen at list **1**. The new building was built in the 1980s and is called the Causewayside building and has a very pleasant outside appearance.

3. National Library of Australia. The library building in Canberra with its own special foun-

tain is built not far from Lake Burley Griffin, giving the building a picturesque view when seen from across the lake. The building was actually designed to resemble the Parthenon in Rome. In the first edition, the Vancouver Public Library, which resembles the Coliseum in Rome, was a winner in the public library building category.

4. National Library of The Netherlands. Known locally as Koninklijke Bibliotheek, or KB, the library building in the Hague is an easily recognized big shiny white building close to The Hague Central Station. The inside, as the photograph shows, also has a shiny white appearance. The European Library Office is based in the building of the library.

5. National Library of Poland. Warsaw. A voter remarked that the library is built within the confines of a large park that looks like Stonehenge in England.

6. National Library of Portugal. Lisbon. Many public buildings in Portugal are multi-colored or have unusual coloring, the most prominent color used on the buildings being blue, green or red. The national library has several pink stripes.

7. National Library of South Africa. The library has branches in Cape Town and Pretoria.

National Library of Scotland, Causewayside building (© Trustees of the National Library of Scotland).

Top: The National Library of Australia building at night with fountain on (courtesy Yvonne Kennedy, National Library of Australia). *Bottom:* The National Library of Australia building at night with fountain off (courtesy Yvonne Kennedy, National Library of Australia).

Top: National Library of The Netherlands building (courtesy Koninklijke Bibliotheek, the National Library of The Netherlands, The Hague). *Bottom:* The National Library of The Netherlands, inside (courtesy Koninklijke Bibliotheek, the National Library of The Netherlands, The Hague).

Top: The National Library of Poland in Warsaw, main building (© Biblioteka Narodowa). *Bottom:* National Library of Portugal in Lisbon.

The National Library of South Africa in Cape Town (courtesy National Library of South Africa, Cape Town).

The photograph shown is the Cape Town branch with the statue of George Grey, a former governor of South Africa, in front of the building.

8. National Library of Canada. The new building in Ottawa was opened June 20, 1967, at a cost of $13 million. The building is an imposing structure of granite, marble, glass and steel. The library building's interior includes four rectangular pillars and gold mosaic tiles. *The Secret Bench of Knowledge* sculpture by the famous Lea Vivot is easily recognized in the front of the building.

9. The National Library of Spain began as the Palace Public Library in Madrid. It opened in 1712. One of the statues in the front of the building is San Isidoro, from Seville. It has the largest collection of books in Spanish for the Hispanic community.

10. Bavarian State Library, Germany. This massive reddish brown library building (photograph at list **1**) is located at Munich's famous

The National Library of Canada in Ottawa (courtesy National Library of Canada, Ottawa).

Ludwigstrasse, which contains the palaces of the former kings of Bavaria. The library was actually founded by a member of the Bavarian royal family. The Bavarian State Library is famous for containing the world's largest collection of incunabula.

The winners for the vote in 2001 were: the U.S. Library of Congress, Washington D.C; the British Library (London); the Berlin State Library (Germany); and the national libraries of Austria (Vienna); Japan (Tokyo); France (Paris); Czech Republic (Prague); Taiwan (Taipei); Malaysia (Kuala Lumpur); and Denmark (Copenhagen).

245
Ten Most Fascinating University Library Buildings

1. **National Taiwan University Library**. Voters noted that approaching the library building in Taipei seems surreal. As the photograph shows, the giant palm trees lining the path give a scenic view.

2. **Kings Norton Library, Cranfield University**. U.K. Based in Cranfield, Bedfordshire, the library building was designed by the famous architect Norman Foster, who also designed famous buildings such as Wembley Stadium in London, the Hearst Tower in New York, and the new Reichstag building (ruined during the war) in Berlin, Germany. The library, completed in 1992, cost $33 million to build and won many awards.

3. **University of California, San Diego, Geisel Library**. U.S. The 100-foot-tall reinforced concrete and glass geometrical building was designed by William Pereira. The pyramid-shaped building looks like a gigantic lantern. The library is named after the famous U.S. writer of children's books, Theodor Seuss Geisel.

4. **University of Edinburgh Library**. U.K. The new modern Edinburgh university building, which is undergoing a $95 million refurbishment, is a great deviation from the style of the former library building. Like many modern office buildings, the new library utilizes its numerous windows to ensure sufficient sunlight

National Taiwan University Library in Taipei (photograph by Liao Yunchi, courtesy of National Taiwan University).

Kings Norton Library at Cranfield University (© Cranfield University).

gets into the building during the daytime. The old Gothic library building still has some collections, notably the rare books collections of the university.

5. **University of Macao Library**. China. The University of Macao is one of the few universities in Asia where lectures are in both Portuguese and Chinese. Hence the library also has the only collection of books in Portuguese in an Asian university library.

6. **Jagiellonian University Library**. Poland. The old library building, Collegium Maius, can be seen at list **68**. The stunning new library building was opened in October 2000. The entire area of the library building is now 161,469 square feet, making it the largest university library building outside Russia.

7. **University of Waterloo Library**. Ontario, Canada. The university has 4 main libraries. The 10-story building, located in a park, houses

library administration as well as materials in the arts, humanities, and social sciences.

8. **Leuven Catholic University Library**. Belgium. The architects of the library building made it look the same as it was in the 15th century, despite being destroyed in the first and second World wars.

9. **John Rylands Library, University of Manchester**. U.K. The new John Rylands Library reopened September in 2007 after a $34 million, three-year restoration project. As well as being a world-renowned research library, the famous neo-gothic building is now a major visitor attraction. During the three year closure, much of the library's massive book and manuscript collection was stored in a Cheshire salt mine for protection. The dry and stable atmosphere provided ideal conservation conditions.

10. **Kyoto University Library**. Japan. Kyoto University Library consists of a Central Library as well as over 60 branch libraries.

Top: Edinburgh University Library's old building (courtesy University of Edinburgh). *Bottom:* Edinburgh University Library's new building (courtesy University of Edinburgh).

Top: The University of Macao Library's new building (courtesy University of Macau). *Bottom:* Jagiellonian University Library's new building in Krakow, Poland.

The University of Waterloo Dana Porter Library in Canada (courtesy Cheryl Kieswetter, University of Waterloo Library).

The winners for the vote in 2001 were: University of Massachusetts W.E.B Du Bois Library, U.S.; Toronto University, Robarts Library, Canada; Yale University Beinecke Rare Book and Manuscript Library, New Haven, U.S.; Mexico National Autonomous University Library, Mexico City; Lancaster University Library, U.K.; Waseda University Library, Tokyo, Japan; Trinity College Dublin, Ireland; Bodleian Library, Oxford University, U.K.; Tamkang University Library, Taipei; Michigan University Library, Ann Arbor, U.S.

246
Ten Most Fascinating Public Library Buildings

1. **Seattle Public Library**. Washington, U.S. The architect was Rem Koolhaas. The $200 million public library opened to the public in 2004. The stunning steel lattice glass walls are a marvelous showpiece of 21st century U.S. craftsmanship. It has 11 floors, with floors 6 to 9 arranged in a spectacular spiral arrangement.

In 2005 the library was awarded the American Institute of Architects Honor Award for Architecture.

2. **Lyon Public Library**. France. It probably has the tallest public library building in France, as one voter noted.

Leuven Catholic University Library in Belgium (photograph © K.U. Leuven).

Seattle Public Library in Washington (photograph by Fred Housel, 2004. Courtesy The Seattle Public Library).

3. **Los Angeles County Pubic Library**. California, U.S. As Los Angles is a big metropolitan city, it is divided into several sections. The photograph shows the spacious interior of the East LA library branch, or *Biblioteca El Este*, in Spanish. The library is very different from the other main public library system in the city, the Los Angeles City Public Library.

4. **Cape Town City Library**. South Africa. This library is located inside the large Cape Town City Hall (the last major Victorian building to be erected in Cape Town), which also houses the Cape Town Symphony Orchestra.

5. **Kuala Lumpur Library**. Malaysia. Jalan Raja's famous public library is an interesting

building of Moorish façade capped with rustic bronze domes, reminiscent of the British colonial era in Malaysia. It recently underwent a $6 million makeover that expanded the building to include an auditorium and conference and seminar facilities.

6. **Dallas Pubic Library**. Texas, U.S. The library has 20 branches around the city. One of the most intriguing branches is the J. Erik Jonsson Central Library, which a voter noted looks much better than a 5-star hotel inside and outside. First Lady Laura Bush is a famous former member of staff.

7. **Bournemouth Public Library**. U.K. Located on the seaside suburb of south England, the $27 million public library building either

Lyon Municipal Public Library in France.

Top: The East Los Angeles County branch of the Los Angeles Public Library (courtesy Los Angeles County Public Library). *Bottom:* Dallas Public Library's J. Erik Jonsson Central Library (courtesy Texas/Dallas History & Archives Division, Dallas Public Library).

Dallas Public Library's J. Erik Jonsson Central Library, inside (courtesy Texas/Dallas History & Archives Division, Dallas Public Library).

resembles a big glass ship or a big transparent whale. The fully glazed north-facing elevation opens the library interior to the street, inviting people in as well as enabling people to look out. Glass roof panels and south-westerly facing windows allow light to flood into the library spaces, reducing the need for artificial lighting and cooling and thereby ensuring that energy costs are minimized. Built on a former derelict site, the library has seen a threefold increase in visitor numbers since it opened. At night with the lights on, the building makes a mesmerizing sight. It received the Prime Minster's Best Building Award.

8. Cincinnati and Hamilton Public Library. Ohio, U.S. Was voted because it is the largest public library building in the state of Ohio and the 2nd largest in U.S.

9. Lee Kong Chian Public Reference Library. Singapore. It is the largest reference library in Singapore and also has one of the largest public library buildings in Asia (it is a 7-story building). It is named after Singapore's most famous philanthropist and is a premier resource for works on Singapore.

10. Folger Shakespeare Library. This public research library in Washington, D.C., founded in 1929, has the world's largest collection of the William Shakespeare's works. A voter noted that the library building architecture earned it a listing in the U.S. National Register of Historic Places.

The winners for the vote in 2001 were: Handley Public Library. Winchester, Virginia. U.S. The Hague Public Library. The Netherlands. Peckham Public Library and Media Center. London, U.K. San Francisco Public Library. U.S. Derby Central Library. U.K. Helsingborgs City Library. Sweden. Architect Vancouver Public Library. British Columbia, Canada. Pasadena (California) Public Library. U.S. Newark Public Library. U.S. Nottinghamshire. U.K. Rotterdam Municipal Library.

The Netherlands. Phoenix (Arizona) Central Public Library. U.S. Malmö City Library. Swe-

den. Shanghai Library. China. Harold Washington Library Center. Chicago, Illinois, U.S.

247
Ten Other Fascinating Library Buildings

Here are 10 other libraries taken from the library "votes" submitted by the respondents. They did not make the top 10 list, but there is something about them that makes them tick!

1. **João Library** (*Biblioteca Joanina*). This famous library building in the University of Coimbra in Portugal was constructed between 1717 and 1728 for the Portuguese King Dom João V. It is a mesmerizing showcase of 18th century baroque architectural design. The interior of the library has so many designs and decorations in every nook and corner rivaling those found in the Vatican Library, especially on the exotic jacaranda wood tables, the beautiful painted frescoed ceilings, and the stunning bookshelves. Some students complain that these excess designs make it a big distraction to study seriously in the library. Others claimed that the library was better suited for visiting than reading, despite the fact that it has over 200,000 books on a variety of subjects such as science, medicine, the humanities and law.

2. **Tsar Nicholas II Library at the Hermitage Museum**. St. Petersburg, Russia. The famous collection of the State Hermitage Museum, including the Fabergé Eggs, are housed over 5 buildings, and one of them is a neo-gothic styled library founded in 1762. It has over 610,000 books covering such topics as sculpture, pottery, visual arts and paintings stored in several locations of a library whose interior very much resembles the painted ceilings of the Vatican Library. The other famous library nearby is the Winter Palace Library. The Winter Palace was the main residence of the Russian tsars from 1760, so much of its collection passed through many owners. Just after Tsar Nicholas II was overthrown by Lenin and the Bolsheviks, many important rare book and manuscript collections in both libraries were smuggled out to the West.

3. **National Library of Economics**. Kiel, Germany. It has gone through many names since it was established in 1919. It was formerly called the Kiel Institute for the World Economy Library, and before then called the Royal Institute for Maritime Traffic and World Economy Library. It is also known as Leibniz Information Center for Economics. The architects gave it a more business-like design, as seen in corporate buildings, to take into account its sole role as an economics library. The expensive library budget of 20 million Euros ($18 million) is financed jointly by the federal and state governments, not surprising, as the large building houses the world's largest economic library.

4. **National Library of Wales**. U.K. This Victorian Gothic (Neo-Gothic) building created by Sidney Greenslade in the city of Aberystwyth is one of the 3 national libraries in the U.K. It is known locally as *Llyfrgell Genedlaethol Cymru*.

5. **Victoria State Library**, Melbourne, Australia. It has some of Australia's rarest and most precious manuscripts relating to the early European settlement of the state of Victoria. The most amazing view of the library building, opened in 1856, is at night, when the whole place is lit up inside and outside, showing the magnificence of architect Joseph Reed's design.

6. **National Institute for Policy & Strategic Studies Library**. Kuru, Nigeria. The NIPSS was conceived as a high level center for reflection, research and learning with the primary objective of serving as Africa's foremost policy think-tank. The peculiar shaped library is located close to a lake in Kuru, near the city of Jos. The two circular shaped concrete parts of the building house the main book collections.

Top: The German National Library of Economics, based in Kiel (courtesy Lukas-Roth, Cologne/German National Library of Economics, Kiel, Germany). *Bottom:* The National Library of Wales (© Llyfrgell Genedlaethol Cymru/The National Library of Wales).

Top: The Victoria State Library in Melbourne, Australia (© Joyce N. Church) *Bottom:* The National Institute for Policy and Strategic Studies Library in Kuru, Nigeria (courtesy of the Nigeria High Commission, London).

Top: El Escorial Library in Spain. *Bottom:* Coimbra University Library is the oldest academic library in Portugal, and the building shown dates to the seventeenth century (courtesy Coimbra University).

Palmerston North City Library, New Zealand (© Palmerston North City Library).

7. San Lorenzo de El Escorial Monastic Library. Spain. Based north of Madrid, it was planned by Juan de Herrera, who also designed the library's eye-catching shelves. The style of the building is Gothic, one of the favored styles in the West before the 1700s.

8. University of Coimbra. Portugal. Although Portugal is famous for having so many existing historic buildings, several of the ancient buildings housing the University of Coimbra library have been replaced with modern buildings to take into account expanding book collections.

9. Ambrosian Library. Milan, Italy.

10. Palmerston North City Library. New Zealand. The building, which opened in 1996, won an architectural award for its design by architect Ian Athfield. There are 5 branches of the library.

The libraries listed in this category for the votes in 2001 were: Alexandria Library in Egypt; Silesian University Library, Katowice, Poland; The Hague Public Library, The Netherlands; Dong-Eui University Library, Pusan, South Korea; the Vatican Library, Rome; Temasek Polytechnic Library, Singapore; National Library of Egypt, Cairo; King's College London, Central Library, U.K.; and the Chester Beatty Library, Dublin, Ireland.

WORLD RECORDS FOR LIBRARY CATALOGS, DATABASES AND TECHNOLOGY

248
Oldest Library Classification Scheme

A good classification scheme makes it easy for library users to quickly locate a book in a library; this is particularly useful when locating books in large libraries with thousands or millions of books. Each book has a unique classification mark or class number for identification, which is typically a combination of numbers and letters. In 1876 U.S. librarian Melvil Dewey put forward the Dewey Decimal Classification or DDC, the first successful attempt by a librarian to classify books by subject. A few years later Dewey went on to set up the first university course in the world for training librarians. DDC has been revised several times the last major one being the 22nd edition in 2003, while the DDC 22 abridged edition 14 was released in 2004. The DDC is also the most widely used classification scheme in the world, at least in the English speaking world, but it has been published in over 35 languages. An international version of the DDC known as the Universal Decimal Classification also ex-

ists. Today other classification schemes are available alongside DDC, such as BLISS Classification and Colon Classification. In the U.S., a different system, called the Library of Congress Classification, has been in use since 1898; however, DDC is maintained at the DDC Division of the Library of Congress. The DDC version for classifying documents on the Internet is called WebDewey.

Before DDC or the Library of Congress Classification was translated into major languages, libraries wanting to adopt the system but whose official language was not English faced a dilemma. For example, the National Library of France abandoned the use of the Library of Congress Classification because no French version was available. And with only an abridged version of the DDC translated into French, the national library, when it was based at the old building, continued to use an indigenous Clement Classification originally developed by Nicolas Clément in 1670.

249
Most Popular Library Cataloging Principles

While a classification scheme identifies a single item in a library such as a book, a cataloging rule standardizes the way entire collec-

tions in a library such as books, maps and periodicals are indexed. Hence a catalog is the list of the entire collection in a library. If the catalog includes the combined collections of several libraries, then it is called a union catalog. For centuries, catalogs were typically filed on paper index cards, but from the 1970s they have increasingly been filed on computers as Online Public Access Catalogs or OPACs. Given the international use of English, the Anglo-American Cataloging Rules 2 or AACR2, first set up in 1966, is the most popular in the world. Well more than half of the libraries in the world use the AACR2 as it has been translated into 25 languages and is in use in 45 countries.

Although AACR2 unifies cataloging principles throughout the English-speaking world, it is based on the 1961 Paris Principles introduced at the International Conference on Cataloging Principles where discussions focused on creating a single standard for cataloging. It is the Paris Principles that several non–English speaking countries used to set up their own indigenous cataloging rules, such as the RAK (Regeln für die Alphabetische Katalogisierung) cataloging rules in Germany, the AFNOR (Normes de Catalogage Publiées par l'Association Française de Normalisation) cataloging rules in France, and the Nippon Cataloging Rules or NCRT in Japan. The very first catalog of a major library is attributed to the one called Pinakes, and compiled by a librarian of the ancient Alexandria Library in Egypt in the 4th century B.C. From 2009, the three major English-speaking libraries in the world, the Library of Congress, the British Library, and the Library and Archives Canada will be replacing the AACR2 with a new cataloging rule that takes into account the now numerous digital items or new-media information in libraries today such as digital images, digital recordings and digital publications. The new rule is to be called Resource Description and Access or RDA. At one point RDA was to be called AACR3.

250
Largest National Union Library Catalogs

The computerized National Union Catalog of the U.S., which includes the collections of the Library of Congress, currently has over 25 million books, 2.5 million recordings, 12 million photographs, 4.5 million maps, and 60 million manuscripts. The British Library's computerized catalog is by far the largest in Europe, a factor in this being the international use of English. Every new book received by the British Library is published regularly in the *British National Bibliography* or *BNB*. In 1997 an Internet version called OPAC 97 was introduced.

A search of the British Library's computerized catalog will come up with the oldest known Valentine's Day message in the English Language. It was written in 1477 by Margery Brews to her fiancé.

The computerized French Union Catalog or CCFR (*Catalogue Collectif de France*), has a combined total of over 13.3 million books, encompassing collections from the National Library of France as well as those held by the major university and public municipal libraries. Included in the catalogue are 15 million engravings and photographs, 800,000 maps and 350,000 periodicals

Similar large catalogs exists in Italy (*Catalogo Unico Indice / Sistema Bibliotecario Nazionale SBN*); Germany (*Verbundkatalog Deutschland*); Belgium (CCB or *Catalogue Collectif de Belgique / Collectieve Catalogus van België*); Norway (BIBSYS); Portugal (Catálogo Colectivo Portugués/PORBASE); Sweden (LIBRIS); and Russia (Ruslan). There exists a single large union catalog of Scandinavia and Baltic States libraries called NOSP. In Canada the national union catalog is called AMICUS. Other national union catalogs around the world are- Brazil (*Rede Cooperativa de Bibliotecas Brasileiras*); Singapore (NLB) and Israel (MAL-MAD). In Africa, the Sabicat union catalog, maintained in Cape Town, covers major South African and 6 other southern African libraries.

251
Largest Union Library Catalogs in Europe

Union catalogs of university, public, state, provincial or research libraries have been extremely popular and hundreds of such catalogs exist. It will be impossible to list half of them in this book, so a selection of the major ones in each continent is given here.

University/Research Libraries. Since 1987 the Consortium of University Research Libraries, or CURL, provides a unified access to the catalogs of more than 20 of the largest university research libraries in the U.K. and Ireland. Over 13.3 million books are included in the catalog along with thousands of periodicals. The computerized catalog of CURL is better known as COPAC, and the main computer system hosting the catalog is based at the John Rylands University Library in Manchester. The French university library catalogs are listed in the *Système universitaire de documentation*, or

SUDOC union catalog. Other European university union catalogs are: Germany (SWB, GBV HEBIS , KOBV, BVB; all these are interstate union catalogs, for instance SWB or *Suedwestdeutschen Bibliotheksverbund* covers southwest states of Germany such as Baden-Wurttemberg); Ireland (IRIS); Italy (*Catalogo collettivi regione/SBN*); Spain (*Catálogo Colectivo de la Red de Bibliotecas Universitarias Españolas*/REBUIN); The Netherlands (*Nederlandse Collectieve Catalogus*); and Switzerland (RERO and NEBIS, representing French and German language university libraries respectively).

Public Libraries. U.K. (Project WiLL, covering all public libraries in London); Spain (*Catálogo de las Bibliotecas Publicas del Estado*/BPE); Belgium (Vlaamse Centrale Catalogus); and Finland (MANDA).

252
Largest Union Library Catalog in the Americas

University/Research Libraries. The MELVYL union catalog (the name given to the combined catalog of the University of California libraries and the California State University libraries) currently includes over 26 million books, making it larger than the Harvard University Library catalog (the largest individual university library catalog in the world). Other union catalogs are RLG (Research Libraries Group union catalog, covering major research and academic libraries in the U.S., Canada and Latin America, and a great deal of libraries in Europe and the Asia-Pacific region, such as China, Russia, Australia, New Zealand, Saudi Arabia, Japan. It available in over 400 lan-

guages. It is the second largest union catalog in the world, after WorldCat); Center for Research Libraries union catalog (Union catalog of the consortium of North American academic and independent research libraries, mostly serials and dissertations); Washington, D.C. (ALADIN); California (PHAROS and Link+); Illinois (ILLINET); Michigan (MiLE); Brazil (*Catálogo de Libros*/Librunam); Canada (Virtual Canadian Union Catalogue/vCuc).

Public Libraries U.S. (Link +, MOBAC, Bibliomation, SunLink, WVLC etc.). Several of the national and university union catalogs listed above also cover public libraries.

253
Largest Union Library Catalogs in Africa

University/Research Libraries. In Africa, there are very few union catalogs at the moment, as limited library resources make setting up and maintaining union catalogs unattractive. The Sabicat union catalog listed above also covers public libraries in southern Africa.

254
Largest Union Library Catalogs in Asia

University, Research and public Libraries. Japan (WebCatPlus; NACSIS catalog covers all university libraries in Japan and is produced by the National Center for Scientific Information System and covers over 400 Japanese universities); Australia (KINECTICA, COOLKAT); China (CALIS; Chinese Sciences Digital Library [CSDL] Union Catalog); Taiwan (NBINET); India (INFLIBNET); DELNET. The DELNET union catalog has 2,855,821 bibliographic records of member libraries (817 in India and 12 outside India from Nepal, Oman, the Philippines, Sri Lanka, United Arab Emirates, and the U.S.). It is run by the Delhi Library Network in New Delhi.

255
Largest Union Library Catalogs in the Middle East

University, Research and public Libraries. Israel (MALMAD and ULI) and Egypt (Egypt Library Network).

256
Largest Unified International Library Catalog

WorldCat, a union catalog maintained and updated daily by OCLC (Dublin, Ohio, U.S.) since 1971, covers library items held by 60,000 libraries in 94 countries and territories on the OCLC network. Over 95 million records of books, periodicals, newspapers, maps, music, audio-visual materials, manuscripts, are included in the catalog, and in 470 languages and dialects. The database continues to grow at a rate of more than 2 million records per year or a new record added every 10 seconds, making it the world's largest bibliographic database. The Research Libraries Group union catalog (see list **252**) is the world's second largest union catalog.

257
First Computerized Catalog or OPAC

Today to find a book in a library we consult a computer or technically a computerized catalog or an OPAC. The first libraries to set up OPACs were Canada's Guelph University Library and University of Waterloo Library in 1976 and 1977, respectively. They both used OPACs designed by Geac (the model name was GEAC 8000). Significantly this system was used before the IBM PC launched in 1981, meaning librarians (catalogers) were among the first office workers to use computerized systems at work.

Prior to the introduction of computerized catalog in libraries, paper cards were used to index library items. For large libraries this meant thousands if not millions of cards. For instance, the New York Public Library once employed the use of some 10 million cards in over 10,000 drawers for its catalog. The first step towards computerizing catalogs was the introduction of MARC. First developed in the U.S. in 1965, MARC or Machine Readable Cataloging, is a standard for cataloging library materials in computerized format, for easy access with a computer. In short MARC is a sort of standard for creating database records on library items. A MARC record is typically arranged according to the cataloging principles such as AACR2, and each field in a MARC record lists variables such as title or author and a class mark such as a DDC number. Such computerized catalogs or OPACs are now very widespread in libraries around the world. But in many developing countries OPACs are still gradually replacing the older tradition of card-based cataloging, while in industrialized counties, very few libraries are without an OPAC. Today different versions of MARC are used around the world, such as CANMARC in Canada, IBERMARC in Spain, JPNMARC in Japan and RUSMARC in Russia. Harmonization between the different MARC versions are ongoing projects in major libraries. With the introduction of the Internet, many OPACs can now be accessed with a web browser, and this means one does not necessarily have to be in a library to access its OPAC.

258
First Library OPACs in the U.S.

The Ohio State University Library in Columbus and Princeton University Library in New Jersey installed a Geac OPAC in 1979. In 1980, the University of Arizona Library in Tucson was the third library to install a Geac OPAC in the U.S.

259
First Library OPAC in Europe

Hull University Library in the U.K. began using the Geac OPAC in 1980.

260
First Library OPAC in Australia

Deakin University Library, Victoria, began using the Dataphase OPAC, and the Tasmania University Library, Hobart, began using URICA OPAC, both in 1982.

261
First Public Library OPAC in the U.K.

Librarians at Somerset County Public Library were the first in a British public library to use the Geac OPAC in 1982.

262
First Library OPAC in Asia

The National Library of Japan in Tokyo was the first Japanese library to install an OPAC in 1985.

263
First Library OPAC in Africa

In 1991, the SABINET database service in Cape Town helped set up the first OAPC in Africa at the National Library of South Africa branches in Cape Town and Johannesburg.

264
First Companies to Develop Library OPACs

Geac Library Automation Systems was established in 1976. A Canadian company based in Markham, it originally developed the Geac OPAC for libraries from computer systems sold to financial institutions, such as banks. In 2002, Geac became the first library automation company to introduce an OPAC operated by voice commands to aid the visually impaired library users.

Three other strong candidates that began similar library automation products in the late 1970s were CLSI (Computer Library Systems Inc.) in 1977, Dataphase in 1976 and Gaylord in 1978.

In 1966 the National Library of Germany in Frankfurt was the first library to compile a national bibliography with the aid of computers. Going back in 1941, an experimental electromechanical library automation system was installed at the Newark (New Jersey) Public library in the U.S. And in the 1930s, the University of Texas Library and the Boston Public Library both introduced library circulation and acquisition systems using punched cards. For many years Libertas was the favorite OPAC for university libraries in the U.K., but today both Geac and Talis are the leading OPACs.

265
First Library to Make Use of Microfilm

The National Library of France began providing microfilm copies of some of its collections in 1884. René Dagron in France had improved the technique of creating microfilms following its invention by British optician John Dancer in 1852. Libraries eventually began using microfilms (to preserve items such as newspapers), made with the technology developed by Eastman-Kodak, in 1935, with the *New York Times* the first ever newspaper on microfilm. Since 1938 Harvard University Library in the U.S. has had the oldest and largest microfilm collections in the world. Today, thanks to computer technology and the Internet, libraries can now digitize their collections, relying much less on microfilm except where absolutely necessary.

The microfiche was invented in 1939 by C.H. Kleukens, and for a while it was used principally in European libraries, as the technology did not gain much acceptance in the U.S. and elsewhere.

266
First Major Library to Digitize a Large Portion of Its Collections

In 1997 the French national library was the first library to provide full-text access to a great deal of its collections via the Internet. The special catalog called Gallica also provides photographs and illustrations from the publication (cover page digital image and/or digital images from inside the publication). In total, over 80,000 digitalized books were available to access, including access to important publications in print that had once had restricted access such as the French Academy of Sciences printed publication (*Procès Verbaux de l'Académie des Sciences*). A Google project to be released as Google Book Library involves several large U.S. and overseas university libraries collaborating to provide up to 10 million books from their collections available for digitization and access through Google's search engine.

267
First Major Computer Database

The very first crude databases were developed during the 1950s. The first and most important database developed was the U.S. Census Bureau's office database, released in 1951. The custom designed database software was run on a UNIVAC mainframe computer supplied by Remington-Rand (now part of Unisys Corporation). This database was thus used 5 years after ENIAC, the world's first general-purpose electronic digital computer (essentially the first mainframe) was developed at the University of Pennsylvania in 1947).

The relational database theory was developed by E. Codd in 1972 at IBM laboratories. The first commercial relational database package for a desktop computer was Aston Tate's (now Borland) dBASE version 2 for CP/M computers (1980) and for MS-DOS computers (1982). dBASE was developed from an early popular database package invented in the late 1970s for UNIVAC mainframes. Microsoft Access, the major database package today, was released in 1992. The first commercial SQL database package was developed by Oracle in 1980. Databases with Graphical User Interface or GUI, such as buttons to press and input boxes for entering data, became feasible when the Palo Alto Research Center, PARC, in the U.S., released the first computers to use GUI as a means of input. The first two from PARC were the Dyna Book computer in 1973 and the Xerox Star computer in 1979. Both these computers influenced the later development of the first successful commercial computer to use GUI, the Apple Macintosh, launched in January 1984, and the development of the first successful GUI operating system for PCs, Windows 3 in 1990. CD-ROM databases (available from the middle 1980s) were among the first GUI databases.

268
Largest Computer Database

Patent databases tend to be the largest kind of databases produced. Several patent databases covered have more than 60 million records, with each record having very detailed information, increasing the computer size of the database to over several thousand gigabytes. Currently the two largest patent databases with the largest number of records are the Delphion Patent Database with over 80 million records and the European Patent Office's International Patent Documentation Database, or INPADOCDB, with over 63 million patent records. The computer size of the Delphion Patent Database in gigabytes is 150,000 gigabytes, or the hard disk capacity size of just over 1000 personal computers. This makes the Delphion Patent Database full-text database the largest in the world. Patent databases are covered in this book in more details at lists **346** to **351**. The WorldCat, a union catalog (see list **252**), is world's largest bibliographic database as over 2 million records are added each year. WorldCat covers about 95 million records.

The British Library is actively digitizing several of its rare books and manuscripts for general access. The digital manuscript system in the photograph, one of several in the national library, is the *Magna Carta*, a thirteenth century manuscript on parchment.

269
First and Largest Database Host

Apart from books and periodicals, libraries, especially university and special libraries, are increasingly offering access to several CD-ROM, Internet or online databases covering a wide variety of subjects. Most public libraries tend to offer the cheaper CD-ROM databases, while academic and special libraries, such as business and law libraries, in addition to CD-ROM/DVD ROM, also offer more expensive online access to databases via the Internet and commercial Wide Area Networks or WANs such as X.25 networks. Some databases are used for finding articles in periodicals such as in journals (i.e., electronic journals), newspapers and magazines, or searching directories, indexes or registries. Other databases contain specific data and information, such business data (e.g., share price information), biological data (e.g., DNA structures), chemical data (e.g., chemical composition) or legal data (e.g., law cases). Big libraries such as university and national libraries often subscribe to one or more database hosts. Database hosts are online services proving access to dozens or hundreds of databases, allowing a single access point and thus a single subscription to several databases, the bulk of these databases being produced by different companies and not the database host itself. The first commercial online database host was DIALOG database host, introduced in 1972. Lockheed Missile and Space Corporation originally developed it for a NASA database project in 1965. In 1988 DIALOG (based in Cary, North Carolina, U.S.) was sold to Knight-Ridder Information and in 2000 it became a subsidiary of Thomson Corporation (Toronto, Canada). DIALOG, used in over 120 countries, offers over 600 huge international databases to access from. DIALOG's detailed list of its databases is interestingly called Bluesheets.

SDC's Orbit database host (now part of Questel-Orbit) is also a strong candidate for the first commercial online database host, as it began developing online information retrieval systems as far back as late 1960 and began a commercial service in the early 1970s.

270
Oldest and Largest Database Hosts in Europe

In 1969 the European Space Agency's Information Retrieval Service or ESA-IRS database host, located in Frascati, near Rome in Italy, became Europe's first online database host. In 1988 ESA-IRS became part of the British Library initiative called European Information Network Services or EINS. It offers access to over 200 scientific, technical and medical databases, some provided by other European database hosts.

Télésystèmes-Questel database host was introduced in 1979. It merged with Orbit in 1994 to become Questel-Orbit and is based in Paris, France. Over 160 databases can be accessed with Questel Orbit. Its coverage is mostly on intellectual property information such as scientific and technical patents and trademarks.

The largest French language scientific and technical database is PASCAL, produced by the National Center for Scientific Research in Paris.

BLAISE database host was introduced by the British Library bibliographic services in London back in 1978. It provides access to several bibliographic databases such as the British National Bibliography (which is also available in print form) the U.S. National Library of Medicine MEDLARS databases, such as MEDLINE and U.S. Library of Congress MARC records.

The German Institute for Medical Documentation and Information in Cologne established the DIMDI database host in 1975. It currently offers access to over 100 databases mostly in the biomedical field.

Radio Suisse, Bern, Switzerland, introduced the DataStar database host in 1980 in Switzerland. It offers access to over 350 databases. In 2000 it became a subsidiary of Thomson Corporation (Toronto, Canada). It is the second largest database host in the West after DIALOG.

Russia's Integrum-Techno database host in Moscow offers over 400 databases covering legislation of Russia and the Commonwealth of Independent States as well as political, business, commercial, investment, legal, scientific databases, most of which are available in Russian and English. It is the largest bibliographic database host after DIALOG.

With over 70 databases, Sweden's Info-Torg (operated by Sema InfoData, Stockholm) is the largest database host in Scandinavia.

271
Oldest and Largest Database Hosts in Asia

Based in Tokyo, PC VAN (operated by NEC), NIFTY-Serve (operated by Fujitsu) and G–Search are Japan's three largest and most popular online services with subject coverage in multidisciplinary fields. Between them they have over 5 million subscribers in Japan. Although the information services display data in Japanese ideograms, NIFTY-Serve and G-Search offer their services in both Japanese and English. By linking to the Japan Information Center for Science and Technology (see list **283**), the two services further provide access to PATOLIS and JOIS, the largest science and technology information databases in Japan.

Founded in April 2000, and based in Tokyo, the National Institute of Informatics (NII) provides the information services and portals for the academic community in Japan

The German Institute for Medical Documentation and Information, or DIMDI, in Cologne, is the largest provider of biomedical databases in Germany.

in various multidisciplinary fields such as the humanities and science in the Japanese language. The biggest online database portal is GeNii (also called GiNii) covering humanities, social sciences, and natural sciences). From GeNii other huge databases can be accessed including: CiNii (full text and citation of Japanese scholarly and academic journals and magazines); Kaken (scientific research projects in Japan); Nii-DBR (academic research database repository for specialized academic information such as Japanese doctorial dissertations); Nii-REO (repository of electronic journals and online publications, offering both full-text and bibliographic access); and WebCatPlus (database for books, magazines, in Japanese and English).

The major well known Korean general database hosts include Chollian (LG Dacom) and Hitel. Based in Seoul, the Korean Database Promotion Center, or KDPC, offers access to over 900 Korean language databases covering multidisciplinary fields.

The Korea Institute of Industry & Technology in Seoul produces the KINITI IR academic database host, which offers over 40 databases in Korean covering scientific and medical abstracts, Korean patent abstracts in English, directory of Korean databases, union catalog of Korean periodicals, research and development reports, and commodities and manufacturers. Developed in 1983 it was the first Korean database host. It also provides access to overseas database host such as DIALOG and STN for university libraries in Korea.

CrimsonLogic, formerly SNS (Singapore Network Services) is the largest provider of databases in Singapore covering law (Singapore Academy of Law LawNet database), medicine and finance.

Based in New Delhi, India, the DELNET database host produces over 20 databases. These include the full text JAIN database; the database of Hindi and Urdu manuscripts; the DEVINSA sociology database; and Indian theses and dissertations database.

The Indian National Information System on Science and Technology, NISSAT, produces the largest Indian scientific and technical databases covering the chemical and pharmaceutical industries, manufacturing, food technology, metal working, oceanography, sugar industry, textiles industry and microbiology.

The Malaysian Science and Technology Information Center, or MASTIC, in the city of Putrajaya, is the main provider of science and technology information in Malaysia. It collects and disseminates information related to science and technology research activities. Its database host provides access to several databases such as MASTIClink, a database on current science and technology research projects in Malaysia. The information in the database comes from several sources including institutes of higher learning and government research institutes in Malaysia.

The Institute of Scientific and Technical Information of China (ISTIC) and Wanfang Data (based in Beijing and an affiliate of the Chinese Ministry of Science & Technology) produces several large comprehensive databases such as China Online Journals database (the only product of this kind in China), Dissertations of China database, Academic Conferences in China database, Chinese Companies & Products database, Policies and Laws of China database, Chinese Science Citation Index database and the National Scientific Awards and Scientific Achievements database. They are all available in Mandarin, Cantonese and English. The availability of English versions means several overseas libraries subscribe to the databases, such as the U.S. Library of Congress, the British Library and libraries of Oxford and Yale universities.

272
Oldest and Largest Database Hosts in Africa

The oldest and largest African database host is South Africa's SABINET service. Started in 1986, the database service covers subjects such as business, law, medicine, religion, science and the humanities. It also offers access to over 150 electronic journals published in southern Africa.

273
First Database Host to Introduce Networked CD-ROM Access

Bibliographic Retrieval Services (BRS online), a database host, introduced networked CD-ROM access to its databases in 1986. Established in 1976 at the State University of New York in the U.S., it became part of Ovid Technologies (a pioneer in CD-ROM information retrieval) in 1994. Ovid Technologies (now part of Wolters Kluwer, Amsterdam, The Netherlands), offers over 100 databases.

274
First Indexing Service

With the proliferation in the publication of periodicals in the Victorian age, William Poole, a U.S. librarian, indexed by subject over 100 Victorian periodicals from 1802 to 1881, and published the results as *An Index to Periodical Literature*. This was the first attempt to provide an indexing service for scholars. Poole's brilliant work is the forerunner of *Reader's Guide to Periodical Literature*, a popular index, first published in 1901, to the periodicals found in the English language. Today automated or manual indexing services are an essential part of the production of bibliographic databases.

275
First Citation Indexes

Shepard's Citations, covering cited works in legal information and first published in 1873, was the first major citation index. It is now part of the huge legal databases of Lexis-Nexis. Twelfth century Hebrew citations called *Analysis of Judaica* are the earliest authentic citation index.

276
Largest Citation Index Database Service

Citations indexes for science, arts, humanities and social science literature developed from 1958 by Professor Eugene Garfield of the Institute for Scientific Information or ISI (Philadelphia, Pennsylvania, U.S.), are the largest in the world. Citations from over 8,000 journals published in 35 languages are indexed. The ISI citation indexes have now evolved into the ISI Web of Science database. The combination of this database and several other ISI and non–ISI databases make up the ISI Web of Knowledge database. See also list **310**. ISI is now part of Thomson Corporation (Toronto, Canada).

277
First Major KWIC Indexing Service

KWIC, or Key Word in Context, indexing was an efficient method of indexing words developed by Hans Peter Luhn, a German inventor. In 1960 the American Chemical Society adopted Luhn's method to index the journal *Chemical Titles*. Today, there are KWIC indexes in almost every branch of knowledge.

278
First Table of Contents Database

The Institute for Scientific Information (Philadelphia, Pennsylvania, U.S.) Current Contents database was released in 1984. It is also the largest table of contents database.

279
First and Largest Full-Text Databases

Lexis-Nexis began full-text databases in the 1970s with Lexis in 1973 to provide legal databases, and Nexis in 1979 for news and business databases. It was originally introduced in 1966 by Data Corporation, becoming Mead Data Central in 1968. The Anglo-Dutch giant Reed Elsevier bought the company in 1994.

280
Largest Commercially Available Microform Collection

UMI, or University Microfilms Inc., one of the ProQuest Information and Learning services, and a Bell & Howell company (Ann Arbor, Michigan, U.S), contains over 5.5 billion page images (microfilm and microfiche) drawn from thousands of literary, journalistic, and scholarly works such as dissertations. About 37 million images are added each year. Eugene Power founded UMI in 1938, after successfully microfilming rare and foreign books in the British Museum. Bell & Howell acquired UMI in 1985.

281
Largest Electronic Information Services

Thomson Corporation (Toronto, Canada), founded in 1989, owns some of the leading electronic database producers, database hosts and information providers and online publishers such as Westlaw, DIALOG, Data-Star, Information Access Company, Micromedex, Sweet & Maxwell, Gale Group, Derwent and the Institute for Scientific Information or ISI. It had global sales of over $8 billion in 2006, and its business is very diverse, covering a wide variety of subjects such as scientific, financial and legal information. There are five main divisions. The science division of the business is called Thomson Scientific, while the business information division is called Thomson Financial. Thomson itself is a pioneer in the old print economy, and helped create the electronic age with early proprietary online systems and CD-ROM products. The other multinational conglomerate and second big player and competitor with multiple information services (following acquisitions and mergers, as with Thomson) is the Anglo Dutch giant Reed Elsevier, which owns, among others, Lexis-Nexis, Kompass, ScienceDirect, EMBASE, Elsevier Science and a large book and journal publisher arm. It was founded in 1993 by the merger of Dutch and British businesses and has a company structure similar to other Anglo-Dutch businesses (like the oil company Royal-Dutch Shell) by having its headquarters in London and Amsterdam and two CEOs from each country. Sales in 2006 were $5.7 billion. Like Thomson, its businesses are very diverse.

282
Largest Periodicals Directory Database

Ulrich's International Periodicals Directory (R.R. Bowker, New Providence, New Jersey, U.S.) indexes information and contact details for over 250,000 periodicals and serials from 80,000 publishers in 200 countries on a range of different subjects. It also lists over 14,000 newspapers.

283
Largest Databases with Electronic Journals and e-books

With globalization of businesses, some of the databases listed below can also be seen as database hosts, as the publishers of the electronic journals or e-books featured in the electronic journal database host may come from several different companies worldwide, and on a broad range of multidisciplinary subjects. There are also very specific databases that only contain electronic journals on specific subjects such as law, engineering, business, science or medicine. These are detailed in lists **290** to **337**.

The CISTI catalog of the Canada Institute for Scientific and Technical Information (or CISTI), based in Ottawa, gives access to over 50,000 periodicals and more than 800,000 scientific and medical (STM) reports and conference proceedings.

Swets Information Service (Lisse, The Netherlands) allows its subscribers access to some 17,000 periodicals. Full text articles are available from over 2,500 of these journals. Subject coverage spans the majority of academic disciplines including arts, business, geography, history, language, management, marketing, medicine, philosophy, religion, sciences, social sciences and technology.

EBSCO*host* (Ipswich, Massachusetts, U.S.) provides access to over 10,700 electronic journals and over 136 databases.

OCLC's FirstSearch database service (Dublin, Ohio, U.S.) has a collection of over 7,500 electronic journals from a wide variety of subjects. OCLC's ArticleFirst database indexes articles from 12,000 journals.

Ingenta (Bath, U.K.) offers more than 5,400 academic and professional electronic journals. This service is primarily involved in providing access to databases for the academic community. Ingenta also provides full-text access to over 2000 periodicals for which there is a print subscription. The Uncover Plus section of Ingenta is an indexing service only and does not incorporate full-text.

Science Direct (part of the Amsterdam-based Elsevier Science in The Netherlands) gives its users access to more than 6000 scientific, technical and medical electronic journals. In addition it also links up to external databases giving a grand total of over 10,000 electronic journals.

Wiley InterScience (Wiley-Blackwell, Hoboken, New Jersey, U.S.) offers 2,500 electronic journals.

The Journals@Ovid service of Ovid Technologies (part of Wolters Kluwer based in the, Amsterdam, The Netherlands) is the largest scientific and medical full-text electronic journal service. Over 920 journals from over 68 different publishers are currently available for searching in the journal database.

Cambridge Scientific Abstracts or CSA (Bethesda, Maryland, U.S.) database CSA Illumina provides 70 databases linking to more than 5,000 full-text journals.

The Tokyo-based Japan Information Center for Science and Technology (Japan Science and Technology Corporation) JICST database has over 9 million records, sourced from Japanese, Asian and selected overseas journals and other materials, covering, scientific, biomedical and technical research in Asia. Its two largest databases are PATOLIS and JOIS.

Sage (Thousand Oaks, California, U.S.) provides access to over 80,000 full-text articles from over 510 peer-reviewed journals covering the social sciences.

JSTOR (or Journal Storage) is essentially a digital archive collection of core scholarly journals, providing full-text searches of digitized back issues of thousands of journals, dating back to 1665. Hence, it includes the contents of *Philosophical Transactions* (see list **176**). Founded 1995 by the Andrew W. Mellon Foundation, JSTOR offers researchers the ability to retrieve high-resolution scanned images of journal issues and pages as they were originally designed, printed, and illustrated. The journals archived in JSTOR span many disciplines in the arts and sciences.

Zetoc provides access to the British Library's Electronic Table of Contents of around 20,000 current journals and around 16,000 conference proceedings published per year. The database covers 1993 to date and is updated on a daily basis.

Informaworld (Taylor & Francis, London,

U.K.) offers over 1,100 electronic journals and 10,000 e-books.

SpringerLink (Berlin, Germany) offers 1,250 STM electronic journals and adds 3,000 new e-books every year.

The Digital Book Index or DBI (Westport, Connecticut, U.S.) provides access to more than 110,000 e-books from commercial bestsellers to specialized research documents in variety of formats such as Adobe PDF format, HTML, ASCII text and Microsoft Reader.

Books@Ovid offers access to over 5000 e-books.

NetLibrary (a division of OCLC) offers the largest e-book subscription service, with more than 140,000 titles available.

Factiva, Profound, ProQuest, Intelligence Data, HighBeam, Lexis-Nexis, Thomson Gale, H.W. Wilson, Northern Light, DIALOG and Datastar are other leading subscription-based information services that also provide abstracts or full text of thousands of electronic journals in multidisciplinary fields. Many journals and some scholarly magazines (on the second page) now provide the name of the database which provides the electronic version, or provide the internet address of the web version.

Google Scholar (from Google) and Windows Live Academic (from Microsoft) are examples of two major free databases providing bibliographic access to electronic journals. But these types of services are limited in content scope and coverage quality and quantity, compared to the subscription-based databases. For instance, because it is free, Windows Live Academic is either slow or difficult to access at peak times. Wiley InterScience Backfile Collections currently has one of the oldest electronic journal coverage. While most electronic journals go back to issues published from the early 20th century, Wiley InterScience Backfile Collections covers journals published from 1799. Project Gutenberg, started by Michael Hart at the University of Illinois, in the U.S., in 1991, is the world's largest free electronic library. It contains over 10,000 public domain texts and e-books of non-copyrighted books (e.g. pre–1923), such as novels and reference texts, among which are books written by William Shakespeare and Lewis Carroll. Dictionaries, maps and encyclopedias are also available in the electronic library. In March 2002, the 5,000th e-book was added: The Notes of Leonardo Da Vinci. *An average of about 200 books is added per month to Project Gutenberg.*

284
First Major Reference Book on CD-ROM

The first encyclopedias were all in print format and spread over several heavy individual volumes. Then Sony and Phillips introduced the compact disk, then later the CD-ROM. Suddenly massive amounts of information could fit in a disk, such as the entire encyclopedia, which you could easily grasp in your hand without sweating. *Grolier Electronic Encyclopedia* on CD-ROM was the first major electronic encyclopedia published in 1986. An earlier minor encyclopedia by Grolier had been published on CD-ROM in 1985 titled *Academic American Encyclopedia*.

The next 5 digitized encyclopedias available on CD-ROM were Compton's Interactive Encyclopedia *(1989),* Hutchinson Electronic Encyclopaedia *(1991),* World Book Encyclopedia *(1992),* Microsoft Encarta Encyclopedia *(1993), and* Encyclopædia Britannica *in 1994. Most now have Internet versions as well, and some such as* Microsoft Encarta Encyclopedia *have a DVD-ROM version to cater for huge audio and video multimedia files.*

285
Oldest Electronic Newspaper Coverage

Gale Group (a subsidiary of Thomson, Toronto, Canada, and now known as Thomson Gale), which provides access to a number of U.K. electronic newspapers, reached an agreement with *The Times* newspaper of London (the oldest U.K. broadsheet) to provide access to digitized back issues of the newspaper from 1785. The database will be ready by 2004. Prior to this you had to use a microfilm reader to look at 18th century copies of the newspaper. In 2006, Google (famous for its search engine) expanded its internet news service to include stories up to 250 years old. Hence it is possible to use the service (called Google News Archive) to read newspaper reports on such items as the British response to the U.S. declaration of independence in 1776. When its news service was introduced in 2002, it was limited to stories up to 30 days old.

In October 2007, the British Library and Gale/Cengage introduced a database covering the full text contents of leading U.K. newspapers from the 1800s. It is one of the largest databases of its kind in Europe.

286
Largest Producers of Newspapers Online and on CD-ROM

Lexis-Nexis (part of Reed Elsevier) provides over 12,000 worldwide newspapers online, making it the largest electronic newspaper source. The service began in 1979. CD-ROM databases produced by NewsBank (Naples, Florida, U.S.) offer access to over 200 U.S. newspapers. Its databases can also be accessed via the Internet. EBSCO, Factiva, HighBeam, InfoTrac (Gale Group), DIALOG and Datastar are some other leading information services that also provide abstracts or full text of numerous major world newspapers either online (via the Internet) or on CD-ROM / DVD-ROM. The electronic journal services given in list **283** also provides access to online newspapers as well.

287
Largest Database on the Latest Books Published in English

BookBank (Whitaker Information Services, Farnham, U.K.) provides monthly updates and prices on CD-ROM of over 2 million forthcoming English language publications as well as current titles from several of the largest English speaking countries including the U.K., the U.S., South Africa, Nigeria, India, Australia and New Zealand. It also holds out-of-print titles since 1970. In 2002 BookBank merged with Nielsen BookData (part of Dutch group VNU in the Haarlem, The Netherlands). The entity provides over 3 million titles. Nielsen BookData also collects data on English language books from over 70 countries, including non–English speaking countries. A sister company, Nielsen BookScan, operates the world's largest continuous retail sales monitoring service for books.

The other main source of new books published in English is R.R. Bowker's Global Books in Print (New Providence, New Jersey, and a division of Reed Elsevier). It lists over 5.9 million English titles. The database contains in-print and forthcoming books, audios and videos, as well as books, audios and videos declared out-of-print or out-of-stock-indefinitely since 1979. There are many country versions. The U.K. version is called Books in Print or BIP database (from Bowker-Saur, East Grinstead, U.K.) and has over 1.8 million titles. The databases of both R.R. Bowker and Nielsen BookData are available on DVD-ROM, the Internet and other formats such as microfiche, hardback print and tape. But the Internet version is the most current, as it is updated weekly.

Google Book Search is the largest free database service offering full downloads of copyright-free books (in Adobe PDF format).

288
Largest Database Covering Reviews of New Books in English

Gale Group's Book Review Index is the most used source for searching for reviews on newly published books. So popular is the database that if a new book is not mentioned in BRI, it is likely to be overlooked by the majority of acquisition librarians in the English-speaking world ordering new books for the library. Book Review Digest database from H. W. Wilson (New York, U.S.) provides 733,000 records on reviews for English-language fiction and non-fiction books excluding reviews of textbooks, government publications, and technical books in law and the sciences.

289
Largest Live Financial Information Services

In the financial world the three largest providers of live financial data such as on equities, i.e., share and stock prices, commodity futures, stock market index points, etc., to investors and stockbrokers, are Reuters, based in London, U.K.; Bloomberg (New York, U.S.) and Thomson Financial Services (Toronto, Canada). All major stock exchanges around the world employ the services of at least one of these big three, which supply thousands of specialized computer terminals giving real-time financial data.

290
Largest Business and Financial Information Databases

The Kompass database (part of Thomson Corporation, Toronto, Canada) lists over 85 million public and private businesses in over 70 countries around the world. The D&B database (Dun & Bradstreet, Parsippany, New Jersey, U.S.) lists over 100 million businesses worldwide. Printed versions of both databases are also available. They provide detailed company information such as company addresses, company products and services, number of employees, key staff members, financial figures such as company sales (turnover or revenue), and profit/loss for the financial year.

Hoover's (Austin, Texas, U.S.) is the second largest provider of company information in the U.S., giving access company records of over 14 million businesses. It is part of D&B services.

Bureau Van Dijk (Amsterdam, The Netherlands) produces the Orbis and MintGlobal databases, which both provide data on 33 million private companies and 46,000 listed companies. The Global Insight database provides access to market analysis reports on 30 million companies worldwide. The largest mergers and acquisitions database is the Zephyr database (from Bureau Van Dijk).

The Securities and Exchange Commission or SEC EDGAR database provides the most comprehensive company filings data in the U.S.

The largest provider of daily business news and newswires are Dow Jones Interactive (which is now merged with Reuters business news to form Factiva) and Nexis business news databases (part of Lexis-Nexis, and a Reed Elsevier service). The online versions of major daily financial newspapers such as the *Wall Street Journal* (published in New York, U.S.) and the *Financial Times* (London, U.K.) are other chief sources of daily business news.

The four largest databases on company credit ratings are those compiled by Moody's (New York, U.S.); Standard & Poor's (New York, U.S); Experian (Costa Mesa, California, U.S.) and Equifax (Atlanta, Georgia, U.S.).

291
Largest Business Directory Database in the U.S. and Canada

ReferenceUSA database (Omaha, Nebraska) contains contact information such as addresses and telephone numbers on more than 14 million U.S. businesses and 180 million U.S. residents. In addition it has coverage for 1.3 million Canadian businesses and 12 million Canadian residents.

292
Largest Database on Businesses in Europe

ICC British Company Directory database produced by ICC (Hampton, U.K.) indexes over 3.6 million U.K and Irish registered companies. Thomson Directories Database lists over 5 million U.K. and Irish businesses. The Fame database produced by Bureau Van Dijk has data on over 2 million U.K. and Irish companies.

Genios (a division of Handelsblatt Publishing Group, Düsseldorf, Germany) has the largest source of business databases in Germany.

Bureau Van Dijk's Amadeus database supplies information on about 8 million major public and private companies in 38 countries in Europe. EuroInfoPool database, produced in Goteborg, Sweden, provides data on periodic European company filings from 18 million companies on the continent (it is the equivalent of the SEC EDGAR database in the U.S.).

Datamonitor provides over 3000 industrial profiles and market analysis reports on 15 million companies in Europe. Similar large European market analysis and reports are also produced by Euromontor (based in London, Shanghai and Chicago).

293
Largest Database on Businesses in Asia

Teikoku Databank provides the latest information for over 300,000 Japanese companies. The database is in the English language and produced by Teikoku Databank America in New York City, U.S. Nikkei Economic Electronic Database, or NEEDS, has over 5 million records in Japanese on financial and economics data. The largest provider of financial information services in Japan is Nikkei Telekom in Tokyo. The various databases given in lists **290**, **292** and **296** also cover over 10 million companies in Asia (including Australia). CrimsonLogic, formerly SNS (Singapore Network Services), is the largest provider of databases in Singapore covering finance.

294
Largest Database on Businesses in Africa

The various databases given in lists **290**, **292** and **296** also cover over 30,000 African companies. South Africa's SABINET database host service in Cape Town has a number of online database covering business and finance.

295
Largest Database on Businesses in Latin America

The various databases given in lists **290**, **292** and **296** cover over 2 million Latin American companies.

296
Largest Database on Economics and Business Management

Based in London, the Economist Intelligence Unit, or EIU, produces the largest and most comprehensive international databases on economics covering areas such as country economic forecasts, economic indicators and market analysis. The largest economics database in the U.S. is EconLit, from the American Economic Association in Pittsburgh, Pennsylvania. It contains 800,000 plus records sourced from 750 economics journals from 1969. ABI/Inform database, produced by ProQuest Information and Learning (Ann Arbor, Michigan, U.S.), indexes over 2,002 journals in over 2.8 million records in the fields of business management and economics. EBSCO*host* (Ipswich, Massachusetts, U.S.) provides access to over 2300 business and management journals.

297
Largest Collection of U.S. and Canadian Legal Databases

Westlaw databases (now part of Thomson Corporation), totaling over 9000, are the largest databases on law in the U.S., and they include legal electronic journals. West Publishing Company developed the database host back in 1976 with help from the Ohio Bar Association. Lexis databases (part of Lexis-Nexis, and a Reed Elsevier service), released in 1973, are the second largest source of legal databases in the U.S. QuickLaw database host, developed in 1975 by QuickLaw (Kingston, Ontario), provides over 2500 databases covering recent civil and criminal Canadian law cases from all jurisdictions in Canada, as well as some Australian and British legal materials.

298
Largest Collection of European Legal Databases

Lexis databases are by far the largest of its kind used Europe. Butterworths, Lawtel, and Sweet & Maxwell databases are the largest U.K. produced databases for professional lawyers (known as solicitors and barristers), as well as law school students in the U.K. Juris, the German legal information service, offers several large online and CD-ROM legal databases, covering German and European legal information.

299
Largest Collection of African Legal Databases

The databases given in lists **297** and **298** are the primary sources for online legal material. Other important African legal texts and journals remain in print format. South Africa's SABINET database host service in Cape Town has a number of online database covering law and legislation.

300
Largest Collection of Asian legal Databases

The Institute of Scientific and Technical Information of China (ISTIC) and Wanfang Data (based in Beijing and an affiliate of the Chinese Ministry of Science & Technology) produces the largest legal databases for China, Hong Kong and Macau. CrimsonLogic, formerly SNS (Singapore Network Services), is the largest provider of databases in Singapore covering law. The database is called Singapore Academy of Law LawNet database.

301
Largest Collection of Middle Eastern Legal Databases

The databases given in lists **297** and **298** are the primary sources online legal material. Other important Middle Eastern legal texts and journals remain in print format. Israel has a number of locally produced legal database covering Israeli laws. The PDOR database is produced by the Israeli Bar Association. Takdin database provides access to over 360,000 case laws and legislations, mainly in Hebrew. It is Israel's premier legal database and is produced by C.D.I. Systems, which produces several other Israeli legal databases such as Dinime Ve-Od. In Amman, Jordan, Arab L@w Net is the largest Arab legal services. Databases are available in both Arabic and English. The United Nations Development Programme: Programme on Governance in the Arab Region (UNDP: POGAK) in New York has sponsored the development of several Arabic legal and legislative databases.

302
Largest Medical and Nursing Database

MEDLINE database was released in October 1971 by the U.S. National Library of Medicine, following an experimental project which began in 1966 with help from New York University's SDC database host. It has over 15.8 million records and abstracts from over 10,621 biomedical journals from 75 countries. It also employs the largest database thesaurus in use, called MeSH from the words Medical Subject Headings. Today over 500 million searches are done on the database each year. Coverage period goes back to 1965 and it is updated daily, meaning the most updated version is the online version and not the disk versions. The CINAHL database from Ovid (Wolters Kluwer, Amsterdam, The Netherlands) indexes journals from the fields of nursing and allied health, from 1937. It offers complete coverage of English-language nursing journals covering nursing, biomedicine, health sciences librarianship, alternative/complementary medicine, consumer health and 17 allied health disciplines. In addition, this database offers access to health care books, nursing dissertations, selected conference proceedings, standards of practice, educational software, audiovisuals and book chapters. EBSCO Publishing database Health Source: Nursing/Academic Edition provides nearly 550 scholarly full text journals, including nearly 450 peer-reviewed journals focusing on many medical disciplines. Also featured are abstracts and indexing for nearly 850 journals.

MEDLINE is just one of several large medical databases hosted by the U.S. National Library of Medicine MEDLARS database host. Other major medical databases that can be accessed include CancerLit, PopLine, SDLine, SpaceLine, ToxLine, HistLine and ChemID.

303
First and Largest Printed Medical Indexing Service

U.S. surgeon John Billings, who served in the field and in hospitals during the American Civil War, developed *Index Medicus* in 1879. It is the printed version of the MEDLINE database. Since the 2000s, *Index Medicus* has been gradually phased out in preference to MEDLINE, due to the sheer number of medical data now available that make it uneconomical to produce in print. Before the start of the 1990s, more researchers around the world used the printed version, *Index Medicus*, than the computer version, MEDLINE, and in many university libraries, the numerous volumes of the printed version occupied large precious spaces in the library. Although *Index Medicus* was the first major medical bibliography compiled, the first professional medical bibliography was written by James Douglas, a Scottish anatomist, in 1715.

304
Largest Biomedical and Pharmaceutical Database

EMBASE database produced by Elsevier Science in Amsterdam, The Netherlands, contains over 12 million records, with 400,000 records added annually. It is the electronic version of the printed version known as *Excerpta Medica*. As with *Index Medicus* above, the printed version has been phased out in preference to EMBASE.

The largest pharmaceutical database covering drug research and development is the Ensemble database, produced by Prous Science (Barcelona, Spain). It covers over 100,000 bioactive chemical compounds being developed into potential drugs. Updated daily the IDdb³ or Investigational Drug Database, developed by Current Drugs (Philadelphia, U.S. and now part of Thomson Scientific), is the largest pharmaceutical database covering the development of drugs from discovery and clinical trials, right up to eventual launch and marketing. Thomson Pharma database, part of Thomson Corporation, contains detailed data on over 20,000 pharmaceutical drugs. Pharmacopeia are huge databases, issued by an officially recognized authority in a country, describing every single drug, chemical, and medicinal preparation on the market and serving as a quality, strength and purity standard for current and new drugs, etc. The largest such database is the U.S. Pharmacopeia. The international Pharmacopeia is an initiative of the Geneva-based World Health Organization aimed at minimizing or eliminating variations among national pharmacopoeial standards.

305
Largest DNA and Molecular Biology Databases

GenBank DNA database maintained by the U.S. National Center for Biotechnology Information (a division of the U.S. National Library of Medicine and the U.S. National Institutes of Health) currently contains over 32,549,400 sequence records with more than 37 billion nucleotide base pairs (individual units in a strand of DNA) from over 100,000 species including humans. Because of the rate at which scientists from around the world submit new DNA sequences to be added to the database, GenBank grows at an exponential rate, with the number of nucleotide bases doubling approximately every 14 months. There are other major DNA sequence databases around the world, though smaller in size, notably the DNA DataBank of Japan or DDBJ and the database of the European Molecular Biology Laboratory or EMBL in Heidelberg Germany. The largest protein sequence databases are the SWISS PROT, produced and maintained by the European Bioinformatics Institute and Geneva University in Switzerland, and the Protein Information Resource (PIR) database, produced by Georgetown University Medical Center in the U.S. PIR was established in 1984 by the U.S. National Biomedical Research Foundation as a resource to assist researchers in the identification and interpretation of protein sequence information. The Geneseq database is the largest DNA database containing patented sequences. It is produced by Thomson Derwent Information.

In early 2001 GenBank DNA database received the eagerly anticipated data from the multi–million dollar global Human Genome Project, which had released a draft DNA sequence of the human genome. The draft covered all 3 billion nucleotide base pairs of the human genome, representing 50,000 to 100,000 genes. The international collaboration was carried out in labs primarily in the U.S., the U.K., Italy, Russia, Japan, France, and The Netherlands. The project was finally completed in 2003.

306
Largest DNA Database for Forensic Investigations

DNA and protein are not the only materials of human origin that have been extensively recorded; in the field of forensic science several countries have huge national fingerprint databases with millions of records. The British national DNA database, also known as the UK National Criminal Intelligence DNA Database, contains the DNA profiles of about 5 million individuals, covering 8 percent of the population. It was established in 1995. See also list **338** for details on the largest fingerprint database.

307
Largest Agriculture, Animal Science and Botany Databases

The U.S. National Agricultural Library's Agricola database, available since 1970, has over 3.9 million records, sourced from 850 journals and other materials. The United Nations Food and Agricultural Organization (FAO, based in Rome) Agris database, introduced in 1975, contains roughly 2.3 million records. The CAB Abstracts database provides a large collection of over 1 million full-text records on agriculture, veterinary science, botany and entomology (some going back to 1910) and a collection of specific data on plants. It is produced by scientists at the CABI (Center for Agriculture and Biosciences International) a not-for-profit publisher of bibliographic databases, journals and books in the applied life sciences, based in Oxon, Britain. The BIOSIS Previews database (see below) also covers a large selection of botanical and animal science data. Biological and Agricultural Index database from H. W. Wilson covers botany, animal husbandry, entomology, forestry, genetics, horticulture and soil science. The database coverage starts from 1983 and has 1.6 million records.

The largest databases on food science and nutrition are those produced by Leatherhead Information Services (Foodline database), and the International Food Information Service (Food Science and Technology Abstracts database).

308
Largest Biology Databases

Biosciences Information Service or BIOSIS (Thomson Scientific) produces the BIOSIS Previews database which indexes and abstracts over 6,000 biological (mainly botany, zoology and microbiology) journals and has over 18 million records going back to 1969.

The largest biotechnology database is Biotechnobase, from Elsevier Science (Amsterdam, The Netherlands). There are over 1.5 million records, dating back to the early days of commercial biotechnology in 1980. Frankfurt-based German Society for Chemical Apparatus, Chemical Engineering and, Biotechnology, DECHEMA also produces major databases on biotechnology, biochemical engineering and industrial biochemistry, in Europe.

309
Largest Zoology and Microbiology Databases

Zoological Record database (produced by Thomson Scientific) contains over 2.2 million records dating from 1864, making it also the oldest-continuing database in animal sciences.

The sources are over 600 zoological journals. The U.K. Zoological Society of London Library helps to produce the database.

The largest international microbiological databases are those produced by the World Data Center for Microorganisms in Japan, the American Type Culture Collection in the U.S. and the United Nations Microbial Strain Data Network. The BIOSIS Previews database (see above) also covers a large selection of microbiological data.

310
Largest STM Abstracting, Indexing and Citation Databases

Both the ISI Web of Science database, launched by Thomson Corporation, and the Scopus database, launched in 2004 by Reed Elsevier, are aiming to create the world's largest abstracting, indexing and citation database in the fields of science, technology and medicine, or STM combined. Both enable researchers and students to search titles in thousands of peer-reviewed journals, not only in the STM field, but also in social sciences and physical sciences.

311
Largest Chemistry Databases

Chemical Abstracts Service or CAS, of Columbus, Ohio, U.S., was founded in 1907 and is a division of the American Chemical Society. Its CAS databases (available via a database tool called SciFinder) now number over 19 million records, extracted from over 2000 periodicals in chemistry. CAS also introduced (with Germany's FIZ Karlsruhe and Japan's Science and Technology Agency) the well-known STN database host in 1984, which provides access to over 220 databases including CAS databases among others. A unique feature of STN is the ability to search for matching chemical structures. The CAS Registry System, better known as the CAS number, currently holds information on over 31 million chemical substances, making it the largest chemical register in the world. Every 9 seconds, a new record is added to the CAS Registry database.

In the field of organic chemistry, the CAS databases is one of the largest. But the largest specific organic chemistry database is the Beilstein database. It currently has extensive details of over 8 million organic compounds. The database is produced by the Beilstein Institute in Frankfurt, Germany. The main source of the database was originally published as a handbook by Russian chemist Friedrich Beilstein in 1881 in Germany.

The Russian Institute of Scientific and Technical Information, or VINITI (Vserossiisky Institut Nauchnoi i Tekhnicheskoi Informatsii), also has a very similar large chemical abstracting and indexing database service, like CAS, and produces the huge chemical database known as RZK or Referativnii Zhurnal Khimiya. But a great proportion of the literature is in Russian, hence it does not have wide international usage outside Eastern Europe.

312
Largest Engineering Databases

Engineering Information (Hoboken, New Jersey, U.S.) produces the major database Ei Compendex (the electronic version of the publication *Engineering Index*), which provides abstracted information from the world's significant engineering and technological literature. About 8.5 million records are available for searching; the sources are more than 2,600 engineering journals. Each year, over 220,000 new abstracts are added from 175 disciplines and major specialties. Besides applied engineering, coverage also extends to manufacturing, quality control, and engineering management issues.

313
Largest Civil Engineering Databases

International Construction Database, or ICONDA, covers worldwide technical literature on civil engineering, urban and regional planning, architecture, and construction. Fraunhofer Informationszentrum in Stuttgart, Germany, produces the database. The Archi-Text Construction Index is a comprehensive annotated index of articles covering over 50 journals relating to architecture, building design, and the construction industry.

314
Largest Electrical and Electronic Engineering Database

The Information Services for the Physics and Engineering Communities, or INSPEC, database has over 9 million records, indexed from almost 4000 journals. The database is produced by INSPEC Inc. (Edison, New Jersey, U.S.) and the Institution of Electrical Engineers (now renamed The Institution of Engineering and Technology or IET from 2006) in London, U.K. A subset of the database called INSPEC Archive provides access to over 870,000 records covering the period 1898 to 1968. The database is available via the electronic journal database host EBSCO*host*.

The largest central resource for government-funded scientific, technical, engineering, and business related information is the National Technical Information Service of NTIS. Based in Springfield, Virginia, it was established in 1952. But the origins of the NTIS go back further to the days of the OSS, the predecessor of the CIA. Before the CIA was founded in 1947, the NTIS was part of the library acquisition service of the OSS, until it was taken over by the Office of Technical Services. The NTIS has well over 2 million publications covering over 350 subject areas.

315
Largest Technical Standards Database

IHS Engineering databases (Englewood, Colorado, U.S.) are the largest source of technical standards, specifications, and regulations for the industry and the military, with data obtained from 450 of the world's largest standards-developing organizations. Techstreet, from Thomson Scientific, is the largest database covering engineering codes and standards.

316
Largest Geology Databases

The GeoRefS from the American Geological Institute contains over 2.8 million records indexed from 3,500 journals and other sources on geology and earth sciences, as well as geophysics, palaeontology, marine ecology and hydrology. The database coverage is from 1785.

The U.S. NASA Earth Science Data Search and Order System (EOSDIS) database is the largest of its kind, providing earth science and geological data from various geological information centers around the globe. Much data is also from weather and climate satellites. Established in 1949 and based in Calgary, Canadian Stratigraphic Services produces the Canstart geology database. The U.S. Geological Survey in Reston, Virginia, apart from producing geological maps, imagery, and publications, also maintains a selection of geology databases.

317
Largest Geography Databases

Geobase, produced by Elsevier Science, (The Netherlands), is the largest bibliographic geographical database covering human, social and physical geography, geology, geomechanics and ecology. Its 2 million records from 1,800 geography journals cover 1980 to present. The largest provider of GPS map, road and street atlas databases, allowing search by postal or ZIP codes of addresses for most cities in the Americas, Europe, and Asia, are Navteq (based in San Francisco, California) and Tele Atlas (based in The Netherlands). The largest online database of satellite and aerial images is DigitalGlobe (Longmont, Colorado, U.S.)

318
Largest Petroleum Database

The American Petroleum Institute (Washington, D.C., U.S.), the national trade association of the U.S. oil and natural gas industry, produces the APILOT database which provides the most comprehensive information on crude oil production.

319
Largest Astronomy Databases

NASA and the University of Maryland Astronomical Data Center work with collections of astronomical data and provide data services to the scientific community. The center receives guidance from a scientific steering committee made up of representatives of the astronomical research community. The Encyclopedia of Astronomy & Astrophysics Online database is produced by Taylor and Francis Group. It is the online version of the 4 volume print version produced by the Institute of Physics and Grove's Dictionaries, edited by Paul Murdin, the famous British astronomer. Finally there is the Astrophysics Data System (ADS), a NASA-funded project with Harvard University, which maintains three bibliographic databases containing more than 5.9 million records: Astronomy and Astrophysics; Physics; and arXiv e-prints databases. Johns Hopkins University in Baltimore, Maryland, and its Sky Query Service gives access to the three large ADS astronomy databases.

320
Largest Nuclear Physics Databases

While Ei Compendex and INSPEC databases described above cover data on nuclear physics, there are some specific nuclear physics databases. The National Institute for Standards and Technology, a non-regulatory federal agency, founded in 1901 within the U.S. Department of Commerce, produces the Atomic Spectra Database and the Bibliographic Database on Atomic Energy Levels and Spectra Online, as well as several related databases.

321
Largest Military and Weapons Databases

Specific military information is secret, hence commercial military databases cover military information that is already in the public domain. The largest military information database used in military academic institutions such as West Point Military Academy is Military Periscope database. Available since 1986, Military Periscope has been the defense industry's premier online database for accurate open-source global defense information. Coverage includes orders of battle, equipment inventories, plans and programs for more than 165 nations, as well as descriptions, specifications, and technical characteristics of virtually every major weapon, platform and system worldwide. It is produced by United Communications Group of Rockville, Maryland.

Jane's Information Group, based in Coulsdon, U.K., was founded in 1865 by a former MI5 agent. At first it provided information in print format in the form of books, newsletters and periodicals. CD-ROM and online databases of its products began in 1989. Content includes defense procurements, global defense budgets, and naval construction markets, arms, weapons systems and components used in armies, navies and air forces. There is no main database, but a group of several related databases.

The Defense Technical Information Center (DTIC) Scientific and Technical Information Network (STINET) database, produced by the DTIC at Fort Belvoir, Virginia, contains unclassified and classified military documents that have been entered into DTIC's Technical Reports Collection. Sources include Air University Library Index to Military Periodicals, Staff College Automated Military Periodical Index, Department of Defense Index to Specifications and Standards. Only the unclassified version is available to the public.

322
Largest Movie Database

The Internet Movie Database or IMDB is the largest database on movies (films) around the world. It was set up in 1996. Information about practically every single movie, dating from the first silent motion pictures can be accessed from the database. There is a free version of the database and a more detailed premium version (available via a subscription). The Modern Language Association (founded in 1883, in New York, U.S.A.) MLA International Bibliography database includes a coverage of books, dissertations, and articles on dramatic arts (film, radio, television and theatre). There are over 7,000 indexed electronic periodicals from 1000 publishers in the database from 1926 to the present, giving a total of 1.9 million records. In 2006 EBSCO unveiled a major database for TV and movie information called Film & Television Literature Index, a bibliographic database indexing over 600 related journals, newspapers and reports.

323
Largest Literature, Music and Songs Database

Humanities Abstracts from H. W. Wilson contains abstracts covering diverse subject areas of the humanities including classics, folk lore, linguistics, music, performing arts, philosophy and literature. iTunes, run by Apple Computers, has the largest downloadable music database. The MLA International Bibliography database described in list **322** above also covers electronic journals and other publications in literature, music and songs. RILM Abstracts of Music Literature is an international bibliographical database of scholarly writings on music and related disciplines and is produced by RILM, which was founded in 1966 with help from the International Musicological Society and the International Association of Music Libraries. RILM is based in the U.S. at City University of New York. The International

Bibliography of Theatre & Dance database provides full text of journal articles on all aspects of theater and performance, plus indexing for books, book articles and dissertation abstracts. IBTD with Full Text is a multicultural and interdisciplinary research tool for theater students, educators and professionals. IBTD was initiated by the American Society for Theatre Research and is produced by EBSCO.

324
Largest History Databases

The database Historical Abstracts covers literature on the history of the world except the United States and Canada from 1450 to the present. All branches of world history are included: political, diplomatic, military, economic, social, cultural, religious, and intellectual history, and the history of science, technology, and medicine. The database contains citations to journal articles, books, dissertations, and collections indexed from 1982 to the present. Articles in the database are ab-

stracted from 2,100 journals in 50 languages worldwide.

The largest source of biographical data is Marquis Who's Who, with over 1 million biographies hosted on a web database based in New Providence, New Jersey. The company has been producing a printed version since 1899. The H.W. Wilson biographical database, titled Biography Index, covers writers, artists, world leaders, sport figures, politicians, and others.

325
Largest Social Sciences and Sociology Databases

Sociological Abstracts, produced by Cambridge Scientific Abstracts (Bethesda, Maryland), has over 815,730 records from 1,800 sociology, social and behavioral sciences journals. The database covers 1952 to present. CSA also produces another sociology database, PAIS International, which is stronger in international relations and policymaking.

Launched in 2005 by EBSCO (Birmingham, Alabama, U.S.), SocINDEX with Full Text indexes approximately 620 journals in the subject area of sociology with selective coverage of a further 1570 journals. Date of coverage begins at 1895 for some journals. It is very comprehensive, with subject areas covering all aspects of criminology, demography, anthropology, religion, ethnic and racial studies, religion, social psychology and social work.

Arts and Humanities Search (AHSearch),

produced by Thomson Scientific, has 2.9 million records from over 1,136 journals in the fields of arts, social science and humanities. Its coverage is from 1980.

The International Bibliography of the Social Sciences database is the largest and most comprehensive social science database in the world, with access to over 2 million records. Current data is taken from over 2800 international social science journals and around 7000 books per year.

The DEVINSA database produced by the Indian DELNET service in New Delhi contains nearly 20,000 records on journal articles, books and unpublished materials on socio-economic issues in India, Bangladesh, Pakistan, Maldives, and Sri Lanka.

The South Asian Association for Regional Cooperation produces the SAARC social sciences and humanities database covering books, periodicals and electronic sources (CD-ROMs, web sites, audio/video cassettes, etc.) published from SAARC countries such as Bangladesh, Bhutan, India, Maldives, Nepal, Pakistan and Sri Lanka in the fields of social sciences and humanities. It is compiled by the National In-

formation Services Corporation in Hyderabad, India. In Russia, the world's largest social sciences library, the Institute for Scientific Information on Social Sciences Library, INION, produces a bibliographical database with more than 1.5 million records covering all branches of social sciences and humanities.

326
Largest Databases on Art and Architecture

Bibliography of the History of Art is the most comprehensive database on art bibliographies available worldwide, covering European and American visual arts from late antiquity to the present. It encompasses the fine arts as well as decorative and applied arts. Over 750,000 records are available, indexed from 4,300 art journals and other materials. Coverage is from 1973 and it is produced by Getty Research Institute in Los Angeles.

Art Museum Image Gallery database (from H.W. Wilson, New York, U.S.) contains over 96,000 art images, including selections from art museums.

Another large art database from H.W. Wilson is Art Abstracts with over 700,000

records indexing 475 journals on art, art history, architecture, interior design, sculpture, folk art, graphic arts, painting, visual to performing arts, archaeology, television and video. The database gives references to articles, reviews, exhibition listings and many other types of material. Coverage period is from 1984. Information on the largest digital images databases is at list **345**.

The Avery Index to Architectural Periodicals database from the Getty Research Institute in Los Angeles has over 600,000 records indexed from 3000 journals from 1741 covering architecture, urban planning, interior design and urban design.

327
Largest Database in Psychology, Religion and Anthropology

The PsycINFO database (American Psychological Association, Washington, D.C.) has more than 2.4 million bibliographic records starting from 1806, providing access to the largest source of international literature related to behavioral and social sciences, including psychiatry, sociology, anthropology, and linguistics. The sources are 2000 journals in 45 countries.

The American Psychological Association also maintains the largest full-text database in

psychology. In the field of anthropology the largest databases are Anthropology Plus (from OCLC), by far the largest, indexing 3,678 journals and AnthroSource (from the American Anthropological Association.

In the field of religion and theology, the ATLA Serials Database from the American Theological Library Association or ATLA (Chicago, Illinois) has over 175,000 records from 1949.

328
Largest Genealogy Database

Ancestry Plus databases, produced by Gale Group (a subsidiary of Thomson, Toronto, Canada), have over one billion names in more than 3,000 databases. This is a commercial product. The local database of the Family History Library has over 2 billion records (see list **86**).

329
Largest Academic Reference Databases

Blackwell Reference Online database, produced by Blackwell Publishing (Wiley-Blackwell, Hoboken, New Jersey, U.S.), is currently the largest academic reference collection, composed of almost 300 volumes in 5 major disciplines including business, economics, history, psychology and sociology. EBSCO Publishing offers a database called Science Reference Center, which contains over 600 full-text titles including encyclopedias, reference books, and bibliographies. Cambridge Scientific Abstracts or CSA (Bethesda, Maryland, U.S.) is the largest publisher of scientific research bibliographic databases. Its Internet Database Service contains over 50 technical and scientific databases used by more than 4,000 research institutions worldwide. As a multi-disciplinary reference tool, its databases also cover other subjects such as the social sciences and humanities.

330
Largest Doctoral Theses Database in Europe and North America

Dissertation Abstracts Online from ProQuest Information and Learning (Ann Arbor, Michigan) has over 2 million records on masters and doctoral theses and dissertations from Canada, the U.S, and Europe. The coverage is from 1861 to present. The British Library in collaboration with more than 70 higher education institutions in the U.K. has begun the Ethosnet project to digitize all available U.K. Ph.D. theses. The resulting full-text database called Ethos (Electronic Theses Online Service) is the largest of its kind in Europe and is expected to roll out in 2009.

331
Largest Database on Government Policies and Politics

The U.S. government, through the GPO or Government Printing Office, provides access to several databases covering the daily mechanisms of the government such as yearly budgets, congressional bills, GAO reports, comptroller general decisions, and GILS records for over 25 federal agencies. It also provides access to the *Code of Federal Regulations* and the *Federal Register* both of which are also available in print format. The databases produced by the European Union are the second largest of their kind. Databases produced include TED (for business opportunities in Europe via open competition tenders); CELEX (EU laws and directives); RAPID (press releases and news briefings of the EU institutions); and SCAD (EU legislation, government policies and related data). International Political Science Abstracts database includes current indexing and abstracts of the world's leading journals in political science. It is produced by the International Political Science Association and distributed by EBSCO Publishing.

332
Largest Database on Pulp and Paper Industries

Paperbase is world's most comprehensive database for the pulp and paper industries. More than 300 international trade and technical journals as well as conference papers are scanned to provide weekly updates for the database. Paperbase is a joint venture partnership of the Center for Paper Technology in France, Keskuslaboratorio Centrallaboratorium in Finland, Pira International (U.K.) and the Swedish Pulp and Paper Research Institute. International Paper, based in Stamford, Connecticut, in the U.S., is the largest manufacturer of paper in the world with sales of over $21 billion in 2004.

333
Largest Database on Mathematics and Computer Science

The MathSciNet database provides access to over 60 years of *Mathematical Reviews* and *Current Mathematical Publications* (from 1940 to the present). Both provide timely reviews or summaries of articles and books that contain new contributions to mathematical research. It is produced by the American Mathematical Society. The largest computer journal and books databases are Computers & Applied Sciences Complete, Safari Tech Books Online, Oxford Reference and Computing. See also lists **312** to **315**. The Computer Abstracts database from Cambridge Scientific Abstracts provides online access to over 100,000 abstracts from the foremost journals in computer science.

334
Largest Database on Education

The Washington, D.C.–based U.S. Department of Education funded ERIC database (Educational Resources Information Center) contains over 1.2 million records on education-related documents and journal articles dating from 1966. It is the world's largest index to journal articles and documents on education, policy and practice. Sources include 630 journals and 350 organizations contributing non-journal literature. The largest and most updated database for research and education funding opportunities is the FEDIX (Science-Wise) database, produced by the ResearchResearch. It has offices in Washington, London, Brussels, Amsterdam and Sydney.

335
Largest Bibliographic Database on Transportation Information

With 500,000 records, the Transportation Research Information Services, or TRIS, database is produced by the U.S. Transportation Research Board, in Washington, D.C. The TRIS database contains worldwide abstracts of published articles and reports, or summaries of ongoing or recently completed research projects relevant to the planning, development, opera-tion, and performance of transportation systems and their components.

336
Largest Air Travel Reservation Databases

In the airline and travel industry the four largest airline reservation databases (known as GDS or global distribution system) are SABRE, Amadeus, Galileo, and Worldspan. Every major travel agency around the world, as well as airlines, uses at least one of these four databases to book airline seats. The first and largest GDS database was SABRE, introduced in 1964. It materialized when an IBM employee and an employee of American Airlines happened to be sitting next to each other on a flight to Los Angeles and began talking about improving the booking and reservation system on American Airlines. The largest provider of airline and rail transport timetables and schedules is OAG (based in Downer's Grove, Illinois, U.S.). OAG data is also available in print format and is the most comprehensive information for the air traveler (except booking seats, which has to be done with a GDS database). So popular are OAG databases for looking up data such as last minute checks on departure or arrival times, airport and airline information, etc., that in addition to access from a PC or laptop, OAG databases exist in formats suitable for access from a cell phone, a PDA or other handheld computers with internet access. For instance, well-known application Worldmate is an example of third-party software using OAG data.

337
Largest Immigration Database

The largest immigration database is the Schengen Information System II, or SIS second generation database. Based in Strasbourg, France, and set up in 1995, the data is a secure governmental database pooled from 15 European countries' immigration departments. In 2006 there were over 15 million records. The database has a dual function use, first for processing immigration information such as issuance of normal visas, transit visas, or granting of residence permits, second, for maintaining and distributing information related to border security and law enforcement. It has been called Europe's largest database because of the length of data in each field of a record. As a secure database, it is not accessible by the public, but information from the database for the public domain is used for such things as statistical figures on immigration movements in Europe.

338
Largest Fingerprint Database

The FBI fingerprint database based in Clarksburg, West Virginia, and known as Automated Fingerprint Identification System or AFIS, is the largest in the world, containing over 40 million records.

339
Largest Library and Information Science Abstracting and Indexing Service

The librarian's firm favorite since 1969, the Library and Information Science Abstracts database, or LISA, contains over 180,000 records covering library and information science research, information retrieval and information management. Bowker-Saur (East Grinstead, U.K.) produces the LISA database.

The largest online purchasing directory for library and information professionals in the U.S. is the Librarian's Yellow Pages, which also exists in print with the same name. The database (accessed via the Internet and produced in New York) currently covers over 1000 companies supplying library products and services.

340
First Commercial Information Brokerage

FIND/SVP, based in New York, U.S., was the first comprehensive information brokerage in the world. It was created in 1937 as SVP and known from 1969 as FIND/SVP. Today over 1100 information consultants worldwide provide specialized business consulting and advice.

341
Most Popular Stand-Alone Bibliographic Database Software

A study has shown that academic researchers, lecturers and university students writing up projects, theses and dissertations are more likely to use either Reference Manager, Endnote or ProCite database software to organize their journal references and bibliography.

342
Largest Online Information Events in Europe

Every year since December 1977, a major exhibition and conference for information professionals and librarians called Online Information has been held in London. The global event held at London's Olympia Exhibition Hall is the world's largest and oldest event for the information industry, with an average 15,600 visitors from 46 countries and over 300 exhibitors. The 33rd Online Information meeting was held in early December 2007. The two other large annual online events in Europe are Infobase — International Fair for Information, held annually at Messe Trade Center in Frankfurt since 1986. From 2002 the event has been held during the Frankfurt International Book Fair every October. IDT is held annually in Paris. The 24th IDT event with more than 160 exhibitors was held in May 2007.

343
Largest Online Information Event in North America

The Online World and National Online Meeting, held annually in different cities in the U.S., has been discontinued. National Online Meeting was replaced with InfoToday Conference & Exhibition. The annual Computer in Libraries meeting is the largest technology conference and exhibition for librarians and information managers in North America. The 22nd meeting was in April 2007. It is organized by the publishers of the popular periodic publications for librarians and information professionals such as *Online* and *EContent* magazines and *Information Today* newspaper. A list of the largest North American book fairs is at list **231**.

344
Largest Online Information Event in Asia and Africa

Separate online expos and conferences for information professionals and librarians are not normally held in Asia or Africa; instead, they are held as part of the program of events at book fairs. The largest Asian and African book fairs are given at lists **232** and **235**.

345
Largest Digital Images Database

The Corbis Collection has over 65 million digital images (photographs, art and illustrations). Part of this collection is accessible via the Internet as the Corbis Picture Experience. Microsoft's Bill Gates founded the Corbis Collection in 1989, and its headquarters is in Seattle, Washington, U.S. Image Bank, Corel and Archive Photos are examples of other huge commercial digital images databases. The Corel database in particular specializes in travel photographs of countries, objects and people around the world. Information on the largest art image databases is at list **326**.

346
Largest Patent Databases

The Delphion Patent Database (set up in 1997 by IBM and maintained by Thomson Scientific) is the largest patent database in the world. The latest estimates suggest that the database has over 45 million patent records and over 40 million records on technical reports and bulletins from over 70 worldwide patent offices (giving a total of over 80 million records). Questel-Orbit database host (Paris, France) offers over 160 databases on trademarks and patents, making it the largest online patent database host in the world. MicroPatent (East Haven, Connecticut, U.S.) has built up a collection of over 5,000 CD-ROMs since 1989 on patent and trademark information. Over 33 million patents and 50 million trademarks are covered. Its databases are also accessible via the Internet.

*WorldCat (see list **256**) is the world's largest bibliographic database with over 95 million records.*

347
Largest Patent Databases in Europe

Apart from Questel Orbit, above, Derwent Information (London, U.K., part of Thomson Scientific) produces the Derwent World Patents Index database, which indexes over 9 million patent records covering over 13 million patents, sourced from over 40 international patent-issuing authorities, since 1963. It has the largest specialist collection of European patents. The European Union's European Patent Office has consolidated data from all member countries and the end result has been the huge International Patent Documentation Database, or INPADOCDB. This database has over 63 million patent records (mid–2007). Due to the large number of chemical patents covered by the database, the German chemistry database service FIZ Karlsruhe (which runs the huge STN database host jointly with Chemical Abstracts Service in the U.S. and Japan's Science and Technology Agency) became the first to offer access to the INPADOCDB database outside the European Patent Office.

The U.S. Patent and Trademark Office Library is the largest patent library in the world. The British Library in London has the world's largest collection of patent specifications in a national library, while the Swiss Federal Institute of Technology Library in Zürich, founded in 1855, has the largest patent library in Europe in an academic library. The All Russian Patent Technical Library founded in 1896 in Moscow is the largest in Eastern Europe. The largest patent office library is at the Munich-based German Patent Library, with over 900,000 books.

348
Largest U.S. Patents Database

IFI/Plenum, based in Wilmington, North Carolina, U.S., has the largest specialist collection of U.S. patents, called CLAIMS. IFI began indexing U.S. patents in 1955 and today its databases cover over 4.5 million United States patents. The U.S. Patent and Trademark Office has offered large free databases on patents since 1976, but searching is limited to text terms.

349
Largest Database of Patents in Asia

The Tokyo-based Japan Information Center for Science and Technology JICST database (Japan Science and Technology Corporation) has the largest collection of Asian patents, apart from the Western produced database, above, which also covers Japanese, Taiwanese, Korean and Chinese patents, among others.

350
Largest Database on Trademarks

Trademark Scan, from Thomson & Thompson (North Quincy, Massachusetts, U.S.) is the largest trademarks database in the world. The trademarks database of Questel-Orbit is the largest in Europe with over 14 million records.

351
Largest Database on Chemical and Pharmaceutical Patents

Available since 1998, the Merged Markush Services, or MMS (run by both Thomson Derwent Information in the U.K., and the French Patent and Trademark Office), has over 300 million chemical substances listed, which can be searched by chemical structure. Since chemical and pharmaceutical patent applications give diagrammatic information on how the substance was synthesized, the MMS database is very popular among scientists, especially those working in the pharmaceutical industry. Chemical Abstracts Service (Columbus, Ohio, U.S.) databases contain the second largest number of chemical patents in the world. Incidentally, in today's competitive global market a huge amount of a major pharmaceutical company's annual budget is often allocated for fighting lawsuits on patent infringements and cheap generic copies from rival companies. Thomson Pharma database contains information on over 23 million records, as well as information on 20,000 drugs. As it is part of Thomson Corporation, the database is actually an integration of other Thomson services that also exist separately, such as Derwent, Delphion, Micromedex, Newport and Gardiner Caldwell, to name a few.

352
Most Popular CD-ROM Information Retrieval Software Used in Libraries to Access Networked CD-ROM databases

SilverPlatter's SPIRS and Ovid Technologies (both part of Amsterdam-based Wolters Kluwer) search and retrieval software are both widely used for accessing CD-ROM networked databases and are available in more libraries worldwide than any other similar product.

353
First Major CD-ROM Database Used in Libraries

The InfoTrac CD-ROM database, released in 1984 by Information Access Company (now part of Gale Group, and a subsidiary of Thomson, Toronto, Canada), was originally a general reference database helping libraries to track down and retrieve periodical documents.

354
Largest Search Engines

By summer 2007, the three largest search engines were Yahoo (founded in 1994), indexing 19.2 billion web pages and 1.6 billion images; Google (founded in 1998), indexing 8.2 billion web pages and 2.1 billion images; and AllTheWeb (founded in 1997 in Sweden), indexing an estimated 6 billion web pages.

355
Largest Archives of Web Pages and First Library Websites

The Internet Archive is a non-profit venture founded in 1996 and based in San Francisco, U.S. Its database, called Way-Back-Machine, archives an estimated 30 billion web pages, dating back to 1996. Over 80 percent are thus old web pages, some first appearing on the web as far back as 1993 (when Mosaic was the only popular web browser widely available). Standard search engines such as Google, Yahoo and Alta Vista no longer pick up these old web pages because the web pages have long been deleted or moved from the hosting web server.

Today the largest Internet cafe is easyInternetCafé in New York City, U.S. Founded in 1999 by Stelios Haji-Ioannou, the Internet cafe currently offers about 800 Internet terminals. Each month over 2 million people use easyInternetCafé's 22 stores in the U.S. and Western Europe. It is hard to imagine that back in 1993 very few people outside the scientific community had ever heard about the Internet. The very first Internet node (more commonly called Internet host today) goes back much further, when the University of California Library in Los Angeles set up the earliest node in 1969, one of four U.S. academic institutions setting up an Internet node in 1969. Credit for designing the first website (i.e., installing the first web server) goes to Tim Berners-Lee's group at the Swiss-based research institute CERN in December 1990. His group used a NeXT computer as the web server, and their web browser (called WorldWideWeb) was non-graphical, as navigation was achieved by typing in text commands, very much like DOS before Windows was available. info.cern.ch was the domain name address of the CERN web server, and one of the first websites was the address book of CERN employees. In recognition of the pioneering work of Tim Berners-Lee, the name of his web browser, i.e. WorldWideWeb, or just the Web, was adopted as the general name of the graphical Internet system used today with browsers such as Netscape Navigator and Internet Explorer. Several text-based web browsers and crude graphical web browsers appeared between 1991 and 1993, such as libwww, Pello, Erwise, ViolaWWW, Midas, Samba, Lynx, Cello, Arena and Mosaic. But it was the Mosaic browser, developed at the computer department of the University of Illinois, Urbana-Champaign, that proved the most popular, as it later gave rise to both Netscape and Internet Explorer browsers.

In early 1994, the University of Illinois library became the first library to set up a website. St. Joseph County Public Library, in South Bend, Indiana, U.S., set up the very first public library website in late 1994. The first European public library to set up a website was Helsinki Public Library in Finland in 1995. Today over 90 percent of all major public libraries and universities around the world now have a website. The most important part of a library website is access to the library catalog. An alternative to the web is the Wireless Application Protocol or WAP. This is a technology that makes it possible to view a customized website with a WAP-compatible cell phone or a hand-held computer also known as a PDA. Vienna Public Library in Austria established its WAP site back in May 2000, becoming the first library in the world to do so. Its WAP site ensures that one does not need a computer to get information on the library. The central library of Hampshire County in the U.K. set up its own WAP site in June 2000. WAP is not the only new technology being harnessed by public libraries; increasingly a number of public libraries in the West now offer e-books or electronic books for members of the public to borrow, which are can be read with laptop computers or PDAs.

356
Largest Library Document Supply and Inter-Lending Service

The British Library Document Supply Center based at Boston Spa in West Yorkshire handles up to 4 million requests, for inter-library loans or photocopies of periodical articles or book extracts, a year. In 2001 it delivered its 100 millionth document.

357
Largest Scientific Document Supply Services

ISI Document Solution (formerly The Genuine Article), which is the document delivery service of the Institute for Scientific Information (Philadelphia, Pennsylvania, U.S., now part of Thomson Corporation), and the document delivery service of the Chemical Abstracts Service (Columbus, Ohio, U.S.) both handle over 2 million requests for scientific literature a year from around the world. Other large commercial document delivery services include CISTI, Adonis, CatchWord, Doc Deliver, Faxon, Infotrieve, Swets, and UnCover. The largest French scientific document delivery service is the one provided by INST-CNRS, based in Nancy. It has a library of 26,000 French and international periodical titles.

Because there are more journals in the various fields of medicine, science and technology, compared to other subjects such as law and business journals, several countries have a central or national medical, scientific and technical document supply center, which is also part of a national institute or a library, such as the U.S. National Library of Medicine; the Canada Institute for Scientific and Technical Information (CISTI); the French National Institute for Scientific and Technical Information (INIST); the Japan Information Center for Science and Technology (JICST); and the Indian National Scientific Documentation Center (INSDOC). In Turkey, the Documentation Center of the Turkish Scientific and Technical Research Council in Ankara, known as TUBITAK-TURDOK, has a collection of over 800 periodicals on science and technology, making it the largest periodicals library and document supply service in the Middle East.

358
Largest Library Network or Consortium

OCLC founded in 1967 as a non-profit computer library service and research organization and based in Dublin, Ohio, in the U.S. has a membership of more than 9000 libraries. More than 40,000 libraries in 76 countries and territories use OCLC's products and services.

The largest information consortium is the Electronic Information for Libraries Direct. Formed in 1999 by EBSCO and the Open Society Institute (part of the Soros Foundation Network), it encompasses libraries in 39 countries in Europe, Africa, and Latin America. Members have access to all EBSCO's full-text electronic journals.

359
Largest Providers of Subscription Services for Libraries

EBSCO Subscription Services, based Birmingham, Alabama, U.S., and founded in 1958 by Elton B. Stephens, works with over 78,000 publishers in 21 countries. Its subscription services help libraries buy bulk copies of books and periodicals. Its database covers over

300,000 titles. Swets Information Services (Lisse, The Netherlands) handles more than 2 million subscriptions each year, dealing with about 65,000 publishers from 20 countries. It maintains a database of 250,000 titles. Ingenta (Bath, U.K.) works with over 30,000 publishers worldwide providing libraries and researchers with access, via subscription or pay-per-view, to a huge base of books, reports and periodicals.

360
Oldest Providers of Subscription Services for Libraries

Everetts in London began offering book and subscription services to libraries in 1793. Baker & Taylor, based in Charlotte, North Carolina, in the U.S., has been providing wholesale subscription services to libraries and bookstores since 1828 and is the largest such service in the Americas. Its databases cover over 1 million titles.

361
Largest Electronic Trading Services for Libraries in the U.K.

Located in Tonbridge, First Edition has provided a large scale EDI trading network (a standard for transmitting information and commercial messages), for library acquisitions services. The network encompasses publishers, booksellers, library suppliers and the libraries themselves.

362
Twelve Greatest Inventions Used in Libraries Today

1. **Paper**. A.D. 105. Inventor: Ts'al Lun, China. Main use: manufacture of books and periodicals.

2. **Book Printing**. A.D. 1450. Inventor: Johannes Gutenberg, Germany. Main use: manufacture of books and periodicals.

3. **The Internet**. Late 1960s. Inventors: various people invented the many components that make up the Internet as we know it today. It began as ARPANET, and in 1969 the first Internet host was set up at the University of California, Los Angeles, in the U.S. Main use: searching for information, browsing library catalogs and online publishing.

4. **Microfilm**. 1852. Inventor: John Duncan, U.K. Main use: preservation of periodicals, especially newspapers.

5. **Electric bulb**. 1879. Inventor: Thomas Edison. Main use: illuminating the library.

6. **Television**. 1926 and 1927. Inventors: John Logie Baird, U.K., and Philo Farnsworh, U.S. Main use: watching videos and DVDs in the library.

7. **Photocopying**. 1938. Inventor: Xerox, U.S. The Xerox 914 was the first office photocopier. Main use: duplication of printed works.

8. **Personal Computer**. 1973. Inventors: like the Internet, various people invented the many components that led to the personal computer. French company R2E marketed a PC called Micral in 1973. But Ed Roberts built the first personal computer kit in 1975 and called it the Altair. Microsoft's Bill Gates and Paul Allen wrote the first personal computer software for the Altair. Main use: too much to list here.

9. **CD-ROM disk**. 1984. Inventors: Sony in Japan and Philips in The Netherlands. Main

use: storage of reference databases and huge books such as encyclopedias.

10. **e-book**. 1993. Inventors: Adobe Corporation. When the U.S. company Adobe introduced the Acrobat PDF format in 1993, it was only used on PCs and laptops for reading electronic documents. Very few PDA devices and no smartphones were available that could read PDF documents. In 1994 e-books appeared in HTML format. Once again HTML was only used on PCs and laptops. In 1998, NuroMedia released the first custom-made handheld e-book reader (today hundreds of companies make similar products). Once popular pocket PCs and palm PDA devices that could read PDF or HTML documents became widespread, the publishers Simon & Schuster, in 1999, brought out the idea of selling books in PDF and other formats for the handheld devices. They called their new imprint ibooks. Also in 1999, the National Institute of Standards and Technology in the U.S. held its first e-book conference, while Microsoft declared that e-books were the future of reading. Soon the e-book boom was born, with Microsoft and others releasing free e-book readers. E-book pilot trials in libraries began in 2000. Many libraries now offer e-book access to users via services like NetLibrary and Questia. The big

advantage of an e-book is the ability to search it quickly. Main use: an alternative small size for borrowing a book, allowing one to carry lots and lots of books in one go, to read on a PDA or computer.

11. **DVD-ROM disk**. 1995. Inventors: Several Japanese companies, including Sony and Toshiba. Main use: storage of large databases or huge books such as the Microsoft Encarta Encyclopedia Reference Suite or Encyclopædia Britannica Ultimate DVD, which is rich in huge multimedia files that cannot fit in a CD-ROM disk.

12. **WiFi**. 1997. The standards for WiFi emerged in 1997, following its invention in 1991 and were ratified in 1999 and 2000. Apple was the first to include WiFi hardware in its computers as standard under the name Airport in its new iBooks in 1999. When Windows XP arrived in 2001, WiFi software was included as standard. Starting from late 2002 (first in the U.S., then elsewhere a year later) libraries began to offer WiFi hotspots. Initially only university, college and special libraries around the world offered WiFi hotspots. But soon public and national libraries also began to offer WiFi hotspots. Main use in library: using one's laptop to access the Internet in a quiet place.

WORLD RECORDS FOR LIBRARY AND INFORMATION SCIENCE ORGANIZATIONS

Prior to the late 16th century, librarians were generally scholars with special interests in book and manuscript collecting. With the organization and opening of larger libraries in the late 16th and early 17th centuries, the work of a librarian came to be recognized as requiring special expertise and skills, if not specialized education. Soon librarians became more involved in the organization of library facilities and its services to the user. While the first library school was not introduced until the 19th century, several early important publications on the work of librarians included Gabriel Naudé's *Advis pour dresser une bibliothèque,* published in 1627 in France, and John Duries's *The Reformed Librarie-Keeper,* published in 1650 in Scotland.

363
First Library School

The Columbia University School of Library Service in New York City was set up in 1887. Its founder, Melvil Dewey, had in 1876 constructed an expandable scheme for classifying books, known today as the Dewey Decimal System. The library school was closed in late 1992, but many of the original librarianship book collections used by Dewey are still in existence and part of the Columbia University Library.

364
Oldest Accredited Library School in North America

The American Library Association provides a list of library schools that it finds to meet a high standard. Pratt Institute School of Information and Library Science in New York was the first library school to be accredited, having been established in 1890.

365
First Five University Library Schools in the U.S.

1. Columbia University School of Library Service, New York City. Founded 1887.

2. Pratt Institute School of Information and Library Science in New York. 1890.

3. Emporia State University, School of Library and Information Management, Kansas. 1902.

4. University of Washington Information School, Seattle. 1911.

5. Emory University, Division of Librarianship, Atlanta. 1926.

The University of Toronto's Faculty of Information Studies is the oldest in Canada.

366
First Five University Library Schools in Europe

1. George August University library school, Göttingen, Germany. Founded 1888.

2. Munich University library school, Germany. 1905.

3. Leipzig University library school, Germany. 1914.

4. Copenhagen University library school, Denmark. 1918.

5. University College library school, London University. UK. 1919.

367
Oldest University Library Schools in Asia

The Bangkok Library Association in Thailand was founded in the 1890s by British Librarian Jennie Neilson Hays, who also founded the largest English library in Thailand, the Neilson Hays Library. Wuhan University library school in China was founded in 1910 by the American librarian Mary Elizabeth Wood, who gave English lectures in China and who also signed on China's behalf the membership charter of the International Federation of Library Associations when it was founded in 1927. The first Japanese library school was at Keio University in Tokyo in 1951.

368
First University Library School in the Middle East

The library school of Hebrew University, Jerusalem, Israel, was founded in 1956.

369
First University in the U.S. to Offer an Extensive Program in Information Science

Unlike the librarian whose job is very familiar to those who use libraries, information scientists are rather a rare sight. They are more likely to be working in specialist libraries such as biomedical, pharmaceutical or legal libraries and less likely in national, public and university libraries, which are open to members of the public. Typically, information scientists are primarily involved in creating, retrieving, organizing or disseminating information, and their work involves much use of computer technology. Georgia Institute of Technology, in Atlanta, began teaching information science in 1963.

370
First University in Europe to Offer an Extensive Program in Information Science

In early 1961 City University School of Informatics in London became the first university in the world to train professional information scientists. Over the years more than half of all qualified information scientists in the U.K. who reside in London studied at City University, including the author of *Library World Records.*

371
Top Fifteen U.S. Library Schools for the Year 2008

The list is based on *U.S. News and World Report* magazine survey of U.S. LIS schools in 2007 offering master's degree programs in the United States that are accredited by the American Library Association.

Just as law, business and engineering schools have specialized courses within the core main subject to cater to the increasing complexity of the different aspects of the core subject, some library schools offer specialized courses in core areas of library and information studies. The top three library schools for five major specialized divisions, including the general library and information studies, are:

City University in London.

General Library and Information Studies

1. University of Illinois library school, Urbana-Champaign.
2. University of North Carolina library school, Chapel Hill.
3. Syracuse University library school, New York.

Law Librarianship

1. University of Washington information school, Seattle.
2. Catholic University of America library school, Washington, D.C.
3. University of Texas library school, Austin.

Medical and Health Librarianship

1. University of Pittsburgh library school, Pennsylvania.

2. University of North Carolina library school, Chapel Hill.
3. University of North Texas library school, Denton.

Archives and Preservation

1. University of Texas, Austin library school.
2. University of Maryland–College Park library school.
3. University of Michigan library school, Ann Arbor.

Children and Youth Librarianship

1. Florida State University library school, Tallahassee.
2. University of Illinois library school, Urbana-Champaign.
3. Rutgers University library school, New Brunswick, New Jersey.

372
Largest National Library Association

The American Library Association, or ALA, was founded in 1876 in Philadelphia. It is also the world's first library association. Melvil Dewey, who invented the Dewey Decimal Classification, helped in the establishment of the ALA. It has over 55,000 members today.

*With over 11,000 members, the U.S. Special Libraries Association, or SLA, formed in 1909, is the second largest library and information related association in the world. The first Canadian library association was founded in 1900 for librarians in On-*tario. *The Brazilian Library Association (Federação Brasileira de Associaçoes de Bibliotecarios), founded in 1938 in São Paulo, was the first in Latin America. The largest international library association is the International Federation of Library Associations and Institutes, or IFLA. It was founded in 1927 and more than 1783 library organizations from 154 countries are members. Each year annual conferences are held in various capitals of member countries. The IFLA Secretariat headquarters is at The Hague, in The Netherlands.*

373
Largest and Oldest National Library Association in Europe

The Library Association, London, was founded in 1877. It has over 5,000 members. It is now called CILIP, or the Chartered Institute for Library and Information Professionals.

Some of the other earlier library European associations were those founded in Austria in 1896, *France (1906), Belgium (1907), Germany (1918), and Italy (1930). The British equivalent of the Special Library Association in the U.S. is the Association of Special Libraries and Information Bureaux, better known today as ASLIB.*

374
Oldest National Library Association in Africa

The first and largest African library association was the South Africa Library Association in 1930. Since 1997 it is called the Library and Information Association of South Africa. The name change is common around the world. Many organizations have merged the separate organizations for librarians and information professionals. For instance, in the U.K. the Library Association changed its name to the Chartered Institute for Library and Information Professionals in 2002, when it merged with the then Institute of Information Scientists.

375
Oldest National Library Association in Asia

The Japan Library Association in Tokyo (*Nihon Toshokan Kyokai*) was set up in 1892.

376
Oldest National Library Association in the Middle East

The Egyptian Library Association was founded in 1946 in Cairo.

The first Sub-Saharan African library association was the South Africa Library Association in 1930.

377
Largest National Information Science Association

The American Society for Information Science, formed in 1937 as the American Documentation Institute, is the largest of its kind in the world, with over 6000 members. The substitution of Information Science (for Documentation) happened in 1955. Paul Otlet (Belgian lawyer), who co-founded the International Federation for Documentation, FID (then known as the International Institute of Bibliography), in 1895, is generally considered to be the first major pioneer of the general principles of information science in the world.

378
Most Prestigious Award for Information Scientists

Each year the U.K. Chartered Institute for Library and Information Professionals, or CILIP, offers the Jason Farradane Award to an individual or organization for an outstanding contribution to the information field or in recognition of an advancement in the field of information science. It is named after one of the founding fathers of information science in Europe who taught at City University in London and was the first person in the U.K. to be recognized academically as an information scientist. The American Society for Information Science and Technology offers the annual Award of Merit, given to individuals who have made a noteworthy contribution to the field of library and information science.

379
Famous First Full-Time Librarians

National Library of Australia, founded in 1901: Harold Leslie White, first librarian in 1947. U.S. Library of Congress, founded in 1800: George Watterson, first librarian in 1815. Chetham Library, founded in 1653: Richard Johnson was appointed by Chetham Library in Manchester in 1653 and given a salary of £15 per annum. Harvard University Library, founded in 1636: Solomon Stoddard, first librarian in 1643; Bodleian Library Oxford University, founded in 1320 and 1602: James Bodley, first librarian in 1602.

380
Six Libraries with More Than 800 Staff Members and Their Annual Budgets

1. Library of Congress, Washington, D.C., U.S. 4,360 staff/$462 million.

2. Russian State Library, Moscow. 2,500 staff/$24 million.*

3. British Library, London. 2,410 staff/$201 million.*

4. National Library of France, Paris. 2,800 staff/$196 million.*

5. National Library of China, Beijing. 1,600 staff/$38 million.*

6. National Library of Japan, Tokyo. 860 staff/$235 million.*

The largest annual library budget is the U.S. National Security Agency Library budget of over a billion dollars. The university library with the largest budget is Harvard University Library at over $140 million, while the New York Public Library has the largest public library budget, around $100 million a year. For centuries, the rich, members of royal families, politicians, and others have made generous donations of books or money to libraries. In terms of the largest financial donations made to libraries by billionaires to date, two individuals have given grants of more than $300 million combined up to 2006 — George Soros (through his Soros Foundation Network) and Bill Gates (through the Bill & Melinda Gates Foundation). No philanthropist has yet to match the generosity achieved by Andrew Carnegie, who personally financed the construction of over 1500 libraries in the U.S. This has been called the greatest gift to American libraries.

*Based on local currency exchanges rates for the U.S. dollar.

381
The 345 Largest and Most Important Libraries

This list focuses only on the largest and most important libraries, in each country, with 2 million or more books.

Omissions: both Russia and the U.S. have dozens of academic, research, special and public libraries with more than 2 million books. This list of largest libraries has thus excluded the following: U.S. university libraries with fewer than 6 million books, and public libraries with fewer than 4 million books and research and special libraries with less than 3 million books. For Russia, omitted are Russian university, research and special libraries with fewer than 2.5 million books. Russia in particular has over 130 research and special libraries with more than 1 million books.

Five other omissions include Ukrainian special libraries and Chinese provincial and special libraries, with less than 3 million books, and German, Chinese and Japanese university libraries with less than 3 million books.

Rank	Name	Location	Volume of books (millions)
1.	Library of Congress	Washington, D.C.	30
2.	National Library of China	Beijing	27
3.	Russian State Library	Moscow	24.2
4.	National Library of Germany	Frankfurt and Leipzig	17
5.	National Library of France	Paris	15.3
6.	Harvard University Library	Cambridge, Massachusetts, U.S.	15
7.	Russian Academy of Sciences Library	St. Petersburg	14.2
8.	The British Library	London	14.5
9.	Boston Public Library	Massachusetts, U.S.	14
10.	National Library of Ukraine	Kiev	13
11.	INION Library	Moscow, Russia	12.8
12.	National Library of Russia	St. Petersburg	12
13.	Metropolitan London Borough Libraries	London, U.K.	12.1
14.	Yale University Library	New Haven, Connecticut, U.S.	12
15.	Lomonosov Moscow State University Library	Russia	11
16.	Berlin State Library	Germany	11
17.	National Library of Italy	Rome and Florence	11
18.	RASLNS Library	Moscow	11
19.	National Library of Canada	Ottawa and Montreal	11
20.	University of Illinois Library	Urbana-Champaign, U.S.	10.5
21.	Los Angeles County Public Library	California, U.S.	10.4
22.	University of California Library	Berkeley, U.S.	10
23.	National Library of Japan	Tokyo	10
24.	Romanian Academy Library	Bucharest	9.8
25.	Cincinnati & Hamilton County Public Library	Ohio, U.S.	9.6
26.	University of Toronto Library	Ontario, Canada	9.5
27.	Shanghai Library	China	9.3
28.	Tokyo University Library	Japan	9.2
29.	Columbia University Library	New York, U.S.	9.2
30.	Bodleian Library, Oxford University	U.K.	9
31.	University of Texas Library	Austin, U.S.	8.9
32.	National Library of Romania	Bucharest	8.3
33.	Stanford University Library	California, U.S.	8.2
34.	University of Michigan Library	Ann Arbor, U.S.	8.1
35.	Bavarian State Library	Munich, Germany	8
36.	Beijing University Library	China	8
37.	University of California Library	Los Angeles, U.S.	8
38.	Vernadsky Central Scientific Library	Kiev, Ukraine	8
39.	UNWM Library	U.S.	7.9
40.	Cornell University Library	Ithaca, U.S.	7.7
41.	University of Calgary Library	Canada	7.6
42.	Detroit Public Library	Michigan, U.S.	7.5
43.	Toronto Public Library	Ontario, Canada	7.6
44.	St. Petersburg State University Library	Russia	7.5
45.	Nanjing Library	China	7.4
46.	University of Chicago Library	Illinois, U.S.	7.4
47.	National Library of Australia	Canberra	7.3
48.	RSPLST Library	Moscow	7.3

Rank	Name	Location	Volume of books (millions)
49.	Indiana University Library	Bloomington, U.S.	7.2
50.	NSTL Library	Kazakhstan, Almaty	7
51.	Lithuanian Technical University Library	Riga	7
52.	Kyoto University Library	Japan	7
53.	National Library of Armenia	Yerevan	7
54.	University of Paris, I–XIII Libraries	France	7
55.	Queens Borough Public Library	New York, U.S.	7
56.	Chinese Academy of Sciences Library	Beijing, China	6.7
57.	University of Washington Library, U.S.	Seattle, U.S.	6.9
58.	Free Library of Philadelphia	Pennsylvania, U.S.	6.5
59.	University of Minnesota Library, U.S.	Minneapolis	6.6
60.	Princeton University Library, New Jersey	U.S.	6.5
61.	Los Angeles Public Library	California, U.S.	6.4
62.	Cambridge University Library	U.K.	6.4
63.	Ohio State University Library	Columbus, U.S.	6
64.	Azerbaijan Scientific and Technical Library	Baku	6
65.	Kyrgyzstan Scientific and Technical Library	Bishkek	6
66.	Kazakh Academy of Sciences Library	Almaty	6.3
67.	National Library of Kazakhstan	Almaty	6.5
68.	Berlin Free University Library	Germany	6.4
69.	National Library of the Czech Republic	Prague	6.3
70.	Carnegie Library of Pittsburgh	Pennsylvania, U.S.	6.3
71.	Nanjing University Library	China	6.3
72.	National Library of Scotland	Edinburgh, U.K.	6
73.	National Library of Georgia	Tbilisi	6
74.	National Library of Austria	Vienna	6
75.	Chicago Public Library	Illinois, U.S.	6
76.	New York Public Library	New York, U.S.	5.9
77.	University of London Libraries	U.K.	5.8
78.	Vienna University Library	Austria	5.8
79.	SFIT Library	Zürich, Switzerland	5.6
80.	University of Dhaka Library	Bangladesh	5.5
81.	National Library of Lithuania	Vilnius	5.5
82.	National Library of Latvia	Riga	5.4
83.	National Library of Bulgaria	Sofia	5.4
84.	National Library of Spain	Madrid	5.4
85.	St. Cyril & St. Methodius National Library	Sofia, Bulgaria	5.4
86.	Central House of the Russian Army Library	Moscow	5.3
87.	Laval University Library	Quebec City, Canada	5.3
88.	Lund University Library	Sweden	5.3
89.	Uppsala University Library	Sweden	5.2
90.	Vilnius University Library	Lithuania	5.2
91.	National Library of Belgium	Brussels	5.1
92.	Waseda University Library	Tokyo, Japan	5.1
93.	Armenia Scientific and Technical Library	Yerevan	5.1
94.	Sydney University Library	Australia	5.1
95.	McGill University Library	Montreal, Canada	5
96.	Brooklyn Public Library	New York, U.S.	5
97.	Brno State Scientific Library	Czech Republic	5
98.	National Library of Turkmenistan	Ashkhabad (Ashgabat)	5

Rank	Name	Location	Volume of books (millions)
99.	National Library of Wales	Cardiff, U.K.	5
100.	National University Library	Strasbourg, France	5
101.	National Library of Belarus	Minsk	5
102.	National Library of Medicine	Bethesda, Maryland, U.S.	5
103.	National Library of Denmark/ Copenhagen University Library	Denmark	5
104.	Kazan State University Library	Russia	4.9
105.	Simferopol State University Library	Ukraine	4.9
106.	John Rylands University Library	Manchester, U.K.	4.8
107.	Leipzig University Library	Germany	4.8
108.	Hanover Technical University Library	Germany	4.8
109.	Hebrew University Library/ Israel National Library	Jerusalem	4.8
110.	Kansai University Library	Osaka, Japan	4.8
111.	Sichuan University Library	Chengdu, China	4.8
112.	MRSLF Library	Moscow, Russia	4.8
113.	University of Alberta Library	Edmonton, Canada	4.8
114.	Central Research and Technical Library	Sofia, Bulgaria	4.7
115.	Zhejiang Provincial Library	Hangzhou, China	4.7
116.	National Library of Sweden	Stockholm	4.6
117.	Martin Luther University Library	Halle-Wittenberg, Germany	4.6
118.	Utrecht University Library	The Netherlands	4.6
119.	Dresden University Library	Germany	4.6
120.	University of British Columbia Library	Vancouver, Canada	4.6
121.	San Diego Public Library	California, U.S.	4.5
122.	University of Frankfurt Library	Germany	4.5
123.	Akhundov M.F. Azerbaijan State Library	Baku	4.5
124.	National Library of India	Calcutta (Kolkata)	4.5
125.	Mitchell Library	Glasgow, U.K.	4.5
126.	Oslo University Library	Norway	4.5
127.	National Library of New Zealand	Wellington	4.4
128.	National Library of Poland	Warsaw	4.4
129.	CISTI Library	Ottawa, Ontario, Canada	4.3
130.	Heidelberg University Library	Germany	4.3
131.	Dallas Public Library	Texas, U.S.	4.3
132.	Montpellier University Libraries	France	4.3
133.	Islamic Azad University	Tehran, Iran	4.3
134.	Miami-Dade Public Library	Florida, U.S.	4.2
135.	Saxony State Library	Dresden, Germany	4.2
136.	Irkutsk State University Library	Russia	4.2
137.	National Library of Ireland	Dublin	4.1
138.	Beijing Society of Library Science Capital Library	China	4.1
139.	State and University Library	Århus, Denmark	4.1
140.	Fudan University Library	Shanghai, China	4.1
141.	Alisher Navoi State Public Library	Tashkent, Uzbekistan	4.1
142.	Cleveland Public Library	Ohio, U.S.	4.1
143.	Moravian Library Brno	Czech Republic	4.1
144.	George August University Library	Göttingen, Germany	4.1
145.	National Library of Korea	Seoul, South Korea	4
146.	Lvov State Scientific Library	Ukraine	4

Rank	Name	Location	Volume of books (millions)
147.	Florence University Library	Italy	4
148.	Houston Public Library	Texas, U.S.	4
149.	National Library of Hungary	Budapest	4
150.	Amsterdam University Library	The Netherlands	4
151.	Hunan Provincial Library	Changsha, China	4
152.	Buenos Aires University Library	Argentina	4
153.	National Library of Chile	Santiago, Chile	4
154.	National Center for Documentation	Sofia, Bulgaria	4
155.	Humboldt University Library	Berlin, Germany	4
156.	National Taiwan University Library	Taipei, Taiwan	4
157.	Lithuanian Academy of Sciences Library	Riga	4
158.	New South Wales State Library	Sydney	4
159.	Cologne University Library	Germany	4
160.	Frankfurt University Library	Germany	4
161.	Russian Central Epidemiology Institute	Moscow	4
162.	National Library of Mongolia	Ulan Bator	4
163.	University of Waterloo Library	Canada	4
164.	Leuven Catholic University Library	Belgium	4
165.	Estonian Academic Library	Tallinn	4
166.	Russian State Medical Library	Moscow	3.9
167.	Shandong Provincial Library	Jinan, China	3.9
168.	Jagiellonian University Library	Kraków, Poland	3.9
169.	Chernyshevsky State Library	Bishkek, Kyrgyzstan	3.9
170.	Sichuan Provincial Library	Chengdu, China	3.9
171.	Zhengzhou University	Henan, China	3.9
172.	Trinity College Library, Dublin University	Ireland	3.8
173.	Hampshire County Public Libraries	Winchester, U.K.	3.8
174.	Zhejiang Provincial Library	Hangzhou, China	3.8
175.	Munich University Library	Germany	3.8
176.	Russian State Public History Library	Moscow	3.8
177.	São Paulo Federal University Library	Brazil	3.7
178.	Kyushu University Library	Fukuoku, Japan	3.6
179.	Guangdong Provincial Library	Guangzhou, China	3.6
180.	Taras Shevchenko University of Library	Kiev Ukraine	3.6
181.	Tsinghua University Library	Beijing China	3.6
182.	Sichuan Union University Library	China	3.6
183.	Halle University Library	Germany	3.6
184.	National Library of Moldova	Chisinau	3.6
185.	Rostock University Library	Germany	3.5
186.	Babes-Bolyai University Library	Cluj-Napoca, Romania	3.5
187.	Berlin Technical University	Germany	3.5
188.	U.S. National Agricultural Library	Washington, D.C.	3.5
189.	Kent County Public Libraries	Maidstone, U.K.	3.5
190.	Mickiewicz University Library	Poznan Poland	3.5
191.	Tomsk University Library	Russia	3.5
192.	Hubei Provincial Library	Wuhan, China	3.4
193.	Georgian Academy of Sciences Central Library	Tbilisi	3.4
194.	National Library of The Netherlands	The Hague	3.4
195.	National Library of Finland/Helsinki University Library	Finland	3.4

Rank	Name	Location	Volume of books (millions)
196.	National Library of Switzerland	Bern	3.4
197.	Heidelberg University Library	Germany	3.3
198.	Soochow University Library	Taipei, Taiwan	3.3
199.	Swiss Federal Institute of Technology Library	Zürich	3.3
200.	Tajikistan State Library	Dushanbe	3.3
201.	Charles University Library	Prague, Czech Republic	3.4
202.	Humboldt University Library	Berlin, Germany	3.3
203.	Birmingham Public Library	U.K.	3.3
204.	National Parliamentary Library	Kiev, Ukraine	3.3
205.	Chongqing Library	China	3.3
206.	Odessa University Library	Ukraine	3.3
207.	Hokkaido University Library	Sapporo, Japan	3.3
208.	Wroclaw University Library	Poland	3.3
209.	Bremen State University	Germany	3.3
210.	St. Clement Ohridski & University Library	Skopje/Bitola, FYR Macedonia	3.3
211.	National Library of Mexico/NAU Library	Mexico City	3.3
212.	Innsbruck University Library	Austria	3.2
213.	Tübingen University Library	Germany	3.2
214.	Baden Württemberg State Library	Stuttgart	3.2
215.	Munich City Library	Germany	3.2
216.	Tbilisi State University Library	Georgia	3.2
217.	Jena University Library	Germany	3.2
218.	Hebei University Library	China	3.1
219.	State Central Polytechnic Library	Moscow	3.1
220.	Berlin Central Library	Germany	3.1
221.	Kobe University Library	Japan	3.1
222.	Lyons University Library	France	3.1
223.	Würzburg University Library	Germany	3.1
224.	Nankia University Library	Tianjin, China	3.1
225.	Seoul National University Library	South Korea	3.1
226.	Tartu University Library	Estonia	3.1
227.	Khakiv State University	Ukraine	3.1
228.	Belarus National Academy of Science	Minsk	3.1
229.	Central Library, Armenian Academy of Science	Yerevan	3.1
230.	Zurich Central Library	Switzerland	3.1
231.	University of Basel Library	Switzerland	3.1
232.	Regensburg University Library	Germany	3.1
234.	Hiroshima University	Japan	3.1
235.	Montreal University Library	Canada	3.1
236.	University of Western Ontario London	Canada	3
237.	Russian Academy of Agriculture Library	Moscow	3
238.	Saskatchewan University Library	Saskatoon, Canada	3
239.	Hamburg University Library	Germany	3
240.	Gent University Library	Belgium	3
241.	Munchner Library	Munich Germany	3
242.	National Library of Argentina	Buenos Aires	3
243.	Malmö City Library	Sweden	3
244.	National Library of Estonia	Tallinn	3
245.	Saratov University Library	Russia	3

Rank	Name	Location	Volume of books (millions)
246.	Birmingham University Library	U.K.	3
247.	Wuhan University Library	China	3
248.	National Library of Greece	Athens	3
249.	Lancashire County Public Libraries	Preston, U.K.	3
250.	Melbourne University Library	Australia	3
251.	Graz University Library	Austria	3
252.	Liverpool Public Library	U.K.	3
243.	Nagoya University Library	Japan	2.9
254.	Rome "La Sapienza" University Library	Italy	2.9
255.	Complutense University Library	Madrid, Spain	2.9
256.	Kaya University Library, Kyungbuk	South Korea	2.9
257.	Groningen State University Library	The Netherlands	2.9
258.	New South Wales University Library	Sydney, Australia	2.8
259.	Rostov State University Library	Russia	2.8
260.	Concordia University Library	Canada	2.8
261.	Helsinki City Library	Finland	2.8
262.	Essex County Public Libraries	Chelmsford, U.K.	2.8
263.	Center for Research Library	Chicago, U.S.	2.8
264.	Lyons Municipal Library	France	2.8
265.	National Library of Venezuela	Caracas	2.7
266.	Voronezh State Library	Russia	2.7
267.	U.S. National Agricultural Library	Washington, D.C.	2.7
268.	Edinburgh University Library	U.K.	2.7
269.	Madrid Autonomous University Library	Spain	2.7
270.	National Library of Taiwan	Taipei	2.7
271.	National Library of Cuba	Havana	2.7
272.	Moscow Technical University Library	Russia	2.7
273.	Turin University Library	Italy	2.6
274.	Basel University Library	Switzerland	2.6
275.	Hamburg Public Library	Germany	2.6
276.	National Library of Portugal	Lisbon	2.6
277.	Air University Library, MAF	Alabama, U.S.	2.6
278.	Bucharest University Library	Romania	2.5
279.	Toulouse University Library	France	2.5
280.	Russian State Public Historical Library	Moscow	2.5
281.	Eotvos Lorand University Library	Budapest, Hungary	2.5
282.	Stockholm University Library	Sweden	2.5
283.	National University of Ireland Library	Dublin	2.5
284.	Leeds University Library	U.K.	2.5
285.	Ryukoku University Library	Kyoto, Japan	2.5
286.	Lviv Ivan Franko State University	Ukraine	2.5
287.	Ottawa Public Library	Canada	2.5
288.	Azerbaijan Academy of Science Library	Baku	2.5
289.	National Library of Greece	Athens	2.5
290.	Leiden State University Library	The Netherlands	2.4
291.	University of Trondheim Library	Norway	2.4
292.	Warsaw University Library	Poland	2.4
293.	National Library of Thailand	Bangkok	2.4
294.	V.I. Lenin State University	Tashkent	2.4
295.	National Library of Norway	Oslo	2.3
296.	National Chengchi University	Taipei, Taiwan	2.3

Rank	Name	Location	Volume of books (millions)
297.	Latvia University Library	Riga	2.3
298.	Northeast Normal University Library	Changchun, China	2.3
299.	National and University Library	Ljubljana, Slovenia	2.3
300.	Marie Curie-Sklodowska University Library	Lublin, Poland	2.3
301.	Turku University Library	Finland	2.3
302.	Vancouver Public Library	Canada	2.3
303.	Aix-Marseille University Library	Marseille, France	2.3
304.	Hitotsubashi University Library	Japan	2.2
305.	University of Adelaide University Library	Australia	2.2
206.	Stockholm City and County Library	Sweden	2.2
307.	Malaya University Library	Kuala Lumpur, Malaysia	2.2
308.	Pyongyang Academy of Sciences Library	North Korea	2.1
309.	Korolenko State Scientific Library	Kharkov, Ukraine	2.1
310.	Australian National University Library	Canberra, Australia	2.1
311.	Dublin City Library	Ireland	2.1
312.	Belarus State University	Minsk	2.1
313.	Yonsei University Library	Seoul	2.1
314.	Astan Quds Razavi Documentation Library	Mashhad, Iran	2.1
315.	Moldovan State University Library	Chisinau	2.1
316.	Nijmegen University Library	The Netherlands	2.1
317.	Baku State University	Azerbaijan	2.1
318.	Okayama University Library	Japan	2.1
319.	National Library of Egypt	Cairo	2
320.	Aristotelian University of Thessaloniki Library	Greece	2
321.	National Library of Vietnam	Hanoi and Ho Chi Minh City	2
322.	Rio de Janeiro Federal University Library	Brazil	2
323.	Louvain Catholic University	Belgium	2
324.	Bern University Library	Switzerland	2
325.	Coimbra University Library	Portugal	2
326.	Rotterdam Municipal Library	The Netherlands	2
327.	University College Library	Ireland, Dublin, Galway and Cork	2
328.	National Library of Italy	Naples	2
329.	Marciana National Library	Venice, Italy	2
330.	Tenri University	Japan	2
331.	Victoria State Library	Melbourne	2
332.	Moscow City Public Library	Russia	2
333.	Keimyung University Library	Taegu, South Korea	2
334.	University of London Library at Senate House	U.K.	2
335.	Queensland University Library	Brisbane, Australia	2
336.	Belarusian National Technical University	Minsk	2
337.	Salzburg University Library	Austria	2
338.	National University Library	Bosnia & Herzegovina, Sarajevo	2
339.	St. Clement Ohridski University Library	Bulgaria, Sofia	2
340.	University of Manitoba	Canada	2
341.	Montreal City Library	Canada	2
342.	University of Hong Kong Library	China	2
342.	Comenius University of Bratislava Library	Slovakia	2
344.	Monash University Library	Clayton	2
345.	Mikhail Eminescu University Central Library	Iasi, Romania	2

These 345 libraries have a grand total of over 1 billion books.

Abbreviations

CISTI. Canada Institute for Scientific and Technical Information.

INION. Institute for Scientific Information on Social Sciences Library.

MAF. Maxwell Air Force Base.

MRSLFL. M. I. Rudomini State Library for Foreign Literature.

NAU. National Autonomous University.

NSTL. National Science and Technology Library of Kazakhstan, Almaty.

RASLNS. Russian Academy of Sciences Library for Natural Sciences.

RSPLST. Russian State Public Library for Science and Technology Moscow.

SFIT. Swiss Federal Institute of Technology Library.

UNWM Library. University of Wisconsin–Madison Library U.S.

N.B.: The figure for the National Library of Canada in Ottawa includes that of the National Library of Quebec in Montreal.

382
The 145 Oldest Libraries

This list focuses only on the oldest significant libraries (excluding private libraries) that are still in existence today (all but 11, founded before 1600). For information on the earliest libraries in the world (but which no longer exist intact), see list **123**. World records on the oldest library buildings are at list **236**.

Rank	Name and Location	Year founded (A.D.)
1.	Al-Qarawiyin University Library, Fez, Morocco	circa 859
2.	Hunan University Library, Changsha, China	976
3.	Al-Azhar University Library, Cairo, Egypt	985
4.	Al-Nizamiyah University Library, Baghdad, Iraq	1070
5.	Bologna University Library, Italy	1088
6.	Padua University Library, Italy	1122
7.	Modena University Library	1160
8.	Hacettepe University Library, Ankara, Turkey	1206
9.	Vicenza University Library, Italy	1204
10.	Salamanca University Library, Spain	1218
11.	San Domenico Library Bologna, Italy	1218
12.	Sorbonne University of Paris Library, France	1230
13	Mustansiriya University Library, Bagdad, Iraq	1233
14.	Montpellier University Library, France	1240
15.	Perugia University Library, Italy	1243
16.	Sienna University Library, Italy	1245
17.	Piacenza University Library, Italy	1248
18.	Arezzo University Library, Italy	1252
19.	Parma University Library, Italy	1255
20.	Salerno University Library, Italy	1265
21.	Vercelli University Library, Italy	1270
22.	Valladolid University Library, Spain	1290
23.	Macerata University Library, Italy	1290
24.	Coimbra University Library, Portugal	1290
25.	Lisbon University Library, Portugal	1291
26.	Toulouse University Library, France	1292

Rank	Name and Location	Year founded (A.D.)
27.	Complutense University Library, Madrid, Spain	1293
28.	Seville University Library, Spain	1295
29.	Naples University Library, Italy	1297
30.	Lleida University, Spain	1297
31.	Valencia University Library, Spain	1298
32.	Rome University Library, Italy	1304
33.	Orleans University Library, France	1306
34.	Florence University Library, Italy	1321
35.	Grenoble University Library, France	1339
36.	Cahor University Library, France	1342
37.	Pisa University Library, Italy	1343
38.	Angers University Library, France	1345
39.	Cambridge University Library, U.K.	1347
40.	Charles University, Prague, Czech Republic	1348
41.	Perpignan University Library, France	1350
42.	Pavia University Library, Italy	1361
43.	Avignon University Library, France	1363
44.	Jagiellonian University Library, Kraków, Poland	1364
45.	Vienna University Library, Austria	1365
46.	Orange University Library, France	1365
47.	National Library of the Czech Republic, Prague	1366
48.	Pécs University Library, Hungary	1367
49.	National Library of Austria, Vienna	1368
50.	Rupert-Charles University Library, Heidelberg, Germany	1386
51.	Cologne University Library, Germany	1388
52.	Ferrara University Library, Italy	1391
53.	Erfurt University Library, Germany	1392
54.	Sungkyunkwan University Library in Seoul, South Korea	1398
55.	Würzburg University Library, Germany	1402
56.	Turin University Library, Italy	1404
57.	Leipzig University Library, Germany	1409
58.	St. Andrews University Library, U.K.	1410
59.	Aix-Marseille University Library, France	1413
60.	Rostock University Library, Germany	1419
61.	Franche-Comté University Library, Besançon, France	1423
62.	Louvain (Leuven) Catholic University Library, Belgium	1425
63.	Barcelona University Library, Spain	1430
64.	Caen University Library, France	1431
65.	Poitiers University Library, France	1432
66.	Bordeaux University Library, France	1441
67.	Catania University Library, Italy	1444
68.	Vatican Library, Rome, Vatican City	1451
69.	Malatesta Monastic Library, Cesena, Italy	1452
70.	Glasgow University Library, U.K.	1451
71.	Istanbul University Library, Turkey	1455
72.	Greifswald University Library, Germany	1456
73.	Freiburg University Library, Germany	1457
74.	Basel University Library, Switzerland	1460
75.	Astan Quds Razavi Documentation Center Library Mashhad, Iran	1460
76.	Rennes University Library, France	1461
77.	Comenius University of Bratislava Library, Slovakia	1465
78.	Marciana National Library, Venice, Italy	1468
79.	Munich University Library, Germany	1472

Rank	Name and Location	Year founded (A.D.)
80.	Eichstatt-Ingolstadt Catholic University Library, Germany	1472
81.	Mainz University Library, Germany	1476
82.	Uppsala University Library, Sweden	1477
83.	Tübingen University Library, Germany	1477
84.	National Library of France, Paris	1480
85.	Saragossa University Library, Spain	1480
86.	Copenhagen University Library, Denmark	1482
87.	Aberdeen University Library, U.K.	1494
88.	Granada University Library, Spain	1494
89.	Santiago de Compostela University, Spain	1495
90.	Martin Luther University Library, Halle-Wittenberg, Germany	1502
91.	University of Évora, Portugal	1502
92.	Royal College of Surgeons Library, Edinburgh, U.K.	1505
93.	Madrid Autonomous University Library of Library, Spain	1510
94.	Frankfurt University Library, Germany	1511
95.	Tianyi Ge Library, Ningbo, China	1516
96.	Royal College of Physicians Library, London, U.K.	1518
97	Zürich University Library, Switzerland	1523
98.	Latvian Academic Library, Riga	1524
99.	Magdeburg Public Library, Germany	1525
100.	Lyons Municipal Library, France	1527
101.	Bern University Library, Switzerland	1528
102.	Santiago de Compostela University Library, Spain	1532
103.	Gazi Husrebegov Library in Sarajevo, Bosnia and Herzegovina	1537
104.	University of Lausanne Library, Switzerland	1537
105.	Santo Domingo Autonomous University Library, Dominican Republic	1538
106.	National University Library, Strasbourg, France	1540
107.	St. Nicholas of Hidalgo Michoacán University Library, Morelia, Mexico	1549
108.	Mexico National Autonomous University Library, Mexico City, Mexico	1551
109.	San Marcos National University Library, Lima, Peru	1552
110.	Pontifical Gregorian University Library, Rome, Vatican City	1553
111.	National Library of Malta, Valetta	1555
112.	National Library of Belgium, Brussels	1559
113.	Bavarian State Library, Munich, Germany	1558
114.	University of Geneva Library, Switzerland	1559
115.	Lille University Library, France	1560
116.	Deventer Municipal Library, The Netherlands	1560
117.	Eotvos Lorand University Library Budapest, Hungary	1561
118.	San Lorenzo de El Escorial Monastic Library, Madrid, Spain	1563
119.	Palacky University Library, Olomouc, Czech Republic	1566
120.	Vilnius University Library, Lithuania	1570
121.	Laurentian Library, Florence, Italy	1571
122.	Leiden State University Library, The Netherlands	1575
123.	Amsterdam University Library, The Netherlands	1578
124.	Santo Tomás University Library, Bogotá, Colombia	1580
125.	Edinburgh University Library, U.K.	1580
126.	San Jose Seminary Library, Bogotá, Colombia	1581
127.	University of Utrecht Library, The Netherlands	1584
128.	Ecuador Central University Library, Quito	1586
129.	Trinity College, Dublin University Library, Ireland	1592
130.	Puebla Autonomous University Library, Mexico	1598
131.	Edward Kardelja University Library, Ljubljana Slovenia	1595
132.	Polish Academy of Sciences, Warsaw	1596

Rank	Name and Location	Year founded (A.D.)
133.	Cuzco University Library, Peru	1598
134.	Francis Trigge Grantham Library, U.K.	1598
135.	St. Benedict Monastery Library Rio Janeiro, Brazil	1600
136.	Bodleian Library, Oxford University, U.K.	1602
137.	Rotterdam Municipal Library, The Netherlands	1604
138.	National Library of Croatia, Zagreb	1606
139.	Ambrosian Library, Milan, Italy	1609
140.	Norwich City Library, U.K.	1608
141.	University of Oviedo, Spain	1608
142.	Córdoba National University Library, Argentina	1615
143.	Groningen State University Library, The Netherlands	1615
144.	Yucatan Autonomous University Library, Mérida, Mexico	1624
145.	San Francisco Xavier Royal Pontifical University Library, Sucre, Bolivia	1625

*With the exception of Padua University in Italy, all the libraries in existence before 1452, when the Malatesta Monastic Library, Cesena, Italy, was founded, have had newer buildings built for the libraries, replacing the older library buildings. Malatesta Monastic Library remains the oldest library building in the world. The five oldest libraries in the U.S. are Harvard University in Cambridge, Massachusetts, founded in 1636; Sturgis Library in Barnstable, Massachusetts (on the Cape Cod peninsula), founded in 1644; William & Mary College, Williamsburg, Virginia, founded 1693; a library founded in 1698 at Charleston, South Carolina; and Yale University Library, New Haven, Connecticut, founded in 1701. Cambridge University (#39) was originally founded in the 13th century. The Bodleian Library at Oxford University was re-founded in 1602, even though the library was originally founded in 1320. Palencia University Library in Spain was founded in 1210, but it was closed near the end of the 13th century because of the prominence of Salamanca University, so it has been excluded. Córdoba University was the first of its kind in Europe, as the original university was founded in 10th century A.D. (so older than Bologna University). But it was re-founded in 1972. Nanjing University in China existed in A.D. 258 as the Imperial College of Emperor Sun Xiu. But modern Nanjing University was re-founded in the early 20th century. The Corviniana Library in Hungary was founded in 1460 but was wrecked when the Turkish Ottoman Empire overran Hungary in the 1526 Battle of Mohács. Also excluded from this list is Kaliningrad University, which was founded as Königsberg University in 1544, but was destroyed in the Second World War. Avignon University (#43) was originally founded in the 13th century. The Vatican Library (#68) original founding date goes back to the 14th century. Istanbul University (#71) was founded as Constantinople University in A.D. 430. Some book collections of the National Library of France (#84) date back to 1368. The libraries of Copenhagen University (#86) and Mexico National Autonomous University Library (#108) are also part of the national library in those countries. Lambeth Palace Library (official library of the Archbishop of Canterbury in the U.K.) was founded in 1610, but omitted as it is also a religious archive. Several other significant old library collections, such as religious libraries (e.g., libraries in cathedrals, monasteries and mosques), still exist today, some dating back to the 5th century A.D. See lists **60, 62, 63, 123** and **236** for more details.*

SAINT JEROME, THE LIBRARIAN'S PATRON SAINT

St. Jerome is the patron saint for librarians and libraries. Born in Italy, he was a passionate lover of books. He was taught by the famous Latin grammarian Aelius Donatus. Apart from being ordained a priest in the 4th century A.D., he also worked for some time in Rome as a prolific translator of the Bible from Hebrew and Greek to Latin, and revised existing Latin versions of the Bible, previously incorrectly translated from Greek by other writers. The Bible by the beginning of 4th century A.D. was mainly composed of Old Testament in Hebrew and New Testament in Greek and very few accurate Latin versions. His first translations of the Bible remained unchanged for more than a thousand years.

In fact one of his major translations of the Bible finished circa 384 A.D. is the Vulgate edition of the Bible, which is the basis for the Bible used in Roman Catholic churches today, as it was adopted by the Council of Trent as the official Roman Catholic Bible in 1546. It was later generations of this original vulgate edition of the Bible that Gutenberg symbolically chose from other choices of handwritten parchment manuscripts to print his very first book in 1455. During St. Jerome's time working on his translations in Rome, he kept a well stocked personal library, meticulously cataloged.

One of St. Jerome's most remarkable feats was to seek solitary refuge in Syria's Chalcis desert for five years, just reading, praying and fasting!

BIBLIOGRAPHY

Books

Abdulrazak, Fawzi. *Arabic Historical Writing: An Annotated Bibliography of Books in History from All Parts of the Arab World*. London: Mansell Information, 1976.

American Library Directory. 52nd ed. New York: Bowker, 1999.

Bartram, Alan. *Five Hundred Years of Book Design*. New Havener: Yale University Press, 2001.

Betz, Paul, and Mark Carnes, eds. *American National Biography*. New York: Oxford University Press, 2002.

Boyer, Paul. *The Oxford Companion to United States History*. New York: Oxford University Press, 2001.

The Cambridge Biographical Encyclopedia. 2nd ed. Cambridge, U.K.: Cambridge University Press, 1998.

Campbell, Gordon. *The Oxford Dictionary of the Renaissance*. New York: Oxford University Press, 2003.

Casson, Lionel. *Libraries in the Ancient World*. New Haven, CT: Yale University Press, 2001.

Chambers Dictionary of World History. Edinburgh, Scotland: Chambers, 2005.

Chronology of European History, 15,000 B.C. to 1997. Pasadena, CA: Salem Press, 1997.

Columbia Encyclopedia. 6th ed. New York: Columbia University Press, 2000.

Coulmas, Florian. *The Blackwell Encyclopedia of Writings Systems*. Oxford, U.K.: Blackwell Publishers, 1999.

De Hamel, Christopher. *The Book: A History of the Bible*. New York: Phaidon, 2001.

Edwards, Edward. *Memoirs of Libraries*. London: Trübner Co., 2 vol., 1859, repr. 1964.

Encyclopædia Britannica, 2002 ed. Chicago: Encyclopædia Britannica, 2001.

Encyclopedia of the Renaissance. New York: Scribners, 1999.

Finkelstein, David, and Alistair McCleery, eds. *The Book History Reader*. New York: Routledge, 2002.

Feather, John, ed. *International Encyclopedia of Information and Library Science*. London: Routledge, 1997.

Harris, Michael H. *History of Libraries in the Western World*. 4th ed. Metuchen, NJ: Scarecrow, 1995.

Hutchinson Encyclopedia 2002 (CD-ROM). 10th ed. Oxford, UK: Helicon, 2001.

Irwin, Raymond. *Origins of the English Library*. London: Allen & Unwin, 1958, repr. 1981.

Jiangzhong, W., ed. *New Library Buildings of the World*. Shanghai: Kexue-Jishu Wenxian-Chubanshe, 1999.

Kagan, Neil, ed. *National Geographic Concise History of the World: An Illustrated Time Line*. Washington D.C.: National Geographic, 2006.

Landau, Thomas, ed., *Encyclopedia of Librarianship*. 3rd ed. New York: Hafner, 1966.

Lerner, Fred. *The Story of Libraries*. New York: Continuum, 2001.

McMurtrie, Douglas C. *The Book: The Story of Printing and Bookmaking*. New York: Oxford University Press, 1962.

Microsoft Encarta Encyclopedia 2007 (DVD-ROM). Richmond, WA: Microsoft, 2006.

Mueckenheim, Jacqueline K., ed. *Gale Directory of Databases 2006*. London: Thomson Gale, 2005.

Nakanishi, Akira. *Writing Systems of the World: Alphabets, Syllabaries, Pictograms*. Rutland, VT: C. E. Tuttle, 1995.

Savage, Ernest Albert. *The Story of Libraries and Book-collecting*. London: Routledge, 1909, repr. 1969.

Schniederjürgen, Axel, ed. *World Guide to Library, Archive and Information Science Education*. 3rd ed. Munich: K. G. Saur, 2007.

Schottenloher, Karl. *Books and the Western World:*

A Cultural History. Jefferson, NC: McFarland, 1989.

Stam, David H., ed. *International Dictionary of Library Histories.* 2 vols. Chicago: Fitzroy Dearborn, 2001.

Stern, Madeleine B., and Leona Rostenberg. *Bookman's Quintet: Five Catalogues About Books, Bibliography, Printing History, Booksellers, Libraries, Presses, Collectors.* Newark, DE: Oak Knoll, 1980.

Tolzmann, Don Heinrich, ed., et al. *Memory of Mankind: The Story of Libraries Since the Dawn of History.* New Castle, DE: Oak Knoll, 2001.

UNESCO Statistical Yearbooks. Paris: UNESCO, 2006.

Wedgeworth, Robert, ed. *ALA World Encyclopedia of Library and Information Services.* 2nd ed. Chicago: American Library Association, 1986.

Wiegand, Wayne, and Donald Davis, eds. *Encyclopedia of Library History.* New York: Garland, 1994.

Winckler, Paul A. *History of Books and Printing: A Guide to Information Sources.* Detroit: Gale Research, 1979.

The World Almanac and Book of Facts 2007. 139th ed. London: World Almanac, 2006.

World Book Encyclopedia 2007. Chicago: World Book, 2006.

The World of Learning. 57th ed. London: Europa, 2006.

Periodicals and Newspapers

Alexandria: The Journal of National and International Library and Information Issues
American Libraries
Archives
The Bodleian Library Record Libraries and Culture: Exploring the History of Books, Collections, and Society
Bookseller
The Boston Globe
Computers in Libraries
Digital Librarian
E-Content
The Guardian
Herald International Tribune
IFLA Journal
inCite
Information Technology and Libraries
Information Today
Information World Review
Journal of Digital Information
Journal of Information Science
Journal of the American Medical Library Association
Journal of the American Society for Information Science
KMWorld
Liber Quarterly
Libraries & Culture
The Library
Library Hi Tech
Library History
Library Journal
Library Management
The Library Quarterly
Libri
Managing Information
New Library World
The New York Times
Online
Publishers Weekly
School Library Journal
Searcher
The Times
Washington Post

INDEX

References are to entry numbers.